SUPERPOWER ARMS CONTROL

SUPERPOWER ARMS CONTROL
Setting the Record Straight

Edited by
ALBERT CARNESALE
and
RICHARD N. HAASS

BALLINGER PUBLISHING COMPANY
Cambridge, Massachusetts
A Subsidiary of Harper & Row, Publishers, Inc.

International Standard Book Number: 0-88730-228-9 (CL)
0-88730-229-7 (PB)

Library of Congress Catalog Card Number: 87-1372

Printed in the United States of America

Library of Congress Cataloging-in-Publication Data

Superpower arms control.

Includes index.
1. Nuclear arms control—United States. 2. Nuclear arms control—Soviet Union. I. Carnesale, Albert. II. Haass, Richard.
JX1974.7.S96 1987 341.7'34 87-1372
ISBN 0-88730-228-9
ISBN 0-88730-229-7 (pbk.)

CONTENTS

v

LIST OF FIGURES AND TABLES

PREFACE

Nuclear arms control has been a central theme of superpower relations for at least a quarter of a century. Everyone agrees that there are valuable lessons to be learned from those decades of experience: the disagreements arise only when attempts are made to identify those lessons. Individuals and organizations advocate policies based on their own vivid perceptions of arms control's past—perceptions often derived more from emotion and ideology than from evidence and analysis.

In this volume, we test the views held by important actors in the arms control process against the historical record of negotiations and accords, and we identify those lessons that are consistent with the evidence and those that are not. Our goal is to present an accurate and objective picture of arms control's past. Although we make no attempt to predict or prescribe its future, we believe that our findings can serve as a useful foundation for thinking about what might come to pass. In any event, we fully expect that readers will have little difficulty in formulating their own versions of implications for the future. Our intention and aspiration are for this study to be of interest and utility to many different kinds of readers, including policymakers, experts, students, and members of the general public who care about the role that arms control might play in altering the risk of war.

This book is based largely on a research project, "Learning from Experience with Arms Control," conducted during 1985 and 1986 at Harvard University's John F. Kennedy School of Government under the direction of Albert Carnesale. The project was sponsored by the U.S. Arms Control and Disarmament Agency. We are indebted to ACDA and its director, Kenneth Adelman, for providing not only financial support but also the encouragement and freedom essential to truly objective scholarly inquiry. This study benefitted also from our association with Harvard's Project on Avoiding Nuclear War, which is funded by the Carnegie Corporation of New York.

Researchers actively engaged in the arms control project met biweekly to review work in progress. Participants in this working group were Professors Albert Carnesale, Ashton Carter, and Joseph Nye; Drs. Charles Glaser, Stephen Flanagan, Richard Haass, and Fen Hampson; doctoral candidates Andrew Bennett, Robert Beschel, Ivo Daalder, Thomas Graham, Elisa Harris, Sean Lynn-Jones, James Miller, and Kiron Skinner; and research assistant John Wertheimer. Valuable advice and counsel was provided by an advisory committee comprised of Graham Allison, Robert Blackwill, Paul Doty, Samuel Huntington, William Kaufmann, Ernest May, Stephen Meyer, Robert Murray, Joseph Nye, and Richard Pipes.

A two-day workshop to review a preliminary draft of this volume was conducted at Harvard on May 7–8, 1986. The researchers and advisors were joined at this workshop by Abram Chayes, Antonia Chayes, Jonathan Dean, Lynn Eden, Sidney Graybeal, Steven Miller, Michael Mobbs, Louis Nosenzo, Thomas Schelling, Jane Sharp, and Herbert York. Still others commented along the way on ideas, outlines, and drafts. These drafts were "processed" by Betty Miele with skill, patience, and assorted combinations of computer hardware and software.

Those of us who performed this research are grateful to all of these people for the help we've received. Credit for what's good in this book is to be shared with all of them: blame for what's bad is ours alone.

Finally, we note that views expressed in this report are those of the authors and do not necessarily reflect the views of Harvard University or of the U.S. Arms Control and Disarmament Agency.

1 INTRODUCTION
Framework for Analysis

Albert Carnesale

What can we learn from our arms control experience with the Soviet Union? The step-by-step approach to arms control pursued in the 1960s and 1970s did not aim to alter drastically the defense plans and programs of the two sides but attempted instead to identify areas where mutual compromise might codify a rough balance, reduce tensions, and, equally important, pave the way for more extensive limitations. Measured solely in terms of the number and scope of agreements reached, the approach seemed to work: it produced the Limited Test Ban Treaty, the Nuclear Non-Proliferation Treaty, the Biological Weapons Convention, the Accidents Measures Agreement, the Anti-Ballistic Missile Treaty, the SALT I Interim Agreement on Offensive Arms, the SALT II Treaty, and other agreements.

But did this process and the measures it produced further the traditional arms control objectives of lessening the likelihood and destructiveness of war and reducing defense expenditures? By the early 1980s there was a growing belief in the United States that the step-by-step approach to arms control had not lived up to expectations, but there was no consensus on what went wrong and why.

Some observers pin the blame squarely on the Soviet desire to seek military advantages (by halting promising U.S. programs, by resisting meaningful limitations on their own arsenal, or by cheating on agreements where practicable) and to lull the United States into a false sense of security. Others attribute the blame to both sides for failing to curb the qualitative arms competition. Still others say that the problem stems less from arms control's meager accomplishments than from the unrealistically high expectations generated by the Nixon, Ford, and Carter administrations.

Though few would doubt the utility of a systematic assessment of the efficacy of past U.S. arms control efforts, such evaluations are not easily made. To assert simply that what was achieved was somehow flawed compared to what might hypothetically have been accomplished fails to take into account the military, diplomatic, and political forces that shape superpower nuclear arsenals and glosses over the exigencies of the bargaining process. Even a good arms control agreement compares poorly with an imaginary better one and still more poorly with the best.

Rather than compare real arms control negotiations and agreements with imaginary ones, in this study we try to compare prior expectations about the results of real negotiations and agreements with actual outcomes. What did various U.S. participants and constituencies involved in the arms control process expect to be the results of specific arms control negotiations, and how do those expectations compare to the agreements that emerged? What did these participants and constituencies expect to be the effects of the agreements reached, and how do those expectations compare to what actually happened? To what might the differences between expectations and outcomes be attributed? What lessons can be learned?

Expectations cannot readily be extracted from the public record. The difficulty lies in distinguishing between individuals' true beliefs of what the future holds in store and the rosey or bleak futures that they paint to support the policy positions they advocate. Proponents of arms control tend to recite an exhaustive list of favorable future conditions that, they claim, are likely to flow from the negotiation or agreement under consideration. They provide also a comparably long list of unfavorable conditions depicted as likely consequences of failing to heed their pro–arms control advice. Opponents of arms control present their own lists of delightful and catastrophic consequences and merely reverse the sign of the proponents' argument.

Our approach has been to examine the public record of arms control debates in the United States—as reflected in speeches, testimony, editorials, and other public documentation—and, on the basis of the views and expectations expressed therein, to formulate more general hypotheses about arms control and to examine their validity. The ten hypotheses listed in Table 1-1 are the resulting backbone of this approach.

Five focus primarily on the prerequisites for and processes of arms control, and the other five deal largely with its effects. Together they have served and continue to serve as the underlying structure of arms control debates in the United States, and they represent the conceptual framework for this study.

Each hypothesis underlies one or more important actors' basic view on an important aspect of arms control. Inconsistencies among the hypotheses reflect the diverse views of the actors. Hypotheses selected in this manner are unlikely to be simply true or false: in most cases the evidence is mixed, although the weight of evidence may well favor one view over the other. It is useful to know which of the contradictory yet fervently held views about arms control are consistent with the historical record and which are inconsistent. Recognizing the realities of arms control's past can help us to shape its future.

This book examines these hypotheses in the context of seven case studies, each of which is the subject of a separate chapter. Chapter 2 deals with the Limited Test Ban Treaty; Chapter 3, the Accidents Measures Agreement; Chapter 4, the SALT I ABM Treaty and Interim Agreement; Chapter 5, the SALT II Treaty; Chapter 6, the 1977–79 negotiations on Antisatellite Weapons; Chapter 7, the Superpowers and the Non-Proliferation Treaty; and Chapter 8, the Biological Weapons Convention. The cases dealing with the Non-Proliferation Treaty (NPT) and the Biological Weapons Convention (BWC) were not included in the original 1985–86 Harvard University project on "Learning from Experience with Arms Control." (That project focused on bilateral nuclear arms control, whereas the NPT is multilateral in essence and the BWC does not deal with nuclear arms.) Inclusion of the NPT and BWC cases in this volume serves to expand the historical record on which the analyses and conclusions are based. In addition to the analyses contained in the individual case studies, three chapters deal with sets of issues that arise in most of the cases and that were deemed sufficiently important to warrant separate treatment. These cross-cutting analyses are set forth in Chapter 9, on the Lulling and Stimulating Effects of Arms Control; Chapter 10, on Linkage; and Chapter 11, on Verification and Compliance. The conclusions appear in Chapter 12.

Table 1-1.   Arms Control Hypotheses.

---

1. Bargaining from Strength

Progress in arms control takes place only when

1. The United States has the advantage.
2. Neither side has an advantage.
3. The Soviet Union has the advantage.

2. Genies in Bottles

Meaningful constraints on any particular category of weapons can be achieved only if neither side

1. Really wants the weapon.
2. Has tested the weapon.
3. Has invested heavily in the weapon.

3. Unilateral Restraint

Unilateral restraint by the United States

1. Induces reciprocal restraint by the Soviet Union.
2. Induces counterproductive action by the Soviet Union.
3. Increases the likelihood of achieving bilateral arms control agreement.
4. Decreases the likelihood of achieving bilateral arms control agreement.

4. Linkage

The arms control process influences and is influenced by

1. Soviet behavior in other policy areas.
2. U.S. behavior in other policy areas.

5. Effect on Arms

The arms control process and arms control agreements

1. Redirect the arms competition in productive ways.
2. Codify existing defense plans.
3. Redirect the arms competition in counterproductive ways.

6. Uncertainties

The arms control process and arms control agreements reduce uncertainties in estimates and projections of each other's forces.

7. Verification and Compliance

1. The Soviets do not comply with the spirit or the letter of agreements.
2. The political requirements for verification and compliance are more demanding than the security requirements.
3. Ambiguity does not offer a solution to verification and compliance problems.

Table 1-1. continued

8. *Lulling*

The arms control process and arms control agreements

1. Lull the United States into spending less than it should on defense.
2. Stimulate the United States to spend more than it should on defense.

9. *Political Support*

1. Political support for an arms control agreement depends less on the provisions of the agreement than on other factors.
2. Congressional support for an arms control agreement depends upon the extent of Congressional participation in the arms control process.
3. The public will support any negotiated arms control agreement.

10. *Asymmetry*

The arms control process and arms control agreements serve Soviet interests more than U.S. interests.

ARMS CONTROL NEGOTIATIONS AND AGREEMENTS

2 THE LIMITED TEST BAN TREATY

Ivo H. Daalder

When Averell Harriman left for Moscow on July 12, 1963, the subject of a ban on nuclear testing had been on the East-West negotiating agenda for eight years. Formal negotiations among the United States, Great Britain, and the Soviet Union had borne no fruit for over five years. Yet it took Harriman, the British delegate Lord Hailsham, and Soviet Foreign Minister Andrei Gromyko only ten days to initial an agreement banning nuclear testing in the atmosphere, underwater, and in space. The Limited Test Ban Treaty (LTBT) was formally signed by the foreign secretaries of the three countries—Dean Rusk, Lord Home, and Gromyko—on August 5 in Moscow. The Senate advised ratification of the treaty by a vote of eighty to nineteen on September 24, and President John F. Kennedy ratified it on October 7, 1963. Three days later the treaty entered into force. In less than three months, the three countries succeeded in negotiating, signing, and ratifying a treaty that had been sought in one form or another since the "spirit of Geneva" breathed the first spell of fresh air into the Cold War climate in 1955.

The LTBT represents a specific form of arms control. The treaty addressed a process within the defense research and development framework. Rather than seeking to alter or manipulate the structure of the respective force postures, and rather than focusing on numbers of systems or their characteristics, it sought to prohibit certain forms of knowledge acquisition in the R&D phase. That such prohibitions ultimately affected the utility and effectiveness of certain weapon systems or their characteristics (as was to be the case with antiballistic missile defenses) was a by-product of the agreement and not its conscious aim.

An examination of the public record reveals that current conventional wisdom about the accord appears to be somewhat mistaken. There is a general belief that radioactive fallout was the crucial issue in the LTBT debate and that public pressure for a ban on atmospheric testing ultimately forced the United States to sign and ratify the agreement. There is little doubt that such pressure was instrumental in getting the nuclear testing issue on the negotiating table and crucial in persuading the Eisenhower administration to seek a test ban. The public record provided by Senate hearings, congressional debate, and executive statements of the time, however, points to the very limited role played by the fallout issue in the LTBT ratification debate, both before and after the treaty was signed. Rather, as will be seen, the two crucial issues were the existing climate of relations between the United States and the USSR following the Cuban Missile Crisis in October 1962 and the treaty's potential effect on the development of an optimal ABM system.

NEGOTIATING A LIMITED NUCLEAR TEST BAN

The idea of negotiating a ban on all nuclear testing became prominent following a 1954 U.S. test on the Bikini atoll of a 15 megaton (MT) nuclear device that resulted in the contamination of surrounding areas, including a Japanese fishing boat, *Lucky Dragon*, whose crew suffered from radiation sickness and one of whom died. The resulting public outcry over testing meant that the idea of banning such testing became part of the public agenda of disarmament deliberations.[1] Negotiations for a test ban were taken up in 1955 by the Subcommittee of Five (composed of the United States, the Soviet Union, the United Kingdom, Canada, and France) of the U.N. Committee on Disarmament. Separate negotiations among the United States, Great Britain, and the Soviet Union on a test ban commenced in October 1958. At that time, following the convening in July and August 1958 of an international panel—the Conference of Experts—to determine possible ways of detecting and identifying nuclear tests should these be banned, the three nuclear powers embarked on an unsigned yet mutually agreed moratorium on nuclear tests in all environments.

Despite the informal moratorium, negotiations were stuck on one key point—verification. The West generally insisted on some form of on-site inspection (OSI) to identify the origin of suspicious events. The identification of low-yield nuclear explosions performed underground was particularly problematical given that the seismic signals of a small nuclear explosion are difficult to differentiate from those of an earthquake. Until 1962 the Soviet Union refused any form of OSI, however, and saw the establishment of control posts as an unwarranted interference with its internal affairs.

Despite these problems surrounding the verification provisions, the continuing moratorium and the apparent adherence to it by all parties kept hopes alive of an eventual agreement. These hopes were shattered, however, by the Soviet announcement of August 30, 1961, that it would resume testing in the atmosphere. The announcement, followed by three atmospheric tests in less than a week—one with an estimated yield of 58 MT—caught the United States by surprise. The Soviet decision was interpreted as a calculated affront to the good will of the West in pursuing arms control negotiations. That the Soviet Union had always said that it would not test unless a Western power tested first, and that its announcement came after the French had tested their first atomic weapon, seemed to matter little, given the scope of the Soviet testing series, which indicated months if not years of preparation. The "breaking" of the moratorium and the ensuing test series in 1961 and 1962 strengthened opposition in the United States to the entire idea of arms control negotiations and were, consequently, to play a major role in the LTBT ratification debate.

Following the Soviet resumption of testing, the debate within the United States on whether to resume atmospheric testing was vigorous. Having been caught off guard by the Soviet decision, the United States proved to be totally unprepared for resuming atmospheric testing, although, just two weeks after the first Soviet test, underground testing resumed in tunnels dug during the moratorium. In November 1961 the Presidential Committee on Atmospheric Testing submitted a report to Kennedy setting out the rationale for atmospheric testing. Such testing was needed, the report argued, in order (1) to develop antiballistic missile defenses, (2) to ensure that U.S.

missiles and warheads would survive a Soviet attack and could subsequently penetrate Soviet ABM defenses, and (3) to acquire knowledge on the effects of nuclear explosions on hardened silos, missiles, warheads, radars, and communications.[2] These requirements for testing were to form the essential basis of the military and strategic discussions surrounding the LTBT some two years later. In the absence of a test ban and given these testing requirements, Kennedy decided that the United States had to resume atmospheric testing. A test series codenamed DOMINIC was started on April 25, 1962.

Even though both the United States and the Soviet Union had resumed atmospheric testing, a key event was to transform relations between the two countries. The Cuban Missile Crisis of October 1962, in which both superpowers stood at the brink of nuclear war, had a profound influence on the U.S. (and probably Soviet) evaluation of East-West relations. Kennedy was deeply affected by the crisis. As Arthur Schlesinger recalls, Kennedy believed that Cuba "made vivid the sense that all humanity had a common interest in the prevention of nuclear war—an interest far above those national and ideological interests which had once seemed ultimate."[3]

The Cuban Missile Crisis thus pointed to the urgent need to seek some form of accommodation and to tackle the Cold War issue head on. As Secretary of State Rusk told the Senate Foreign Relations Committee during hearings on the treaty, "I think it is important for us to understand that something new in history, perhaps, happened this past year, and that is that nuclear powers had to look actually and operationally at what a nuclear exchange could mean, and I think that this was an experience that those who carried the responsibility on all sides recognized that one does not go through as a weekend avocation."[4] The administration, however, was convinced that while the post-Cuba climate might see an improvement in East-West relations, the time was short. Hence, all efforts were to be expanded to solidify such improvements by way of lasting agreements. As a consequence, the negotiating efforts employed during early 1963 were more strenuous than ever before.

In December 1962 an exchange of letters between President Kennedy and Soviet General Secretary Nikita Khrushchev seemed to provide a new opening, as the Soviet leader suggested that in order for the president to overcome congressional obstacles he might be willing to accept two or three on-site inspections a year. With the

Americans unofficially willing to go down to six, the gap between the two countries seemed to be of manageable proportions.[5] More important, perhaps, the perception of a new danger—nuclear proliferation—added urgency to Kennedy's search for an agreement. The times were ones of rapid advance, with France obtaining an operational nuclear capability and China widely seen as achieving such a capability in the near future. A test ban was believed to be one way of halting what was perceived as the new and present danger of nuclear proliferation. As Kennedy declared in a press conference on March 21, 1963, "the reason why we keep moving and working on this question [of a test ban], taking up a good deal of energy and effort, is because personally I am haunted by the feeling that by 1970, unless we are successful, there may be 10 nuclear powers instead of 4, and by 1975, 15 or 20."[6]

The president apparently believed that his concern with nuclear proliferation was shared by the Soviet Union and that the signing of a treaty by both powers would codify this concern. As he argued, there "is no guarantee, if we sign a nuclear test ban, that it will end proliferation. It is, however, our feeling that the Soviet Union would not accept a test ban unless they shared our view that proliferation was undesirable, and it might be a weight in the scale against proliferation, and I so regard it."[7] As such, any United States–Soviet agreement was seen by Kennedy as symbolizing a mutual concern for nonproliferation and possibly impeding the spread of nuclear weapons.

Throughout early 1963 the president expended much effort to get the test ban negotiations going again. To Kennedy the window of opportunity, opened by the Cuban Missile Crisis the fall before, was rapidly closing. By early June the effort seemed to be paying off. On June 8 Kennedy received word that Khrushchev had agreed to resume test ban negotiations in Moscow the following month. Two days later, the president delivered the American University commencement address. The speech was a broad appeal to peace and ended with Kennedy announcing the impending meeting in Moscow. The president further stated that as of that day the United States would halt all atmospheric testing as long as the Soviet Union would too.[8] On July 2, just thirteen days before the Moscow meeting was to open, Khrushchev announced in East Berlin that he was willing to conclude a ban on testing in space, in the atmosphere, and underwater. The road to an agreement, albeit a partial one, was open. Just twenty-three days later, a Limited Test Ban Treaty was negotiated and initialed.

THE DEBATE OVER THE MAJOR ISSUES

Both the Senate and the public debates focused on two different sets of issues. First were the political-diplomatic implications of the treaty, its effect on Soviet-U.S. relations, and its significance for an emergent arms control process. Second and more controversial were discussions of the military-strategic implications of the treaty.

Political-Diplomatic Issues

The most important political-diplomatic issues concerned the possible effect the reduction of East-West tensions resulting from the treaty would have on U.S. national security. Other major issues were the treaty's effect on the negotiation of future agreements, on the national mood, and on radioactive fallout levels.

The LTBT's Effect on Tensions. Many individuals, particularly in the administration, argued that the treaty marked a symbolic beginning of a changing political climate. Kennedy, when announcing the initialing of the treaty, said, "it is an important first step—a step toward peace—a step toward reason—a step away from war." He went on to say that the treaty's symbolic value was twofold, both as the end of an era and the beginning of a new one: "Nuclear test ban negotiations have long been a symbol of East-West disagreement. If this treaty can also be a symbol—if it can symbolize the end of one era and the beginning of another—if both sides can by this treaty gain confidence and experience in peaceful collaboration—then this short and simple treaty may well become an historic mark in man's age-old pursuit of peace."[9] Similarly, the Joint Chiefs of Staff made clear that their support for the treaty was predicated on the belief that the possible political advantages resulting from a reduction of tensions outweighed any possible military disadvantages the treaty might have.[10]

The hope that tensions might be reduced lay not only in the symbolic value of the treaty but also in the fact that limitations on parts of the armament expansion might contribute to such a reduction. Kennedy, in a July 26, 1963, address on the treaty, pointed to the interrelation of tensions and armaments: "Each increase of tensions has produced an increase of arms; each increase of arms has produced an increase in tensions."[11] The expressed hope was that the LTBT, as an arms control agreement, could at least contribute to breaking this vicious circle.

Although the administration continued to stress the symbolic value of the treaty, opponents or skeptics stressed that (1) Soviet behavior had not changed with the signing of the treaty, (2) arms control measures, if acceptable to the Soviet Union, were tactical calculations by the East to undermine the West, and (3) a reduction of tensions might be counterproductive. Thus, Senator Strom Thurmond argued that "it is . . . my judgment, before we can hope to stabilize international relations with the Communists, or have a peaceful environment in which to seek a resolution of differences between countries, the Communists have got to abandon their goal of world domination."[12] Nothing in the record, Senator Thurmond argued, had shown that the Soviet Union had abandoned that goal.

The second point, that arms control might in itself be detrimental to U.S. security, was forcefully expressed by Edward Teller: "We need strength to be able to leave the initiative to others. I think that through our policy of arms limitations we already lost our superiority. . . . And I think we might repeat the tragic mistake of the 1930s where war has not been the consequence of an arms race, but the consequence of a race in disarmament."[13] Third, many a commentator pointed out that a reduction in tensions might not only be unhelpful but in fact could be counterproductive and dangerous. Robert Strausz-Hupé, then director of the Foreign Policy Research Institute, testified before the Senate Foreign Relations Committee that he disagreed with the last paragraph of the Moscow communiqué, issued July 25, which spoke of the pursuance of "other measures, directed at a relaxation of tensions." Strausz-Hupé commented that the "desirability of such a goal in dealing with an opponent who seeks world domination and frequently speaks of burying us is questionable."[14]

Whether a reduction of tensions in fact occurred in the aftermath of the treaty, and whether such a reduction contributed to U.S. security, are matters open to debate. The competition between East and West continued unabated; 1963 was definitely not a time of a more general détente, nor, indeed, did Soviet objectives seem to have changed fundamentally. On the other hand, some reduction of tensions did occur. An in-depth content analysis by Sophia Peterson of Soviet statements six months prior to as well as after the signing of the LTBT points out that from the Soviet side a visible lessening of hostility had taken place.[15] A second indication of reduced tensions might lie in the marked improvement in European–Soviet and later U.S.–Soviet relations. By 1964 President Charles de Gaulle of France was openly courting the Soviet Union, and even West Germany was cautiously treading the steps that eventually led to the success of *Ostpolitik*. Hence, tensions were clearly reduced following the LTBT. It is difficult to tell, however, whether reduced tensions resulted more from the surrounding environment within which the treaty was signed (notably the post–Cuba atmosphere and the Sino–Soviet conflict) than from the treaty itself. Nevertheless, whether as a symbol of improved relations in the aftermath of the Cuban crisis or on its own terms, as the first concrete achievement in Soviet–U.S. arms control, the LTBT clearly was a turning point in the Cold War.

The LTBT's Effect on Future Agreements.   Running parallel to the belief that the LTBT would reduce tensions was the argument that it would induce additional agreements in the future, either on similar issues or on the more intractable political issues that divided the United States and the Soviet Union. Theodore Sorensen reports that the "political change in the atmosphere was even more important than the physical one, in John Kennedy's view. The treaty was a symbolic 'first step,' a forerunner of further agreements. It facilitated a pause in the cold war in which other, more difficult problems could be stabilized."[16] The notion of the LTBT as a "first step" was an important one to the administration and others alike. It was therefore also an often repeated one. In a memorandum to the president by William Foster, director of the Arms Control and Disarmament Agency (ACDA), written shortly before Harriman's mission to Moscow, the expectation was expressed that in the "perspective of the next ten years, the significance of a nuclear test ban lies more in the political doors which it might assist in opening than in the military doors which it might close."[17]

Others disagreed with this perspective, however. Some feared that the LTBT, containing no provisions for inspection, might set a dangerous precedent for uninspected and unverifiable agreements made for their apparent political benefit rather than their inherent military and security advantages. Thus, Strausz-Hupé argued that "It would be a serious lapse from a previously held, and a strongly held, position if the United States were to lose interest, for all practical purposes, in international inspection and control as an essential condition of disarmament."[18] Second, the argument was made that, the treaty being partial, a more comprehensive disarmament agreement might elude future negotiators. The point was made, again, that having conceded the principle of an agreement without inspection, future negotiations could well be thwarted on the issue.[19]

Subsequent events could be interpreted as confirming either point of view. Thus, those who believed that the LTBT would stimulate future agreements can point to the successful negotiations of agreements directly related to the LTBT (such as the Non-Proliferation Treaty in 1968, the Threshold Test Ban Treaty in 1974, and the Peaceful Nuclear Explosions Treaty in 1975) as well as a host of other agreements, most notably the SALT I and II accords and the ABM Treaty. Moreover, at least until 1980 every U.S. administration supported the negotiation of a comprehensive test ban treaty, and actual talks to this effect were held during the Carter administration. Most important, perhaps, the LTBT was the start of a transitional process in nuclear diplomacy, putting arms control effectively on the table as a central component of East-West relations.

On the other hand, despite the treaty's promise in the preamble that the parties seek to "achieve the discontinuance of all test explosions of nuclear weapons for all time," a comprehensive treaty, notwithstanding longstanding negotiations, has eluded the parties. The OSI issue remained intractable and, until recently, was seen as the principal obstacle to progress.

The LTBT's Effect on the National Mood. A surprising unanimity existed at the time of the treaty's signing as well as during the hearings that its effect might well be to "soften up" the public mood to the extent that prudent vigilance would be discarded in a wave of "peace euphoria." Warning against this danger of lulling, it was argued, could maintain both the inherent benefits of the treaty without thereby reducing national security. The administration believed that a warning against euphoria would be sufficient. Sorensen summed up Kennedy's attitude on this issue:

> He took pains—partly for political reasons, perhaps, but also because it was his substantive belief—to warn the Administration and the general public against any sunny feeling that the millennium had arrived and that everything

would be rosy in our relations with the Russians from here on out. He felt that our military strength, our willingness to use that strength, and our vigilance of being alert to the possible using of that strength had played a part in achieving the test ban treaty. While he hoped for further agreement, he remained to the end extremely cautious in his expressions of optimism and extremely anxious not to lower our guard, even though tensions were hopefully lessened.[20]

Both Secretary of Defense Robert McNamara and the Joint Chiefs of Staff testified that the greatest military danger in the treaty would be the emergence of euphoria.[21] By recognizing the problem immediately, they hoped to stem its possible tide in the future.

The same recognition of the dangers of lulling was recognized by the treaty's opponents. To them, however, the treaty was in no small part an expression of this general psychological climate rather than its cause. As such, the belief was that the atmosphere could not be prevented, as it could in the administration's view, but that it was inevitable. This lulling effect was well expressed by Senator Bourke Hickenlooper: "the psychology of the people of this country is being fed by the idea that this is a great step toward a reliable peace, toward the guarantee of peace, and the cessation of atomic warfare. . . . [T]he effect on the American people is one that is apt to be considerably dangerous here and will lull them into a state of unwarranted security in connection with this treaty."[22]

One can interpret the outcome of the lulling expectation in two ways. First, no excessive euphoria occurred; within less than two years the United States was fighting a war in Vietnam against Communist subversion and had invaded the Dominican Republic for the same reason. Whatever the immediate effect might have been, the long-term implications were negligible. Second, however, the expectation that lulling might occur led perhaps to an excessive emphasis on what the treaty would *not* do. In an effort to sell the treaty to the nation and the Senate, President Kennedy clearly set out the treaty's limits. In his Address to the Nation on July 26, 1963, and his message to the Senate asking for its advice and consent, Kennedy mentioned the following thirteen points:

1. The treaty permits continued underground testing.
2. Any nation which signs the treaty may withdraw from it upon three months' notice.
3. The treaty is not an end to the threat of nuclear war.
4. It will not reduce nuclear stockpiles.

5. It will not halt the production of nuclear weapons.
6. It will not restrict nuclear use in time of war.
7. It reflects no concessions by the Soviet Union.
8. It will not resolve all conflicts, or cause the Communists to forego their ambitions, or eliminate the danger of war.
9. It will not reduce our need for arms or allies or programs of assistance to others.
10. The Moscow talks reached no agreement on any other subject.
11. The Soviet Government is still unwilling to accept inspection.
12. No one can predict with certainty what future agreements, if any, can be built on the foundations of this one.
13. The familiar contest between choice and coercion, and the familiar places of danger and conflict, are still there, including Berlin, the Congo, Cuba, Vietnam and German reunification.[23]

At the end of the Senate hearings, some believed that the negative turns the hearings had taken had seriously impeded the process for additional agreements that the treaty was meant to initiate. Kennedy became convinced that he had to go to the United Nations to renew his "strategy for peace" and persuade the world that despite the vociferous domestic debate, the United States remained committed to the course that the LTBT had charted.[24] *The New York Times* felt that perhaps it was already too late: "The nuclear test ban treaty is coming into the world like an unwanted child," it argued in an editorial on August 23. "Even those who favor it and believe in it seem to be doing everything they can in Senate committees and public statements to persuade the American people that it really doesn't mean much. . . . A treaty smothered in a blanket of fear and distrust represents a poor foundation for further progress."

The LTBT's Effect on Fallout.   In addition to its expected effect on proliferation and East-West tensions, the LTBT's contribution to a reduction in fallout was seen by the administration as one of the primary benefits provided under the treaty. Kennedy argued that "this treaty can be a step toward freeing the world from the fears and dangers of radioactive fallout. . . . Continued unrestricted testing by the nuclear powers, joined in time by other nations which may be less adept in limiting pollution, will increasingly contaminate the air that all of us must breathe."[25] The last point was one that carried much weight; even if present levels of testing had produced only limited fallout, the continuation of testing would only increase the health hazard.

Although no one argued that fallout was a good thing, many, if not most, testified that it was much less of a problem than popularly believed. Moreover, the question of fallout had to be weighed against the standards of military security that might or might not require testing in the atmosphere. John Foster, director of Livermore, argued before the Senate Committee on Foreign Relations that "from the technical point of view it [the fallout issue] has no bearing on the major issue."[26] Similarly, Glenn Seaborg, chairman of the Atomic Energy Commission, believed that the issue had little to do with the treaty,[27] while Teller claimed that "these two questions, the test ban and fallout, are linked only by propaganda."[28]

The halting of atmospheric testing by the superpowers did reduce the amount of fallout in the air. As Seaborg reported in 1981, "On the matter of test fallout, the treaty has had its anticipated beneficial effect. . . . The United States has reported atmospheric tests by other powers—France, China, and India. While there has been measurable fallout from these tests, the total amount has remained at such low levels as to constitute a negligible biological risk."[29] An important question is, however, to what extent the treaty was decisive in reducing the risks of fallout. Arthur Dean, chief negotiator in Geneva at the time, testified before Congress that he believed that, in the absence of an agreement, the United States would be forced by public opinion to halt testing in "2, or 3, or 4, years."[30] Nevertheless, in expecting a reduction in fallout, the outcome confirmed the positive expectation.

Military-Strategic Issues

Although the administration would have much preferred to stress the long-term political implications and argue that the treaty had few if any strategic-military implications, congressional hearings tended to discuss the military and strategic aspects to a much greater degree. Within this context, primary attention was paid to an exploration of the technical balance in the expectation that what was now to be frozen would later turn into a de facto balance of power. As Senator Henry Jackson put it, "We are freezing something here if the test ban goes through, and I am trying to find out as best as I can, in the exercise of my constitutional responsibility as a Senator, just what we are freezing."[31] One's views on the balance as prevailing in 1963, therefore, directly influenced one's expectations of the ensuing strategic environment. That is to say, the future nuclear balance, the course of the arms race, the need for parity or superiority, and so forth were issues whose expectations tended to be based on an a priori evaluation of the technical balance.

The LTBT's Effect on the Technical Balance.   In discussing the balance of technical knowledge in 1963, it was conceded that the Soviet Union had made relative gains in this area as compared to the balance prevalent in 1958 when the three-year testing moratorium was initiated. Nevertheless, the administration was confident of the present balance, at least to the extent that the knowledge gained by the Soviet Union in its 1961–62 test series did not then, nor would it in the future, impair the U.S. deterrent capability. Moreover, any limitations that the treaty imposed would affect both sides, and no guarantee existed that in the absence of a treaty the United States would always be the first in making the strategically significant breakthrough.

The relative technological balance was assessed by the Joint Chiefs in the Senate hearings. There they argued that the Soviet Union was ahead in the high-yield spectrum (above 15 MT)—both in terms of weapons effects knowledge and in yield-to-weight ratio of warheads—that parity in the midyield spectrum (1–15 MT) had been attained by the Soviet Union, and that the United States was far ahead at the low-yield and tactical warhead level (KT range). Moreover, they argued that the United States would continue to have sufficient nuclear power to inflict maximum damage on the Soviet Union in a retaliatory strike.[32]

Regarding the treaty's effect on limiting the attainment of further knowledge, Harold Brown, Director of Defense, Research and Engineering, argued that such limitations were mutual: "the main question, in my mind is, Does it [the LTBT] inhibit us from getting knowledge but allow the Soviets to get knowledge that will have an important effect in a decisive area? And there my answer is that it will not."[33] It was also believed that in the absence of treaty limits, the technical breakthrough that might lead to significant strategic advantages could be made by either side. As Rusk argued in March 1963, there is "one proposition which we must keep in mind despite confidence and understandable national pride: Nature does not yield up its secrets with political favoritism."[34]

More pessimistic assessments were presented by those who believed that, as a result of their test series in the early 1960s, the Soviet Union had made significant gains in overall nuclear knowledge since 1959. The disparity in testing between the United States and the Soviet Union at that time was emphasized by a number of statistics: the Soviet test series started massively in September 1961, catching the United States totally off guard, while the United States did not resume its atmospheric testing until April of the following year; Moscow had tested about 100 devices compared to twenty-eight atmospheric tests by the United States between the end of the moratorium and the signing of the treaty; and in the high-yield spectrum, the USSR tested more devices above 1 MT than the United States had in its entire history, exploding ten times more megatonnage than the United States in the comparable timeframe. Only in underground testing did the United States have a decisive edge, testing up to ninety devices, where the Soviet Union exploded but a few.[35]

It was statistics like these that led some, like Air Force Chief of Staff General Curtis LeMay, to argue that the knowledge balance had shifted adversely: "The Soviets are therefore in a position to use the information from their last test program in their laboratory work. In this way they may possibly advance further in weaponry than we could with the results that we obtained in our last series."[36] The advances in the high-yield spectrum made by the Soviet Union in their test series, advances conceded by all, led some to question the overall evaluation of the nuclear technology balance as presented in administration testimony. The area in which the United States was said to be ahead was carefully scrutinized by opponents of the treaty. As Teller argued, in the "important subkiloton range, we have no knowledge of the Soviet progress. There is no objective justification to assume as is usually done that in this area we are ahead. . . . In those cases where we can make a comparison we have reason to believe they are ahead. In those cases where we have no basis of comparison, we claim superiority."[37] The resulting effect of the disparate knowledge balance in 1963 was succinctly stated by Teller: "I think there is a disparity of knowledge, and a disparity of knowledge today means a disparity of power tomorrow."[38]

The expectation that the 1963 disparity of knowledge would turn into a disparity of power, however, was not fulfilled. But little more can be said than just that. Given that data on the 1961–63 testing series (apart from the numbers and yields) remain classified, it is difficult if not impossible to judge who was ahead at that time. More important, perhaps, despite who was ahead, the eventual knowledge and nuclear balance would seem to have been little affected by the balance then actually prevailing. The importance of these negative and positive assessments concerning the technical balance lie there-fore elsewhere—namely, in buttressing the arguments made on other issues.

The LTBT's Effect on the ABM.   The central argument put forward by administration officials concerning the development and eventual deployment of an antiballistic missile defense was that, whatever the desirability of such a defense, the LTBT would not inhibit its devel-opment. The basis of this argument was fourfold: (1) the relative bal-ance of deployable systems was currently in the United States' favor or at least not in favor of the Soviet Union; (2) atmospheric testing of system components would not be crucial to the system's develop-ment; (3) in order to decide the wisdom of deploying an ABM, atmo-spheric testing was not needed; and (4) countering the argument that an operational test would be impossible under the treaty, it was argued that such operational tests were in any case impossible short of nuclear war.

McNamara set out his view of the present ABM balance before the Foreign Relations Committee as follows:

> The best present judgment is that our design efforts are comparable in magni-tude and success with those of the Soviets. Any deployed system which the Soviets are likely to have in the near future will probably be less effective, almost certainly not more effective, than the Nike-Zeus system. It should be noted that the United States decided not to deploy the Nike-Zeus because its effectiveness was inadequate.[39]

McNamara's conclusions were buttressed by Harold Brown in a wide-ranging discussion of the treaty's implications for ABM development before both the Committee on Foreign Relations and the Prepared-ness Subcommittee of the Senate Armed Services Committee. Brown repeatedly stressed his belief that (1) the ABM problems still to be worked out were unrelated to atmospheric testing; (2) an appropriate warhead for an ABM interceptor missile had been developed and could be improved through underground testing; and (3) one could overcome the problems posed by the potential blackout of radars.[40]

The second major expectation concerning the ABM was related to the effect of an atmospheric test ban on the system's development. Here the belief was expressed that the limitations imposed by an atmospheric ban, particularly on examining the blackout phenomenon on radar and communications, could be overcome through theoretical extrapolation of presently held data, duplication of radars, and general overdesign. More important, the consensus was expressed that the major ABM problems had nothing to do with atmospheric testing—indeed, not even with the nuclear component—but rather with the problems of missile accuracy and speed and of discriminating reentry vehicles from decoys. Most people, even those much more skeptical, agreed that the warhead development for an ABM would not be impeded by the treaty, given the possibility of underground testing. McNamara time and again defended these points.[41] Moreover, McNamara's judgment on this score was echoed not only in Brown's various statements but also by the professional military. Both General Maxwell Taylor, chairman of the JCS, and Army Chief of Staff General Earl Wheeler, the man primarily responsible for the ABM, confirmed that the primary problems in ABM developments lay outside the nuclear field.[42]

Third, whatever the limitations an inability to test in the atmosphere placed on ABM development, the administration argued that such limitations would not be crucial in deciding whether to deploy the system. As Brown put it before the Preparedness Subcommittee, "atmospheric nuclear tests are important in producing an optimum system, but they will not, by themselves, determine whether the system is effective enough to warrant deployment."[43] Last, operational testing of an ABM would be impossible under any circumstance (that is, with or without a test ban), and, hence, this objection to the LTBT would not hold. The central problem of operational testing, it was argued, lay not so much in the uncertainties concerning the system's performance, as in the nature of the attack it was to withstand.[44] Short of an actual nuclear war, this could never be known.

There were those, however, who disagreed with the above assessment and did so essentially for two reasons. First, because the Soviet Union was judged to be ahead in the crucial area of nuclear effects knowledge that they obtained in the 1961 and 1962 test series, a ban on the U.S. ability to attain similar knowledge would prove to be a disaster, leaving the Soviet Union with an effective ABM and the United States with none whatsoever. Second, an ABM needed operational testing. To deploy a weapon system without such testing would be self-defeating.

The view that the Soviet Union was ahead of the United States in the ABM field was expressed by the Joint Chiefs of Staff. In closed hearings before both the Senate Foreign Relations Committee and the Preparedness Subcommittee, General Taylor affirmed that in "the anti-ballistic-missile field, there is evidence that the Soviets are further advanced than the United States.[45] Teller also argued that if the Soviet Union was ahead in this field, then such an advantage now, given the LTBT, would be translated into a strategic advantage later.[46]

Second, there existed the express belief that, as Admiral Lewis Strauss argued, "[n]o matter how well in theory the components of a weapon will behave on paper, there is no assurance that they will work dependably together until they are put together and tried, and an anti-ballistic missile system cannot be tested underground and therefore no nation, our Nation could not put one safely into production and stockpile it which had never been tested."[47] What was true of every weapon system was even more applicable to ABM, given its inherent complexity.[48]

The ABM story is particularly important today when strategic defenses are again under serious consideration. The LTBT did impede the acquisition of relevant knowledge (particularly in the area of radar blackout) required for the development of a ground-based ABM. How crucial such information was for the actual development of an ABM is difficult to gauge. Not only are the ABM-relevant data obtained through atmospheric testing still highly classified, but also in 1972 the United States and the Soviet Union jointly relinquished the right to build significant missile defenses.

Some judgment about the outcome can, however, be made. Although the administration was correct that the major problems confronting the development of an optimal ABM system lay outside of the treaty's scope, these problems were eventually solved. Once solved, the limitation imposed by the LTBT did increase the uncertainty associated with the system's performance. These limitations included the phenomenon of radar blackout as a result of an atmospheric nuclear explosion; the possibility of an electromagnetic pulse (EMP) created by a high-altitude nuclear explosion, thus crippling electronic communication; and the possibility that incoming warheads might suffer from the effects of fratricide—that is, the destruction of a warhead as a result of the explosion generated by a previous nuclear warhead. Although the EMP problem was not discussed in the open literature at the time of the LTBT ratification debate, Herbert York argued that it was discussed behind the veil of secrecy.[49] Over time it proved possible to ameliorate somewhat the effects of EMP and the fratricide phenomenon, primarily through hardening of the relevant materials.

The remaining problem of radar blackout came to occupy a prominent position in the ABM debate in the latter part of the 1960s. The blackout phenomenon presented two different problems. According to Hans Bethe, "our knowledge of blackout is mainly theoretical."[50] Bethe argued that the United States acquired its weapons effect knowledge during the two test series of 1958 and 1962, in which about seven devices were exploded of various yields and at altitudes ranging from ten to 250 statute miles. Because not every yield was investigated, the gap had to be filled through theoretical extrapolation, and, hence, there was "some uncertainty about the exact extent of blackout in certain cases."[51] It is these ranges of uncertainty that could not be cleared in the absence of atmospheric testing. Although Bethe, Herbert York, and others claimed that the "important conclusions [about ABMs] are essentially independent of these uncertainties,"[52] such uncertainties could not but affect the ultimate performance of an ABM system.

A second problem associated with the blackout phenomenon was that the Soviet Union *had* tested the various yields that the United States had not and, as such, might be in the possession of weapons effect knowledge that was denied the United States under the treaty. Whether the Soviet Union actually possessed the relevant data is difficult to say. The fact remains, however, that the USSR decided to deploy an ABM system before the United States did and continued to deploy the system around Moscow even after the ABM Treaty was signed.

Nevertheless, the effect of the LTBT on the future development of an ABM system remains indeterminate, given the ABM treaty and given a lack of publicly available data. The most that can be said is that although the expectation that the nonnuclear elements were the key to an effective ABM was mostly correct, once these problems were solved the limitations on nuclear effects knowledge imposed by the LTBT did become important if not crucial.

The LTBT's Effect on U.S. Nuclear Advantage.   The administration argued that the treaty would not halt U.S. nuclear progress and that, to the extent that the United States was ahead in 1963, such superiority would be prolonged or even maintained indefinitely. As Kennedy claimed, this "treaty does not halt American nuclear progress. The United States has more experience in underground testing than any other nation; and we intend to use this capacity to maintain the adequacy of our arsenal."[53] According to McNamara, the treaty would at least delay Soviet achievement of technical parity, a condition many in the administration saw as inevitable.[54]

Some, however, went further than McNamara, arguing that the treaty's acceptance by the Soviet Union codified U.S. nuclear superiority. Sorensen attributes this argument to Kennedy, who was said to believe that "even a limited test-ban treaty required a Soviet acceptance of permanent American superiority in nuclear weapons."[55] Arthur Schlesinger similarly argued that the treaty meant a Soviet "acquiescence in American nuclear superiority." The Soviet acquiescence, Schlesinger went on, "showed not only a post–Cuba confidence in American restraint but a new understanding of the theories of stable nuclear deterrence."[56]

Others were less sanguine about the future nuclear balance, believing that the treaty's limits applied asymmetrically. Thus, James Kendall, chief counsel to the Preparedness Subcommittee argued, "I state frankly that I can't quite see the compatibility with our national security of a provision which would give them the opportunity to catch up to us in the low-yield weapons [through underground testing], where we are assumed to be ahead, and would deny to us the opportunity to catch up with them in the high-yield weapons [by prohibiting atmospheric testing], where they are assumed to be superior."[57]

The United States did eventually lose its advantage in the nuclear balance. The effect of the LTBT on this development was, however, marginal at most. The evolution of the balance was determined by factors not related to the treaty, primarily because the treaty did not limit areas crucial to the quantitative and qualitative expansion of nuclear arsenals. Indeed, the treaty's limits, whatever the prevalent nuclear balance, did not influence the capability on either side to expand and elaborate their respective offensive nuclear stockpiles.

The LTBT's Effect on the Arms Race. Some believed that the treaty's effect on the nuclear arms race might be to curb it, if not halt and reverse it altogether. This argument was political in nature, in that the treaty was seen as stimulating additional agreements limiting further expansion of the nuclear arsenals and even genuine disarmament measures. Kennedy cautiously pointed to this potential benefit in his address to the nation on July 26, 1963: "this treaty can limit the nuclear arms race in ways which, on balance, will strengthen our nation's security far more than the continuation of unrestricted testing. For, in today's world a nation's security does not always increase as its arms increase when its adversary is doing the same."[58]

Others argued that the immediate effect of the treaty would be to stimulate the arms race. In anticipation of the lulling effect, the JCS argued that they could support the treaty only if the following four safeguards were implemented: (1) continued and vigorous underground testing, (2) maintenance of national laboratories, (3) performance of the necessary preparations to ensure a speedy resumption of atmospheric testing if needed, and (4) vigorous development of national technical means (NTM) to verify Soviet compliance.[59] Kennedy, in a letter to Senate minority leader Everett Dirksen and majority leader Mike Mansfield sent during the Senate's floor debate (which was to sway the minority leader's vote in the treaty's favor), promised to implement all JCS safeguards.[60] Implementation of the safeguards was expected to increase rather than decrease the number of future tests. Thus, the Chief of Naval Operations Admiral David McDonald argued that "there is a possibility that this treaty, together with the safeguards that we have laid down, will perhaps stimulate our test program."[61]

The implementation of the JCS safeguards had the undeniable effect of increasing the number of tests performed. In large part this was assured when the Senate Armed Services Committee adopted an amendment by Senator Henry Jackson predicating its support for the treaty on the implementation of the safeguards. In 1968 Jackson reported to the Congress that he was "pleased with the way the administration has continued to support and implement its promise to the Senate to carry out the safeguards."[62] From 1971 to 1974 the Senate Armed Services Committee created a permanent subcommittee on Nuclear Test Ban Safeguards chaired by Senator Jackson, thus ensuring their implementation even ten years after the treaty had been signed.

The actual number of tests performed before and after the treaty tells the full story. The United States exploded ninety-five devices in the period 1951–57 compared to 119 in the period 1966–72. The comparable figures for the Soviet Union were thirty and 111, respectively.[63] Hence, in this instance, it was the anticipation of the lulling effect that led to the United States spending more on defense.

The LTBT's Effect on Nonproliferation. Despite the central role that the nonproliferation argument played before the treaty was signed, once signed, the potential contribution of the LTBT to nonproliferation tended to be downplayed. President Kennedy was one of the few people to stress the connection: "this treaty can be a step toward preventing the spread of nuclear weapons to nations not now possessing them. . . . This treaty can be the opening wedge in that campaign."[64]

Two justifications for this belief were put forward. First, the example of halting testing in three environments would increase the means available to dissuade nations to acquire nuclear weapons. As William Foster wrote in a memo for the president, a treaty "would increase the leverage the United States might exert and would open the way for the development of new combinations of inducements and persuasions, possibly on an international scale, which are difficult to set in motion as long as the United States itself continues to test. Accordingly, over the next decade, the United States might expect to approach this problem more successfully on the basis of a test ban than without it."[65] Second, by limiting testing to the more costly and difficult underground environment, the LTBT placed another hurdle in the way of those states interested in acquiring nuclear weapons. McNamara argued that testing underground was both more costly and more difficult and would therefore dissuade others from testing.[66]

Although no one saw the prospect of nuclear proliferation as a gain for U.S. security, not all believed that the treaty addressed the issue. In fact, general agreement emerged that the proliferation problem ought to be addressed as soon as possible, but this treaty did little, if anything, to do so. On a more specific point, Teller countered McNamara's argument that cost might dissuade potential acquisition of nuclear weapons, with the argument that the added cost of underground testing was not really much of a deterrent: "once a nation has gone to the expense of developing a nuclear explosive, the additional single million dollars that is needed for underground testing will certainly not be a financial deterrent."[67]

The contribution of the LTBT to nonproliferation would appear to be negligible. It is true that since its signing only two additional countries declared that they had tested a nuclear device—China and India—and India tested only underground. On the other hand, the absence of a LTBT would hardly seem to have directly contributed to an increase in the number of nuclear weapons states. This is not to say that the treaty might not have had an indirect positive effect on the proliferation issue. For one, the first arms control agreement following the signing of the LTBT was the Non-Proliferation Treaty. For another, reduced tensions that might have accompanied the treaty's signing could have obviated the need for other states to acquire nuclear weapons, particularly in Western Europe. But the overall effect of the treaty on proliferation was probably limited even though it did perhaps contribute to establishing a testing norm and as such provided timely warning of an impending decision to detonate a nuclear device underground.

The Effect of Noncompliance on U.S. Security.   The issue of compliance may be subdivided into two related factors: (1) To what extent can compliance be verified, and what are the effects on security of successful cheating? And (2) what are the risks of surprise abrogation, and what mechanisms exist to guard against such abrogation?

On the adequacy of verification, once the treaty allowed for underground testing, verification with national technical means was deemed to be sufficient. Harold Brown, testifying before the Preparedness Subcommittee, reaffirmed that the United States could detect and identify all significant violations with NTM.[68] As to the effect of successful cheating, Kennedy reassured the Senate on this score in the message accompanying his request for the Senate's advice and consent:

> Under this treaty any gains in nuclear strength and knowledge which could be made by the tests of any other power—including not only underground tests but even any illegal test which might escape detection—could not be sufficient to offset the ability of our strategic forces to deter or survive a nuclear attack and to penetrate and destroy an aggressor's homeland.[69]

This conclusion was shared by the JCS.[70] Moreover, the treaty safeguards put forward by the JCS would ensure that no clandestine testing could result in an adverse balance of power.

The risks of surprise abrogation were minimized by two factors. The successful implementation of the JCS safeguards would entail an instant readiness to address any such abrogation through a testing program directed at correcting any imbalances that might occur. The fact that anyone could withdraw from the treaty within ninety days also reinforced the sense of security. Moreover, an abrogation of the treaty would be unlikely to lead to an instantaneous shift in the balance.[71]

The judgment that Soviet secret noncompliance would not affect the overall strategic balance was challenged by Edward Teller. Teller, arguing that shallow underground bursts were legal under the terms of the treaty as long as venting of radiation would be confined to national territory, put forward the hypothesis that such testing, if combined with undetectable atmospheric testing in the subkiloton range, could threaten the survivability of the retaliatory forces.[72] The threat posed by a Soviet surprise abrogation was also viewed adversely. Admiral Lewis Strauss, former chairman of the AEC, argued that a "radical new weapon discovery or a breakthrough in countermeasure systems, suddenly tested and found workable, could put the possessor nation in command of world events. We ourselves were twice in that position, first with our invention of the fission bomb and later of the fusion bomb."[73]

The issue of compliance with the LTBT has not been a major one since the treaty was ratified. Undetected cheating cannot, by definition, be known, and, should this have occurred, its effect on the military balance cannot be known either. Because other developments in the nonnuclear field have proven to be more important to the overall balance, however, it might be a proper inference to argue that, should undetected cheating have occurred, such events did not affect the balance.

There have been incidents in which underground tests resulted in radioactive venting beyond the confines of the national territory. Such incidents occurred on both sides, if only because some form of venting is inevitable even if not always detectable. In the mid- to late 1960s, however, the Soviet Union did explode a number of devices causing large amounts of radioactive debris to cross its national boundaries. At least one of these tests was performed in a shallow underground environment.[74] The venting that resulted from this latter test may be viewed as predictable and, as such, as a meaningful violation of the terms of the treaty. Up to 1984 each side was satisfied that the remaining incidents of venting were technical violations of the terms of the treaty but that neither the intention nor the effect was worth serious questioning of the continued compliance with the treaty. In October 1984, however, the Reagan administration's General Advisory Committee on arms control and disarmament mentioned the venting issue as part of a series of significant Soviet treaty violations.[75]

CONCLUSIONS

What does the Limited Test Ban Treaty tell us about the competing claims made concerning arms control? What, in short, are the LTBT's lessons for arms control? Given that the Limited Test Ban Treaty dealt with procedural rather than structural factors in the forces of both sides and that the treaty was the first major postwar arms control agreement between both sides, its effects were felt more in the political than in the strategic-military realm. Nowhere was this more apparent than U.S.-Soviet relations. Clearly the LTBT was a product of the crisis over the Cuban missiles of October 1962. The most immediate effect was a consciously sought deescalation in both the rhetoric and the reality of foreign policy behavior by each side. Immalleable negotiation positions began to give way to the give-and-take negotiations that are the sine qua non of reaching agreements. In this sense, then, the LTBT was a clear product of the surrounding U.S.-Soviet environment that was marked by a search for rapprochement in the aftermath of both sides having stood on the brink of war.

The longer-term effect of the LTBT on U.S.-Soviet relations is more difficult to judge. Some evidence presented above did point to a change in at least the tone and content of Soviet statements following the treaty. Since the treaty was signed within a climate of improving relations, however, its precise effect on these relations is uncertain. The most one can say is that the treaty reinforced the search for a rapprochement and as such contributed to the improvement of relations. The arms control process operated within the wider environment of U.S.-Soviet relations. As the latter changed, the former was invariably affected. To the extent that the arms control process itself served to reinforce the existing trend in U.S.-Soviet relations, the two worked to reinforce each other.

What of the LTBT's effect on reducing uncertainties in force estimates and projections of each other's forces? The test ban negotiations induced all sides, but particularly the United States, to think through the problems of and develop the means for effective verification. Improvements in the Atomic Energy Detection System (AEDS), the Conference of Experts, the VELA project for space detection, as well as the Sound and Surveillance systems for underwater sound detection were all products of an eight-year effort to negotiate an effective and verifiable ban on nuclear testing.[76] These verification instruments could be used not only for monitoring arms control compliance but also as intelligence instruments for the estimation and projection of the other's armed forces.

On the other hand, the actual agreement increased uncertainty about the opposing force structures by forcing testing underground. Not only did the testing process become less transparent, but the fact that atmospheric testing was barred meant that the intelligence tool of radioactive debris sampling would henceforth be denied to both sides. As the Preparedness Subcommittee reported in its interim report opposing ratification, "By driving Soviet testing underground this intelligence will be denied the United States with the result that with the passage of time knowledge of the Soviet state of the art in weapons undergoing tests will be seriously degraded. The effect of the treaty will be to reinforce the difficulties already imposed on the United States by Soviet secrecy."[77] Not only was the treaty's effect to increase uncertainty of estimating the *opposing* forces, but one's own force posture would also become subject to growing uncertainties. Thus, the appropriate hardness of missile silos, the penetrability of reentry vehicles, and the survival of one's deterrent force became a matter more of extrapolation from uncertain data than of full-scale testing. Had it been deemed desirable (or should it today be seen as desirable) to develop an ABM system, similar, if not greater, uncertainties would have been present in this area.

The lulling proposition was very much discussed during the debate of the LTBT. Both arguments—that the United States would spend more and that it would spend less on defense as a result of the treaty—were made. However, as a result of the anticipated lulling effect, both Congress and the administration adopted measures (in the form of the JCS safeguards) that ensured that the former would be the case. Moreover, the actual terms of the treaty directly contributed to increased defense spending (at least as far as the AEC budget was concerned) by forcing testing underground, an environment in which testing is more expensive than elsewhere. The anticipation of lulling by all sides on the issue was important in directing U.S. attention to the perceived need for vigilance. Whether the actual result was more (or less) than required remains, in the final analysis, a matter of judgment.

The verification issue lay at the heart of much political controversy, more as a result of doubts about the Soviet Union's trustworthiness, however, than of the actual ability to verify compliance. Although the argument was made that the Soviet Union would cheat, the administration convinced many that even if it should occur, such undetected cheating could only be so marginal as not to affect the security of the United States. In fact, the political requirement to ensure appropriate verification proved to be more demanding than the security requirements, as the Jackson amendment to make the JCS safeguards a law were to demonstrate.

The above discussion indicates that political support for the treaty was more related to factors outside of the terms of the agreement than to the actual provisions of the treaty itself. The one exception to this rule is the fact that the halting of atmospheric testing did address the popular issue of fallout directly. In general, however, it was the president's strength in the aftermath of the Cuban crisis, the improved U.S.-Soviet relations following this episode, and the large measure of executive branch support for the treaty (including, most important, that provided by the Joint Chiefs) that led many to believe that the treaty would make a positive contribution to U.S. security. As to congressional support for the treaty, this was more related to those factors just mentioned, as well as to the political outlook of the Senate in general, than to the direct congressional participation in the process itself, which was virtually nonexistent.[78]

Last, the proposition that the arms control process and arms control agreements serve Soviet interests more than U.S. interests was one openly and vigorously argued by the opponents of the treaty. Many times opponents argued that the Soviet Union signed the treaty only because it believed the LTBT to be to its advantage. Further, the belief that the USSR would in any case cheat while the United States as an open society could not meant that the treaty necessarily favored Moscow to the detriment of the United States. The Kennedy administration, on the other hand, effectively argued that the treaty served both U.S. and Soviet interests and that arms control was reflective of mutual interests rather than reducible to a zero-sum interpretation.

In conclusion, it appears that the treaty affected military-strategic issues far less than it affected the climate of East-West relations. The terms of the LTBT did not directly address, nor indeed contribute to, the traditional arms control goals: reducing the likelihood of war, decreasing the costs associated with the preparation for war, and decreasing the destructiveness of war.[79] Offensive systems could be and, in fact, were developed at an accelerated rate on both sides. The treaty did pose an impediment to the development of an optimum antiballistic missile system, although its effect on this should not be overstated.

Yet the treaty was an undoubted success, most notably in the intangible realm of international politics. With nuclear testing and the absence of a ban on such activity having been symbolic of the Cold War, the agreement's signing performed the powerful symbol of marking a change in that relation. All the positive political expectations were more or less fulfilled, although the direct contribution of the LTBT to these outcomes remains a matter of debate. Nevertheless, the treaty was symbolic of a changed climate and, as such, represented the culmination of the Cuban Missile Crisis's peaceful resolution. Where prior to its signing the road of East-West interaction was strewn with the failures of summits in Paris and Vienna, confrontations over Berlin, Cuba, Laos, and the Congo, and a general distrust of motives and sentiment that spilled over into the domestic political arenas, subsequent to the Moscow signing new tones of voices were raised and different issues emerged. Henceforth the mood of relations was marked by "bridge-building" concepts, the search for and signing of new agreements such as the NPT and SALT, and the rise of a more general détente. Whether a cause or not, the LTBT marks a turning point as the first concrete achievement in postwar arms control.

NOTES

1. On the negotiations of a nuclear test ban see particularly the account of Harold K. Jackobson and Eric Stein, *Diplomats, Scientists and Politicians:*

The United States and the Nuclear Test Ban Negotiations (Ann Arbor: University of Michigan Press, 1966), and Ronald Terchek, *The Making of the Test Ban Treaty* (The Hague: Martinus Nijhoff, 1970). See also the inside account of Glenn Seaborg, *Kennedy, Khrushchev, and the Test Ban* (Berkeley: University of California Press, 1981).

2. Seaborg, *Kennedy, Khrushchev and the Test Ban*, pp. 123–25.

3. Arthur Schlesinger, *A Thousand Days* (Greenwich, Conn.: Fawcett Crest, 1965), p. 815.

4. U.S. Senate Committee on Foreign Relations, *Hearings on the Nuclear Test Ban Treaty*, 88th Cong., 1st Sess. (Washington, D.C.: U.S. Government Printing Office, 1963), p. 67 (hereafter cited as Committee on Foreign Relations).

5. See Seaborg, *Kennedy, Khrushchev and the Test Ban*, pp. 179, 187–88.

6. In U.S. Arms Control and Disarmament Agency, *Documents on Disarmament, 1963* (Washington, D.C.: U.S. Government Printing Office, 1964), p. 113 (hereafter cited as ACDA, *Documents on Disarmament, 1963*).

7. ACDA, *Documents on Disarmament, 1963*, p. 60.

8. ACDA, *Documents on Disarmament, 1963*, p. 221.

9. ACDA, *Documents on Disarmament, 1963*, pp. 252–53.

10. See, e.g., the statement by General Curtis LeMay, in Committee on Foreign Relations, p. 358.

11. ACDA, *Documents on Disarmament, 1963*, p. 250.

12. U.S. Senate Preparedness Investigation Subcommittee of the Committee on Armed Services, *Hearings on the Military Aspects and Implications of Nuclear Test Ban Proposals and Related Matters*, 88th Cong., 1st Sess. (Washington, D.C.: U.S. Government Printing Office, May-Aug. 1963), p. 644 (hereafter cited as Preparedness Subcommittee).

13. Preparedness Subcommittee, p. 564.

14. Committee on Foreign Relations, p. 515. See also the representative statements of Senator Hickenlooper and Admiral Lewis Strauss in *ibid.*, pp. 413, 691.

15. Sophia Peterson, *The Nuclear Test Ban Treaty and Its Effect on International Tensions* (Los Angeles: UCLA Security Studies Project No. 9, 1967).

16. Theodore C. Sorensen, *Kennedy* (New York: Harper & Row, 1965), p. 740.

17. William C. Foster, "Memorandum for the President: Political Implications of a Nuclear Test Ban," ACDA Memorandum, July 12, 1963, National Security File Box #256, ACDA–Harriman Trip to Moscow, Part II, John F. Kennedy Library, Mass., p. 4.

18. Committee on Foreign Relations, p. 514.

19. See, for example, the statement by Senator Mundt in Committee on Foreign Relations, p. 88.

20. Sorensen to Carl Kaysen in "Oral History Project" interview, April 26, 1964, John F. Kennedy Library, pp. 85–86. See also Kennedy's statements to this effect in his July 26 Address and Message to the Senate of August 5, in ACDA, *Documents on Disarmament, 1963*, pp. 257, 302.

21. See, for example, Committee on Foreign Relations, pp. 109, 276.

22. Committee on Foreign Relations, p. 75. See also Strausz-Hupé's argument in *ibid.*, p. 516.

23. Cited in James H. MacBride, *The Test Ban Treaty: Military, Technological and Political Implications* (Chicago: Henry Regnery, 1967), pp. 120–21.

24. See the comments by Kennedy in Schlesinger, *A Thousand Days*, p. 839.

25. ACDA, *Documents on Disarmament, 1963*, p. 254.

26. Committee on Foreign Relations, p. 622.

27. Committee on Foreign Relations, p. 243.

28. Committee on Foreign Relations, p. 455.

29. Seaborg, *Kennedy, Khrushchev and the Test Ban*, p. 286. See also "A Nuclear Unthreat," *The Economist* (March 29, 1986), p. 35, and Herbert York, "The Great Test-Ban Debate," *Scientific American* (Nov. 1972), p. 300.

30. Committee on Foreign Relations, p. 818.

31. Preparedness Subcommittee, p. 428.

32. Committee on Foreign Relations, p. 273.

33. Committee on Foreign Relations, p. 543.

34. Statement before the Senate Foreign Relations Committee, March 11, 1963, in *Department of State Bulletin* (April 1, 1963), p. 486.

35. McBride, *The Test Ban Treaty*, pp. 26–28.

36. Preparedness Subcommittee, p. 357.

37. Preparedness Subcommittee, p. 544. See also General LeMay's and Dr. John Foster's statements in *ibid.*, pp. 429, 729.

38. Committee on Foreign Relations, p. 475.

39. Committee on Foreign Relations, pp. 103–04.

40. See, e.g., his statement in Committee on Foreign Relations, pp. 530–31.

41. See, for example, Committee on Foreign Relations, pp. 103–04.

42. See, e.g., statements by Taylor, Wheeler, and Brown in Committee on Foreign Relations, pp. 314, 378, 559, 571.

43. Preparedness Subcommittee, p. 858. See also McNamara's statement to this effect in Committee on Foreign Relations, p. 138.

44. See, for example, the testimonies of Herbert York in Committee of Foreign Relations, p. 760, and of Norris Bradbury in Preparedness Subcommittee, p. 436.

45. Preparedness Subcommittee, p. 588.

46. Committee on Foreign Relations, p. 439.

47. Committee on Foreign Relations, p. 692.

48. See, for example, Edward Teller in Committee on Foreign Relations, p. 424.

49. See York, "The Great Test-Ban Debate," p. 297.

50. Hans A. Bethe, "Countermeasures to ABM Systems," in Abram Chayes and Jerome Wiesner, eds., *ABM* (New York: Signet Books, 1969), p. 139. See also Hans Bethe and Richard Garwin, "Anti-Ballistic Missile Systems," *Scientific American* (March 1968).

51. Bethe, "Countermeasures to ABM Systems," p. 139.

52. Bethe, "Countermeasures to ABM Systems," p. 139, and York "The Great Test-Ban Debate," pp. 295–97.

53. ACDA, *Documents on Disarmament, 1963*, p. 300.

54. See, for example, Committee on Foreign Relations, pp. 104–05. The JCS shared McNamara's views on this. See *ibid.*, p. 316.

55. Sorensen, *Kennedy*, p. 734.

56. Schlesinger, *A Thousand Days*, p. 831.

57. Preparedness Subcommittee, p. 395.

58. ACDA, *Documents on Disarmament, 1963*, p. 255.

59. See U.S. Senate Preparedness Investigating Subcommittee of the Committee on Armed Services, *Military Implications of the Proposed Limited Test Ban Treaty: An Interim Report*, 88th Cong., 1st Sess. (Washington, D.C.: U.S. Government Printing Office, Sept. 9, 1985), pp. 9–10, 16–24.

60. See Seaborg, *Kennedy, Khrushchev and the Test Ban*, p. 279. See also Kennedy's press conference of August 20, 1963, in which he detailed the steps taken by the administration to implement the safeguards, in ACDA, *Documents on Disarmament, 1963*, pp. 390ff.

61. Committee on Foreign Relations, p. 367.

62. See the remarks by Senator Henry Jackson on nuclear test ban safeguards in the *Congressional Record—Senate*, Sept. 25, 1986, pp. 28131–32.

63. The specific periods for comparison were chosen for the following reasons: (1) they are of equal duration; (2) the 1951–57 period is the only period where both the Soviet Union and the United States tested and was before the moratorium; and (3) the 1966–72 period was chosen in order to allow development and construction of drilling and diagnostics technologies. Figures for the earlier period are from *Bulletin of Atomic Scientists* (Nov. 1963), p. 46. Figures for the later period are from SIPRI, *The Arms Race and Arms Control, 1982* (London: Taylor and Francis, 1982), p. 135. It should further be noted that since 1961 the United States pursues a policy of not announcing all the tests that it conducts so that the actual figures for the latter period are likely to be higher. Indeed, as Senator Jackson told the Senate, "a large number of additional tests have not been announced in consonance with the policy established in 1961." *Congressional Record—Senate*, Sept. 25, 1968, p. 28129.

64. ACDA, *Documents on Disarmament, 1963*, pp. 254–55.

65. Foster, "Memorandum for the President," p. 4.

66. Committee on Foreign Relations, p. 108.

67. Committee on Foreign Relations, p. 421.

68. Preparedness Subcommittee, pp. 864ff.

69. ACDA, *Documents on Disarmament, 1963*, p. 301.

70. Preparedness Subcommittee, p. 647.

71. See, e.g., the testimony of Dr. George Kistiakowsky, in Committee on Foreign Relations, p. 875.

72. Preparedness Subcommittee, p. 549.

73. Committee on Foreign Relations, p. 673.

74. The information on these tests was provided by Herbert York at a Conference at the John F. Kennedy School of Government, Harvard University, May 8, 1986.

75. Report by the General Advisory Committee on Arms Control and Disarmament, *A Quarter Century of Soviet Compliance Practices under Arms Control Agreements, 1958–83* (Washington, D.C.: The White House, October 1984), p. 5.

76. See also the Congressional Research Service report, *Fundamentals of Nuclear Arms Control: Part IV—Treaty Compliance and Nuclear Arms Control*, Report Prepared for the House Subcommittee on Arms Control, International Security and Science of the House Committee on Foreign Affairs, 99th Cong., 1st Sess. (Washington, D.C.: U.S. Government Printing Office, June 19, 1985), pp. 7ff.

77. Senate Committee on Armed Services, *Military Implications of the Proposed Limited Test Ban Treaty*, p. 8.

78. See Terchek, *The Making of the Test Ban Treaty*, pp. 139–82.

79. Thomas C. Schelling and Morton Halperin, *Strategy and Arms Control* (New York: Twentieth Century Fund, 1961).

3 THE ACCIDENTS MEASURES AGREEMENT

Andrew Bennett

The Accidents Measures Agreement (AMA) was for a number of reasons the subject of the least intense and divisive expectations of all the cases in this study, making it a potential model for "quiet" arms control. The most important feature of the AMA that sets it apart from the other cases in this study is that it was considered to be peripheral to the arms negotiations of which it was a part—peripheral first in the sense of being secondary in importance to the other issues discussed in the SALT I talks and later in the sense of being delinked from those issues. In addition to being considered a peripheral agreement, the AMA was an executive agreement and hence did not require Senate ratification. The administration briefed congressional committees on the implications of the agreement following its negotiation, but the negotiation process itself was less open to public and congressional influence than that of any of the other agreements in this study. Yet another reason for the agreement's low profile was that expectations of its effects were essentially consensual, positive, and noncontroversial. In this and other respects, there has been substantial continuity between the expectations of the AMA and those of previous and later efforts to prevent accidental war (the 1963 Hot Line Agreement, the 1972 Incidents at Sea Agreement, the 1975 Helsinki Confidence Building Measures, and the 1971 and 1982 agreements to update the Hot Line). Moreover, the Congress, the public, and interest groups seemed satisfied with their limited roles in reaching the agreement, although some members of the press were somewhat dissatisfied with the secrecy that surrounded the accord. Finally, and perhaps most important, the AMA was considered to be peripheral to discussions of offensive and defensive forces because it did not involve constraints on the numbers or operations of those forces. Thus, executive departments and agencies, as well as the Congress, the public, and the media, did not play a very active role in formulating U.S. positions in the accidents measures negotiations. This case study examines how these low levels of public, congressional, executive, and media interest and involvement in the AMA affected its negotiation and implementation, highlighting the advantages and limitations of the agreement as a model for quiet arms control.

NEGOTIATION AND PROVISIONS OF THE AGREEMENT

Negotiation of the Agreement

After the Soviets raised the subject of accidents measures in preparatory exchanges for the SALT talks in 1968, in a Gromyko speech to the Supreme Soviet in 1969 and in an exchange between Soviet Ambassador Anatoly Dobrynin and the U.S. chief arms negotiator Gerard Smith just weeks before the opening of SALT talks in Helsinki in November 1969, Smith indicated that the United States was interested in discussing accidents measures once the main SALT negotiations were well underway. Smith's caution, according to Raymond Garthoff, who was serving as the senior State Department advisor on the U.S. delegation, "reflected a concern in Washington that the accident problem not delay or distract from the task of limiting strategic arms."[1] After Vladimir Semenov, the chief of the Soviet SALT delegation, raised the issue of accidental war in the very first working session of the SALT talks, the United States agreed to discuss the issue. Discussions on accidents measures intensified following the U.S. government's completion of an interagency study on accident measures as one of fifteen analytical arms control tasks studied in preparation for the April 1970 Vienna session of SALT I.[2]

During the fall 1970 recess the U.S. Verification Panel, an ad hoc interagency group chaired by Kissinger that made the key U.S. arms control policy decisions on SALT I,[3] developed a firmer U.S. position on accidents measures. The panel recommended that the United States seek an agreement providing for notification of unauthorized missile launches or other accidents involving nuclear weapons, mutual exchange of information in the event of detection of unidentified objects by missile warning systems or signs of interference with these systems, and advance notification of planned missile launches and strategic aircraft takeoffs (the U.S. government later reversed itself on notifications of aircraft takeoffs at the suggestion of its negotiating delegation).[4] President Nixon agreed to the panel's recommendations, with the sole reservation that any "accidents" agreement would have to be part of a strategic arms limitation agreement.

Once the strategic arms talks were well underway, a parallel set of negotiations on accidents measures began in earnest in the spring of 1971, managed by a Special Technical Group established in mid-April and headed on the U.S. side by Ambassador J. Graham "Jeff" Parsons. Talks on the agreement proceeded rapidly, and by the beginning of the July 1971 Helsinki session, only two and one-half months after the establishment of the Technical Group, the AMA was almost in final form. The most important remaining issue was whether the agreement would be signed separately from a strategic arms agreement, as the Soviets wanted, or only as a part of a wider agreement, as the United States desired. President Nixon soon decided that a separate agreement was acceptable, possibly persuaded by Ambassador Smith's arguments that as a separate accord, the agreement could help balance recent U.S. moves toward China and make the Soviets more forthcoming on other SALT issues.[5] Secretary of State Rogers and Foreign Minister Gromyko signed the agreement in Washington on September 30, 1971.

Provisions of the Agreement

In its final form, the AMA has five major provisions. First, each side agreed to improve its own organizational and technical control of nuclear weapons to prevent accidental or unauthorized use of these weapons. Each side was left free to determine which organizational and technical changes it deemed necessary to prevent accidents, and neither side was required to report or verify its actions in compliance with this provision. Second, each side agreed to notify the other immediately "in the event of an accidental, unauthorized or any other unexplained incident involving a possible detonation of a nuclear weapon which could create a risk of outbreak of nuclear war" and to "make every effort . . . to render harmless or destroy such weapon without its causing damage." As with command and control improvements, each side was left free to define for itself which incidents might entail a risk of accidental war and would therefore require notification. Third, the two sides agreed to "notify each other immediately in the event of detection by missile warning systems of unidentified objects, or in the event of signs of interference with these systems." At U.S. insistence, this provision also contained the qualifying clause "if such occurrences could create a risk of outbreak of nuclear war," a judgment that was again left for the parties to make for themselves. Fourth, both sides agreed to give advance notification of any planned missile launches beyond their national territories and in the direction of the other country. Finally, each party agreed that in "other situations involving unexplained nuclear incidents" it would "act in such a manner as to reduce the possibility of its actions being misinterpreted by the other party." "In any such situation," the agreement concluded, "each Party may inform the other Party or request information when, in its view, this is warranted by the interests of averting the risk of outbreak of nuclear war." "Transmissions of urgent information" and "notifications and requests for information in situations requiring prompt clarification" were to be made via the Hot Line, and less urgent communications were to be made through other means, including diplomatic channels.

It is important to note the provisions proposed by the Soviets that were *not* included in the final agreement. Among these were Soviet proposals for notification of mass takeoffs of aircraft, limitation of the flight paths of nuclear-armed bombers to the national territorial airspace of each country, and limitation of the patrolling areas of nuclear-armed submarines and aircraft carriers. Although the United States had given some consideration to notifications of mass takeoffs of strategic aircraft, U.S. negotiators eventually rejected all of these Soviet proposals because they would clearly place greater operational constraints on U.S.-NATO forces than on Soviet-Warsaw Pact forces.[6] The United States was firmer still in rejecting Soviet proposals to discuss "no first use" and possible provocative attacks by third parties. The Soviets did not reject any major U.S. accidents measures proposals.

EXPECTATIONS

The expectations inspired by the AMA were limited by the agreement's secondary status in SALT I, by the administration's management of the negotiations, and by the Congress's low level of involvement in arms control in general. The AMA was also wholly negotiated by the negotiating teams in Vienna and Helsinki rather than the Kissinger-Dobrynin "back channel," perhaps as good an indication as any of the relatively lower priority accorded to accidents measures during SALT I. The provisions and even the very negotiation of the agreement, however, were kept a complete secret from the public and, as far as the public record shows, from the Congress as well, until after the United States agreed to sign the AMA as a separate agreement. Prior to the first leaked reports that the agreement was awaiting formal signature, the only oblique hint that the public had that such an agreement was being contemplated was an announcement in late March 1971 that the United States and the Soviets were discussing ways to "improve and modernize" the Hot Line.[7] News coverage of the accord essentially ended after a few articles in the three weeks preceding and one week following its signature.

It is not entirely clear why the AMA negotiations were kept even more secret than those on offensive and defensive arms. The most likely explanation is the administration's fear that the Soviets would exploit politically sensitive accidents measures issues, most notably that of provocative attack. In addition, the administration initially feared that accidents measures discussions could distract attention from the main issues in SALT I. In retrospect, the most striking aspect of the complete secrecy surrounding the accord is not that it was effectively maintained but that as far as the public record indicates, no one in Congress strenuously objected to not being kept informed of the talks on accidents measures. When members of Congress were briefed on the accords in closed committee hearings, they raised some substantive questions but appeared content with the secret process through which the accords were reached.[8] This was in keeping with the Congress's general lack of involvement in arms control issues in the early 1970s and its preoccupation with the war in Vietnam.[9] Only *The Washington Post* complained loudly, in an editorial by the editorial board, that "we see no good reason why the matter had to be kept secret so long."[10]

Strategic Expectations

The expectations of informed government officials and agencies during the agreement's negotiation were for the most part consensual and positive, as were public expectations following the accord's announcement—no one opposes the prevention of accidental nuclear war. The most general expectation among officials and the public was that the AMA would slightly reduce the risks of false alerts, unauthorized or accidental launches or other nuclear accidents that could involve nuclear detonations and misunderstandings in crises.

The agreement was expected to reduce these risks in two ways. First, it was expected to lead to greater attention on both sides toward establishing safeguards in their command and control of nuclear forces. This subject led to one of the few sources of disagreement within the U.S. government on the accord because some, most notably the Joint Chiefs of Staff, were concerned that discussions of C^3I safeguards might give the Soviets valuable information on U.S. technologies and standard operating procedures involving nuclear weapons.[11] The Chiefs therefore objected to giving the Soviets a detailed briefing on U.S. safety procedures unless they agreed to reciprocate. All other agencies argued that the provision of information that might improve Soviet safety measures would be in U.S. interests regardless of whether the Soviets provided information on their own safety procedures. In the end, the White House compromised by withholding a detailed presentation on U.S. safety procedures that had been prepared, while having Ambassador Smith give a more general presentation and invite the Soviets to engage in a more detailed discussion. The Soviets declined, giving instead a very general assurance that their safety procedures were adequate.

This episode suggests that U.S. and Soviet views of the AMA may have differed in a fundamental way. The Soviets, whose safety procedures were presumed to be inferior, may have been more concerned about preventing retaliation for accidents than preventing accidents themselves. This might help explain why they took an unusual amount of initiative in pushing for accidents measures and why, if initial news reports were accurate,[12] they preferred to look on the AMA in terms of a pledge against retaliation more than a means of preventing accidents. The United States, on the other hand, preferred to focus on the AMA as a means of preventing accidents, even to the point of unilaterally providing the Soviets with information on safety procedures.

A second way in which the agreement was expected to reduce the risk of accidental nuclear war was by facilitating communications to prevent misunderstandings in situations involving nuclear accidents, nuclear alerts, or other incidents that could lead to direct U.S.-Soviet nuclear crises. The popular image of the "red telephone" in the White House, which contrasts sharply with the reality of the telex that only recently added a White House terminal to its facilities in the Pentagon, underlines the public expectation of relatively frequent and easy use of the Hot Line during crises. In a more general way, it was hoped that discussions of accidents procedures would provide something similar to what Thomas Schelling has termed "focal points," or congruent mutual expectations of behavior, facilitating cooperation and accident prevention in crises.[13]

Perhaps the most significant negative expectation associated with the agreement was the concern voiced by some that it might enable the Soviets to launch a surprise attack on the United States after first giving warning of an "accidental" missile launch. This issue was reportedly raised by at least one congressman in hearings on the agreement, and it has since been raised by strategic analysts as a general concern with "confidence-building measures" such as the AMA.[14] Fear that the agreement might aid a deceptive attack was not widespread, however, and it was generally overshadowed by positive expectations of a lowered risk of accidental war.

One other expectation was central to the implementation of the AMA. This was the understanding, following a suggestion from Ambassador Smith to Soviet chief negotiator Semenov, that the Standing Consultative Commission (SCC) would oversee implementation of the AMA.[15] Although the SCC was under discussion in June 1970 when Ambassador Smith proposed this arrangement, the signing of the AMA preceded the formal establishment of the SCC by eight months. The AMA itself contained only a general provision for consultations on implementation "as mutually agreed," (Article 7), and it was not until the signing of a Memorandum of Understanding in December 1972 that the SCC was specifically given responsibility to "promote the objectives and implementation" of the AMA.[16] By making the implementation of the AMA dependent on the successful completion of the strategic arms talks, U.S. negotiators signaled that they placed high expectations on successful SALT talks and low priorities on implementation of the AMA.

Political Expectations

Like the 1963 Hot Line Agreement, the AMA was generally heralded as "the first tangible if modest result of nearly two years of secret negotiations on the limitation of strategic arms."[17] As such, the most prominent political expectation placed on the agreement was that it signaled and could contribute to an improvement in the prospects for an agreement limiting strategic arms.[18] This expectation represented an ironic twist on the administration's previous expectation that holding out on an accidents measures agreement would provide the Soviets with incentives to be more amenable to U.S. positions on strategic arms and the converse concern that negotiations on the accidents measures would divert attention from strategic arms. *The Washington Post* appropriately captured this switch in stating that the agreement "was to have been a postcript to an agreement on strategic arms. Instead, it has become a curtain raiser."[19]

A second political expectation was that the agreement would give some modest impetus to an improvement in overall U.S.-Soviet relations.[20] Soviet Foreign Minister Gromyko met with President Nixon on the day following the signing ceremony, and although their meeting was substantively unrelated to the AMA, *The New York Times* reported that it had persuaded the Nixon administration that "its relations with Moscow are better now than at any time in the last three years."[21]

A third set of political expectations associated with the agreement was that it would be what *Newsweek* termed a "global morale booster,"[22] improving confidence in the United States and among U.S. allies that the United States was behaving responsibly both in its control of its nuclear forces and in its arms control approach and relations with the Soviet Union.

Finally, some in the administration, including Kissinger, were concerned during the negotiations that the Soviets would use the issues of U.S. "forward-based" nuclear systems in Europe, "no first use" of nuclear weapons, accession to the agreement by other parties, and "provocative attacks by third parties" to disrupt U.S. relations within NATO and the U.S. rapprochement with China.[23]

Compliance and Verification

As noted above, essentially no provision was made for mutual verification of compliance with the terms of the accord. Each side was given full freedom to decide which changes in the command and control of its nuclear forces were necessary to reduce the risk of accidents, without any obligation to reveal or verify the steps, if any, taken toward this end. Even more important was the wide latitude that each side was permitted in defining which accidents involving nuclear weapons could raise the risk of nuclear war and would therefore require notification. The United States, in fact, insisted that in the case of nuclear alerts, each side be required to give notification of only those incidents that it believed raised the risk of war.[24] In this case, then, the United States encouraged ambiguity in order to preserve its flexibility in implementing the AMA, even at the cost of allowing the Soviets similar latitude.

Some analysts have argued in retrospect that it was unrealistic to expect either side to comply fully with the agreement. One report, for example, notes that "Article 3 of the agreement requires notification 'in the event of detection by missile warning systems of unidentified objects . . . if such occurrences could create the risk of outbreak of nuclear war.' Is this a feasible response to what may be perceived as a surprise nuclear attack?"[25] Evidently, U.S. officials knew that verifying compliance would be problematic but felt this to be a lesser evil compared to the difficulties of negotiating a common definition of incidents that could raise the risk of accidental nuclear war.[26]

OUTCOMES

Arms Control Objectives

Most analysts, in summing up the effects of the agreement, cite its potential for reducing the probability of war as its greatest contribution.[27] Indeed, although the most likely causes of a nuclear war are a subject of debate, some analysts believe that accidents or miscalculations would play a critical role in the most likely scenarios that lead to a nuclear war.[28] This is so, they argue, because a nuclear war would cause such great mutual destruction that neither side would intentionally begin such a war.[29] The AMA's capability to prevent accidental nuclear war, however, is cast into doubt by the lack of evidence of its effective implementation and use.

Implementation

Probably the most important outcome of the AMA is that both the agreement and the general goal of establishing joint U.S.-Soviet measures to prevent accidental nuclear war continue to enjoy widespread bipartisan acceptance. Yet it is difficult to point to tangible benefits from the agreement's central provisions for notifications of accidents and false alerts involving nuclear weapons—provisions that, according to the public record, have never been invoked.[30]

The absence of any publicly acknowledged instances in which notifications were made in accordance with the agreement does not in and of itself call into question the agreement's implementation—after all, there have been no accidental nuclear wars. The more troubling fact, however, is that several situations since 1971 have been of the kind that the AMA's negotiators might have expected to lead to notifications or requests for clarifying information. Yet there is no information in the public record suggesting that either side has ever notified the other of accidents or false alerts. Taking just the period from the beginning of 1979 to the end of June in 1980, for example, the United States experienced 147 "Missile Display Conferences," the lowest level of alert in which experts are convened to evaluate information from missile warning systems indicating a potential threat to the United States.[31] On four occasions in this period, the evaluation process moved to the next highest level of alert, called a "Threat Assessment Conference," one step short of the highest alert level, which would involve the president (this level of alert, a "Missile Attack Conference," has never been reached). In one of these instances, ten U.S. fighters from three separate bases were scrambled and sent airborne, while in another, about one hundred B-52 bombers were readied for takeoff, as was the president's emergency airborne command post.[32] Although the Soviets may have detected these developments, there is no publicly available information suggesting that they were notified by the United States nor that they or the United States requested clarification, as was each party's prerogative under the 1971 agreement.

Similarly, there is no evidence in the public record that the United States immediately notified the Soviets of U.S. accidents involving nuclear weapons such as the explosion of missile fuel at a missile complex near Damascus, Arkansas, on September 19, 1980, and the burning of a Pershing II rocket motor in Germany on January 11, 1985. The 1980 accident killed one person while "belching flames and debris 500 feet skyward" from the silo, and the Pershing II missile fire killed three U.S. soldiers.[33] In neither case was there any danger of an accidental launch or nuclear detonation (the Pershing II missile warheads are reportedly stored separately from the missiles as a precaution against accidents). Both of these accidents could have been observed by the Soviets' national technical means, however, and either could have been misinterpreted by them as a nuclear launch (and an imminent nuclear detonation). This places these incidents in the gray area of the AMA's provisions on "unexplained nuclear incident(s) involving a possible detonation of a nuclear weapon" (Article III) and other "unexplained nuclear incidents" (Article V). Much less is known about whether the Soviets have, without notifying the United States, experienced false alerts or nuclear accidents of the kind that U.S. officials in 1971 expected would lead to notification.

Any conclusions drawn from the above incidents are subject to two important caveats and must remain tentative at best. First, it is possible that notifications were in fact made in the course of some or all of these incidents but were not made public. Second, the incidents described above may not have been of the kind that negotiators in 1971 intended or expected to lead to notifications. The scenarios that preoccupied negotiators—both in their discussions and in the language of the agreement—were accidental missile launches, nuclear detonations, and advanced false alerts. They gave much less consideration to the more likely but less immediately threatening gray areas of nonnuclear explosions and fires at missile complexes and less advanced false alerts, such as those described above. Still, accidents like these might reasonably fall under the definition of raising the risk of nuclear war because they might be observed by national technical means and misinterpreted as launches. Because of the ambiguity of the requirement for notifications of accidents that "could create a risk of outbreak of nuclear war," however, there are no grounds for suggesting that either side has violated the terms of the AMA, even if no notifications were made in any of the above incidents. The parties observing the above and other accidents and false alerts may have believed, wrongly in the view of this author, that they did not create a risk of outbreak of nuclear war.

These caveats notwithstanding, the point remains that notifications may not have been made in situations where officials—both negotiators in 1971 and decisionmakers observing the above incidents—might have expected them. If indeed no notifications have been made, the failure to negotiate a more precise operational definition of when notification is required may have led to a situation in which it is unreasonable to expect any notification at all, particularly of false alerts. If notifications have not been made with low-level alerts, is it reasonable to expect notification of high-level alerts in times of crisis with high levels of tension and distrust? If notifications of possible false alerts or of nonnuclear accidents that look like launches are made for the first time in a crisis, particularly when similar previous incidents have been ignored, will those notifications be credible? Further, the possible lack of any notifications by either side begs the question of whether each side has defined for itself situations requiring notification and established procedures for notification as an automatic step in its operating procedures. It may well be that the United States has decided, without making the decision public, that the Soviets would be notified of the possibility of a false U.S. alert whenever the United States convenes a Missile Attack Conference, the highest stage of alert. If the United States and the Soviets have not incorporated into their standard operating procedures such unilateral definitions of when notification is required, it is less likely that they will make timely notifications of nuclear accidents and false alerts.

Although it remains unclear whether the AMA's provisions on notification of accidents and false alerts have been properly implemented, the AMA has enjoyed at least one unambiguous success. Since 1971 both sides have refrained from testing missiles on flight paths in the direction of the other (Article 4).[34] In addition, the United States has adopted a number of measures in its command and control of nuclear forces consistent with its commitment to provide safeguards against nuclear accidents, including computer-constructed key codes, coding devices and interlocks, a sealed authenticator system, permissive action links, overlapping communications systems, a personnel reliability program, emergency destruction devices and procedures, and a two-man rule.[35] Many of these predate the 1971 Agreement, however, and the Soviets have not publicly disclosed any measures they have taken along these lines.

U.S. and Soviet Standing Consultative Commission representatives achieved another modest success in meeting operational expectations when they agreed in 1976 on a code for transmitting as rapidly as possible the nature of accidents involving nuclear weapons. Even this instance, however, suggests that the two sides have not given high priority to implementing the 1971 Agreement. First, the fact that it was five years before the code was set up indicates a lack of intense interest in operationalizing the agreement. Second, if the two sides could agree on a code for categorizing accidents, why did they not agree on which accidents require notification? The slow implementation of the Hot Line update suggests a similar pattern of sporadic interest. The satellite system, originally expected to become operational "sometime after 1973," became operational only in January 1978, after numerous delays "to work out technical and procedural arrangements, including the construction of satellite earth stations required to support use of INTELSAT and MOLNIYA."[36] These and other technical and political difficulties with the AMA and the Hot Line update undoubtedly contributed to implementation delays, but it is equally true that implementation could have been speeded and strengthened had these agreements been a higher priority for both sides. The original Hot Line, for example, although admittedly an easier technical task than the satellite upgrade, was activated less than two months after it was agreed on.

Political Outcomes

In retrospect, expectations that the AMA would have a substantial political effect of any kind were exaggerated. The agreement was not considered important enough by either side to provide either leverage in or distraction from the strategic arms issues on center stage in SALT I. In addition, the substantive issues involved in accident prevention were easily separated from those of strategic arms limitations, although the United States made some effort to link the two.[37] The agreement had no greater linkage effects as a curtain raiser than as a postscript, although it may have made a modest improvement in the atmosphere of the talks judging from the statements of U.S. and Soviet officials cited above. After the conclusion of the accidents agreement, talks on strategic arms proceeded much as they had before, with few references to the accidents measures. Similarly, the agreement had little effect on the continuing improvement of U.S.–Soviet relations, which had deeper roots in domestic and international politics—the Nixon-Kissinger "grand design" of triangular politics and a "web" of interests, the fitfull U.S. withdrawal from Vietnam, Soviet desires to parlay Soviet military power into global political power, and U.S. domestic politics under the shadow of Vietnam. The mutual desire to improve relations, even if for widely conflicting reasons, probably helped the negotiation of the agreement more than the agreement helped improve relations. As for building confidence at home and abroad in U.S. arms control policies, the agreement may have played a small role as a "global morale booster," but the suddenness with which it appeared and was forgotten in the press and the public suggests that these effects were also negligible.

Fears that the Soviets would use the subjects of no-first-use, forward-based systems, accession to the agreement by other parties, and third-party provocation as political footballs to disrupt U.S. relations with NATO and with China were not substantiated by the pattern of Soviet involvement in these issues. The Soviets quickly dropped the subject of no first use and studiously avoided that of forward-based systems, indicating their seriousness on reaching an accidents accord.[38] Regarding the accession of other parties to the agreement, the Soviets later concluded agreements with France and Great Britain similar to the AMA, indicating that this, too, was in their view a serious matter. Finally, in 1985, U.S. and Soviet representatives agreed at a regular SCC meeting to expand the 1976 message code to include prepositioned Hot Line messages dealing with the possibility of a nuclear incident instigated by a third country or terrorist group.[39]

In sum, several uncertainties underlie any assessment of the outcomes, costs, and benefits of the 1971 agreement. Although there have been a number of false nuclear alerts and accidents involving nuclear weapons, none has led to the detonation of a nuclear weapon or a spiral of misinterpretations and military escalation. It is not clear, however, to what extent this outcome can be attributed to improvements of U.S. and Soviet safety procedures motivated by the

AMA. It is even less clear how much credit is due to the AMA's provisions for notification of accidents and false alerts, provisions that, at least according to the public record, have never been invoked despite numerous situations of the kind that the agreement's negotiators may have expected to lead to notification. The major uncertainty that therefore remains more than fourteen years after the AMA's conclusion is whether it will be used effectively should accidental nuclear war become an imminent danger, particularly if it is indeed the case that the agreement has gone unused in ambiguous but potentially dangerous circumstances in the past.

MANAGING THE ARMS CONTROL POLICY PROCESS

The presumed asymmetry between U.S. and Soviet safety procedures did not allow either side to "bargain from strength," nor did it preclude reaching an agreement. It is possible that the differing accident procedures and strategic doctrines of the two sides led them to interpret the agreement very differently. The Soviets may view the AMA at least partly in terms of insurance against retaliation, while in the U.S. view the accord serves as a safeguard against accidents. In any case, the actual provisions of the accord, and the limited efforts to implement it, have focused on the goal of preventing accidents. This appears to benefit both sides, whether or not one assumes that one side is more likely than the other to have an accident.

The one clear asymmetry in the AMA was the United States' unilateral release of information on safety procedures. At least in this case, a unilateral concession did not elicit a corresponding response. Yet it cannot be said that the Soviets clearly gained more than the United States through the unilateral U.S. disclosure because the United States benefits if Soviet safety procedures improve. Also, it is not clear that the United States was really interested in hearing about Soviet safety procedures in general terms—the Joint Chiefs' objections to a unilateral disclosure rested more on principle than substance.[40] In general, the unusual circumstances of this case limit its applicability to other possible unilateral actions.

No one really raised concerns of a "lulling" effect in the context of the AMA. The concern that came closest to such an effect was perhaps Nixon's concern that the AMA could detract from interest in other SALT issues. This concern did not materialize, nor did the AMA appear to diminish interest in other accident-prevention measures. In part, this may be attributable to the fact that the Nixon administration did not in any sense "oversell" the provisions of the accord. In fact, the AMA received only passing mention in administration statements to Congress between its signing and the conclusion of the ABM treaty.[41]

If the public record is correct in suggesting that no notifications of nuclear accidents or false alerts have been made, then the AMA provides evidence that vague provisions are inadequate, even when those provisions are in the clear interest of the two sides and are therefore supposedly self-enforcing. Where the AMA's provisions are the vaguest—on the definition of when accidents and alerts require notification—the AMA's implementation, according to the public record, has been weakest. The AMA's implementation has been strongest, on the other hand, on its most specific provision, which called for advance notification of missile tests in the direction of the other party. Negotiators knew that they were trading off compliance versus flexibility of implementation and ease of negotiation, but they may have underestimated how much ambiguity would detract from the value of the AMA. Instead of creating room for agreement, the vagueness of the AMA's provisions has created room for the very misunderstandings it was to prevent.

A Model for "Quiet" Arms Control?

Some of the factors that gave the 1971 Agreement a low public profile—a quiescent Congress and public with regard to arms control issues, bipartisan support and uniform expectations, continuity of expectations with previous and other agreements—are particular to the substantive issue of accident prevention and the domestic politics of the late 1960s and early 1970s. Four factors that contributed to the low level of interest in the agreement, however, are common to many other possible arms control agreements, making the 1971 AMA a potential model for "quiet" arms control. First, the agreement was an executive agreement and did not require Senate ratification. Second, the agreement concerned an arms control issue that was considered to be peripheral to the main issues in U.S.-Soviet arms control negotiations. Third, the agreement was negotiated through a policy process that was largely closed to public and congressional participation. Finally, the AMA did not involve extensive changes in the structures or operations of the two sides' nuclear or conventional forces, and thus executive departments played a limited role in its negotiation. What, then, are the lessons of the 1971 Agreement that might be applicable to negotiations and agreements that share some or all of these attributes?

Closed Policy Processes and Peripheral Issues

The closed process through which the agreement was negotiated offered many apparent advantages for the executive branch. Most important, the Congress and the public could not attempt to alter the agenda or timing of the AMA talks. To take only one example of the flexibility this allowed, President Nixon was able to decide without any outside pressure whether to sign the agreement separately from a strategic arms agreement. Even the executive departments with a stake in the agreement could not take their concerns—such as the Joint Chiefs' worry over discussing U.S. safety procedures—to the media. It was largely because of the closed negotiating process, then, that the agreement was very quickly and easily reached once talks began in earnest.

At the same time, the closed process prevented the Congress, the public, and some of the executive departments from playing a potentially beneficial role in the agreement's negotiation and implementation. Because none of these groups played a role in the negotiations process, none were able to challenge the ambiguous definition of incidents requiring notification and the lack of verification measures. Furthermore, because none of these groups had a role or stake in the negotiation of the agreement, none took a deep interest in overseeing its implementation. It is possible that the low priority attached to accidents measures may have discouraged interest in the AMA even if its negotiation had been made public. Still, the "quiet" negotiating process is probably at least partly responsible for the five-year lapse between the agreement's signature and the development of a code for relaying accidents messages. The "quiet" process no doubt also contributed to the dearth of academic interest in the agreement—in contrast to the other cases in this study, there are virtually no books or even articles that deal with the agreement at length.[42] Thus, the closed process allowed the administration to avoid any controversy over the agreement, but controversy may have improved the agreement by pushing negotiators to use less ambiguous formulas and focusing attention on the bureaucracy as it implemented the agreement. If the quiet process kept the agreement from generating committed opponents, it also deprived it of committed implementers.

In addition, the SCC, with its many other responsibilities, limited organizational resources, and infrequent meetings, was in some respects not very well suited for implementing the accord.[43] There was no organization in a better position to implement the accord, ensure its incorporation into the SOPs of both sides, and generate sufficient bureaucratic momentum to overcome technical and procedural problems. Without a high priority mandate from political leaders to implement the AMA, however, and with the SCC's self-perceived mission tied more directly to implementing agreements on central strategic systems like SALT I and SALT II, implementation of the AMA seemingly fell through the organizational cracks. In contrast, the Incidents at Sea Agreement—also a "peripheral" agreement but one that the navy held dear and was in a natural position to implement—has been effectively implemented. Extensive joint U.S.-Soviet SOPs and periodic meetings on the Incidents at Sea Agreement have provided military to military contact at the operational level, successfully monitoring implementation and compliance.[44] The lesson here, then, is that if peripheral agreements are to be effectively implemented despite low levels of public, congressional, and executive interest, they must be implemented by organizations with both a strong interest in and sufficient resources for their implementation.

A more fundamental tradeoff involved in the closed process is that between secrecy and democracy. Of course, much information concerning U.S. negotiating positions is rightly classified so that U.S. negotiators are not deprived of negotiating leverage and fallback positions. Even so, the unnecessarily complete secrecy that surrounded the accidents agreement—and the congressional and public backlash against the secrecy of back-channel negotiations in SALT I—suggest the need for a more consistent public information policy. Although it is impossible to devise a general rule for disclosing information on negotiations, U.S. decisionmakers should continue to consider whether the U.S. government is releasing so much information that U.S. positions are endangered or so little that the Congress and the public cannot participate in the policy process in an informed way.

The dilemmas of secret versus public negotiations are particularly important in view of the increasing role that Congress and the public have expected to play in arms control policy. Although the "quiet" arms control model may still be applicable to executive agreements on "peripheral" issues, it is doubtful that even here today's Congress and public would accept a policy process as closed as the one used in the accidents agreement. Clearly, the closed policy processes of "quiet" arms control are even less applicable to treaties or executive agreements on central strategic issues.

One final lesson of this case is that agreements considered to be "peripheral," or both secondary in importance and functionally unrelated to the central issues of U.S.-Soviet negotiations, can be separated from other negotiating issues and from the overall state of U.S.-Soviet relations. This was particularly true of the accidents measures agreement because prevention of accidental nuclear war has enjoyed bipartisan support during periods of both confrontation and détente; indeed, accident prevention is generally recognized to be of greater importance in periods of confrontation. More generally, because positions on "peripheral" subjects provide little leverage in talks on more central issues and have little effect on overall U.S.-Soviet relations, peripheral issues can be separated from both of these areas.

Unfortunately, the perception of secondary importance often leads U.S. decisionmakers to try to link peripheral to central issues in hopes of helping along central issues. In the case of the Accidents Measures Agreement, linkage between accidents measures and strategic arms talks provided little leverage in the strategic talks but slowed discussions of accidents measures and could have ended them altogether if the United States had continued to link the two and if the strategic talks then stalled. Also, "peripheral" issues are often the first to be linked to Soviet behavior and hence called off in response to Soviet misdeeds, just as a decade of U.S.-Soviet incidents at sea conferences were temporarily interrupted because of the unrelated Soviet killing of Sergeant Nicholson, a U.S. military observer in East Germany.

CONCLUSIONS

The AMA amply demonstrates that the process of "quiet" arms control is no panacea for growing disillusionment with the SALT/

START style of negotiations. The factors that made the AMA easy to negotiate quietly—low involvement by Congress and the executive departments, bipartisan support, continuity of expectations, growing détente, "peripheral" subject matter, executive agreement status, and so on—may not apply to historical periods unlike the early 1970s or issues unlike those addressed by the AMA. Some of the same factors that made the AMA easy to negotiate quietly also stymied its full implementation. Thus, between the secrecy of the negotiations process and the low priority devoted to its implementation, the AMA may not have realized its full potential for either reassuring the public or establishing operational safeguards against accidental nuclear war. The vagueness of the agreement further hindered its implementation, even though the provisions were clearly self-interested and supposedly self-enforcing. Finally, the linkage between the AMA and offensive and defensive arms talks provided little leverage in those talks but slowed and at times threatened the successful conclusion of the accidents negotiations.

Despite these and other limitations, the accidents measures agreement still provides some hope for greater returns from those issue areas where a quiet negotiating process is applicable. Because it was a "peripheral" issue, the AMA could be and eventually was separated from other issues in SALT. Future negotiators can gain from this lesson by avoiding intentional linkage of functionally unrelated negotiations when such linkage promises to be unproductive. Moreover, the quiet negotiating process and "peripheral" subject matter of the AMA did not make poor implementation of the AMA a foregone conclusion, as the Incidents at Sea experience suggests. Armed with foreknowledge of the implementation problems to expect with agreements like the AMA, policymakers can devote more organizational and political resources to implementation. Finally, with a clearer view of the consequences of ambiguity, negotiators may be willing to devote more time and effort to hammering out well-defined agreements. These and the other lessons of the 1971 accidents measures agreement case can help guide future discussions on accident prevention, crisis management and prevention, war termination, transparency and communication and other CBMs, "incidents in the air," and other forms of "arms control with and without agreements."[45]

NOTES

1. Raymond Garthoff, "The Accidents Measures Agreement," in John Borawski, ed., *Avoiding War in the Nuclear Age* (Boulder, Colo.: Westview Press, 1986), p. 57.
2. Gerard C. Smith, *Doubletalk: The Story of the First Strategic Arms Limitation Talks* (Garden City, N.Y.: Doubleday, 1980), p. 281.
3. *Ibid.*, pp. 108–09.
4. *Ibid.*, pp. 287–88.
5. *Ibid.*, p. 295.
6. Garthoff, "The Accidents Measures Agreement," pp. 61–62; see also Smith, *Doubletalk*, p. 288.
7. "U.S. and Soviet Discuss Modernizing Hot Line," *The New York Times*, April 1, 1971, p. A2.
8. See Smith, *Doubletalk*, pp. 296–97.
9. See Alan Platt, *The U.S. Senate and Strategic Arms Policy, 1969–1977* (Boulder, Colo.: Westview Press, 1978).
10. *The Washington Post*, Sept. 17, 1971, p. A26.
11. This discussion is based largely on Garthoff, "The Accidents Measures Agreement," pp. 60–61.
12. See Smith, *Doubletalk*, p. 296. See also Tad Szulc, "Accord Reported to Prevent Atomic War in Error, *The New York Times*, Sept. 13, 1971, p. A1, and Marilyn Berger, "Accident Pacts Were to Be P.S. to SALT," *The Washington Post*, Sept. 16, 1971, p. A14.
13. Thomas Schelling, *The Strategy of Conflict* (Cambridge, Mass.: Harvard University Press, 1980, 1960). See also Smith, *Doubletalk*, p. 289, and Garthoff, "The Accidents Measures Agreement," pp. 68–69.
14. Smith, *Doubletalk*, p. 297; see also Jim Hinds, "The Limits of Confidence," in Borawski, *Avoiding War in the Nuclear Age*, p. 192.
15. Garthoff, "The Accidents Measures Agreement," p. 67.
16. *Ibid.*, p. 67.
17. Szulc, "Accord Reported to Prevent Atomic War in Error." *The Washington Post* used similar language in describing the accidents measures agreement and the Hot Line update, calling them "the first concrete measures to come out of the SALT negotiations" (Marilyn Berger, "Arms Talks Progress Claimed," *The Washington Post*, Sept. 25, 1971, p. 1).
18. Szulc, "Accord Reported to Prevent Atomic War in Error." See also Smith, *Doubletalk*, pp. 283, 297.
19. Berger, "Accident Pacts Were to Be P.S. to SALT," p. A14.
20. Marilyn Berger, "U.S.-Soviet SALT Pacts Signed," *The Washington Post*, Oct. 1, 1971, p. A14.

21. Terence Smith, "U.S. Encouraged by Soviet Talks," *The New York Times*, Oct. 3, 1971, p. 25. The *Times* reported that administration officials attributed the trend toward détente not to the arms agreements or the SALT talks but to a Soviet desire to solidify the Soviet position in East Europe, codifying the postwar division of Europe in a security conference after a rapprochement with the West.

22. *Newsweek* (Sept. 27, 1971), p. 64.

23. Raymond Garthoff, *Détente and Confrontation* (Washington, D.C.: Brookings, 1985), pp. 176–80.

24. *Ibid.*, pp. 286, 288.

25. Richard Williamson, ed., Supplement to *Beyond the Hotline: Controlling a Nuclear Crisis*, prepared for the U.S. Arms Control and Disarmament Agency by the Nuclear Negotiation Project, Harvard Law School, Contract #AC2PC110, 1984, p. 68.

26. See, for example, Smith, *Doubletalk*, p. 288.

27. See, for example, Garthoff, "The Accidents Measures Agreement," p. 69; Smith, *Doubletalk*, pp. 297–98.

28. See, for example, Graham Allison, Albert Carnesale, and Joseph S. Nye, Jr., eds., *Hawks, Doves, and Owls* (New York: Norton, 1985), p. 17.

29. *Ibid.*, pp. 9–10; see also Smith, *Doubletalk*, p. 281.

30. Garthoff, "The Accidents Measures Agreement," p. 68; see also Williamson, *Beyond the Hotline*, p. 68.

31. Senator Gary Hart and Senator Barry Goldwater, *Recent False Alerts from the Nation's Missile Attack Warning System*, Report to the Senate Committee on Armed Services (Washington, D.C.: U.S. Government Printing Office, Oct. 9, 1980).

32. Paul Bracken, *The Command and Control of Nuclear Forces* (New Haven: Yale University Press, 1983), pp. 54–55.

33. See Wendell Rawls, "Missile Silo Explodes, 1 Killed 21 Injured," *The New York Times*, Sept. 20, 1980, p. 1, and James Markham, "3 G.I.s Die at German Base When Missile Catches Fire," *The New York Times*, Jan. 12, 1985, p. 3.

34. Williamson, *Beyond the Hotline*, p. 69.

35. *Ibid.*, p. 67.

36. Terence Smith, "U.S. and Soviet Sign Two Nuclear Accords," *The New York Times*, Oct. 1, 1971, p. 14, and Sally K. Horn, "The Hotline," in Borawski, *Avoiding War in the Nuclear Age*, pp. 47–48.

37. See Smith, *Doubletalk*, pp. 284–85.

38. Garthoff, "The Accidents Measures Agreement," p. 62.

39. *Ibid.*, p. 68; see also "'Understanding' with Soviet on War Risks Is Described," *The New York Times*, July 5, 1985.

40. Garthoff, "The Accidents Measures Agreement," p. 60–61.

41. See, for example, Philip Farley's statement to the House Appropriations Committee summarizing progress in the SALT negotiations, *Departments of State, Justice, and Commerce, the Judiciary, and Related Agencies Appropriations for 1973*, 92d Cong., 2d Sess. (Washington, D.C.: U.S. Government Printing Office, April 11, 1972), pp. 219–38.

42. The notable exceptions to the lack of academic interest in the 1971 agreement are Gerard Smith's chapter and Raymond Garthoff's article, both cited abundantly above. Perhaps the most damning evidence of a lack of interest is the absence of an acronym for the agreement. It is only with great trepidation, and at the risk of friction with the American Medical Association (the number of possible three letter acronyms is, thankfully, finite), that I have added the acronym *AMA* to the already overburdened language of arms control.

43. For a more sanguine view of the SCC's implementation of the AMA, see Robert Bucheim and Dan Caldwell, *The US-USSR Standing Consultative Commission: Description and Appraisal*, Working Paper #2, Center for Foreign Policy Development, Brown University, May 1983, pp. 13, 16.

44. Sean Lynn-Jones, "Avoiding Incidents at Sea," in Borawski, *Avoiding War in the Nuclear Age*, pp. 82–84.

45. Kenneth Adelman, "Arms Control with and without Agreements," *Foreign Affairs* (Winter 1984–85), p. 261.

4

SALT I
Interim Agreement and ABM Treaty

Fen Osler Hampson

What is striking about the record of the Anti-Ballistic Missile (ABM) Treaty and the Interim Agreement on Offensive Strategic Arms (SALT I) is how much expectations differed among individuals and groups in the government and the public. But what is readily apparent is that there were few illusions about what had been achieved. Although there was strong support for the agreements, it was coupled with deep reservations and considerable skepticism about the future. Although the worst fears expressed by some were not realized, subsequent developments did little to allay many of the suspicions that were expressed at the time the agreements were signed. These concerns in turn played an important role in shaping the debate over SALT II.

BACKGROUND

The Johnson Administration

SALT I had its beginnings in the Johnson administration. The official announcement of strategic arms limitation talks between the United States and the Soviet Union came with the signing of the Non-Proliferation Treaty on July 1, 1968.[1] However, the seeds of

SALT I were sown with the U.S. ICBM and SLBM build-up in the early 1960s, which may have directly or indirectly led to a similar build-up on the Soviet side starting in 1964 after Soviet efforts to place medium-range missiles in Cuba were foiled. The growing arms race in the mid-1960s was a source of concern to senior defense and arms control officials in the United States, as was Soviet construction of a crude defense system around Leningrad in 1962.[2] Although construction of the latter stopped two years later, it was shortly followed by the construction of a similar system around Moscow. The United States feared that the Soviets might be constructing a nationwide ABM system, and this helped to accelerate the Pentagon's development of the MIRV and eventual work on an ABM system for the United States. These developments also precipitated a spate of studies within the Joint Chiefs of Staff (JCS) and the Arms Control and Disarmament Agency about the desirability of controlling nuclear weapons through arms control.

In December 1966 President Johnson instructed U.S. Ambassador to the Soviet Union Llewellyn Thompson to sound out the Soviets about bilateral talks on strategic arms limitations. Johnson had been persuaded by Secretary of Defense Robert McNamara that there was a growing danger of an ABM race between the United States and the Soviet Union that had considerable potential to lead to a new offensive arms race as well. McNamara also feared that ABM defenses would be strategically destabilizing if they impaired the assured destruction capabilities of the United States and its ability to retaliate in the event of a Soviet first strike. He urged Johnson to begin serious negotiations with the Soviets to limit or ban ABMs on both sides. Whether Johnson agreed because of the strategic merits of these arguments or for domestic political reasons (or both) is unclear. However, he did face growing pressure on Capitol Hill to move forward with ABM deployments, and there was enthusiasm in the military for strategic defenses.[3] There was also an upcoming election in 1968, and Johnson may have felt that talks with Soviets would be an asset in the upcoming campaign, particularly in the face of his mounting political difficulties over the war in Vietnam.

The Soviets agreed in principle to offensive and defensive arms limitation talks in January 1967. But the date for starting talks was left open. McNamara pressed Soviet Prime Minister Alexei Kosygin for a date at the Glassboro summit meeting but without success. Talks were delayed for almost a year and a half as the Kremlin wrestled with the problem of deciding whether such talks were indeed desirable.

The domestic debate during this period was marked by growing differences of opinion about the desirability of strategic defenses. Some feared that ballistic missile defenses would threaten strategic stability. Others, however—notably civilian analysts in the Department of Defense—were keen on developing strategic defenses.

The administration also found itself under growing congressional pressure to deploy defenses to counter Soviet ABM deployments. In September 1967 McNamara announced that the administration had decided to deploy a "thin" ABM system to protect the United States from Chinese missile attack or attack by some other third party or accidental missile launch.[4] It was quite apparent that the administration rejected the notion that ABM could limit damage from a Soviet missile attack. This viewpoint prevailed until the end of the Johnson administration. In his last report to the Congress, Secretary of Defense Clark Clifford stated that "We remain convinced . . . we should continue to give primary priority in the allocation of available resources to the primary objective of our strategic forces, namely assured destruction."

The idea of using ABM as a bargaining chip for arms control also gained credence in the 1968 congressional debate on the Sentinel ABM system, even though the term had not yet entered political discourse.[5] It was reinforced as the Soviet position on defenses began to turn in June 1968, when Soviet Foreign Minister Gromyko announced that the Soviets were ready for "an exchange of opinion" on limiting strategic arms, including ABMs.

MIRV was also developed as a bargaining chip in the internal politics of the Johnson administration. The program was not just a response to the Soviet ABM program. It was also a bargaining chip against a military bureaucracy that wanted to expand the Minuteman missile force.[6]

Progress on strategic arms limitation talks came to an abrupt halt in August 1968. On the eve of the public announcement of new arms control talks and the Leningrad summit, the Soviets moved into Czechoslovakia. Both the summit and the talks were called off. The invasion was an early manifestation of the importance of linkage in the domestic politics of arms control. Although Johnson was keen on having a summit and getting the arms talks underway, the events in Czechoslovakia made this impossible.

The Nixon Administration

Both President Nixon and his national security advisor, Henry Kissinger, came to office firmly convinced that arms control would help exert a positive restraining influence on Soviet behavior in other areas of the globe. Their approach toward SALT was intimately linked to a broader strategy and a nascent conception of détente. Nixon and Kissinger, however, were reluctant to jump into talks with the Soviets until they had conducted a formal review of U.S. strategic requirements. If the Soviets were anxious for talks all the more reason to wait, and, in the view of Nixon and Kissinger, any progress in SALT would depend on favorable Soviet behavior in the Middle East, Vietnam, and other areas.[7]

Although the Soviets were willing to support movement to an "era of negotiation rather than confrontation," they were quick to reject the notion of linkage and the administration's view that they wanted a SALT agreement more than the United States. The Soviets made it clear that they would begin negotiations only if the United States quietly abandoned the linkage idea.

There were other reasons for the new administration's reluctance to plunge immediately into strategic talks with the Soviets. The United States was no longer as deeply worried about a nationwide deployment of ABM by the Soviets because construction of new sites had halted. The Soviets, however, who had hitherto not been especially worried about ABM, were now deeply concerned and anxious to see some sort of limitation established.

In the case of ABMs, Soviet views had undergone an important change: "It was now accepted that these could play an offensive as well as a defensive role, and that an effective (or comparatively more effective) American ABM system would disrupt the nuclear balance by enabling the United States to lessen the effectiveness of a Soviet nuclear strike."[8]

In addition, the administration found itself under strong domestic political pressure to begin talks with the Soviets on arms control. Public and congressional attitudes toward the deployment of new strategic systems were also changing.

Congress was no longer forcing ABM on a reluctant administration. Opposition to ABM had grown considerably in the Congress and also within the academic and scientific community. In part, this skepticism was based on a growing appreciation of the technical limitations of ABM and its costs, but it also reflected political worries in the Congress about the future location of ABM sites. On February 16, 1969, Representative Chet Holifield, chairman of the Congressional Joint Committee on Atomic Energy, said he would oppose any missile defense against China or antimissile sites close to California.[9] On February 26 Senator Hubert Humphrey said that the administration should "begin as expeditiously as possible negotiation with the Soviet Union on the reduction of offensive and defensive strategic systems."[10] Senator Albert Gore's Subcommittee on Disarmament on March 6 began hearings on ABM defense. All of the witnesses who appeared before the subcommittee were hostile to ABM. They argued that an ABM system was not technically reliable and could be defeated by Soviet countermeasures. The deployment of defenses might also spark a new arms race and weaken the deterrent effect of strategic weapons. The underlying assumption in these arguments was that unilateral restraint by the United States would induce reciprocal restraint by the Soviets and increase the likelihood of achieving bilateral arms control.

Safeguard (a ballistic missile defense system that was the follow-on to Sentinel) also was not popular with some sectors of the public. People living near designated ABM sites believed that they would be more not less vulnerable to a Soviet missile attack. But it is also true that most people did not have especially strong opinions about the issue one way or the other. In response to a Gallup poll taken in 1969—"Have you heard or read about the discussions on the ABM program—that is, the antiballistic missile program?"—69 percent answered yes, and 31 percent said no.[11] Those who had heard about the program were asked "Do you happen to have an opinion about the ABM program as submitted to Congress by President Nixon?"; 40 percent said yes; 60 percent no. Of those who had an opinion and were asked "Do you favor or oppose the ABM program as submitted by President Nixon?" 25 percent favored; 15 percent were opposed; but the majority, 60 percent, were undecided.

MIRV did not arouse the same intense passions as the debate over ABM, but it was, nevertheless, the focus of some concern in the Congress. The MIRV genie was already out of the bottle insofar as Congress had appropriated funds for MIRV testing in 1968. But the final round of tests, due to begin in May 1969, sparked debate. In June 1969 Senator Clifford Case introduced an amendment to an appropriations bill that called for an end to MIRV testing.[12] In the same month, Senator Edward Brooke introduced a resolution for a MIRV moratorium that had forty cosponsors. On June 12 *The New York Times* argued that unilateral suspension of MIRV testing would invite reciprocal restraint by the Soviets. Just over a week later the *Times* gravely predicted that "No decision Richard Nixon will face as President is likely to be more momentous than the decision he faces within the next few days on the proposals to suspend the flight testing of MIRV. . . . Continued testing for even a few more weeks threatens to take the world past a point of no return into an expensive and dangerous new round in the missile race."

Contrary to its critics, the administration believed that unilateral restraint by the United States would be counterproductive. According to Kissinger,

> the Soviet missile arsenal was growing at the rate of two to three hundred missiles a year. If the Soviets were building while we abandoned our programs, what would be their incentive to negotiate limitations in an agreement? Our unilateral restraint would be an incentive for the Soviets not to settle but to procrastinate, to tilt the balance as much in their favor as possible while we paralyzed ourselves. To abandon ABM and MIRV together would thus not only have undercut the prospects for any SALT agreement but probably guaranteed Soviet strategic superiority for a decade.[13]

Pressure from the public and Congress for arms control was also coupled with the growing belief that the emerging parity in strategic forces had created a new "window of opportunity" to freeze the arms race; and there was some feeling that the administration should not use arms control to resolve other disputes with the Soviets. A Council on Foreign Relations study group chaired by Carl Kaysen (Deputy National Security Adviser under President Kennedy) sent President-elect Nixon a report in January 1969 urging an early strategic arms limitation agreement as an "imperative."[14] The report argued that a rare opportunity to limit ABM and MIRV might slip away. A United Nations Association Panel cited the report in urging the need for early talks with the Soviets on arms control.

From a strategic standpoint it is evident that the Soviets were entering a major phase of build-up of their ICBM and SLBM forces and that these programs were gaining momentum. This is reflected in a simple comparison of the strategic balance. By the late 1960s the United States had tested MIRV and was beginning to develop plans to outfit its ICBM forces with new MIRVed warhead packages. In

January 1967 the United States had 1,630 operational ICBMs and SLBMs versus the Soviets' 600.[15] By September 1968, when SALT was scheduled to begin, the ratio of operational ICBMs and SLBMs was reduced to 1,710 to 1,500 in the United States' favor. But the balance was beginning to shift toward the Soviets. By November 1969 when the talks began, the Soviets had 1,900 missiles operational or under construction. When the talks finally concluded in May 1972, the figure stood at 2,348.

Acceptance of parity, however, was not easy for the United States, particularly because U.S. defense planners had for some time assumed that the Soviets would not catch up with the United States.[16] Intelligence estimates in the mid-1960s had tended to underrate future Soviet force deployments.[17]

These early imbalances may have been important in contributing to the delay in getting SALT underway in the 1960s. The strategic force levels of the Soviet Union were considerably lower than those of the United States. It is significant that the Soviets agreed to begin talks only as they began to achieve a rough parity in strategic intercontinental systems in mid-1968. According to Raymond Garthoff, there were at least two other reasons: the Soviets had to reach an internal political consensus "on the strategic context and concept underlying a SALT agreement with the U.S.—especially one limiting ABM strategic defenses to a low level";[18] they also had to get over their lingering suspicions about U.S. objectives in the talks.

Although some felt that emerging strategic parity between the superpowers created the right conditions for arms control, the administration's fear was that parity would be short-lived. President Nixon had come to accept the notion of strategic "sufficiency" over "superiority," thus marking a shift from his campaign rhetoric to establish U.S. superiority. Both he and Kissinger also saw an important opportunity in arms control to slow down the momentum of the Soviet strategic build-up as well as a way to "promote . . . progress on outstanding political problems." But these perceptions were based on a deep-seated fear that the Soviets would rapidly gain the advantage unless their offensive build-up were halted. Nixon and Kissinger also worried that U.S. will to meet this growing threat was lacking. As Kissinger writes, "By the late Sixties, however, the strategic balance was tending toward parity. This should have changed all the assumptions of our postwar strategy. Unfortunately, at the precise moment that our national debate should have concentrated on the implication of this new situation, *all* our defense programs were coming under increasing attack. They were decried as excessive, blamed on reckless leaders, and criticized as contributing to crises and conflicts."[19] Kissinger was alarmed that growing opposition to the military would also lead to an erosion of U.S. commitments abroad.

The shift in the strategic balance was probably the most important factor in bringing the administration to the negotiating table and its announcement that it would begin talks with the Soviets on June 11, 1969. The administration saw a significant opportunity in arms control to halt the Soviet build-up in offensive strategic forces.[20]

A number of other factors were also important in creating impetus for negotiations. There is little doubt, for instance, that the new president had the right set of political credentials to enter into talks with the Soviets. As *The Wall Street Journal* stated, on January 28, 1969,

> One of the strongest arguments for a quick and positive response to the Soviet initiative, though, is that the Nixon Administration is nicely situated to discount the risks. . . . The President's campaign speeches, and the more recent cautious statements on disarmament talks by his Secretaries of State and Defense, are scarcely likely to persuade the Soviets they can trick us into a unilateral freeze. Nor are the same statements likely to give Americans false hopes about the prospects of any talks that may eventuate. . . . From all indications the Nixon Administration can be trusted to keep its eyes open in any talks with the Soviets. With its background and its constituency, a bit of eagerness is something it can afford.

The allies also supported SALT. Although NATO was concerned about the potential inclusion of forward-based systems in accords, there was a widespread desire, especially after the early successes of West German Chancellor Willy Brandt's *Ostpolitik*, to see a rapprochement between the superpowers. However, enthusiasm for SALT was tempered by predictable feelings of concern and a fear that the United States would sell its allies' interests short.[21]

THE NEGOTIATIONS

Style

The formal SALT negotiations began on November 17, 1969, in Helsinki. More than one observer has commented on the striking contrast between U.S. and Soviet negotiating styles.[22] The Soviets showed a preference for agreements incorporating broad general constraints on strategic arms competition. The United States, on the other hand, took a functional approach that emphasized strategic stability. Furthermore, whereas the Soviets sought "agreements in principle" first before disclosing specific details, the United States would often begin a negotiating round by offering a complete package that had been worked out in detail. These differences in style were complemented by real differences in substance and approach toward the issues.

Substance

The SALT I negotiations lasted over two and a half years. The U.S. team was headed by Ambassador Gerard Smith. In the opening round, the United States indicated its preference for discussions limited to "central" strategic forces only (ICBMs, SLBMs, and heavy bombers). The Soviets, however, wanted to include forward-based systems (that is, U.S. tactical aircraft based in Europe and on aircraft carriers capable of striking targets on Soviet territory).[23] The Soviets sought withdrawal of all FBS from within range of their territory and destruction of bases where they were stationed on the grounds that there was no distinction between the ability of these or strategic systems to attack the Soviet homeland. The United States counterargument was that these systems were tactical not strategic and were based in Europe to deter an attack on NATO, not to attack the Soviet Union. Eventually the FBS issue was set aside for the next round of SALT negotiations, along with MIRV and long-range bombers.

Early in the negotiations, the United States advanced two proposals. Both called for ABM defenses restricted to the defense of national capitals only. One of the proposals also called for a ban on MIRV testing and deployment with on-site inspection as means of verification. The United States was ahead of the Soviets at the time, having tested MIRV. The Soviets rejected the proposal and offered instead to ban MIRV deployment and production but not testing. The United States found this unacceptable because it would allow the Soviets to test MIRV and thereby to eliminate the U.S. lead and because it did not provide for on-site inspection. The United States also sought reductions in the number of heavy Soviet ICBMs (the SS-9s). In exchange, the United States proposed to reduce the number of its B-52 bombers.

The next set of U.S. negotiating proposals abandoned the restrictions on MIRV. Limitations on Soviet medium and intermediate-range missiles and sea-launched cruise missiles were also dropped. The Soviets at this time were still insistent on limitations on forward-based systems (that is, tactical fighter bombers in Europe and on aircraft carriers). But the United States stuck firm to its position that these were not strategic systems. At this point, the only concrete Soviet offer was for a limit on ABMs.

The Soviets sought to restrict negotiations to ABMs, maintaining that offensive limitations should be deferred. The U.S. position was that defensive and offensive limits had to be negotiated concurrently.

There was no real progress until May 20, 1971, when the results of a secret set of negotiations being conducted through backchannels between Henry Kissinger and Anatoly Dobrynin, the Soviet ambassador to Washington, and through letters between President Nixon and Prime Minister Kosygin, were announced.[24] The two governments agreed to work out ABM limitations and "certain measures with respect to the limitation of offensive strategic weapons." However, the Soviets were somewhat more ambiguous about their position with respect to SLBMs. It is likely that they favored noninclusion because they were only beginning their SLBM program and were well behind the United States in SLBM deployments. Both sides also agreed in the backchannel not to impose limits on offensive strategic missile modernization. These two issues were to be major stumbling blocks in the negotiations right to the end. Failure to resolve them ultimately made it difficult to get meaningful limits on SLBMs and missile throw-weights through limits on the volume of future Soviet ICBMs.

By the Moscow summit, the ABM Treaty and most of the details of the Interim Agreement on Offensive Limitations had been worked out. Two important specifics were still outstanding, however: SLBM levels; and the definition of the limit on Soviet heavy ICBMs and allowable increases in silo sizes—although the actual freeze ceiling had been agreed on.

In his April 1972 visit to Moscow to prepare for the summit, Henry Kissinger was able to get partial Soviet acquiescence on SLBMs, but only at very high levels.[25] The SALT delegation pushed hard for a freeze on the then-current number of Soviet SLBM launchers on submarines operational or under construction—the figure was 740 and included about 100 SLBMs on older submarines. But the Soviets wanted a higher figure that would be limited to modern submarines. The issue was resolved only when President Nixon agreed at the Moscow summit to omit SLBMs on older diesel-submarines and to a level of 740 modern launchers on nuclear-powered submarines operational and entering sea trials as the trade-in point for the dismantling of older ICBMs. Thus the Soviets initially were permitted 740 modern SLBM launchers versus 656 for the United States, and, if both sides traded in their older ICBM launchers for modern SLBM launchers, the disparity would grow to 950 to 710.[26]

The final agreement on Offensive Forces gave the United States 1,054 ICBMs operational or under construction and the Soviet Union 1,618. Both parties were prohibited from converting light ICBM launchers, deployed before 1964, to heavy launchers. The United States was limited to 710 SLBM launchers and forty-four SSBNs and the Soviets to 950 launchers and sixty-two submarines. The Interim Agreement permitted modernization of strategic systems but limited the increase in ICBM silo launchers to no more than 10 to 15 percent of the existing dimensions. In a unilateral statement, the United States also declared that it would "consider any ICBM having a volume significantly greater than that of the largest light ICBM now operational on either side to be a heavy ICBM."[27] Although the United States tried to get a ban on mobile ICBMs, it was unsuccessful. However, it declared in a unilateral statement that it would regard deployment of mobile ICBMs as inconsistent with the spirit of the agreement.

Genies in Bottles

Neither the United States nor the Soviet Union were keen on extending the arms race into defenses.[28] The sticking point throughout the negotiations was on the extent of offensive limitations, with the United States favoring them and the Soviets opposed. The slow development of ABM in the mid-1960s may have also played an important role in creating the right conditions for an agreement on defenses because there was not strong momentum behind the ABM program.

By contrast, the fact that the MIRV genie was out of the bottle made MIRV limitations difficult if not impossible.[29] MIRV testing had already begun in August 1968. As Ted Greenwood states, "By 1968 the military commitment to MIRV was exceedingly strong. The programs were too far advanced, deployment schedules of Poseidon and Minuteman III were too integrated with maintenance and modernization of existing systems, and too many other programs had been given up along the way for the military to forego or delay the new MIRVed missiles willingly."[30]

Although the momentum behind MIRV made it difficult to stop, some believe that this did not foreclose the possibility of developing meaningful constraints on MIRV. One such possibility for compromise was apparently uncovered during the talks, even though it was not vigorously pursued. The proposal would have banned the flight-testing as well as the production and deployment of the MIRV but would not have required verification by on-site inspection that the Soviets opposed. "The U.S. could have proposed . . . a real and equitable comprehensive ban on further flight testing, production, and deployment of MIRVs, without the demand for an unneeded (and for that matter ineffectual) on-site inspection, which invited certain Soviet rejection of the idea of a MIRV ban."[31] Neither side, however, entertained this possibility very seriously. The United States was not interested for the reasons stated above, while the Soviets may have been concerned about the U.S. lead in MIRV testing. A ban on testing and deployment would have locked the Soviets into an inferior position.

Linkage

Nixon and Kissinger made much ado about linkage at the outset, viewing the SALT negotiations as part of a larger détente policy. In practice, however, the administration did not press the issue or link arms control to promises of good conduct by the Soviets in the Middle East or elsewhere. Linkage does not appear to have been a condition for sustaining the negotiations. However, there is strong evidence that the May agreement on SALT announced on May 20, 1971, was privately linked to a U.S. agreement on major grain sales to the Soviet Union and credit provisions for those sales.[32] This agreement was also followed by White House approval of two major contracts for mining and oil drilling equipment and a series of contracts for equipment for the Kama truck plant in the Soviet Union.

It is important to note that the Soviets did not seek to apply linkage during the SALT I negotiations. Despite the United States' incursion into Cambodia and the mining of Haiphong harbor in 1971, the Soviets stayed at the negotiating table and continued to press for a strategic arms limitation agreement.

THE PROCESS

Politics within the Administration

The NSC staff played an important role in planning for SALT through the standing Verification Panel that was set up by Kissinger. The negotiations in Helsinki and Vienna were complemented by a series of back-channel communications between Kissinger and Dobrynin. The SALT team, however, was sometimes left in the dark, which created considerable friction between the negotiators and the White House. The decision to iron out some of the final details of the agreements at the Nixon-Brezhnev meeting illustrate the difficulties of summitry and dual-track diplomacy, and the Moscow negotiations were hectic and confused. The White House team was ill equipped to deal with the technical details of issues such as the types of ballistic-missile submarines constrained by the Offensive Agreement; the stage of construction at which SLBMs would be counted as operational systems; and definitions tied in with provisions regarding conversion of launchers for light missiles to heavier launchers.

Executive-Congressional Relations

Congress's role in SALT I was, in many respects, quite limited. Congress did play an important role in slowing movement toward ABM deployment in the mid- to late 1960s. Congress also helped publicize the hazards of MIRV and other qualitative changes in strategic weapons systems, although the MIRV debate was not as intense as ABM, partly because the program had already been funded by the Johnson administration. With the exception of Jackson and a number of other senators, however, Congress was not actively involved or well informed about the negotiations themselves. The Jackson Amendment urging that the principle of equality, reflected in the ABM Treaty, become the standard for SALT II did have an important influence on subsequent negotiations.

There was strong support in Congress for the ABM Treaty and Interim Agreement on Offensive Limitations even though Congress was not actively involved in the arms control process. Because Nixon was Republican and a hardliner, this made it easier to sell the SALT I agreements to Congress. Nixon's record on anticommunism was well known, which mitigated right-wing suspicion, and he was able to carry most of the Congress because moderates were favorably disposed toward the accords anyway.

There also appears to have been a general (if unarticulated) desire to improve relations with the Soviet Union and to view arms control as part of the overall détente process in the Congress and the public at large. The memory of Czechoslovakia had faded by 1972. People had grown weary of the war in Vietnam. SALT I stood as an important symbol of the beginning of a new era of peace and an end to confrontation.

THE AGREEMENTS

The ABM agreement in SALT I was a formal treaty ratified in accordance with constitutional procedures in the United States and the Soviet Union. Two ABM sites were permitted to each side under the treaty, but they had to be at least 1,300 km apart. The treaty was of unlimited duration and is still in effect. Each side was permitted to withdraw from the treaty on six month's notice if it concluded that its national interests were jeopardized.

The Interim Agreement on offensive forces limited each side to the number of launchers for ICBMs and SLBMs operational and under construction at the time the accord was signed. Each side was allowed to replace some of its old ICBMs with new SLBMs. The United States was permitted 1,054 ICBMs and 656 SLBMs, with the option of retiring fifty-four old Titan missiles for SLBMs.[33] The Soviets were allowed 1,608 launchers for ICBMs and 740 for SLBMs, and they could trade in 210 old land-based missiles for SLBMs.

OUTCOMES

The principal hurdle in getting speedy ratification of the SALT I agreements came from those who felt that the administration had betrayed them in getting Congress's approval for the ABM Safeguard program and then trading it away. A number of senators, led by Senator Henry Jackson of the Armed Services Committee, also believed that the unequal force ceilings in the Interim Agreement and the prohibitions on the development of defenses might well place the United States in an untenable military situation vis-à-vis the Soviets. The other key actor was William J. Fulbright, chairman of the Senate Foreign Relations Committee.

Effect on Arms

The prevailing consensus among most moderates on both sides of the political fence was that the agreements would restrain the arms race. In the words of Representative Gerald R. Ford, "What it all comes down to is this. We did not give anything away and we slowed the Soviet momentum in the nuclear arms race."[34] This view accepted the administration's position that, if the Soviet momentum had been allowed to go unchecked, the Soviets would have been able to build an additional 1,000 ICBMs and to increase their modern SSBN force to ninety submarines in the 1972–77 period. It also reflected the belief that the ABM Treaty had prevented a costly and ultimately destabilizing race in strategic defenses. No one really said that the arms competition had been redirected in productive ways; rather, the consensus in the "middle" was that the race had been slowed down.

Those who supported SALT with reservation argued that the agreements had not gone far enough to reduce offensive arms, prohibit MIRVs, and impose controls on qualitative developments. They argued that the Agreement on Offensive Limitations had simply "codified" existing defense plans.

Others, however, argued that the Interim Agreement simply codified Soviet weapons programs, while arresting the United States' ability to catch up. They charged that the quantitative ceilings were high enough to allow the Soviets by 1977 to build to levels they would have probably not exceeded by much without SALT. They charged that the old missile launchers to be traded in under the accords (SS-7s and SS-8s) were obsolete and that the Soviets intended to scrap them anyway. Furthermore, the modernization programs permitted under the agreement would allow the Soviets to upgrade some of their older heavy missiles, even though they could not increase the number of heavy ICBMs under the terms of the agreement. In short, the United States was constrained, but the Soviets were not.

Senator Jackson, in particular, was also alarmed that SALT I would allow the Soviets to deploy the SS-9—and its successor the SS-18—both of which would threaten the survivability of the Minuteman force. The senator believed that Moscow would exploit its numerical four-to-one throw-weight advantage during the period of the agreement by MIRVing its heavy missiles. According to Jackson's scenario, the Soviets would possess a destabilizing, first-strike counterforce capability with as many as 6,000 warheads directed against Minuteman before 1977.[35] Jackson also predicted that the ABM Treaty would actually fuel the arms race because land-based forces would be exposed to threats from qualitative improvements of Soviet systems.[36] Measures like superhardening of silos by relocation in hard rock formations or moving them out to sea were prohibited by the accords. He referred to calculations that he and the administration had done earlier in developing the case for the Safeguard system, which indicated that a force of 400 SS-9 ICBMs could destroy approximately 95 percent of the Minuteman force. He got administration witnesses to acknowledge that once the Soviets achieved accuracies equivalent to the U.S. Minuteman force (at that time approximately .2 nm CEP), U.S. land-based missiles would indeed be vulnerable.[37]

Administration officials challenged the scenario, however, on the grounds that the Soviets did not have the technological capability to deploy highly accurate MIRVs in sufficient numbers to threaten an unacceptable percentage of the Minuteman force during the period of the agreement. Moreover, without sophisticated retargeting capabilities they would be unable to compensate for system failures. The most compelling refutation came from Air Force Chief of Staff Ryan.[38] Ryan agreed that a portion of the missile force could become vulnerable if a large number of accurate warheads were programmed to strike at U.S. silos in unison. But he argued that the Soviets would have difficulty coordinating a simultaneous attack by their forces because of the different flight times of their RVs. They would also deplete their arsenal for other operations, and the ragged nature of the attack would leave the United States with ample time to respond. Even if the Soviets achieved high accuracy and targeted all of the Minuteman force, several hundred ICBMs would still survive.

Jackson's arguments, however, had a powerful hold on the minds of conservative critics. His fears were echoed by notables such as Senator Barry Goldwater. Senator James Buckley in hearings before the Senate Foreign Relations Committee also argued that the agreements would erode U.S. deterrent capabilities and permit destabilizing developments in Soviet strategic forces.[39]

Over the longer term, however, the ABM Treaty restricted the competition in strategic defenses. It was the first major qualitative nuclear arms limitation agreement. Its key provision was the prohibition on territorial defense. The treaty also prohibited development, testing, and deployment of land-mobile, sea-based, air-based, and space-based ABM systems.[40] Multiple-warhead ABMs were banned as were rapid-reload systems. The deployment or transfer of ABM systems outside of U.S. or Soviet territory was also prohibited. The deployment of exotic systems that would substitute for ABM radars, missiles, or launchers (such as space-based lasers) was also banned.

It could be argued that, even without the ABM agreement, the United States would still not have deployed an ABM system. Lawrence Weiler, former counselor of ACDA and a member of the SALT delegation, makes this claim: Safeguard "had produced enough opposition to deployment—based on technical, emotional, strategic and arms control grounds . . . only the bargaining chip argument could keep the program alive."[41] There is some evidence to support this assertion. The twelve-site Safeguard system announced in March 1969 aroused considerable opposition in the Congress, and Congress approved construction of two sites by a margin of one vote. The amendment to limit Safeguard to two sites in 1970 was also defeated by a very narrow margin. Nixon's argument about the need to have Safeguard as a bargaining chip was viewed with considerable skepticism in the Congress. It is quite likely that without arms control talks, Safeguard would have probably been defeated (at least construction beyond the two appropriated sites). Nor is it evident that the Kremlin was interested in ABM deployment beyond the system around Moscow. The Soviet commitment to an ABM treaty in the talks was probably an accurate reflection of their reluctance to deploy ABM further.

The really crucial question, however, is whether the desire not to deploy defenses could have been sustained without the ABM Treaty. As one astute observer remarked, "If there is one certainty about the weapons acquisition process, it is that nothing is certain. The coalition of political and technical opponents of the ABM may over time have diminished in strength and effectiveness, and it is conceivable that ABMs would eventually have been deployed."[42] Without SALT the Pentagon might well have upped its efforts to lobby for hard-site defense because of growing fears about Minuteman vulnerability. This did not happen. Neither side began construction of a second site as permitted in the ABM Treaty. At the July 1974 summit meeting, Nixon and Brezhnev signed a protocol agreement limiting each side to one ABM site only. Shortly after the summit, the U.S. Army announced that it would deactivate the site at Grand Forks because of the expense of operating a facility that had no strategic utility.

With respect to offensive systems, the ongoing arms limitation talks may have helped to slow down the pace of new Soviet missile deployments, although this cannot be proven. When the talks began, no construction of new ICBM launchers began for almost a year. When the talks stalemated in late 1970, the Soviets began construction of eighty new ICBM launchers, but, following the May 20, 1971, agreement, the Soviets unilaterally refrained from starting any new ones.[43] In the two and a half years of negotiations only eighty new ICBM launchers were initiated, versus 650 in the same period preceding the talks. The Soviets also did not publicly attempt to claim any advantage from unequal numbers of ICBMs and SLBMs under the Interim Agreement.

U.S. unwillingness to build defenses for the NCA as permitted under the treaty and the eventual dismantling of the ABM site at Grand Forks freed resources for other uses. The United States also may have saved billions (more than the $5 billion in immediate cutbacks of programmed expenditures) because of potential restraint on offensive systems exercised by the ABM Treaty.[44] A race in defenses would almost have certainly encouraged each side to develop further offensive penetration capabilities to overwhelm the opponent's defenses. Early estimates that the Soviets would deploy 5,000 to 9,000 ABM missile launchers by the middle of the 1970s were not realized.

SALT I also reduced some of the uncertainties in strategic planning, which is frequently done on a worst-case basis. "With the conclusion of the SALT I agreements, each side knew the range of strategic alternatives available to the other side, and for the first time could discount its worst fears about the other's future deployments."[45] SALT I also brought top-level military and political leaders into the military planning process and served an important educational function in that regard.

Most important, however, SALT I initiated a process that, as was clearly recognized at the time, had to continue if significant progress was to be made in addressing fundamental U.S. strategic concerns. As Ambassador Gerard Smith stated in a unilateral declaration delivered to the Soviets on May 9, 1969,

> The U.S. Delegation has stressed the importance the U.S. Government attaches to achieving agreement on more complete limitations on strategic offensive arms, following agreement on an ABM Treaty and on an Interim Agreement on certain measures with respect to the limitation of strategic offensive arms. The U.S. Delegation believes that an objective of the follow-on negotiations should be to constrain and reduce on a long-term basis threats to the survivability of our respective strategic retaliatory forces. . . . If an agreement providing for more complete strategic offensive arms limitations were not achieved within five years, U.S. supreme interests could be jeopardized. Should that occur, it would constitute a basis for withdrawal from the ABM Treaty.[46]

There is little direct evidence that the Interim Agreement redirected arms competition in counterproductive ways. However, it is the case that the military used the SALT I limitations to lobby for increased expenditures and the development of new systems in unrestricted areas. And some might say that the agreement led to larger missiles (for example, MX), more MIRVs, ALCMs, and so forth as a consequence, although this is difficult to prove one way or the other. There was some obvious prompting from the top to exploit areas not restricted by the agreements. Nixon and Brezhnev, for instance, noted at the Moscow summit that both countries were free to proceed to do whatever was *not* explicitly limited by the agreements. This may have had some impact on the U.S. decision in 1972—scarcely noted at the time—to accelerate research and development on strategic cruise missiles.[47]

To some extent, the Interim Agreement also did "codify" defense plans (such as MIRV and Trident). "As a 'freeze,' it yielded only rather high ceilings on the numbers of Soviet ICBM and SLBM launchers (2,348), while holding the United States to the level that had not changed since 1967 (1710). The Soviet Union was required to dismantle its 210 older SS-7 and 8 ICBM's in order to be allowed to continue to build up the number of SLBM launchers to a total of 950."[48]

The Soviets failed to achieve their objective to limit FBS (tactical aircraft capable of striking the Soviet Union). The United States was also unable to constrain the throw-weight of existing or replacement Soviet ICBMs with the exception of very loose limits on silo dimensions and a limit of 308 large ICBMs.

The SALT agreements also gave a great deal of political publicity to nuclear arms questions. They drew attention to the weapons themselves and added fuel to the debate over Minuteman vulnerability that had gained momentum in the earlier debate over ABM. The relative size of U.S. and Soviet strategic arsenals also became the focus of much concern, as did the issue of quantitative superiority. The Jackson Amendment ensured that numbers would continue to be important in future arms control efforts. Some argue that without the Interim Agreement on Offensive Limitations, Americans might have been less inclined to worry about Soviet numerical superiority in strategic offensive missiles.

Bargaining from Strength

Some feared that the Interim Agreement might "spur the arms race" by those advocating new defense programs as "bargaining chips."[49] SALT was the first instance of widespread use of the term *bargaining chip*. The administration believed that certain military programs could be used as positive inducements in the negotiations, but critics argued that their real purpose was not to bargain systems away but to build them.

The idea of using ABM as a bargaining chip was developed quite early in the Nixon administration.[50] In response to congressional pressure, President Nixon asked for a special interagency review of ABM headed by Deputy Secretary of Defense David Packard. The Packard study, concluded in late February 1969, argued that the Sentinel program should be continued in a modified form and that priority should go to the defense of Minuteman ICBM fields. The administration, however, faced the difficulty of trying to sell the idea to Congress. Nixon and Kissinger agreed with the conclusion that the United States should go forward with ABM and supported a plan for twelve separate sites for area defense of which four would protect

Minuteman. In his official statement, the president argued that "The Soviet interest in strategic talks was not deterred by the decision of the previous administration to deploy the Sentinel ABM system—in fact, it was formally announced shortly afterwards."[51] Nixon's view, however, was not shared by his Secretary of Defense Melvin Laird, who firmly stated, "I believe that this system stands on its own feet, on its merits."

Nixon's announcement that the administration was going ahead with ABM provoked a fierce debate, but on August 6 the Senate approved authorization funds for the ABM program by one vote. A decisive factor was Ambassador Gerard Smith's cable that Safeguard was essential to the talks, which Kissinger shared in his meeting with congressional leaders. Congressional opponents to Safeguard, however, refused to give up. They ultimately were successful in shrinking appropriations from twelve sites to two sites by 1972.

Safeguard was the only program to be actually "cashed in" as a bargaining chip. A number of other programs were justified on similar grounds but were never traded in negotiations with the Soviets. This was true, for example, with Trident. On December 2, 1971, Kissinger wrote to Laird to convey the president's decisions on the defense budget for the forthcoming year. He urged Laird "to give favorable consideration to 'an expanded strategic submarine program' in a way that was highly visible to the Soviets."

The Trident decision was a critical one that had important implications for the SALT process. At the time the United States was building no SSBNs. It had one of two choices: to improve the current version of Poseidon or to build an entirely new Trident submarine. States Kissinger, "If we chose to build improved Poseidons, we would prefer to leave submarine-launched missiles out of the SALT freeze; we would have an opportunity to match the Soviet Union by building new submarines rapidly. If on the other hand we chose to invest in the new Trident program, we would have to insist on the inclusion of SLBMs in SALT so as to freeze Soviet numbers while we used the five-year period to develop our new system." The Pentagon opted for Trident. This put pressure on the administration to go for a freeze on SLBMs, although there were those who also believed that the acceleration of Trident would induce the Soviets to accept SLBM/SSBN limitations and provide additional leverage in SALT II.

Bargaining chips and the importance of offsetting quantitative disparities with qualitative advantages continued to be important in the debate over approval of SALT I. In his appearance before a joint session of Congress following the Moscow summit, President Nixon "called for speedy congressional endorsement of the various accords signed at Moscow as a sign of national unity" but cautioned that "the U.S. must also undertake whatever defense programs necessary to maintain a strategic posture second to none."[52]

Thus, when the administration approached Congress for endorsement of SALT it also sought approval of several strategic programs, including acceleration of Trident and continuation of the B-1 and various supplemental budget items totaling $168 million for prototype development of a site defense system; initial development work on a submarine-launched cruise missile (SLCM); research on improved reentry vehicles for the ICBMs and SLBMs; acceleration of the satellite basing program for the B-52s, which would allow for rapid redeployment of these aircraft to inland bases; improved C^3 and intelligence-processing equipment; and augmentation of verification capabilities.[53]

Secretary Laird was explicit that SALT would not lead to any great savings in defense spending because of the escalating costs of the Vietnam War and other strategic initiatives. The savings of $711 million in fiscal 1973 as a result of the cancellation of ABM construction and deployment would be offset by allocations of $686 million for accelerating several strategic programs, particularly the Trident missile and submarine systems. Laird also stated unequivocally that he "could not support the [SALT] agreement if Congress fail[ed] to act on the movement forward of the Trident system, the B-1 bomber and [these] other programs."[54] Although Nixon and Kissinger eschewed direct linkage between the accords and these programs, they underscored the importance of going ahead with them in order to provide the Soviets with sufficient incentives to negotiate follow-on agreements. Nixon stated at the congressional briefings on SALT on June 15, 1972, that "for the United States not to go forward with its programs—and I am not suggesting which ones . . . would mean that any incentives that the Soviets had to negotiate the follow-on agreement would be removed."[55] Kissinger, however, was explicit that this meant acceleration of B-1 and Trident.[56]

Both of these programs were important domestic bargaining chips and key conditions for the Pentagon's support for the accords. That this was so was no secret. Secretary of Defense Melvin Laird repeatedly affirmed in congressional hearings that his and Admiral Moorer's support for SALT was "predicated upon" congressional approval of the acceleration of these programs.

The idea of using SALT as a justification for further military spending did not sit well with some members of Congress. Senator Fulbright expressed grave reservations about the wisdom of such an approach and argued that it "raised several questions about our determination to accept this agreement in the spirit in which it was negotiated."[57] Although the Senate Foreign Relations Committee approved the treaty unanimously, many of its members shared Fulbright's concerns that these strategic programs would undermine the Kremlin's confidence in the accords. They also worried that the bargaining chips would simply stimulate the arms race further as Moscow tried to meet the threat posed by new weapons deployments. The committee's resolution endorsing the agreement, Senate Joint Resolution 241, pointedly excluded the language suggested by the Nixon administration that would have affirmed that it was U.S. strategic superiority that had enabled realization of the accords as well as the importance of the proposed strategic weapons programs to the success of SALT II.[58]

The bargaining chip issue continued to be important as senators pressured the Senate's leadership to bring the 1973 fiscal military authorization to the floor before the SALT pacts were reviewed. They were led by Armed Services Chairman John Stennis, who openly declared his support for the administration's request for B-1 and Trident.

It should be noted, however, that the Senate Armed Services Committee deleted without prejudice the $110 million supplemental request because it wanted more time to study the proposal.[59] It also denied funds for an NCA ABM site and one-third of the $60 million devoted to MIRV for the Trident II D-5 SLBM, on the grounds that it wanted more time to study the desirability of these systems. The Committee also came close to deleting funds for acceleration of the Trident program because Senators Jackson, Goldwater, and Bentsen, in particular, were not keen on the system and favored the development of a smaller, new SSBN. During the floor debate Bentsen proposed an amendment to remove funds for Trident acceleration, believing that such action would not jeopardize SALT II and would give the Senate time to consider the appropriateness of the Trident design.[60] But it did not pass, largely because it failed to get even Jackson's support.

In the House, the Armed Services Committee endorsed the entire SALT-related weapons package.[61] But in the debate on the floor, several Pentagon critics tried to offer amendments to excise all of the $110 million earmarked for the SALT supplemental procurement request and to cut funds for the NCA and acceleration of the Trident program.[62] Their effort failed.

Lulling

Senator Henry Jackson and other conservative critics of SALT I believed that the Soviets would catch up in MIRV and other technologies where the United States had a short-term qualitative advantage.[63] They also feared that the greater throw-weight available to the Soviets would allow them to deploy many more warheads than the United States and that the United States would fail to maintain a high-cost technological effort in the political climate of future SALT negotiations. This view was vigorously contended by administration officials, particularly Secretary of Defense Melvin Laird.

The assertion that SALT I was oversold demands qualification. Certainly from the perspective of arms control there were few illusions about SALT I in the administration or the Congress, and, if anything, administration officials were remarkably restrained about SALT I's achievements. Views about the accords should be distinguished, however, from general atmospherics and the relationship between SALT and détente where there were obviously high hopes. A Harris poll conducted in early June 1972 showed that more than 80 percent of the U.S. people supported all of the Moscow agreements on arms control and other areas of cooperation.[64] However, Americans had no illusions about the long-term implications of the new "era of détente" for U.S.-Soviet relations. Those surveyed agreed with the president's note of caution about the development of U.S.-Soviet relations. Although 58 percent believed that "a whole new period of peaceful relations between the U.S. and Russia" had opened up, a resounding 65 percent concurred with the assertion that "the Cold War had not ended."

It is also important to note that data on public opinion provide little support for the lulling hypothesis (see Figure 4–1). There was a slight drop in the percentage of Americans who felt that the United States was spending "too much" on defense following the signing of

Figure 4-1. Attitudes Toward Defense Spending, 1969–85.

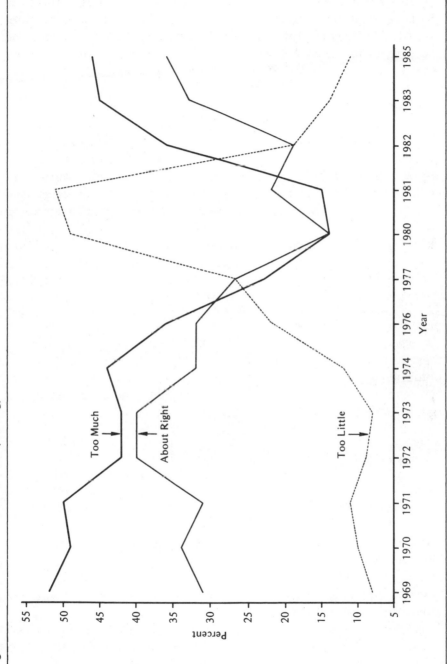

Source: Thomas W. Graham, "The Politics of Failure: Strategic Nuclear Arms Control, Public Opinion, and Domestic Politics in the United States, 1945–1985," Forthcoming dissertation, Massachusetts Institute of Technology.

the SALT I accords in 1972. However, the most abrupt change in attitudes came after the end of the Vietnam war and not the signing of SALT I. But the shift was in the opposite direction—far greater spending on defense, not less. Moreover, the number of Americans who felt that the United States was spending "too little" on defense climbed steadily through the 1970s, while those who felt it was spending "too much" declined.

Of course, the arguments about lulling are more complex than that, and public opinion is only part of the story. Arms control may have had an important impact on internal administration politics and eroded support for new weapons programs over the long run. However, at the level of public opinion, there is little to suggest that SALT I made the public less vigilant about the requirements for a strong defense.

Allies

The United States' Western European allies greeted the SALT I agreements with a combination of skepticism and tepid enthusiasm. At the level of expert opinion within the government (that is, the defense and foreign ministries), attitudes were characterized by disappointment at the limited nature of the agreements but also by concern about the apparent quantitative advantage the agreements gave to the Soviet Union. Nevertheless, the allies were pleased that the United States had made no concessions on forward-based systems and that the ABM Treaty would prolong the deterrent effect of British and French nuclear forces.[65]

Verification

Some feared that national means of detection might not suffice to keep the United States adequately informed of Soviet activity, especially in critical areas of new technology.[66] Others worried that Soviet attempts to attain clear-cut military advantage would be less likely than political exploitation of their "superior" strategic position. The administration's counterargument was that the Soviets had a vested interest in SALT, which validated their achievement of strategic "equality" with the United States. If they cheated, they would be caught and the United States would be able to abrogate the accords.[67]

Generally, however, verification was not a major issue in the debate over the provisions of the ABM Treaty or the Interim Agreement on Offensive Arms. The SALT agreements recognized and legitimized verification by national technical means or nonintrusive methods of intelligence collection. It should also be noted that without effective means of reconnaissance, the accords would have been very difficult to negotiate.

There have been various allegations of Soviet noncompliance with SALT I since the agreements were ratified. The Reagan administration has accused the Soviets of "probable" or "potential" violations of the ABM Treaty with regard to mobile ABMs, concurrent testing of ABM and SAM components, and a territorial ABM defense.[68] There is a growing consensus that some activities constitute breaches of the treaty (such as the Krasnoyarsk radar). There is strong evidence that the Soviets have not fully complied with the spirit or letter of agreement either in the ABM Treaty or the SALT I Interim Agreement.

The first major publicly available review of Soviet compliance of SALT I was conducted in February 1978.[69] The charges of Soviet violations included Soviet flouting of heavy-light missile distinction; concealment of mobile missiles; impediment of U.S. monitoring of telemetry data on Soviet MIRV testing; launch control facilities converted into additional missile silos; testing of the SA-5 radar in an ABM defense mode; installation of an ABM radar on the Kamchatka peninsula; and Soviet failure to dismantle replaced ICBM launchers on time. The extensive review of Soviet behavior indicated that the record of noncompliance was murky. Agreement was reached on a clear demarcation between heavy and light missiles in the SCC and SALT II delegations. The Soviets also acknowledged the discrepancy in meeting requirements for the dismantling of silos for the SS-7 and SS-8 and took further deactivation steps to satisfy the agreements. Although the Report found evidence that Soviet concealment activities had increased substantially in 1974, it argued that this did not prevent verification of SALT compliance, and by early 1975 discussion in the SCC indicated that there was no expansion in Soviet concealment practices. Protested SA-5 radar activity ceased soon afterwards.

One sticky point, however, was the Soviet compliance with the treaty's limits on ABM missile test facilities. Although Sary Shagan was regarded by the United States as an ABM test range at the time of the ABM treaty (and testing at this facility was therefore permissible), the Kamchatka test range was not. Testing at this facility contravened the provision that the establishment of additional ABM test ranges would require the agreement of both parties.

One informed observer argues that Soviet behavior "did at times suggest a 'devil-may-care' attitude about strict compliance with treaty provisions. . . . While these episodes had no appreciable strategic significance—and none violated the letter of SALT I—they did tend to vitiate the 'spirit' of the agreement and cast Soviet motives in a bad light."[70]

Richard Perle takes a different view: "One can debate whether the issues of the 1970s were violations or circumventions or a mix of both. There is no doubt that the Soviets have proven remarkably adroit at exploiting ambiguities in arms control agreements to proceed with activities that it was the intent of one of the parties—us—to preclude by treaty. In doing this, the Soviets have not hesitated to mislead us, deliberately and all too successfully."[71]

The Krasnoyarsk radar has become the focus of recent allegations of Soviet noncompliance with the ABM Treaty. The United States sought to limit construction of large phased-array radars in the ABM Treaty. Both sides, however, wanted to construct LPARs for early warning systems, satellite tracking, and intelligence, but they agreed to limit radars for ABM target acquisition and engagement missions and to restrict deployment of ABM radar at first to two deployment areas and to test ranges and then later to one deployment area as agreed in the 1974 protocol. They also agreed to a ban on the testing of non-ABM components in the ABM mode (although "testing in an ABM mode" was not defined in the treaty) and to limit future early-warning ABM radars to the periphery of each side's national territory, facing outwards. Both sides also agreed not to deploy LPARs exceeding a certain potential (3×10^6 watt meters squared) except as provided for in Articles III (ABM deployment areas), IV (test ranges), and VI (BMEW) or for space-track or NTM.

In 1984 the Reagan administration publicly accused the Soviets of "almost certainly" violating the ABM Treaty. In its February 1985 *Report on Soviet Noncompliance with Arms Control Agreements*, the administration argued that "the USSR has violated the ABM Treaty."[72] The administration argued that the Krasnoyarsk radar was constructed for early warning with an ABM battle management capability, and its location was in violation of ABM Treaty provisions regarding location and orientation of early warning radars.

The administration believes that technical characteristics of the radar are similar to the Pechora-type radars that the Soviets have acknowledged are for early warning. The Soviets have responded in the SCC by arguing that the radar is for tracking satellites and for verification of U.S. compliance with the Outer Space Treaty. The United States, however, believes that the radar is much better suited for early warning than for space tracking.

Controversy has also arisen over Soviet tests in 1983 and 1984 of a SA-12 surface-to-air missile (SAM) system against targets such as the SS-12 tactical ballistic missile. Soviet testing of modular radars has also been controversial as have those of the U.S. ABM testing at Kwajalein.

The administration's February 1985 report concludes that "the aggregate of the Soviet Union's ABM and ABM related actions suggest that the USSR may be preparing an ABM defense of its national territory."[73] This general conclusion is reaffirmed in the administration's December 1985 report and similar concerns were expressed in the president's December 1985 *Report on Soviet Noncompliance to Congress*. Not all concur with the administration's assessment, however. The *National Campaign to Save the ABM Treaty Report* argues that

> the facts do not support the case that the Soviets are on the verge of a break-out of the ABM Treaty. While the Soviets have the potential for such a break-out, the Administration has failed to provide any convincing evidence that they are actually making such a move. . . . There is little doubt that the new ABM–X–3 components could be deployed as part of a nationwide defense. Nor is there any dispute over the fact that the Flat Twin modular radar could be deployed more expeditiously than could the much larger phased-array radars of the Pechora type. But these activities—no more than similar American activities such as the Site Defense effort of the early 1970s—are not necessarily preparations for breaking out of the Treaty. In isolation, any ABM component could be regarded as preparations for a defense of national territory.[74]

Asymmetry

Some argued that SALT I gave the Soviets the quantitative advantage that they would later be able to turn into a qualitative one (that is, MIRVing their heavy ICBMs). The counterargument was that quantitative disparities were more than adequately compensated by

U.S. qualitative superiority, especially in MIRV and delivery accuracy potential. The United States had a lead that the Soviets could not hope to overcome in five years.

There were also those who believed that the asymmetries in SALT I would make negotiations in SALT II harder because the Soviets would be unwilling to give up what they had gained. To ensure that inequities were not worked into a permanent treaty, Senator Jackson sponsored an amendment requesting the president not to accept a treaty that would "limit the United States to levels of intercontinental strategic forces inferior to the limits provided for the Soviet Union."[75] The Interim Agreement on Offensive Arms with the Jackson Amendment tacked on to it passed both houses with comfortable margins.

Whether the process and agreements in SALT I served Soviet interests more than U.S. interests over the longer term is a matter of continuing contention. Some would assert that the most notable achievement was the explicit recognition of "parity" in mutual deterrence. "This situation had been anticipated and widely accepted in the West long before the Soviet Union had achieved a capability even remotely comparable to that of the United States. But by the late 1960s the fact of mutual deterrence, with its corollary of the futility of an unlimited continuing strategic arms race, was recognized by the leaders both of the United States and of the Soviet Union."[76] This assertion, however, begs the question whether recognition of parity was the same as acceptance. The Soviets continued to upgrade their older, heavy missiles as some had feared. In 1975 the Soviets began to deploy a new generation of ICBMs: the SS-17, SS-18, and the SS-19. Both the SS-18 and SS-19 carried MIRVed payloads.[77] By 1977 the Soviet Union enjoyed a slight lead over the United States in the number of ICBM deliverable warheads—2,647 vs. 2,154—but was well behind in SLBM deliverable warheads and those deliverable by long-range bombers. Although the Soviets did not achieve the high levels of accuracy in delivery capability that critics of the Interim Agreement feared they would in the five-year period,[78] SALT I may have provided the basis for Soviet advantages in hard-target and prompt counterforce capability that came later. The vulnerability of U.S. ICBMs was the subject of intense debate in SALT II and the report of the Scowcroft Commission, and the issue is very much alive today. It is nevertheless the case that the vulnerability problem emerged somewhat later than many of the critics of SALT I predicted.

Uncertainties

SALT I may have helped to reduce uncertainties in estimates and projections of each other's forces by the very nature of the dialogue itself. However, it is important to realize, as one close participant observes, that "the process of negotiation sometimes distorted the dialogue. Advocacy and defense of one's own position and proposals, and criticism of those of the other side, may have led to distortions—if only through selective emphases and debating arguments. Matters of agreed positions and those not directly precipitated by the process of negotiation tended to get short shrift or no attention at all."[79] This was particularly true of military doctrinal and operational issues that the Soviets were unwilling to discuss at all.

The Standing Consultative Commission's mechanisms, established in SALT I, provided an institutional basis for maintaining ongoing discussions about forces and programs. Some, like Assistant Secretary of Defense Richard Perle, however, would go so far as to argue that the SCC has served no useful purpose. The Commission was created to implement technical details of the ABM Treaty and the Interim Agreement (such as dismantling of launchers and replacement provisions) and served as a forum for clarifying ambiguous developments that might be viewed as being in violation of the agreements. The SCC conducted the five-year review of the ABM Treaty held in 1977 and 1982. Some matters since then, however, have been raised through separate channels other than SCC.

One of the most important achievements in SALT I was acceptance of the legitimacy of national technical means of verification and a recognized obligation by both parties not to interfere with such systems or their effectiveness. Although there are continuing problems with Soviet encryption, data denial, and other forms of interference with national technical means of verification, one must certainly ask whether, in the absence of such an agreement, the situation would be worse or better than the one today.

Impact on U.S.-Soviet Relations

Whether the SALT I agreements had a decidedly positive or negative effect on U.S.-Soviet relations very much depends on the political disposition and perspective of the observer. However, if one begins with the central assumptions underlying Nixon and Kissinger's approach to SALT I—namely, that the agreements were part of larger strategy aimed at modifying Soviet behavior and encouraging Soviet restraint and responsibility—then the results failed to live up to the architects' initial expectations because of subsequent Soviet activities in Egypt, Angola, Ethiopia, South Yemen, and Afghanistan.[80]

Nevertheless, it would be wrong to draw the conclusion that there was no change in U.S.-Soviet relations as a result of SALT I or that such change was necessarily for the worse.[81] According to Adam Ulam, Soviet emigration policies underwent a significant change prior to the Moscow summit. "Of some 80,000 Jewish petitioners for exit permits between 1968 and 1971, roughly 18,000 had their wish granted. . . . During what might be described as the honeymoon period of détente, 1972–73, some 65,000 were allowed to leave."[82] Following the introduction of the Jackson-Vanik amendment, however, the numbers dropped precipitously, indicating some of the potential hazards of "unintended linkage" from congressional action. Ultimately, although SALT I was the centerpiece of détente in the U.S.-Soviet relationship, its contribution was limited as were the ripple effects.[83]

CONCLUSION

There is considerable evidence to support the proposition that the most important precondition for SALT negotiations in the late 1960s was the situation of emerging strategic parity between the United States and the Soviet Union. The opportunity for strategic arms limitation talks was recognized by many in the Congress and the public at large. In the case of senior administration officials, however, like the president and his national security adviser, what mattered most was not parity per se but the possibility that the balance might shift rapidly in the Soviet's favor. Nixon and Kissinger feared that the political will to sustain defense spending to match the Soviet build-up was lacking in the United States as a result of public opposition to the war in Vietnam. They saw arms control as a way of stopping the Soviets and establishing strategic "sufficiency."

During the debate over ABM deployments and MIRV in the late 1960s, many argued that U.S. restraint would invite reciprocal restraint by the Soviets. There is certainly strong circumstantial evidence that the United States' sluggish development of ABM, and the Soviets' apparent lack of interest in further ABM deployments, increased the possibilities for an arms control agreement on defenses. The experience with MIRV supports the corollary to this hypothesis, which is that meaningful constraints will be difficult to achieve if a system is well on its way to development. The absence of restraint and the momentum behind MIRV by the time the talks got started made it impossible to negotiate meaningful and verifiable constraints.

Linkage was important even before the negotiations on SALT I began. Recall that the Soviet invasion of Czechoslovakia put the talks on hold for a year; the Soviets were also unwilling to come to the negotiating table until the United States stopped its military build-up in Vietnam. Once the talks got underway, however, there was little effort to press linkage: neither U.S. behavior in Vietnam nor Soviet behavior in the Third World had a perceptible effect on the talks' progress. Both sides obviously saw bigger stakes in the negotiations than they did elsewhere, although the United States used the issue of grain sales to wrest some concessions from the Soviets.

The record of SALT I's achievements is mixed. The accords did help reduce some of the uncertainties in strategic planning by putting a ceiling on the "worst-case" analysis of Soviet strategic programs. Intelligence estimates had lurched from complacency in the early 1960s about the Soviets' ability to catch up to wildly pessimistic projections at the end of the decade when the differences in strategic capabilities began to narrow. By initiating a dialogue about force levels and placing a cap on certain offensive and defensive forces, SALT I made the job of military forecasting a little easier.

The ABM Treaty was a major accomplishment because it was a key factor in precluding a destabilizing offense-defense competition and reducing uncertainties about whether the Soviets would deploy defenses or not. The treaty also may have had a positive effect on the offensive side of the equation by reducing the incentive for each side to build additional systems to penetrate the opponent's defenses, although it is certainly the case that the Soviet offensive build-up has continued since the agreement was signed.

The Interim Agreement on Offensive Arms was admittedly less successful because it satisfied no one. Some argued that it froze the United States into a position of strategic inferiority vis-à-vis the Soviets; others argued that it simply perpetuated the arms race by creating an elaborate set of excuses to build more weapons. It is fair to say that fears were exaggerated on both sides. Although the Soviets continued to modernize their strategic forces, they did so subject to the Interim Agreement's restraints, and the much feared "window of vulnerability" did not emerge during the period that the agreement was in effect. Similarly, despite all the worries about a new arms race, the mild acceleration and increase in real levels of spending on strategic forces leveled off fairly quickly. As some of the new programs (such as Trident) reached fruition at the end of the decade, however, spending was on the rise once again.

The question of whether "lulling" occurred during this period is complex and is discussed at greater length in Chapter 9. However, some key programs were accelerated as a direct consequence of internal administration bargaining during SALT I, and public attitudes demonstrated increased vigilance and a desire to spend more on defense, not less, in the aftermath of the Vietnam war.

Congressional involvement in the SALT process was minimal, yet Congress approved the accords by an overwhelming margin. The more important factors appear to have been the president's standing in the eyes of the Congress and the public; a general desire to improve relations with the Soviets and reduce hostilities; and a feeling that half-a-loaf in arms control (and even perhaps a meager one) was better than none.

The most troubling aspects of the historical record have to do with the record of Soviet compliance with the ABM Treaty. Not only have the charges of noncompliance become more serious over time, but the evidence of Soviet violations is more compelling, particularly with respect to the construction of the Krasnoyarsk radar in Central Russia. The Soviets have clearly not done their utmost to be and to appear to be in compliance with the spirit and letter of the agreement. The problem of how to assess this record is addressed more fully in Chapter 11.

The record of SALT I shows that political expectations were complex and varied. But the worst fears were not realized, although some new ones have emerged. This is particularly true with respect to the record of Soviet compliance with the ABM Treaty. Although the terms of the strategic debate have shifted to the president's Strategic Defense Initiative, the recent debates over deployment of the Midgetman missile suggest that certain themes—namely, the continuing problem of Minuteman vulnerability—have not changed markedly since the early 1970s and the United States' and the Soviet Union's first attempt at bilateral arms control.

NOTES

1. For a discussion of the early history of SALT I see John Newhouse, *Cold Dawn: The Story of SALT* (New York: Holt, Rinehart and Winston, 1973).
2. Although this was initially not an ABM system but an air defense system, this was not clear at the time.
3. As Jerome Kahan writes, "U.S. military leaders were quick to explain to Congress that Sentinel has anti-Soviet capabilities and was viewed by the Joint Chiefs of Staff as a first step toward a heavy ABM deployment." Jerome H. Kahan, *Security in the Nuclear Age* (Washington, D.C.: Brookings Institution, 1975), p. 123.
4. The decision has produced a sharp negative reaction from the NATO allies who felt that they had not been adequately consulted beforehand. Kahan, *Security in the Nuclear Age*, pp. 123–24.
5. See Alton Frye, "U.S. Decision Making for SALT," in Mason Willrich and John F. Rhinelander, eds., *SALT: The Moscow Agreements and Beyond* (New York: Free Press, 1974), pp. 74–78.
6. Robert P. Bresler and Robert C. Gray, "The Bargaining Chip and SALT," *Political Science Quarterly* 92 (1) (Spring 1977), p. 6.
7. Henry Kissinger, *White House Years* (Boston: Little, Brown, 1979), p. 129.
8. David Holloway, *The Soviet Union and the Arms Race*, 2d ed. (New Haven: Yale University Press, 1984), p. 45.
9. *Ibid.*, pp. 205–06.
10. *Ibid.*, p. 206.
11. George D. Gallup, *The Gallup Poll: Public Opinion 1935-1971* (New York: Random House, 1979), pp. 2190, 2207.
12. Kissinger, *White House Years*, pp. 210–12.
13. *Ibid.*, p. 212.
14. *Ibid.*, p. 131.
15. Raymond L. Garthoff, "SALT I: An Evaluation," *World Politics* 31 (1) (Oct. 1978), p. 8.
16. Joseph John Kruzel, "The Preconditions and Consequences of Arms Control Agreements," Unpublished dissertation, Harvard University, Cambridge, Massachusetts, 1975, p. 324.
17. See Lawrence Freedman, *U.S. Intelligence and the Soviet Strategic Threat* (London: Macmillan, 1977).
18. Garthoff, "SALT I: An Evaluation," p. 3.
19. Kissinger, *White House Years*, p. 196.

20. See U.S. Arms Control and Disarmament Agency, "Address by Secretary of State Rogers on Strategic Arms Limitation Talks, November 13, 1969," *Documents on Disarmament, 1969* (Washington, D.C.); and U.S. Arms Control and Disarmament Agency, "Message from President Nixon to ACDA Director Smith: Preliminary Strategic Arms Limitation Talks, November 17, 1969," *Documents on Disarmament, 1969* (Washington, D.C.).

21. Ian Smart, "Perspectives from Europe," in Willrich and Rhinelander, *SALT*, p. 188.

22. See Gerard Smith, *Doubletalk: The Story of Salt I* (New York: University Press of America, 1985), and Raymond L. Garthoff, "Negotiating with the Russians: Some Lessons from SALT," *International Security* 1 (4) (Spring 1977), pp. 5–8.

23. A good discussion of the Soviet negotiating position is found in Thomas W. Wolfe, *The SALT Experience* (Cambridge, Mass.: Ballinger, 1979), pp. 49–110.

24. Kissinger, *White House Years*, pp. 1216–22.

25. *Ibid.*, 1229–46.

26. The Soviets chose to trade in their SS-7s and SS-8s for SLBMs whereas the United States chose *not* to trade Titans for SLBMs.

27. Quoted in Smith, *Doubletalk*, pp. 513–14.

28. But this is not to say that the Soviets had no interest in defenses for themselves. They clearly did as their continued maintenance of the Gallosh defensive system around Moscow, which was permitted under the ABM treaty, suggests.

29. For discussions of the origins of the MIRV program see Graham T. Allison, "What Fuels the Arms Race?," in John F. Reichart and Steven R. Sturm, eds., *American Defense Policy*, 5th ed. (Baltimore: Johns Hopkins University Press, 1982), pp. 463–80; Ted Greenwood, *Making the MIRV: A Study of Defense Decision Making* (Cambridge, Mass.: Ballinger, 1975); Ronald L. Tammen, *MIRV and the Arms Race: An Interpretation of Defense Strategy* (New York: Praeger, 1973); and Herbert York, "The Origins of MIRV," SIPRI Research Report, No. 9 (Stockholm, 1973).

30. Ted Greenwood, *The Making of the MIRV*, quoted in Bresler and Gray, "The Bargaining Chip and SALT," p. 76.

31. Garthoff, "SALT I: An Evaluation," p. 20.

32. Raymond L. Garthoff, *Détente and Confrontation: American-Soviet Relations from Nixon to Reagan* (Washington, D.C.: Brookings Institution, 1985), p. 92. Also see Richard Nixon, "U.S. Foreign Policy for the 1970s, A New Strategy for Peace," Feb. 18, 1970, quoted in Congressional Research Service, *Fundamentals of Nuclear Arms Control Part VIII-Linkage: Nuclear Arms in the Broader Context of United States-Soviet Relations*,

prepared for the Subcommittee on Arms Control, International Security and Science of the House Committee on Foreign Affairs (Washington, D.C.: U.S. Government Printing Office, 1986), p. 5.

33. It is important to note that ICBM launchers were limited to those operational and under construction whereas SLBM launchers were limited to *the number* operational and under construction.

34. Quoted in Wolfe, *The SALT Experience*, p. 16.

35. U.S. Senate Committee on Armed Services Committee, *Hearings on the Military Implications of the Treaty on the Limitation of ABM Systems and the Interim Agreement on Limitation of Offensive Arms*, 92d Cong., 2d Sess. (Washington, D.C.: U.S. Government Printing Office, June and July 1972), p. 368.

36. *Ibid.*, pp. 333, 335, 367–68, 468–69.

37. *Ibid.*, pp. 268–69.

38. *Ibid.*, p. 539.

39. U.S. Senate Committee on Foreign Relations, *Hearings on the Strategic Arms Limitation Agreements*, 92d Cong., 2d Sess. (Washington, D.C.: U.S. Government Printing Office, June and July 1972), pp. 256–71.

40. It should also be noted that the then current U.S. view was that the prohibition included exotic technologies.

41. Quoted in Bresler and Gray, "The Bargaining Chip and SALT," p. 71.

42. Kruzel, "The Preconditions and Consequences of Arms Control Agreements," p. 334.

43. Garthoff, "SALT I: An Evaluation," p. 8.

44. *Ibid.*, p. 17.

45. Kruzel, "The Preconditions and Consequences of Arms Control Agreements," p. 338.

46. Smith, *Doubletalk*, p. 512.

47. Bresler and Gray, "The Bargaining Chip and SALT," pp. 77–79.

48. Garthoff, "SALT I: An Evaluation," p. 13.

49. See U.S. Senate Committee on Foreign Relations, *Agreement on Limitation of Strategic Offensive Weapons*, 92d Cong., 2d Sess., Report 92–979 (July 21, 1972); and *inter alia* "Statement of George W. Rathjens, Council for a Liveable World," in U.S. Senate Committee on Foreign Relations, *SALT*, pp. 297–304.

50. See Alton Frye, *A Responsible Congress: The Politics of National Security* (New York: Council on Foreign Relations, 1975), pp. 15–46.

51. Quoted in Kissinger, *White House Years*, p. 209.

52. "Text of President Nixon's Address to Congress, June 1, 1972," *Congressional Quarterly Weekly Report* (June 3, 1972), pp. 1253–56.

53. U.S. Senate Committee on Armed Services, *Hearings on the FY 1973 Authorization for Military Procurement, etc.*, Addendum No. 1, *Amended*

Military Authorization Related to Strategic Arms Limitation Agreements, 92d Cong., 2d Sess. (Washington, D.C.: U.S. Government Printing Office, June and July 1972), pp. 4335–54.

54. U.S. Senate Committee on Armed Services, *Military Implications*, pp. 154–55.

55. "Remarks of the President at a Congressional Briefing on the Arms Limitation Treaty, June 15, 1972," in U.S. Senate Committee on Foreign Relations, *Hearings on the Strategic Arms Limitation Talks*, 92d Cong., 2d Sess., p. 391.

56. "Congressional Briefing by Dr. Henry A. Kissinger, June 15, 1972," in *ibid.*, pp. 393–416.

57. *Ibid.*, p. 402.

58. U.S. Senate Committee on Foreign Relations, Report 92-979, *Agreement on Limitations of Strategic Weapons*, 92d Cong., 2d Sess. (July 21, 1972), in *Documents on Disarmament* 1972, p. 289.

59. U.S. Senate Committee on Armed Services, Report 92-962, *Authorizing Appropriations for FY 1973 for Military Procurement*, 92d Cong., 2d Sess. (Washington, D.C.: U.S. Government Printing Office, July 14, 1972), pp. 3, 26–27.

60. Stephen Joseph Flanagan, "Congress and the Evolution of U.S. Strategic Arms Limitation Policy: A Study of the Legislature's Role in National Security Affairs," Unpublished dissertation, Fletcher School of Law and Diplomacy, Medford, Mass., April 1979, p. 254.

61. See U.S. House Committee on Armed Services, *Hearings on the Military Implications of the Strategic Arms Limitation Talks* (HASC 92-68), 92d Cong., 2d Sess. (Washington, D.C.: U.S. Government Printing Office, July 25 and 27, 1972), pp. 15067–153.

62. *Congressional Record*, June 27, 1972, pp. H. 6144–51.

63. U.S. Senate Armed Services Committee, *Hearings on the Military Implications of the Treaty on the Limitations of Anti-Ballistic Missile Systems and the Interim Agreement on Offensive Arms*, pp. 556–59.

64. Louis Harris, "82% Approve Summit Trip," *The Washington Post*, June 27, A3.

65. Smart, "Perspectives from Europe," p. 193.

66. See, for example, U.S. Senate Armed Services Committee, *Hearings on the Military Implications of the Treaty on the Limitations of Anti-Ballistic Missile Systems and the Interim Agreement on Offensive Arms*, pp. 205–08.

67. Of course, the question of how to deal with cheating has proved to be more complex than was initially thought, and the United States has not abrogated the ABM Treaty despite strong evidence of some Soviet violations.

68. See, for example, Office of the Press Secretary, the White House, "The President's Unclassified report on Soviet Noncompliance with Arms Control Agreements," Dec. 23, 1985; and Secretary of Defense, Memorandum

for the President, "Responding to Soviet Violations (RSVP) Study" (Washington, D.C.).

69. U.S. Department of State, "SALT ONE: Compliance," Selected Documents No. 7, Feb. 1978, in Thomas W. Wolfe, *The SALT Experience* (Cambridge, Mass.: Ballinger, 1979), pp. 279–81.

70. James A. Schear, "Arms Control Treaty Compliance: Buildup to a Breakdown," *International Security* 10 (2) (Fall 1985), p. 152.

71. *Ibid.*, p. 153.

72. Thomas K. Longstreth, John E. Pike, and John B. Rhinelander, *The Impact of U.S. and Soviet Ballistic Missile Defense Programs and the ABM Treaty*, 3d ed. (Washington, D.C.: National Campaign to Save the ABM Treaty, March 1985), p. 31.

73. "The President's Unclassified Report on Soviet Noncompliance," p. 60.

74. Longstreth, *et al.*, *Impact of U.S. and Soviet Ballistic Missile Defense*, p. 60.

75. Office of Senator Henry Jackson, *Strategic Arms Limitation Talks: Legislative History of the Jackson Amendment* (Washington, D.C.: U.S. Congress).

76. Garthoff, "SALT I: An Evaluation," p. 8.

77. *The Military Balance 1977-1978* (London: International Institute for Strategic Studies, 1977), p. 79.

78. They did not achieve the six-to-one superiority in counterforce capability against Minuteman that Senator Jackson had predicted. In 1977 the ratio was only 2.5 to one.

79. Garthoff, "SALT I: An Evaluation," pp. 10–11.

80. See John Lewis Gaddis, *Strategies of Containment* (New York: Oxford University Press, 1982), pp. 310–11.

81. For other assessments of the contribution of SALT I to détente, see Richard Barnet, *The Giants: Russia and America* (New York: Simon and Schuster, 1984), ch. 5; Richard Pipes, *Survival Is Not Enough* (New York: Simon and Schuster, 1984), pp. 133–38; and Morton Schwartz, *Soviet Perceptions of the United States* (Berkeley: University of California Press, 1980).

82. Adam Ulam, *Dangerous Relations: The Soviet Union in World Politics, 1970-1982* (New York: Oxford University Press, 1983), p. 81.

83. Dr. John Steinbruner, "The Purpose and Value of Arms Control Negotiations," in Senate Committee on Foreign Relations, *Perceptions: Relations between the United States and the Soviet Union* (Washington, D.C.: U.S. Government Printing Office, 1978), pp. 364–65.

5 SALT II

Stephen J. Flanagan

The SALT II negotiations spanned three U.S. administrations from 1972 to 1979 and marked a turning point in negotiated arms control. Future negotiations will inevitably build on some of the technical procedures developed in SALT. Yet SALT II's troubled history will remain a source of insight into the problems and limitations of the negotiating process and a stimulus for interest in alternative approaches to restraining the strategic arms competition.

This case covers an era marked by dramatic shifts in the international and domestic U.S. political milieu. The period under consideration ranges from the years when the policy of détente held its greatest promise to its nadir in 1979. During this time, U.S. arms control diplomacy began its shift from a very secretive to an open process. The strategic environment was also undergoing a significant transformation. The USSR, having achieved strategic parity with the United States by 1972, moved during the next decade to a position of superiority in important, but not decisive, measures of military power. This changing military equation had a profound impact on the SALT II negotiations, particularly during their final few years.

STRATEGIC OBJECTIVES

SALT was initiated in 1968 as an effort to regulate aspects of the Soviet-American strategic competition, thereby lessening the risks of nuclear war and avoiding the costs of an unrestrained strategic arms race. It was hoped that this dialogue would reduce tensions and thereby facilitate amelioration of political differences between the two states. As it evolved, SALT became the centerpiece of the Nixon, Ford, and Carter administrations' policies toward Moscow. A number of international developments created a hospitable climate for this dialogue, including growing inter-European détente, ratification of the Non-Proliferation Treaty, deployment of effective national technical means of verification, and, most important, Moscow's achievement of strategic parity.

U.S. policymakers believed that equitable limitations on strategic nuclear weapons would strengthen U.S. and Soviet national security by stabilizing the prevailing military relationship of rough equivalence.[1] The Nixon administration, confronted with very vocal opposition to the construction of the Sentinel antiballistic missile (ABM) system and the continuation of the war in Vietnam, harbored grave doubts about the public's willingness to support a costly strategic force modernization program. Officials in Washington viewed SALT as a way to achieve bilateral constraints on ABM systems and stave off elimination of the U.S. program. The White House also recognized that limitations on strategic offensive missiles would primarily constrain Soviet rather than U.S. programs.[2]

The superpowers' initial objective in SALT was avoidance of a costly and dangerous arms race in defensive strategic weapons, triggered by the development and limited Soviet deployments of ABM systems of dubious effectiveness. Neither state wanted this competition but feared that the other was about to pursue it. The other principal U.S. goal in SALT was to constrain the growth and improvement of Soviet offensive strategic forces, particularly heavy ICBMs. Both these developments threatened to undermine two pillars of deterrence in the nuclear era: the vulnerability of the two superpowers' populations to nuclear annihilation and the inability of one party to launch a disarming first strike against the other's retaliatory forces. Maintaining strategic stability and the survivability of retaliatory forces remained central U.S. objectives throughout the SALT negotiations.

Although the SALT I ABM Treaty has been largely effective in preserving this first pillar of deterrence by sharply limiting ABM systems, unconstrained qualitative improvements in offensive forces during the SALT I period eroded the latter pillar. In the early 1980s the Soviet ICBM force attained a theoretical capability for preemptive destruction of U.S. land-based ICBMs. As the SALT II negotiations dragged on, domestic political pressures on both sides forced accommodation of strategic needs by means of a highest common denominator approach. Agreements became negotiable because they set fairly high numerical force ceilings and allowed for most qualitative improvements.

There was only limited consensus about U.S. objectives in SALT II. The Nixon administration identified achievement of long-term constraints on threats to the survivability of U.S. and Soviet strategic retaliatory forces as a principal objective in SALT II. Indeed, in Unilateral Statement A of the Interim Agreement, the United States declared that failure to achieve more complete limits on strategic offensive arms within five years might constitute a basis for U.S. withdrawal from the ABM Treaty.[3] Some specialists argued that SALT could shape strategic stability,[4] while others felt that SALT could have only marginal impact on the strategic balance.[5] Similarly, while some officials held that SALT should be pursued independently of other aspects of Soviet-U.S. relations, others argued that SALT should be used to moderate Soviet foreign and even domestic policy.[6] Given the absence of widely agreed goals, Presidents Ford and Carter were continually subjected to domestic criticism from right and left in the conduct of the SALT negotiations.

THE POLITICAL CONTEXT

Declining Expectations for Détente

President Nixon articulated and stimulated expectations for the SALT process in his address to a joint session of Congress on June 1, 1972, just after the signing of the SALT I accords, when he said that "we bring back from Moscow . . . the beginning of a process that can lead to a lasting peace."[7] By the time the SALT II negotiations began in earnest during late 1974, however, the policy of détente, of which SALT was the leading edge, was already in decline. The United States entered into the SALT I Interim Agreement recognizing that it did not constrain important qualitative improvements in strategic offensive weapons, which would have to be addressed in subsequent negotiations. However, as the elements of the SALT II Treaty began to emerge after the November 1974 Vladivostok summit, it became questionable whether the new agreement would realize the kinds of "deep cuts" in launchers and tight restraints on qualitative improvements that many in the United States desired. Domestic discontent with these shortcomings of SALT I was exacerbated in 1975 and 1976 by allegations, most of which were subsequently corrected or proven to be unfounded, of Soviet violations of the ABM Treaty and the Interim Agreement.[8]

Domestic support for SALT was further eroded during the late 1970s as it became apparent that progress on arms control was not going to alter Moscow's internal or foreign policies in any fundamental ways. Soviet support to fraternal socialist states and direct and indirect assistance to "progressive forces" in the Third World continued unabated during the decade. The much-heralded era of negotiations and with it the arms control process were undermined by Soviet involvement in conflicts in Angola, Southeast Asia, and the Horn of Africa. Although the fall of Teheran and Kabul at the end of the decade gave the coup de grace to the SALT II Treaty, many of its provisions were still operative nearly a year after their expected lifetime. Moreover, elements of SALT II are certain to form the foundation of any future strategic arms accord. This assessment of the lessons of SALT II is therefore more than a post mortem. It can also provide insights into how the legacy of the SALT process will continue to influence policy options.

Domestic Bargaining

The political process in which SALT II was conducted was much more complicated than it had been at any time in the postwar era. Congress, the allies, and the attentive public were much more willing and able to play a role in the negotiating process. Congressional interest and capabilities to deal with complicated strategic arms issues grew dramatically after 1974, as did the legislature's general reassertiveness in foreign affairs. Those who feared that the SALT process was not sufficiently constraining the expansion and modernization of Soviet strategic forces but was lulling the United States into a false sense of security and neglect of its strategic programs were effective in galvanizing support for force improvements and monitoring the progress of the negotiations.

The SALT II negotiations were conducted during a period when the postwar consensus on foreign policy was coming unraveled. It is important to recall that the early years of the negotiations were dominated by two of the most traumatic events in U.S. political history—the Watergate scandal and defeat in the war in Indochina. At the same time, perennial adversary Moscow became a steady negotiating partner, and Americans were neither comfortable with nor in agreement on how to conduct this new relationship.

Arms control considerations interacted with U.S. strategic planning in several ways. A number of strategic initiatives such as MX, Trident, cruise missiles, and some counterforce programs had been vaunted by the executive branch for their contribution not only to U.S. military capabilities but also to U.S. bargaining strength in SALT II.[9] As President Nixon argued in urging members of Congress to support a series of strategic force modernization programs in 1972, "for the United States not to go forward with [these] programs . . . would mean that any incentive that the Soviets had to negotiate the follow-on agreement would be removed."[10] Throughout the SALT II negotiations, Congress was very receptive to the bargaining from strength thesis and generally supported strategic force modernization efforts.

In another vein, several congressional supporters of arms control believed that new weapons systems of all kinds had been developed with little consideration for arms limitation objectives. Several legislators of this latter persuasion demanded, with mixed success, that authoritative arms control impact statements for all nuclear weapons systems be presented to Congress along with the Department of Defense budget to infuse arms control considerations into congressional review of the military program.[11] Although strong proponents of SALT contended that their concerns were never integral factors in U.S. strategic planning, critics of the SALT process have charged that arms limitation considerations repeatedly distorted defense policy and stymied force modernization efforts. John Lehman has argued that "SALT was a major obstacle to clear thinking and legislative and executive decision making about our defense requirements."[12]

Allied Interests

SALT was not conducted in an international vacuum nor without impact on other key aspects of U.S. foreign policy. SALT addressed aspects of the security interests of U.S. allies by imposing constraints on threatening Soviet weapons and on U.S. nuclear forces that form an extended deterrent. As such, the basic thrust of U.S. policy in SALT was coordinated with or at least acquiesced to by members of the NATO Nuclear Planning Group and Japan, although the allies often complained that this consultative process was inadequate. Furthermore, as SALT II began to deal with the so-called gray area forces—Soviet nuclear weapons targeted on Western Europe or other areas, including some with potential to strike the United States, and U.S. or European nuclear weapons based in Europe—the need to protect allied interests in SALT became more acute.

SALT has had a significant impact on the progress of other components of East-West détente, particularly on the principal negotiating forums. A slowdown in SALT exacerbated the political obstacles that precluded progress in the Mutual and Balanced Force Reduction (MBFR) talks. Conversely, Western participants in MBFR had expected that success in SALT II would give momentum to these efforts to reduce the level of conventional forces in Central Europe. SALT had a similar, though less direct, effect on developments at the Conference on Security and Cooperation in Europe (CSCE).

Inter- and intra-alliance and third-country relationships also interacted with the SALT process. Washington conducted its relations with Eastern European countries and China at various times in ways designed to express displeasure with complications or to bolster progress at SALT. For example, some members of the Carter administration hoped that one of the dividends of normalization of U.S. relations with China in 1978 would be increased Soviet flexibility on several SALT issues.[13] Moscow pursued a similar course with the other NATO countries and Japan. Each of the NATO states has traditionally had distinctive relationships—more (France and West Germany) or less (Britain and Canada)—with the USSR, and Moscow attempted to encourage any divergent tendencies. Thus, when the SALT process and the future of détente became very uncertain in 1980, several of the NATO allies began to consider whether they should pursue their interests with the East more independently of Washington.

THE PROGRESS OF THE NEGOTIATIONS

Early Negotiations

SALT II negotiators had a much more difficult agenda than their predecessors in SALT I. In comparison with the SALT I Interim Agreement, which essentially imposed a freeze on missile launchers, SALT II had to address a number of highly complex issues. SALT I left issues such as restraints on multiple independently targetable reentry vehicles (MIRVs) for missiles, cruise missiles, bombers, and weapons testing—among others—with their attendant verification and political problems, for the next round of negotiations.

The first session of the SALT II negotiations began on November 21, 1972, in Geneva. The central Soviet and U.S. objectives in the talks were evident in both sides' opening proposals. The U.S. delegation suggested conclusion of a treaty that would have imposed equal ceilings on the aggregate number of ICBM and SLBM launchers and heavy bombers, additional equal ceilings on ICBM forces and capabilities, as well as prohibitions against circumvention of the goals of the pact through deployment of unconstrained systems.[14] This proposal was clearly responsive to the stipulations of the Jackson Amendment to the SALT I Interim Agreement, which instructed U.S. negotiators to seek equal limitations on U.S. and Soviet forces in any future accords. More important, with its special ceilings on ICBMs, it sought to reduce the Soviet threat to U.S. land-based ICBMs.

The Soviets favored a permanent treaty that would have continued the asymmetric numerical and volumetric limitations on missile launchers contained in the Interim Agreement, required withdrawal of U.S. forward-based systems (FBS) from Europe, and banned new U.S. weapons such as the B-1 and Trident, with no commensurate restraints on Soviet programs. Such a treaty would allow the Soviets to maintain their numerical and throw-weight advantages and promote a decoupling of European security from the U.S. nuclear guarantee.

At their June 1973 summit, Brezhnev and Nixon were able to agree only to a set of basic principles for the conduct of the SALT II negotiations. Among these tenets were pledges to seek qualitative limitations and to accept supplemental arrangements related to the

Interim Agreement.[15] Secretary of State Kissinger explained the administration's increasingly restrained prognostications on the scope and timing of a SALT II accord as a consequence of the fact that the negotiations could not keep pace with the emergence of new weapons technology.[16]

The Nixon administration attempted unsuccessfully in 1973 and early 1974 to obtain Moscow's agreement to various limitations on MIRVs and the aggregate payload of the two sides' missile forces. The administration was anxious to constrain the number of warheads the Soviets could deploy on their more numerous and larger ICBMs. The SALT I Interim Agreement was negotiated and endorsed by Congress on the assumption that the numerical advantages that it accorded the Soviets in missile launchers would be more than offset by a virtual U.S. monopoly on MIRV technology for the foreseeable future. Little progress was possible during these months because of Soviet inflexibility on key issues, disagreements within the U.S. policymaking community over goals and strategies, and political uncertainty in the United States as the Watergate scandal unfolded. Most important, the Soviets began testing in the summer of 1973, several years ahead of U.S. intelligence predictions, a new generation of MIRVed ICBMs. The Kremlin was unwilling to accept limits on fractionation if only because the United States held an advantage in this area, having deployed more than 500 MIRVed ICBMs by mid-1974.[17]

The Ford Administration Achieves a Framework at Vladivostok

The pace of high-level diplomatic contacts intensified as President Ford moved quickly after his inauguration to breathe life into SALT. After a six-month suspension of front-channel dealings, the negotiating teams sat down in Geneva in September 1974. This activity paved the way for a summit conference at Vladivostok in November 1974, where Ford and Brezhnev agreed in an *aide memoire* to a formula for the completion of a ten-year SALT II treaty. The *aide memoire* included an aggregate ceiling of 2,400 on ICBM launchers, SLBM launchers, heavy bombers, and air-to-surface missiles with a range in excess of 600 kilometers and a limit of 1,320 on launchers of ICBMs and SLBMs equipped with MIRVs. The new accord was to last until

1985 and was to include a provision for further negotiations begin-ning no later than 1980–81 on the question of additional limitations and possible reductions of strategic arms.[18] Kissinger noted that the accord was possible only because the Soviets finally agreed to ex-clude U.S. nuclear weapons based in Europe and predicted that remaining details could be ironed out in time for a mid-1975 Wash-ington summit.[19] Some observers attributed Ford's attainment in three months of what had eluded President Nixon for three years to Moscow's confidence that he could push an accord through Congress and the Soviets' hope that a trade bill extending the preferential tariff benefits of Most Favored Nation status would be approved.[20]

The U.S. public greeted the Vladivostok pact with skepticism. In contrast to precedent, Ford's popularity actually declined following the summit. Polls revealed that only 35 percent of a national sample believed that the Vladivostok accord was "a major breakthrough," although 63 percent felt it "worthwhile." The president's "working for peace" score rose eight points to 60 percent in the Harris survey, but Gallup's results indicated that Ford's overall favorability score declined by more than five points immediately after the summit.[21]

In an unusual display of harmony, hawks and doves on Capitol Hill agreed that the launcher ceilings of Vladivostok were too high. While the former group denounced the accord, the latter reluctantly endorsed it with the express hope that it would serve as a basis for further reductions and limitations on qualitative improvements.[22] Secretary of State Kissinger warned that if a prolonged, bitter debate ensued in Congress, similar to the battle just waged in connection with the trade agreement, Moscow would conclude that détente faced "insuperable" opposition. He argued that the Soviets had made significant concessions at Vladivostok and that if Congress forced the administration to go back and renegotiate the accord, it should be prepared to authorize an additional $5 billion to $10 billion for strategic weaponry.[23]

After Vladivostok, the negotiations were deadlocked, and bureau-cratic infighting and domestic squabbling escalated—symptoms of both technical and political impediments. The issue of how SALT II would limit cruise missiles, which had become an important facet of U.S. strategic modernization plans, and the Soviet Backfire bomber, whose intercontinental capabilities were subject to dispute in the intelligence community, emerged as the most enduring complications at the negotiating table. If cruise missiles were included in the accord, the U.S. ALCM program would be sharply constrained. Mobile ICBMs were not prohibited by the formula, but, if deployed, they would count against the delivery vehicle ceilings, a provision that would also raise verification problems.[24] The Soviets also resisted key U.S. proposals such as the so-called MIRV launcher-type counting rule because it would overstate the total number of Soviet missiles actually deployed with MIRVs.

The deterioration of other aspects of the Soviet–U.S. relationship also began to affect the negotiations. Moscow repudiated the trade agreement, which had been amended to link trade concessions to emigration of Soviet Jews, and increased its involvement in Third World conflicts. By mid-1975, many U.S. officials were also disillusioned with the value of SALT as the Soviets continued their military buildup and exploited several loopholes in the Interim Agreement.

Charges of Soviet violation of the spirit and the letter of both the SALT I and ABM pacts rendered many skeptical of the value of the SALT process and exacerbated concerns about the verifiability of certain limitations. The administration held that there were no Soviet violations of the accords despite this ambiguous behavior. The major problem was Soviet deployment of the SS-19 missile, which, contrary to a U.S. unilateral interpretation of treaty provisions concerning the size of a heavy ICBM, had a volume 50 percent larger than the largest existing "light" ICBM, the SS-11. Congress had endorsed the Interim Agreement based on the Nixon administration's assurances that the accord precluded deployment of ICBMs significantly (more than 30 percent) larger than the SS-11 in existing launchers for "light" ICBMs. Other Soviet activity of concern included possible testing of surface-to-air missile (SAM) components in an ABM mode, construction of a new ABM radar at a test range, concealment of strategic weapons activities, and delays in dismantling certain systems in accordance with agreed procedures. Because allegations of Soviet violations were never fully confronted by the Ford administration, they continued to hamper the SALT II negotiations. A White Paper on SALT I compliance was considered but rejected. Secretary of State Kissinger opted to address some of the issues in press conferences and to have other administration officials brief members of Congress in closed sessions. It remained for the Carter administration to issue a full public accounting.

These emerging doubts about the value of the SALT process, coupled with Soviet intransigence in the negotiations and the approach of the 1976 elections in the United States, constrained progress in SALT during 1975 and 1976. Candidate Ronald Reagan's first campaign address on foreign policy decried prospective limits on cruise missiles and charged that Ford was rushing into a SALT II agreement for political gain.[25] President Ford was able to secure President Brezhnev's acceptance of the MIRV launcher-type counting formula during their June 1975 meeting at the signing of the CSCE Final Act.[26] In January 1976 Kissinger and Soviet Foreign Minister Gromyko agreed in principle that the United States would count cruise-missile-carrying bombers against the Vladivostok formula's 1,320 MIRV subceiling, if the Soviets accepted some constraints on Backfire. However, the cruise missile and Backfire problems, coupled with domestic political considerations and external developments, stymied progress in the negotiations until the end of the Ford/Kissinger tenure.[27] When questioned in 1977 as to why a SALT II accord had not been realized in the previous two years, outgoing Secretary of State Kissinger commented, "I think it was partly the other side, partly the election, and partly disputes within the Administration."[28]

The Carter Administration Realizes a Treaty

President Carter took office committed to reduction of nuclear weapons to levels well below the Vladivostok ceilings. His position was driven by both a moral conviction and political imperatives. His administration's initial, highly publicized SALT proposal of March 1977 called for deep reductions along with sharp constraints on large ICBM force modernization and missile flight testing. President Carter had solicited input from Henry Jackson and other opponents of Vladivostok in formulating this proposal in hopes that it would broaden domestic support for SALT.[29]

Moscow found this "deep-cuts" proposal unacceptable because it would have forced major reductions and stifled Soviet improvements in missiles (requiring, for example, halving the SS-18 force), while leaving U.S. forces unscathed, with the exception of slowing MX. Moscow was also disturbed by the new U.S. administration's eagerness to abandon the Vladivostok formula, which it viewed as the appropriate starting point for the negotiations. These objections, coupled with the public manner in which the proposal was broached, caused Moscow to dismiss it as a propaganda ploy.[30] The administration's fall-back proposal of Vladivostok, with deferral of the cruise missile and Backfire issues, was also rejected at the time. The Kremlin was determined to achieve severe constraints on cruise missiles, where the United States had a clear edge, and to avoid limits on Backfire, which it contended was a theater rather than a strategic system.

Negotiations continued for the next two years in an effort to reconstruct the Vladivostok accord so that it incorporated reductions and some elements of the Carter "deep-cuts" proposal. The administration undertook quiet diplomatic initiatives that yielded a formula for SALT II that was agreed to by Secretary of State Vance and Foreign Minister Gromyko in May 1977. A major breakthrough came four months later, when many of the specifics of this arrangement were established. A three-tiered accord would be pursued: a treaty lasting until 1985 that codified the Vladivostok guidelines with some reductions; a three-year protocol addressing controversial issues; and a joint statement of principles, which would serve as a guidepost for future negotiations.[31] The twenty-one months between the September 1977 breakthrough and the Vienna summit in June 1979 were consumed by negotiations on the nature of limitations to be imposed on cruise missiles, mobile missiles, the Backfire bomber, and several definitional problems (particularly those related to monitoring compliance).

After September 1977 the administration was forced to battle openly with critics of SALT all the way to the Vienna summit. Several nongovernmental groups opposed to SALT II with excellent access to the media had a significant impact on this process. The most effective among them was a bipartisan group of prominent conservative business, academic, and former governmental figures known as the Committee on the Present Danger. Members of the committee conducted briefings on Capitol Hill and wrote numerous newspaper articles and lengthy analyses critical of the Ford and Carter administrations' defense and arms control policies. These articles had wide circulation and influence because of the authors' stature. It was rare for a major foreign policy initiative to encounter such severe criticism from senior former officials. Moreover, the committee's basic message that the United States needed to do more to ensure its security against an inexorable threat from the Soviet Union struck a responsive chord in the American heartland.[32] Many groups that had worked together against the Panama Canal treaties viewed this earlier campaign as a warm-up exercise for the more important SALT II debate. These groups targeted supporters of the SALT and Panama pacts for defeat during the 1978 and 1980 congressional elections. Critics were also effective in attacking selected aspects—some of which were not included in the final text—of the emerging SALT II Agreement. As the details of the September framework became known, these opponents set out to stop the protocol (which they feared would threaten the modernization of U.S. strategic forces) and to modify the treaty.

Supporters of the accords argued that although the limitations were not ideal, the threat to the United States and the countervailing spending on strategic forces that would be required in their absence would be much worse. Proponents also contended that ratification of SALT II was essential if only to ensure the continuation of negotiations that could lead to more significant limitations. This line of argument was barely sufficient to motivate the activist community favorably disposed to arms control, and it was hardly compelling to a general public growing increasingly skeptical of the fruits of détente. The Carter administration undertook a substantial effort to win support for the treaty among the general public. However, this program was not particularly effective, and many observers felt that the president himself was not as deeply involved in the enterprise as he might have been. The efforts of groups supporting the treaty were fragmented. Despite the involvement of several prominent figures with these groups, no readily identifiable spokesman or coherent media strategy emerged.

By the fall of 1978, while still under negotiation, the SALT II Treaty was judged by many observers in and out of government to be at a critical turning point. The slow pace of diplomacy allowed critics of the emerging accord to attack it without full rebuttal. The White House was also fearful that Brezhnev's health was failing and that the Soviet president's incapacitation could force a delay of SALT until the Kremlin succession struggle was resolved. President Carter hoped that the December 1978 announcement of U.S. normalization of relations with China would help solidify congressional support for SALT and put some pressure on the Soviets in the negotiations.[33] The final stages of the negotiations were very complicated because all of the small and several of the major issues that remained had to be resolved together and neither side wanted to make the last concession. Most of these issues were worked out in a series of Vance-Dobrynin meetings, although some issues, such as the limits on Backfire production and deployment, were actually handled at the June 1979 Vienna summit.[34]

OUTCOMES

Strategic Objectives

Throughout the negotiations, there was a general consensus among U.S. officials that SALT II should have a positive effect on the strategic balance and enhance crisis stability. As the agreement developed, attention was directed to the equity of various limitations and their impact on key U.S. strategic forces. Congress also closely scrutinized the administration's contentions that SALT II enhanced U.S. security by preserving the integrity of U.S. strategic forces and obviating major expenditures on these forces, which would have an adverse effect on other vital military efforts.

The congressional debate on SALT II focused on whether the accord did, in fact, impose modest but significant limitations on Soviet strategic forces that would grant the United States additional time and leeway to redress the impressive Soviet momentum. Treaty proponents cited the ceilings on launchers and on numbers of nuclear weapons, certain missiles, and bombers as prime examples of where the Soviets were likely (and in some instances had already demonstrated the capability, as in the case of the SS-18 ICBM) to exceed these ceilings. Executive branch figures noted that, without the treaty's limits on Soviet warheads, the planned U.S. mobile ICBM, the MX (which was to be shuttled among a variety of launch points to conceal its true location from Soviet targeteers), would enter service in 1986 already behind in the race between shelters and warheads that was the system's rationale. Critics countered with the contention that Soviet ICBMs warheads were already so numerous and accurate that future force enhancements would be expected, with or without a treaty, in the area of operational effectiveness rather than numerical expansion.[35]

Most members of Congress, however, found quite persuasive the argument advanced by General David Jones and the Joint Chiefs of Staff that SALT limitations enhanced stability by providing predictability in assessing the evolving threat, thereby improving U.S. force planning.[36] Moreover, a consensus emerged that, just as SALT I was not responsible for the adverse shift in the U.S. strategic posture, so too SALT II alone could not be expected to redress this shift. Legislators recognized that arms control and prudent modernization of strategic forces are collateral means of shaping strategic stability. As the Senate Foreign Relations Committee concluded in its report on the treaty,

> the terms of the SALT I Agreement were not detrimental to the strategic balance, nor will SALT II constrain U.S. efforts to reverse trends in the balance. However, it is undeniable that there are certain unfavorable prospects for the balance in the early 1980's. The Committee therefore recommends that the Senate make clear its intention to support all steps necessary to ensure essential equivalence between the military forces of the United States and the Soviet Union. In making this recommendation, the Committee also recognizes the important contribution that arms control can make toward maintaining an acceptable strategic balance. Nevertheless, arms control can only complement, not replace, the necessary modernization of U.S. strategic forces.[37]

Thus, by the time Senate committee hearings were very far along, the public debate on SALT II had shifted away from the specifics of the treaty toward consideration of the appropriate levels of spending for improvement of U.S. strategic and general purpose forces.

The long vexing problem of Minuteman vulnerability, which many had hoped to forestall by throw-weight and fractionation limits in SALT II, was overtaken by technology and the slow pace of negotiations. Administration officials noted the limited near-term military significance of Minuteman vulnerability given the health of the two other elements of the triad; however, all recognized the destabilizing political implications of this situation and the need to correct this deficiency in the most potent indicator of strategic power.

Thus, the debate turned to other issues. One concern was whether the treaty's bans on deliberate concealment measures and construction of new, fixed ICBM launchers would allow the United States to construct the multiple-launch-point, "shell-game," MX ICBM system. Not completely assuaged by administration assurances that a multiple-launch-point MX could be deployed under SALT II, the Foreign Relations Committee added an understanding to the ratification document that declared U.S. intent to deploy a verifiable MX system of this kind.[38] Because the limitations in the treaty allowed most other likely modernization efforts to continue unabated, the limitations in the protocol became a target of critics. Extension of the protocol's ban on mobile ICBMs and its stiff limitations on cruise missile range were inimical to two important U.S. initiatives and the emerging NATO decision on modernization of long-range theater nuclear forces. Thus, Congress took great pain to reinforce the administration's declaration that there was no implied commitment to extending the protocol's limitations beyond the document's prospective expiration at the end of 1981.

Critics objected to the inequity of provisions that allowed the Soviet Union 308 heavy ICBMs and the United States none and excluded the Soviet Backfire bomber from the aggregate force ceilings.[39] This objection to the heavy ICBM asymmetry was dulled somewhat as it became clear that it was a unilateral U.S. force planning decision to develop light, highly accurate ICBMs and that there were threats to Minuteman other than the SS-18. Opponents charged that the pact's heavy missile limitations were inconsistent with the Jackson Amendment but were unable to secure committee endorsement of an amendment that would have reserved for the United States the right to build an equal number of heavy ICBM launchers.[40] Another narrowly defeated amendment sought to have Soviet Backfire aircraft count as three-quarters of a delivery vehicle. Instead, the Senate reiterated the U.S. right to deploy an aircraft with similar capabilities.[41]

Thus, SALT II's major strategic objective, enhancing the survivability of both sides retaliatory forces, was not realized. However, the treaty did constrain the Soviet threat to U.S. forces somewhat and could have provided the U.S. additional time to redress aspects of the Soviet challenge by unilateral efforts and follow-on negotiations.

The Lulling Effect

It was ironic that one of the initial criticisms leveled at the treaty was that it would have a lulling effect on Congress and the public, creating a false sense of security that would inhibit realization of the several strategic initiatives that most parties believed were necessary. In the end, the final stages of the SALT II debate focused attention on the shifts in the strategic balance and were instrumental in forging a broad consensus that something had to be done to reverse the perception that the Soviets were gaining the upper hand. As the Senate committee hearings drew to a close, the debate had really shifted away from consideration of the merits of the treaty to a battle over what increase in defense spending would constitute a sufficient response to the Kremlin's challenge. Critics of SALT harbored fears that the Carter administration's commitments to increased defense spending and the MX programs were unreliable. In order to allay these fears, the White House stressed the vigor of its five-year defense plans. The SALT debate was transformed into a preparedness debate.

Throughout the SALT II negotiations, both the United States and the Soviet Union continued modernization of their strategic forces and developed programs as hedges against the collapse of the talks. Although the Soviet programs were more visible, the military effectiveness of U.S. qualitative improvements were significant.

During the SALT II period, the United States hardened and modernized the Minuteman force, doubling warhead yield and accuracy; began the MX ICBM program; flight tested and began deployment of the longer-range, more accurate Trident SLBM and continued construction of the new Trident SSBNs; upgraded the survivability and penetrability of the B-52 fleet and equipped it with SRAMs; developed and tested two types of cruise missiles and the Stealth bomber program; and increased the number of deployed strategic nuclear weapons from 5,700 in 1972 to 9,200 in 1980.[42]

During the same period, the Soviet Union fielded three new ICBM types of several MIRVed variants (SS-17, SS-18, SS-19); deployed two new ballistic missile submarines armed with two new types of SLBMs; began development of three types of advanced cruise missiles; tested and deployed more than 300 SS-20 IRBMs, which appear to have replaced the target coverage previously provided by SS-11 ICBMs; began deployments of the Backfire bomber and testing of the Blackjack strategic bomber; and increased their strategic force loadings from about 2,800 weapons in 1972 to about 5,000 in 1979.

Although there were few signs of lulling on either side during the negotiations, the treaty was expected to constrain modestly the number of strategic nuclear delivery vehicles (SNDVs) and force loadings the Soviets could field by 1985. In the absence of SALT II the United States expected the Soviets to deploy as many as 3,000 SNDVs armed with 12,000 to 13,000 weapons by 1985, well above the 2,250 SNDVs and 10,000 force loadings that would be allowed by SALT II.[43]

Genies in the Bottle

By the time the SALT II process gained momentum after 1974 there were few "genies" left to bottle up, except for mobile ICBMs, long-range cruise missiles, further refinements in missile accuracy, and additional MIRVing. However, both sides viewed the first two programs as critical aspects of their strategic force modernization plans. Thus, development of mutually acceptable restrictions on mobile ICBMs and cruise missiles were ultimately placed in the SALT II Treaty's Protocol, which was of three years' duration. By 1977 the United States had invested considerable financial and political capital in cruise missiles, an area in which the United States had clear technological advantage. Cruise missiles were critical to the Carter administration's strategic force modernization program as an alternative to deploying the B-1 bomber and a way to achieve inexpensive fractionation of its forces. Similarly, the Soviets began development of the SS-24 and SS-25 mobile ICBM programs in 1973 as a way to exploit geographical advantages and enhance the survivability of their ICBMs. The Soviets had also been developing a family of long-range advanced cruise missiles: the AS-15, SS-N-21, SS-NX-24, and two new GLCMs.[44]

The protocol's temporary restraint on deployment of long-range ground- and sea-launched cruise missiles (SLCMs) did not really bottle this genie because testing and development of these systems was not prohibited. Such a ban might have enhanced Soviet and U.S. security in certain contexts by obviating the emerging and difficult-to-monitor threat posed by widespread deployment of these systems on a variety of surface ships and submarines. Moscow would have liked to outlaw deployment of long-range GLCMs, if only to undermine the then emerging NATO LRTNF decision. Deployment of the current generation GLCMs, given highly visible basing patterns, limited numbers, and long flight times to target have not had an adverse impact on stability.

The treaty did constrain both the number of ALCMs that could be deployed on a single aircraft and limited the total number of ALCMs that could be deployed by counting all aircraft fitted with ALCMs under 2,250 and 1,320 aggregate limits on strategic delivery vehicles and strategic delivery vehicles with multiple force loadings. Although this particular genie was primarily feared by the Soviets in 1979, an unconstrained Soviet ALCM threat is of increasing concern to the United States, given North America's thin continental air defenses and the growing sophistication of Soviet cruise missile technology.

SALT II failed to constrain significantly many qualitative improvements that have had a major impact on force structure and strategic stability. The treaty precluded the Soviets from increasing their number of heavy ICBM launchers.[45] However, the provisions in Article IV limiting each side to one completely new type of ICBM permitted the Soviets to test and deploy militarily more effective follow-ons to all of their existing ICBMs, and one new, more reliable ICBM, the SS-24, with ten warheads capable of destroying hard targets. Although the treaty restricted the maximum number of warheads all these missiles could carry to about 6,200, these levels would still pose a significant threat to existing and programmed U.S. ICBM deployments. Although a unilateral U.S. move to a land-based force of small, mobile ICBMs might have a stabilizing effect on the balance, the survivability of this force would be questionable in the face of the threat posed by the roughly 12,000 warheads that the Soviets could deploy within SALT II limits.[46]

Verification and Compliance: Monitoring the Verifiers

It was widely known that monitoring of Soviet compliance with the limited provisions of the SALT I Interim Agreement could be accomplished with a high degree of success using available technical intelligence collectors, primarily photoreconnaissance satellites. Unlike the situation with SALT II, there was no history of questionable Soviet compliance to flag the issue, and members of Congress were not nearly as well informed or staffed on arms control matters as they were in the late 1970s. Moreover, President Nixon's record as a hardheaded realist in his dealings with Moscow helped to dampen latent public concerns about Soviet cheating. Thus, verification was not a contentious issue during the SALT I debate. It was clear, however, that the extensive qualitative limitations under consideration for a

SALT II treaty would place much greater demands on U.S. intelligence capabilities. Thus, during the debate on SALT I, the Nixon administration asked for funding to improve the monitoring system so that it could cope with these new demands.

As allegations of Soviet violations of the SALT I accords surfaced and an understanding of the difficulties in assessing certain Soviet strategic weapons characteristics developed, the verification and compliance issues took on greater importance in the domestic SALT debate. Moreover, these allegations of Soviet violations were accompanied by charges that the White House was suppressing or at least restricting the flow of intelligence information concerning such ambiguous Soviet activity and was refraining from raising some of these practices with the Kremlin. Kissinger and other officials sternly denied these allegations of Soviet violations. Although admitting that intelligence data on possible SALT violations had not been widely disseminated, these officials claimed that those who needed to know did.[47] The battle of charges and denials persisted, all of which was complicated by the often ambiguous provisions of the agreements.

The history of SALT I's limitations on silo dimensions provides a classic illustration of how ambiguous provisions, unilateral statements, and excessive zeal in promoting an agreement at home can lead to compliance disputes and disillusionment with the effectiveness of arms control. Article II of the Interim Agreement proscribed the conversion of land-based launchers for "light" ICBMs into launchers for "heavy" ICBMs, essentially freezing the size of the Soviet heavy ICBM launcher inventory at 1972 levels. It was hoped that this provision would also preclude the Soviets from expanding their aggregate ICBM throw-weight considerably. Unable to obtain Soviet agreement on a definition of the size of a heavy ICBM, the White House sought indirect restraints on missile size by means of the limits on silo enlargement. The U.S. SALT delegation was instructed to make a unilateral statement to the effect that it considered any ICBM with a volume significantly (more than 32 percent) greater than that of the largest light ICBM then operational on either side—the SS-11—to be a heavy ICBM.

Against the advice of senior negotiators, administration officials provided numerous assurances to Congress that the combination of these provisions would preclude Soviet deployment of any new ICBMs significantly larger than the SS-11. The negotiators felt that these assurances raised unwarranted expectations about the effectiveness of these marginal provisions.[48] In Common Understanding A, the parties agreed only that a "significant" increase in silo size would be "15 percent of present dimensions." Most U.S. officials interpreted this to mean a total of 15 percent growth in overall dimensions (depth plus diameter), which would allow for a 32 percent expansion in volume. Although SALT I negotiator Paul Nitze admitted that a 15 percent increase in both dimensions would yield a 52 percent growth in volume, he contended that this would be a worst case and would conflict with the U.S. unilateral statement.[49] The administration's confidence in this judgment was bolstered by intelligence available in 1972 but not discussed in public, which indicated that the two new Soviet ICBMs then under development, the SS-17 and SS-19, would be about 15 to 20 percent more voluminous than the SS-11.[50] Although the Soviets did not enlarge their silos by more than 15 percent overall, it was another unforeseen factor, the "cold-launch technique," that enabled them to cram the SS-19, 50 percent larger in volume than the SS-11, into these silos.

During the mid-1970s, the Soviets either corrected, clarified, or stopped most of the military activities, such as use of camouflage, testing of SAM-5 in an ABM mode, and delaying dismantlement of deactivated weapons, that the United States raised in the Standing Consultative Commission (SCC). Kissinger also terminated his system of restricting circulation of information on Soviet compliance. However, the political effect of the controversy was to erode confidence in the verification process—that is, in the Ford administration's resolve to take appropriate political responses when presented with evidence of Soviet violations or ambiguous activity.

The importance of verification waxed and waned in response to a variety of political and technical developments. Due to sanguine judgments by several members of the Senate Intelligence Committee and the focus of attention on the state of the strategic balance, it appeared for a while that verification would be a secondary issue. Then, in March 1979, just three months before the treaty was signed, the United States lost access to intelligence facilities in Iran that monitored Soviet weapons developments. Suddenly, verification was thrust to the top of the political agenda, and Senator John Glenn made it clear that he could not support the treaty until he was satisfied that the capabilities of the Iranian sites were recouped. At about

the same time, the Soviets expanded their use of deliberate concealment measures including encryption of telemetry data that would
complicate monitoring of emerging SALT II provisions.[51]

The unclassified findings of the Senate Intelligence Committee's
1979 report on SALT II noted that, while the treaty's quantitative
and many qualitative provisions could be monitored with relatively
high confidence, there were several provisions where low monitoring
confidence was found, such as counting mobile ICBM deployments
and assessing cruise missile range. Critics focused their attention on
difficult to monitor provisions, while proponents touted the committee's overall judgment that the pact enhanced U.S. capabilities
to monitor aspects of Soviet strategic forces.

The Intelligence Committee's conclusion that "in the absence of
the SALT II Treaty, the Soviets would be free to take . . . sweeping
measures, such as unrestrained concealment and deception, which
could make monitoring these strategic forces still more difficult,"
has been largely validated by the extensive encryption and other concealment measures pursued by the Soviets since 1979.[52] If Moscow
had abided by Article XV of the treaty, which proscribes deliberate
concealment measures, U.S. estimates of certain aspects of Soviet
strategic forces could be developed with greater accuracy. Thus,
SALT II would have reduced uncertainty about Soviet military
capabilities.

Critics of the process argued that the Interim Agreement and the
SALT II Treaty were of too short a duration to enhance predictability. Still others shared Ambassador Edward Rowny's view that the
treaty forced "Soviet efforts into unconstrained and unverifiable
qualitative improvements [undermining] predictability."[53] However, most of the experts who testified to congressional committees
shared the view of the Joint Chiefs of Staff that the treaty gave
greater predictability to Soviet programs by limiting their scope of
action and the range of the threat against which the United States
must hedge its own strategic planning.

In developing language for Article XV's ban on deliberate concealment measures that impede verification of treaty provisions by national technical means, U.S. officials wanted to sharply constrain the
growing Soviet practice of encrypting or encoding telemetry data
from weapons development tests. The United States would need
access to telemetry data in order to develop high-confidence estimates of Soviet compliance with a number of qualitative limitations

under discussion. The intelligence community and other officials in Washington favored a total ban on encryption. However, senior figures in the Pentagon advocated partial restrictions to preserve the right to protect certain U.S. test data from the Soviets. Key State Department and ACDA officials felt a total proscription of this practice was nonnegotiable and also favored the creative imprecision of a partial ban.[54] The intelligence community feared that a partial ban would inevitably be used by the Soviets to draw U.S. officials into discussions of which telemetry data the United States needed for its estimates, thus opening the possibility of permanent compromise of valuable intelligence sources and methods. The formulation that ultimately emerged from the negotiations in Washington and Geneva proscribed telemetry encryption whenever it impeded verification of treaty provisions by national technical means.

Since 1979 the Soviets have encrypted weapons test data to an unprecedented extent and in a way that impedes monitoring of compliance with the treaty.[55] The Soviets have argued that data that they provide in the clear, coupled with other information, is sufficient to verify their compliance with SALT II. It was unclear whether Moscow's political commitment to refrain from actions that would "undercut the goals and purposes of the Treaty" that obligated them to refrain from encryption to the same extent as would have been required had the pact been ratified. Soviet testing practices during this period and past behavior suggest they would have probed U.S. tolerance on the scope of Article XV in any event. However, had the treaty been fully implemented, Moscow might have had considerable political incentives to be more restrained, and Washington might have been able to protest employment of such concealment measures in the Standing Consultative Commission with greater success.

It is too simplistic to suggest that this episode validates the hypothesis that ambiguity does not offer a solution to verification and compliance problems. In this instance, the clarity offered by a ban was objectionable on national security and diplomatic grounds, and the clarity that would have been achieved by designating which telemetry channels could not be encrypted might have jeopardized intelligence sources and methods. Ambiguity was an attractive way to reconcile these two positions. However, by 1979 the Soviets were well aware of U.S. exploitation of their telemetry data and had, as has become all too evident, the capability to deny access to this data. In light of recent Soviet test practices, it would have been preferable if the treaty had more explicitly delineated the extent of encryption allowed, even if this had been restricted to a relatively crude measure such as the percentage of channels that could be coded. This might have preserved access to some telemetry, thereby maintaining the capacity to monitor key provisions of an accord.

The SS-25 case makes a much stronger and clear-cut case about the dangers of ambiguity. It would be much easier to address Moscow's contention that the SS-25 is a follow-on to an existing type of ICBM, the SS-13, in the Standing Consultative Commission if there were an agreed data base on the relevant parameters of current types of ICBMs. Although it might have been possible to establish this baseline data in the Memorandum of Understanding associated with the treaty, this alone would not have obviated subsequent compliance problems. The two sides could still disagree on the validity of their respective estimates about the characteristics of follow-on systems. In this case, there has been disagreement about both types of data. Whatever steps that can be taken to reduce ambiguity are generally advisable; however, at some point compliance judgments must be based on independent assessments of all available information and of the relevant legal obligations.

Linkage

Ultimately SALT was judged more on political than military grounds, and there it suffered from a failure to fulfill unrealistic expectations. A fundamental difference between the Carter administration's SALT diplomacy and that pursued under the guidance of Henry Kissinger during the two previous administrations related to views of the negotiations' relationship to other issues on the Soviet-U.S. agenda. SALT was the touchstone of Kissinger's design for détente. Discord in other aspects of the Soviet-U.S. relationship could not leave SALT unscathed. SALT was fundamentally a political issue pursued in an effort to enable military détente to have a spillover effect on political détente and allow for mutually beneficial cooperation in the economic and scientific realms. Kissinger believed that the United States could manipulate this cooperation, particularly in the trade area, in a way that would induce Moscow's restraint in other areas. The Soviets did not often respond appropriately. At the same time, it should be noted that the Kremlin did not appear to have its own policy of linkage. Brezhnev did not allow Nixon's opening to Peking and the United States' intensified bombing of North Vietnam just before the 1972 Moscow summit to impede the conclusion of SALT I.

In 1972, as is noted in the SALT I case study, many in the West believed that the "era of negotiations" of which SALT was the centerpiece could lead to significant reduction in conflict with Moscow. In this regard, the SALT process was somewhat oversold to Congress and the U.S. public by the Nixon administration. Yet by 1976 allegations of Soviet noncompliance with SALT I provisions coupled with Moscow's direct and indirect military intervention in the Third World brought to the fore enduring U.S. suspicions of Soviet integrity and intentions.

U.S. policymakers failed to educate the public as to what the Soviet leadership was saying about détente and the enduring struggle of social systems. The Soviet world view continued to embrace the notion that lasting peace could be achieved only by promotion of socialism. As Leonid Brezhnev was often quoted, "Détente is not a barrier to social transformation," implying that the support and encouragement to forces engaged in wars of national liberation had to continue. For Moscow, international political relations, particularly between the superpowers, are not "separable from the global class struggle." The Kremlin leadership held no illusions that antagonistic strategic objectives could be bridged by negotiated settlements, as did some in the West.[56] As disillusionment with the SALT process grew, Western analysts began to focus on how arms control could be used as an instrument to promote one of the few strategic interests that the United States and the USSR share, the avoidance of nuclear war.

Thus, the Carter administration moved quickly to eschew the linkage concept. This position, held by some of the leading architects of the administration's SALT policy, was compatible with the president's declared interest in sharply reducing the size of the superpowers' nuclear arsenals. Marshall Shulman, Vance's senior advisor on Soviet affairs, viewed SALT as a process whereby the United States and the USSR could work for mutual interests—such as avoidance of nuclear war and the enhancement of crisis stability—that should be pursued independently of the bulk of other issues where the interests of the two states diverge. Shulman believed that within this two-track design SALT could still have a beneficial effect on other aspects of superpower relations. National Security Advisor

Brzezinski appeared willing to go along with this scheme but believed that the Soviets' commitment to these goals needed to be tested in early SALT proposals. When Moscow rejected the March 1977 "deep-cuts" plan and expanded its intervention in the Third World, Brzezinski argued that the Kremlin could not go unpunished for destabilizing actions in other spheres.[57]

A critical factor in the domestic political equation became the dispute within the Carter administration and between it and a large segment of the Congress over the question of linkage. Many influential legislators firmly embraced this notion as originally enunciated by Henry Kissinger. Indeed, Congress has applied this concept to an extreme that Kissinger did not endorse, by predicating the progress of détente on favorable developments in Soviet domestic as well as foreign policies. The Jackson-Vanik Amendment to the Trade Act of 1974, which tied extension of Most Favored Nation status to the USSR to a loosening of Soviet emigration restrictions, is perhaps the most prominent example of congressional determination to impose this linkage. Similarly, the vigorous objections to conclusion of a SALT II pact while Soviet-supported Cuban intervention in the Angolan Civil War persisted was a major factor in the Ford administration's decision to forgo an accord in 1976. Applications of the linkage concept have not met with success. Secretary Kissinger's effort in early 1976 to trade progress at SALT for Soviet assurance of Cuban troop withdrawals from Angola proved futile. Even though its chief theoretician became disillusioned with its usefulness in the SALT context, linkage retains considerable support.

Despite these disclaimers, the controversy over linkage was never resolved. When Brzezinski declared that the intrusion of Soviet power into the conflicts in the Horn of Africa complicated both the negotiation and ratification of a SALT II accord, he revealed the existence of lingering differences within the administration. Moscow decried Brzezinski's comments as a blackmail attempt. Secretary Vance and ACDA Director Warnke hastened to assert that conclusion of a SALT pact remained in the national interest. Nonetheless, all the official spokesmen who reacted to Brzezinski's statement affirmed his assessment of the domestic political impact of the Kremlin's activities. Clarifying the administration's position, President Carter often noted that although Washington did not initiate the linkage, continued Soviet military presence in Africa would lessen the confidence of Congress and the U.S. people in Moscow's intentions and make it more difficult to ratify a SALT agreement.

With or without a declaratory policy of linkage, the overall tenor of Soviet-U.S. relations influenced the domestic debate on SALT. Congressional perceptions of Soviet credibility and intentions have always colored and may even determine the ultimate fate of the SALT II Treaty. Indeed, the successive shocks of the revelation of the presence of a Soviet combat brigade in Cuba, the fall of the Shah, and the taking of U.S. hostages in Teheran had already made the climate for SALT so inhospitable that the Soviet invasion of Afghanistan was but the final blow that turned U.S. attention from the control of arms to U.S. efforts to rebuild its conventional and strategic might. By 1980 many of its U.S. proponents began to argue that linkage was much too indirect a "punishment" for Soviet interventionism and that a military build-up was a much more effective means of expressing displeasure and alarm.

On January 3, 1980, President Carter asked the Senate to defer its final debate on the SALT II Treaty for an indefinite period while the United States responded to the crisis provoked by the Soviet invasion of Afghanistan. The president contended that although he did not consider it appropriate to put the treaty forward at that time, his commitment to the SALT II accord remained unchanged. The next day an administration spokesman stated that the president expected both the United States and the Soviet Union to refrain from acts that would undermine the goals and purpose of the treaty before it could be ratified. These actions effectively ended the SALT II ratification debate, and the accord entered into an uncertain status.

CONCLUSIONS: LESSONS OF SALT II

The evidence suggests that negotiation of SALT II was possible because neither the United States nor the Soviet Union appeared to have absolute strategic superiority. Rather, a condition of asymmetrical parity existed. Nonetheless, the perception that the Soviet Union had exploited the quantitative limits of SALT I to gain qualitative superiority in prompt hard-target kill capability caused an erosion of domestic U.S. support for the negotiations. Only limitations severely constraining Soviet ICBM throw-weight or warhead totals would be supported with much enthusiasm by the attentive public. Thus, the negotiations were most successful when it was perceived that neither side had a strategic advantage or would be able to achieve such an advantage by adhering to various limitations.

Unilateral restraint by the United States in the fractionation of its ICBM inventory at levels judged to be militarily sufficient for deterrence did not induce reciprocal restraint by the USSR. There is an internal dynamic to Soviet military requirements that is affected only at the margins by U.S. actions. The arms control process and unilateral restraint have little impact on the Soviet requirements process. On the contrary, it appears that Soviet requirements are determining factors in their arms control proposals and their acceptance of any final agreement. The Carter administration's cancellation of the B-1 bomber was not an example of unilateral restraint. It was made on budgetary grounds. No Soviet reciprocal action was or should have been expected. And, indeed, the new Soviet Blackjack strategic bomber was already under development.

The Nixon and Ford administrations were never able to pursue fully their policy of linkage because one of the key incentives they hoped to offer the Soviets for "good" external behavior was taken away by the Jackson-Vanik Amendment. Despite a declaratory policy eschewing linkage, the Carter administration found that the arms control process, most other aspects of Soviet foreign relations, and many facets of Soviet internal behavior are inevitably linked. Unintended, de facto linkage was imposed on the process.

Domestic perceptions of the overall standing of the United States in world affairs play an important role in the arms control process. If the United States is perceived to be respected and strong, the arms control process can go forward. If doubts are created about U.S. capabilities and standing, as in the aftermath of the Iranian crisis of 1979–80, the process falters.

Severe constraints were achieved only on weapons that neither side really wanted (the ban on the SS-16 and heavy SLBMs) or had not tested. The MIRV case illustrates that, once tested by one side or the other, only marginal restraints can be achieved. Thus, rather than the sweeping constraints on fractionation that a MIRV *ban* would have imposed, SALT II yielded MIRV limits to the level of warheads that had been tested as of the time of signature. Two systems that could have been banned by SALT II—mobile ICBMs and cruise missiles—were so central to respective Soviet and U.S. strategic modernization plans that there was insufficient political will to realize any limits other than very short-term restraints that had no impact on deployment schedules. The arms control process can reduce uncertainties in estimates and projections of the other side's forces. Thus, under SALT II the United States could expect the Soviets to have deployed ten MIRVs on their SS-18 ICBMs by 1985. This improved U.S. force planning, given the worst-case estimate that the Soviets could fit twenty to thirty warheads on the missile.

Similarly, and more important, the bans on deliberate concealment and noninterference with national technical means of verification in the SALT I and SALT II treaties gave the United States access to important data on Soviet military capabilities that could otherwise be denied with impunity. Even in the case of SALT II's suboptimal restraints on telemetry encryption, had the SALT II Treaty been fully implemented, Washington would at least have been able to object to the kind of extensive encryption that the Soviets have pursued since 1979. Moreover, Moscow would have had greater political and strategic incentives to be more responsive to these objections than they have had during the past seven years of uncertainty concerning arms control and deteriorating superpower relations.

SALT II largely codified existing defense plans, with some marginal constraints and redirection. Soviet MIRVing may have been somewhat restrained, but the treaty did not require either the United States or the USSR to terminate any ongoing strategic program.

Arms control resulted in increased attention being devoted to the relative size and capabilities of U.S. strategic nuclear forces vis-à-vis those of the USSR. This attention precluded any lulling effect on U.S. strategic force modernization plans. In fact, it helped galvanize support after 1979 for a robust strategic offensive force build-up. Moreover, SALT ensured that defense budget debates within the executive branch and between the Congress and the president were dominated by strategic force issues. This caused a number of strategic programs, such as MX-MPS, to be distorted by the swings of the arms control process and a neglect of certain conventional force capabilities.

Ambiguity is not a solution to verification problems. Indeed, its appearance in SALT I was the source of most of the compliance problems that plagued the SALT II process. The Soviets will attempt to stretch the limits of any agreement and will probe at the edges in an effort to assess U.S. monitoring capabilities. U.S. national technical means of verification are such that most SALT II provisions could be monitored with very high or moderate confidence but always well before any significant erosion of U.S. security could take place. It was the political process, particularly domestic concerns about the administration's resolve to take appropriate actions if Soviet cheating were detected, that set demanding standards with respect to verification.

Political support for an arms control agreement depends on the interaction of a large number of factors, including the president's standing, Soviet internal and external behavior, the negotiating history, the after effects of previous arms control agreements, and the perception of the equity of the provisions themselves.

SALT II yielded marginal military results, but it could have provided valuable political dividends for the United States and the USSR if it had been ratified. Militarily, the United States gained ceilings on Soviet ICBM launchers and missile warhead fractionation, modest constraints on ICBM modernization, and the Article XV "openness" provisions that facilitate access to test data and operational characteristics. The Soviets gained some limits on U.S. cruise missiles, fractionation options, and new types of ICBMs. Had SALT II been ratified, the political climate could well have been conducive to a more productive superpower dialogue on a number of critical issues.

It is easy to blame the prolonged stagnation and unmet expectations of SALT II for the collapse of détente. But this is unfair. The expectations of the U.S. body politic about the fruits of arms control and détente were far in excess of what this process could realistically bear. For a variety of reasons, many U.S. politicians preferred to ignore the fact that Moscow viewed SALT as a very narrow politico-military arrangement. The Kremlin has pursued SALT as a means of managing the strategic competition with the United States. Although this process may have certain political dividends, such as codifying Soviet superpower status, Moscow made it clear that arms control as an element of détente could have only a marginal impact on tempering enduring historical conflicts with Western capitalist societies.[58] In pursuing arms limitations with the Soviets in the future, U.S. officials should have more realistic goals than they did in the 1970s.

NOTES

1. "Address by Secretary of State Rogers on Strategic Arms Limitation Talks, November 13, 1969," in U.S. Arms Control and Disarmament Agency, *Documents on Disarmament* (Washington, D.C.: U.S. Government Printing Office, 1969), pp. 533–34.

2. Henry Kissinger, *White House Years* (Boston: Little Brown, 1979), pp. 195–212; and John Newhouse, *Cold Dawn: The Story of SALT* (New York: Holt, Rinehart & Winston, 1973), p. 168.

3. U.S. Arms Control and Disarmament Agency, *Arms Control and Disarmament Agreements* (Washington, D.C.: U.S. Government Printing Office, 1982), p. 156.

4. U.S. Department of State News Release, "The SALT Process," by Paul C. Warnke, Jan. 19, 1978, p. 3.

5. Edward Luttwak, "Why Arms Control Has Failed," *Commentary* (Jan. 1978), p. 27.

6. For the former view, see U.S. Department of State, "News Conference of Secretary Vance, Feb. 3, 1977," *Department of State Bulletin* (Feb. 22, 1977), pp. 148–49; see also Henry A. Kissinger, "America's Permanent Interests," Speech to the Boston World Affairs Council, March 11, 1976, *Department of State Bulletin* (April 5, 1976), p. 248, for the latter view.

7. "Address by President Nixon to the Congress, June 1, 1972," in *Documents on Disarmament, 1972*, pp. 251–53.

8. For a full discussion of SALT I violations, see U.S. Department of State, *Selected Documents No. 7, SALT I: Compliance* (Feb. 1978).

9. U.S. Department of Defense, *Annual Report of the Secretary of Defense, James R. Schlessinger, to Congress, FY 1975* (Washington, D.C.: U.S. Government Printing Office, March 1974), p. 6.

10. "Remarks to the President at a Congressional Briefing on the Strategic Arms Limitation Treaty, June 15, 1982," in U.S. Senate Committee on Foreign Relations, *Hearings on the Strategic Arms Limitation Agreements*, 92d Cong., 2d Sess. (Washington, D.C.: U.S. Government Printing Office, June 1972), p. 391.

11. U.S. Senate Committee on Foreign Relations and House Committee on International Relations, 95th Cong., 1st Sess., Joint Committee Print, *Analysis of Arms Control Impact Statements Submitted in Connection With the Fiscal Year 1978 Budget Requests* (Washington, D.C.: U.S. Government Printing Office, April 1977).

12. John F. Lehman and Seymour Weiss, *Beyond the SALT II Failure* (New York: Praeger, 1981), p. 97.

13. Zbigniew Brzezinski, *Power and Principle* (New York: Farrar, Straus, Giroux, 1983), pp. 220–21, 412–14.

14. Paul Nitze, "Essential Equivalence Should Be Arms Talk Goal," *Aviation Week and Space Technology* (July 22, 1974), p. 22.

15. "Dr. Kissinger's News Conference, Washington, June 21, 1973," *Department of State Bulletin* (July 23, 1973), p. 135.

16. As Kissinger commented, "The new element in the equation is the rapid evolution of technology, coupled with improvements in accuracy that have—even within the limits of [SALT I]—produced vulnerabilities, perhaps a year or two more rapidly than one expected [in 1972]. . . . So, if things have not gone as well [as I expected] . . . it is simply because technology has been accelerating at a rate that threatens to outpace the capacity to control it. "News Conference Remarks of Secretary Kissinger (extract), December 27, 1973," in *Documents on Disarmament, 1973*, p. 909.

17. Strobe Talbot, *Endgame: The Inside Story of SALT II* (New York: Harper & Row, 1979), pp. 24 and 31–32.

18. "Joint Soviet-American Statement on Strategic Arms Limitation, November 24, 1974," *Department of State Bulletin* (Dec. 30, 1974), p. 879.

19. "Secretary of State Kissinger's News Conference of December 7, 1974," *Department of State Bulletin* (Dec. 30, 1974), p. 910.

20. Victor Zorza, "Kissinger's Breakthrough," *Washington Post*, Nov. 28, 1974, p. A31; and Hedrick Smith, "A Gain toward Détente," *The New York Times*, Nov. 25, 1974, p. 1.

21. Louis Harris, "America Is Skeptical about Arms Breakthrough," *The Chicago Tribune*, Dec. 30, 1974, p. II-4; and John Herbers, "Ford Rating Slips to Low of 42%," *The New York Times*, Dec. 20, 1974, p. 1.

22. John Herbers, "Arms Said to Include 1,200 Vehicles for MIRVs," *The New York Times*, Nov. 27, 1974, p. 1; and Michael Getler, "Schlesinger Backs Pact, Sees Some Raise in Arms," *The Washington Post*, Dec. 7, 1974, p. A1.

23. John W. Finney, "Pentagon Chief Sees Pact Leading to Arms Buildup," *The New York Times*, Dec. 7, 1974, p. 1.

24. Clarence A. Robinson, Jr., "SALT Proposals Facing Hurdles," *Aviation Week and Space Technology*, Dec. 9, 1974, pp. 12–14.

25. Jay Nordheimer, "Reagan Bids U.S. Exploit Missiles," *The New York Times*, Feb. 11, 1976, p. 15.

26. U.S. President, "Statements of the President, August 2, 1975," *Weekly Compilation of Presidential Documents* (Aug. 11, 1975), pp. 815–18.

27. Talbott, *Endgame*, pp. 36–37.

28. "Interview with Henry Kissinger," *The New York Times*, Jan. 20, 1977, p. 16.

29. Jimmy Carter, *Keeping Faith* (New York: Bantam, 1982), p. 67.

30. See Text of Soviet Foreign Minister Gromyko's News Conference, *Tass*, April 1, 1977, in *FBIS-Soviet Union*, April 1, 1977, pp. B1–B10; Jan Lodal, "Carter and the Arms Talks," *The New York Times*, April 12,

1977; and Iona Andronov, "After C. Vance's Visit," *Literaturnya Gazeta*, April 6, 1977, p. 9, in *FBIS-Soviet Union*, April 7, 1977, p. B3.

31. Murrey Marder, "President Discloses Key SALT Elements," *The Washington Post*, May 27, 1977, p. 1; Talbott, *Endgame*, pp. 120–33.

32. Morton Kondracke, "The Assault on SALT," *The New Republic* (Dec. 17, 1977), pp. 19–21; and William J. Lanouette, "The Battle to Shape and Sell the New Arms Control Treaty," *National Journal* (Dec. 31, 1977), pp. 1984–93.

33. Carter, *Keeping Faith*, p. 194.

34. Talbott, *Endgame*, pp. 270–94.

35. See U.S. Senate Committee on Armed Services, 96th Cong., 2d Sess., Report 96-1054, *Military Implications of the Proposed SALT II Treaty Relating to the National Defense* (Washington, D.C.: U.S. Government Printing Office, Dec. 4, 1980), pp. 15–17; and *Hearings on the Military Implications of the Treaty on the Limitation of Strategic Offensive Arms and Protocol Thereto (SALT II Treaty)*, Part 3 (Washington, D.C.: U.S. Government Printing Office, Oct. 1979), pp. 876–977 (hereafter cited as SASC, *SALT II Report*, and *SALT II Hearings*).

36. U.S. Senate Committee on Foreign Relations, *Hearings on the SALT II Treaty, Part 1*, 96th Cong., 1st Sess. (Washington, D.C.: U.S. Government Printing Office, July 1979), pp. 372–73 (hereafter cited as SFRC, *SALT II Hearings*).

37. U.S. Senate Committee on Foreign Relations, 96th Cong., 1st Sess., Report 96-14, *The SALT II Treaty* (Washington, D.C.: U.S. Government Printing Office, Nov. 19, 1979), p. 146 (hereafter cited as SFRC, *SALT II Report*).

38. SFRC, *SALT II Report*, p. 159.

39. SFRC, *SALT II Hearings*, Part 1, pp. 539–41.

40. SFRC, *SALT II Report*, pp. 68–69.

41. *Ibid.*, pp. 65–67.

42. See additional views of Senator Culver in SASC *SALT Report*, p. 45.

43. SFRC, *SALT II Hearings*, Part 1, p. 103.

44. U.S. Department of Defense, *Soviet Military Power, 1986*, pp. 33–34.

45. Heavy ICBM launchers are launchers for ICBMs with a launch weight or throwweight in excess of the SS-19, roughly 90,000 and 3,600 kilograms respectively. See U.S. Department of State, Publication 8986, *SALT II Agreement* (Washington, D.C.: U.S. Government Printing Office, July 1979), pp. 17 and 18–23.

46. U.S. Senate Subcommittee on Strategic and Theater Nuclear Forces of the Committee on Armed Services, and Subcommittee on Defense of the Committee on Appropriations, Joint Session, Testimony of Robert M. Gates and Lawrence K. Gershwin, National Intelligence Council, "Soviet Strategic Force Developments" (Washington, D.C.: U.S. Government Printing Office, June 26, 1985), p. 5 and Figure 5 (mimeograph); and U.S.

Defense Science Board, "Final Report: Task Force on ICBM Modernization" (Washington, D.C.: U.S. Government Printing Office, March 1986).

47.   U.S. House Select Committee on Intelligence, *Hearings of U.S. Intelligence Agencies and Activities: Risks and Control of Foreign Intelligence*, Part 5, 94th Cong., 1st Sess. (Washington, D.C.: U.S. Government Printing Office, Nov. and Dec. 1975), pp. 1602–49, 1927–62; and "Secretary Kissinger's News Conference of December 9," *Department of State Bulletin* (Jan. 5, 1976), pp. 1–12.

48.   Gerard Smith, *Doubletalk: The Story of SALT I* (Garden City, N.Y.: Doubleday, 1980), pp. 400–03, 460–61.

49.   U.S. Senate Committee on Armed Services, *Hearings on the Military Implications of the Treaty on the Limitation of ABM Systems and the Interim Agreement on Limitations of Strategic Offensive Arms*, 92d Cong., 2d Sess. (Washington, D.C.: U.S. Government Printing Office, June and July 1972), pp. 32–33.

50.   "Secretary Kissinger's News Conference of December 9," *Department of State Bulletin* (Jan. 5, 1976), pp. 8–9.

51.   SFRC, *SALT II Report*, pp. 197–99.

52.   U.S. Senate Select Committee on Intelligence, Committee Print, *Principal Findings on the Capabilities of the United States to Monitor the SALT II Treaty*, 96th Cong., 1st Sess. (Washington, D.C.: U.S. Government Printing Office, Oct. 1979), p. 5.

53.   SFRC, *SALT II Hearings*, Part 1, p. 542.

54.   Talbott, *Endgame*, pp. 194–202.

55.   U.S. Arms Control and Disarmament Agency, *Soviet Noncompliance* (Washington, D.C.: U.S. Government Printing Office, 1986), p. 8.

56.   See L.I. Brezhnev, "Address to the 25th Congress of the Communist Party of the Soviet Union," *Pravda*, Feb. 25, 1976, in *Current Digest of the Soviet Press* 28 (March 24, 1976), pp. 3–32.

57.   Brzezinski, *Power and Principle*, pp. 158–62.

58.   David Holloway, *The Soviet Union and the Arms Race*, 2d ed. (New Haven: Yale University Press, 1984), pp. 179–80.

6 THE ANTISATELLITE NEGOTIATIONS

John Wertheimer

In 1977, when Jimmy Carter entered the White House, he brought a firm commitment to arms control with him. His attempt to negotiate, sign, and ratify a second SALT treaty remained a major focus of Carter's foreign policy throughout most of his presidency. But the Carter administration's arms control menu included more than just SALT; it also included several lower-profile items, including the subject of this chapter: an unsuccessful attempt to negotiate an agreement with the Soviet Union limiting antisatellite weapons (ASATs).

THE BACKGROUND

Early ASAT History

When the Carter administration began the first efforts to limit ASATs, antisatellite weapons themselves were nothing new. In fact, the U.S. Air Force began studying ways to attack satellites before the first satellites were launched.[1] U.S. ASAT research began in earnest after the Soviet Union sent Sputnik hurtling into orbit in October 1957. Prototypes of U.S. ASAT systems were tested as early as 1959, but the administration of President Dwight D. Eisenhower suppressed the ASAT program. Eisenhower was extremely concerned about the safety of U.S. reconnaissance satellites and feared that U.S. ASAT development would provoke the Soviet Union to initiate an antisatellite system of its own.[2] By 1963 the legitimacy of reconnaissance satellites had been tacitly accepted by the superpowers, easing U.S. concerns about satellite safety. But the worry was replaced by another one. The Soviet Union was rumored to be developing an orbital nuclear bombardment system (FOBS). In response, President John F. Kennedy instructed the Department of Defense to develop an ASAT system "at the earliest possible time." Following a number of abortive attempts to establish an ASAT system,[3] the Defense Department settled on an air force program employing nuclear-tipped Thor missiles stationed on Johnston Island in the Pacific. Several successful tests were conducted, and the system was declared operational in 1964.[4]

Toward the end of the 1960s the ASAT program began to fall out of favor within the defense establishment. The Outer Space Treaty of 1967, which banned nuclear weapons from orbit, along with the apparent termination of the Soviet orbiting nuclear bombardment system, alleviated U.S. concerns about the Soviet military space threat. Furthermore, the realization grew that the Johnston Island system was slow and inflexible and that use of the system's nuclear kill mechanism against the limited number of Soviet satellites in its range would probably have damaging side effects on nearby U.S. satellites. With the Vietnam War persisting, the air force became less and less willing to divert scarce resources to the ASAT program. In 1970 the Johnston Island system was shut down, although officially it remained operational until 1975. (During these final years, the system hardly deserved the official "operational" label—its reaction time was a glacial thirty days.)[5]

In 1968 the Soviet Union began testing a nonnuclear ASAT. It was a coorbital interceptor, meaning that it was designed to be launched into the same orbit plane as its target, home in, and explode. Testing continued at a leisurely pace for the next three years, after which the system reached something of a technological plateau. Partly due to competing military demands and partly, perhaps, in an attempt to nurture the budding spirit of détente, Soviet testing stopped in 1971.[6]

ASAT Issues Heat Up

For the first half of the 1970s, although both superpowers had developed rudimentary ASATs, antisatellite weapons inspired neither great fear nor great interest. During the final months of Gerald Ford's presidency, however, ASATs became the focus of considerable attention. The main stimulus behind the renewal of U.S. concern was the 1976 resumption of Soviet tests aimed at upgrading the capabilities of that nation's coorbital ASAT.[7] The prospect of an enhanced Soviet ASAT was especially worrisome because of the growing U.S. military dependence on satellites.[8] President Gerald R. Ford responded by directing the Department of Defense to begin work on a new ASAT system. State Department officials, learning of Ford's decision, expressed concern that arms control had not been considered as a possible response to Soviet ASAT activities. As a result, when President Ford, just two days before leaving office, issued a decision memorandum initiating U.S. ASAT development, he included a call for the study of ASAT arms control options.[9]

The Ford administration added arms control to its ASAT policy as an afterthought. Newly elected President Jimmy Carter, however, quickly moved arms control to the top of his ASAT agenda. Less than two months after entering office, Carter suggested to the Soviet Union that the two countries agree to "forego the opportunity to arm satellite bodies and also to forego the opportunity to destroy observation satellites."[10]

A number of arms control measures already affected military activities in space.[11] The 1963 Limited Test Ban Treaty prohibited the explosion of nuclear weapons in outer space. The multilateral Outer Space Treaty of 1967 mandated that no nuclear weapons or other weapons of mass destruction be placed in orbit or on any celestial body. The SALT I Agreement prohibited interference with national technical means of treaty verification, which was understood to include certain reconnaissance satellites. But there was no comprehensive accord governing the possession, testing, or use of antisatellite weapons. It was such an accord that the Carter administration set out to achieve.

THE NEGOTIATIONS

Preparations

In March of 1977 Secretary of State Cyrus Vance traveled to Moscow with a SALT proposal calling for deep cuts in strategic offensive forces. Although Vance's deep-cuts proposal was rejected abruptly by Soviet Foreign Minister Andrei Gromyko, the two officials did agree to establish working groups to consider secondary arms control areas. Antisatellite weapons limitation was the focus of one of these groups.[12]

Before negotiating ASAT arms control with the Soviet Union, however, the Carter administration had to negotiate the same issue within its own ranks. This process dovetailed with a comprehensive review of U.S. space policy, and it took more than a year for the administration to prepare for bilateral ASAT negotiations.[13]

The ASAT strategy finally adopted by the Carter administration became known as the "two-track policy."[14] The first track ordered the pursuit of bilateral arms control negotiations aimed at banning or otherwise limiting antisatellite weapons and their use. The second track instructed the Defense Department to press forward vigorously with development of a U.S. antisatellite system. These two tracks, although they appear contradictory, were designed to be complementary. Carter's preferred destination lay at the end of the first track: antisatellite arms control. Arms control advocates such as Carter saw the ASAT development mandated by the second track as a way to provide U.S. negotiators with bargaining leverage—fuel to propel negotiations down the arms control track. ASAT development also was to serve as a hedge against the failure to achieve an agreement.

The first track of President Carter's antisatellite policy—arms control—was bumpy from the outset.[15] The task of formulating the policy fell to an ad hoc working group chaired by Walter Slocombe, principal deputy assistant secretary for international security affairs in the Office of the Secretary of Defense (OSD). The group joined representatives from the State Department, the Joint Chiefs of Staff (JCS), the Central Intelligence Agency (CIA), and the Arms Control and Disarmament Agency (ACDA). Although the positions of the agencies represented in the working group remain classified, all evidence suggests that sharp disagreements developed regarding U.S. negotiating strategy.[16] In general, a group of representatives from the State Department and ACDA seem to have favored a comprehensive ban on the testing, development, deployment, and use of antisatellite weapons. They reportedly argued that such an agreement would reduce the threat to U.S. satellites—something that a U.S. ASAT system alone would not do—and would serve as a brake on an undesirable space arms race. Furthermore, they believed, by denying the superpowers the means of attacking satellites, an ASAT ban would dampen a tempting fuse that could ignite a dangerous military confrontation. This faction hoped that the second track of the policy, vigorous U.S. ASAT development, would provide negotiators with sufficient bargaining leverage.

The State Department and ACDA representatives who favored ASAT arms control reportedly were opposed by a group of representatives of the JCS and OSD who were averse to comprehensive antisatellite arms control.[17] This group argued that no agreement should be attempted before the United States matched the ASAT capability of the Soviet Union. They felt that as long as an imbalance in operational experience existed, an ASAT ban was unacceptable. Under the terms of a comprehensive antisatellite ban, the Soviet Union would retain the advantage of having tested an ASAT system recently, while the United States by treaty would be denied comparable experience. They believed that arms control compliance could not be verified well enough to assure that the Soviet Union would not exploit this advantage. Furthermore, this faction doubted whether a useful bargain could be reached while the Soviets had the lead in operational capability. Finally, some Pentagon officials opposed ASAT arms control out of a simple desire to deploy a U.S. ASAT system.

The second track of Carter's policy, ASAT development, proceeded more smoothly than the first. The U.S. ASAT was being built for the air force by the Vought Corporation. Although the U.S. system, like its Soviet counterpart, would not be able to attack high-altitude satellites, its design was in many ways superior to that of the Soviet system. The latter consisted of an orbiting interceptor with a nonnuclear warhead that was designed to be launched into space by an SS-9 missile, circle the earth in an orbit similar to that of the target satellite, close at slow speeds, and explode. Because the Soviet ASAT had to enter earth orbit before striking, it required a long time to make its kill; because it was fired from a fixed launch pad and had to wait for appropriate launch windows, it was incapable of striking quickly at satellites in inconvenient orbits. The prospective U.S. system, on the other hand, was designed to be launched in mid-air by a high-performance aircraft. Guided by a sensor, the Miniature Homing Vehicle (MV) was to home in and collide with its target at high speed, destroying the satellite by impact alone. If developed successfully, this direct-ascent system—so called because it was designed to reach satellites directly, without orbiting the earth—would be quicker and more flexible than the Soviet coorbital system. The ASAT program proceeded steadily under Defense Department direction throughout the period of the negotiations.

Because of the duration of President Carter's space policy review, there was a long delay before the ASAT talks began. Nevertheless, a series of events sustained President Carter's conviction that an agreement was worth pursuing. On October 4, 1977, precisely twenty years after Sputnik was launched, Defense Secretary Harold Brown delivered the first public confirmation that the Soviet Union possessed operational antisatellite weapons. Brown pronounced the Soviet ability to attack some low-orbit U.S. satellites to be "somewhat troublesome."[18] Concern about Soviet ASATs was augmented by a series of rumors claiming that Soviet scientists had made dramatic breakthroughs in exotic "death ray" weapons that could lead, among other things, to a new generation of antisatellite weapons.[19] According to some reports, these rumors were started by defense advocates who hoped to stimulate U.S. defense spending and undermine the push for arms control.[20] But the ominous rumors seem to have had the opposite effect of strengthening President Carter's conviction that ASAT arms control was imperative. In the fall of 1977 Carter announced his preference for the types of measures favored by State and ACDA: comprehensive ASAT limitations.[21] In March 1978 he invited the Soviet Union to join the United States in formal ASAT negotiations.

The Talks

U.S. and Soviet negotiators met for three rounds of ASAT talks. The first round, held in Helsinki in June 1978, was no more than an exploratory session. The Soviets appeared to lack familiarity with antisatellite issues. For the most part, they listened to U.S. stances and asked questions. More progress was made during the second and third rounds, held in Bern, Switzerland, from January 23 to February 16, 1979, and in Vienna, Austria, from April 23 to June 17, 1979, respectively.

Apparently, major differences separated the two sides throughout the negotiations.[22] Most significantly, the nations never fully agreed on the underlying goal of the talks.[23] The stated U.S. position held that antisatellite weapons were a mutual menace and should be banned. The two nations had come together in the talks to agree on a ban. The Soviets did not share this view. They felt that certain satellite activities threatened state sovereignty. In such cases, antisatellite weapons would provide a legitimate means of national self-defense. The lack of basic agreement on the objectives of the negotiations was a major impediment to any easy resolution.

U.S. negotiators initially pressed for a comprehensive ban on dedicated antisatellite weapons.[24] But the Soviet Union was unwilling to dismantle its system, even in exchange for U.S. agreement not to build one. Uneager to trade something for nothing, the Soviets apparently attempted to use their bargaining leverage to impose limitations on the U.S. space shuttle program, arguing that the shuttle had the theoretical capacity to tamper with or even kidnap Soviet satellites. As the U.S. delegation had been instructed firmly that the space shuttle was not negotiable, a comprehensive antisatellite ban on these terms was not likely.

The Soviet Union maintained an ASAT test moratorium for the duration of the negotiations. Besides demonstrating that the Soviets took the negotiations at least somewhat seriously, this gesture might have indicated a Soviet interest in an ASAT test ban. The United States, however, was not willing to lock itself into a position of ASAT inferiority by forswearing testing permanently. U.S. negotiators proposed a short-term test ban and nonuse agreement during which time discussions aimed at banning antisatellite weapons might continue. Because the U.S. ASAT was not due to reach the testing phase for several years, a test moratorium of short duration would have affected only the Soviet Union. No resolution was reached in this area.

Perhaps the most feasible prospective agreements were pledges of noninterference with enemy satellites or nonuse of ASAT systems, possibly combined with general agreements concerning the use of space. But even here obstacles existed. The United States allegedly insisted that satellites of all nations be protected from superpower attack; the Soviets, on the other hand, favored a bilateral ban outlawing interference with satellites of the other side but allowing attacks on third-party satellites. This disagreement arose because the United States demanded protection for satellites belonging to its allies, while the Soviets wanted to maintain freedom of action regarding satellites belonging to other countries—especially China. The Soviets also favored a statement in the agreement that would allow attacks on any foreign satellites performing "exceptionally objectionable functions." (When pressed on what might constitute an "exceptionally objectionable function," the Soviets offered the dubious example of a satellite spraying the earth with poison gas. Some people believe that the Soviets were more concerned with direct broadcast satellites.)[25] U.S. negotiators were wary of any statement like this that could provide the Soviets with a legal loophole through which to launch ASAT attacks.

Despite some movement toward a compromise, three rounds of talks yielded no agreement. The third round ended on June 17, 1979, in Vienna, the very day before the SALT II Treaty was signed there. The two negotiating teams regrouped and began preparing for a fourth round. Robert Buchheim, the head of the U.S. delegation, describes what followed: "Nothing. Nobody deliberately axed the negotiations. . . . Just nothing happened."[26] The Carter administration spent the summer and autumn of 1979 immersed in the final stages of the most heated political battle in the history of U.S. arms control: the fight for Senate ratification of SALT II. Because of the intensity of the SALT struggle, the ASAT talks were put on hold, resulting in a loss of momentum. Any remaining possibility of an ASAT agreement during Jimmy Carter's presidency was snuffed out in December 1979 by the Soviet invasion of Afghanistan and the resulting rupture in East-West relations.

ASAT was only one of many arms control efforts undertaken by the Carter administration. Of these, SALT II received the highest priority.[27] Carter spent a substantial amount of political capital on SALT, and his opponents expended a great deal of effort opposing it. Everybody in Washington seemed to want in on the SALT process. In contrast the ASAT negotiations were politically insignificant; few political actors were interested in the process, and fewer still demanded participation therein. As the SALT debate heated up, and as Carter's political troubles mounted, the higher levels of the administration "lost almost all interest in ASAT negotiations."[28]

The lack of attention paid by the public and, increasingly, by the administration to the ASAT talks enabled the OSD and the JCS to hinder what they considered to be undesirable ASAT arms control developments effectively. They did this because they did not trust arms control as a way of rectifying what they perceived to be a dangerous ASAT imbalance. Rather than rely on a treaty to right the inequality, they preferred to rely on their own weapons and judgments, especially in areas of high technology, where the United States enjoys a traditional advantage. Toward this end, they pressed forward with ASAT development while delaying and opposing the arms control process where possible.[29] For example, the second round of ASAT talks, though scheduled for the fall of 1978, did not commence until early 1979. The delay was due in part to the slow progress of a special Pentagon study on antisatellite arms control.[30] In a more clear case of Pentagon recalcitrance, the Joint Chiefs of Staff, who were firmly opposed to ASAT bans, switched representatives to the antisatellite negotiations working group every few meetings. Each new JCS representative had to be briefed—a tedious process that infuriated the State and ACDA representatives. The Joint Chiefs also prepared a briefing of their own about the desirability of U.S. ASATs and the undesirability of comprehensive ASAT limitations and presented it around Washington, D.C.[31] The less-than-cooperative actions of the OSD and the JCS struck some State Department and ACDA officials as deliberate attempts to sabotage the ASAT arms control process.[32]

Although President Carter sought to negotiate a ban on ASATs, he did little to counter those in his own administration who obstructed that goal. He realized that his top arms control priority, SALT II, would have no chance in the Senate without the approval of the Joint Chiefs of Staff and that JCS support of SALT might be jeopardized if the Chiefs were forced to swallow distasteful ASAT limitations first.[33] Once the SALT treaty was ratified, Carter reasoned, "negotiations could go forward more rapidly on banning antisatellite weapons."[34] A similar situation existed during the early 1970s when the Nixon administration was reluctant to conclude the Accidents Measures Agreement before SALT I. President Nixon finally consented, and the Accidents Measures Agreement was concluded first. Despite Nixon's fears that this would have a negative effect on SALT I, it seems that the effect, if anything, was positive. But to conclude that President Carter would have improved the prospects of SALT II by first pressing forward with an ASAT agreement would be incorrect. First, superpower relations and domestic moods were far less hospitable to arms control in the late than in the early 1970s. Furthermore, Jimmy Carter was much weaker politically in 1979 than Richard Nixon was in 1971. The liberal Carter could not afford to spend scarce political resources—especially within the defense community—on an ASAT agreement. Unlike the innocuous Accidents Measures Agreement, an ASAT accord would have been controversial; it would have forced the United States to pay some price (such as the ability to develop an ASAT system). Had advocates of defense increases been asked to pay this sort of price, they would have been even more reluctant than they already were to accept the limitations on U.S. forces included in SALT II. For these reasons, the ASAT talks were left fallow.

OUTCOMES

Because of the secrecy surrounding the talks, and because the negotiations produced no treaty and hence no ratification debate, the public record concerning ASAT arms control is relatively spare. Nevertheless, it is possible to piece together a reasonably clear picture of what was expected of the negotiations to compare with what actually happened.

Bargaining from Strength

There was no consensus about the requirements of bargaining leverage. At the time of the negotiations, while the Soviet Union possessed a crude but operational antisatellite system, the United States had no system at all. Critics of the talks believed that until the United States had a comparable system, there would be no way to budge the Soviets toward a compromise. Although no formal declaration was made, reports left little doubt that the Pentagon "opposed opening [antisatellite] talks before the United States develops a comparable weapon of its own."[35]

Those favoring the talks, on the other hand, believed that arms control progress in a way not adverse to U.S. interests *was* possible when the Soviet Union had the advantage, as long as the Soviets felt their advantage threatened. Although the United States could not match the Soviets' operational ASAT capability at the time of the negotiations, research and development work on the advanced U.S. ASAT was underway. Arms control proponents believed that the Soviets would agree to limit their own system in order to halt U.S. deployment. One White House official summed up this feeling:

"I don't think the Soviets want to force us into the antisatellite business, because with the programs we have under way, we could clean up the sky [of Soviet satellites] in twenty-four hours."[36]

The outcome of the negotiations seems to support the proposition that progress on arms control is difficult when one side has an immediate advantage. This becomes especially evident when the broader sequence of events is examined. During the negotiations, at a time when the Soviets had a working ASAT system and the United States was far from that goal, the Americans were the arms control initiators, and the Soviets were the passive respondents. Soviet negotiators, although well aware of the U.S. ability to develop an effective ASAT, listened to a wide array of U.S. proposals and seemed only to offer counterproposals—such as the one calling for curtailment of the U.S. space shuttle program—that were unlikely to lead anywhere. But as the sophisticated U.S. ASAT got close to the testing stage, the superpowers reversed roles. The Soviet Union began eagerly initiating ASAT arms control proposals to which the United States turned a relatively deaf ear. Relative force levels clearly are key variables in arms control calculations. The absence of essential equivalency in the ASAT case made arms control progress very difficult.

Unilateral Restraint

The history of the superpower ASAT competition provides some interesting examples of the possible benefits and pitfalls of unilateral restraint. In the late 1950s, before either side had antisatellite weapons, President Eisenhower restrained U.S. ASAT development in a deliberate attempt to induce reciprocal restraint by the Soviet Union. The Soviets did in fact refrain from advanced antisatellite development for many years. The extent to which U.S. restraint was responsible for the Soviet delay is, of course, uncertain, but the outcome was the desired one nonetheless.

Years later, in 1970, the United States effectively suspended its ASAT program. Unlike the previous example, this was not a case of deliberate restraint aimed at inducing a reciprocal action by the Soviet Union. Rather, this decision was based on the cost ineffectiveness of the U.S. ASAT system. Nevertheless, the Soviet Union appeared to reciprocate the following year by suspending their own

ASAT testing program. Neither side tested for several years. During this time a tacit regime of mutual restraint seems to have existed. But although the United States, in another unilateral decision based on internal reasons, completely dismantled its system in 1975, the Soviet Union maintained its ASAT. In 1976 the Soviet Union shocked the United States when it suddenly began testing and improving its ASAT again. A number of analysts viewed this as a case of the Soviet Union's taking advantage of naive U.S. restraint. Thus, while some cite the ASAT example as a case in which unilateral restraint "worked," others see in it a classic failure of the same policy. It seems fair to conclude that the lack of a vigorous U.S. ASAT program during the 1960s and 1970s contributed to the low intensity of the Soviet program during that time, but that the complete abandonment of the U.S. ASAT program early in the latter decade allowed the Soviet Union to appear to gain unilateral advantage merely by continuing its low-intensity program of periodic ASAT tests.

Linkage

Linkage played a minimal role in the ASAT negotiations. With some minor exceptions,[37] the ASAT talks were not significant enough to influence or to be influenced by superpower behavior in other policy areas. The only meaningful example of linkage in this case was the U.S. response to the Soviet invasion of Afghanistan. This included the suspension of the ASAT talks and all other bilateral arms control activity.

Genies in Bottles

The White House felt that achieving arms control before the United States matched Soviet ASAT capability was not only possible but was in some ways more likely than it would be after the United States deployed a new ASAT. At the time of the negotiations, the United States did not have a working system, and the Soviet ASAT program, besides being somewhat primitive, was conducted much less intensively than most other Soviet military programs. Because neither side was very committed to ASATs, some believed that an ASAT ban was feasible. Should the United States, in the absence of an agreement, go ahead with production and deployment of the MV ASAT system, a competition would develop that might well reach the point of no return. President Carter expressed this view: "The United States and the Soviet Union have an opportunity at this early juncture to stop an unhealthy arms competition in space before the competition develops a momentum of its own."[38]

Carter saw an ASAT accord as a way to keep the antisatellite genie from wiggling out of its bottle. Negotiators soon realized, however, that there is a large foggy area in which genies are neither completely in nor completely out of their bottles. Although the elementary Soviet ASAT had been tested only sixteen times—and only half of those tests were successful[39]—the Soviets, apparently, were not about to give it up. (When asked to identify the most important barrier to agreement during the 1978–79 talks, a former Antisatellite Negotiations Working Group member replied without hesitation, "The Soviet ASAT."[40]) The Soviet system could not be kept "in its bottle" because it was already out.

Even the U.S. ASAT, although years away from its first test, would not be easy to restrain. Key officials within the Defense Department were determined to deploy the MV. Denial of that goal would not come cheaply. A comprehensive ban on antisatellite weapons obviously would have been far more likely had neither side possessed or desired ASATs.

Effect on Arms

ASAT arms control proponents expected that an agreement would redirect the arms competition in productive ways—away from a destabilizing and dangerous competition in space weaponry. ACDA director Paul Warnke, in private discussions with Soviet ASAT negotiator Oleg Khlestov, expressed this view: "If both of us develop extensive antisatellite capability, we will have contrived still another cause of war."[41] Although the Carter administration did not expect an ASAT ban to assure absolute safety for all U.S. satellites, it did expect that satellites would be much safer with an agreement than without one. (Satellite protection was valued by arms control advocates because satellites, which serve such benign functions as early warning and arms control verification, were considered to be stabilizing. U.S. ASAT development alone, it was argued, would protect

U.S. satellites only to the extent that Soviet ASAT attack would be deterred, and ASAT arms control proponents were very skeptical about the deterrent value of antisatellite weapons.)

Many observers believe that the arms control proponents were right: that the space arms competition unconstrained by formal arms control has in fact proceeded dangerously since the end of the negotiations. Defense scientist J.S. Finan believes that if the ASAT competition is not limited, "the destabilizing elements of this competition could become severe."[42] The Union of Concerned Scientists concurs, arguing that as the competition in space weapons progresses, "the national security of both rivals will inexorably erode. . . . Even in times of peace, a keen rivalry in the development and testing of ASAT weapons is certain to cause friction, increase suspicions, undermine confidence in the ability to deter attack, and perhaps inadvertently spark a conflict."[43]

But not all analysts agree that the effects of an unconstrained ASAT competition are uniformly destabilizing. Thus far, some observers point out, the superpowers have refrained from placing extremely threatening satellites in space precisely because these provocative satellites would be vulnerable to attack. Had the 1978–79 negotiations succeeded in limiting antisatellite weapons and activities, the superpowers might be more likely to use space and space satellites for such threatening purposes as ballistic missile defense and tactical battlefield operations direction. Ashton B. Carter articulates this inherent tradeoff of ASAT arms control:

> [One] problem with ASAT arms control is that not all uses of space are benign and deserving of protection. . . . Paradoxically, any possibility of sanctuary from attack will probably encourage the superpowers to place more and more threatening satellites in space.[44]

One striking aspect of the "unrestrained" postnegotiation ASAT competition is the extent to which it has in fact been restrained. Many observers at the time of the talks believed that in the absence of an agreement, the superpowers would engage in a fast and furious game of ASAT leapfrog. Deployment of the U.S. MV ASAT was expected to be the first leap, followed by a significant upgrading of the Soviet ASAT, and so on.[45] The anticipated explosion in the ASAT arms race, however, has yet to occur. Due primarily to two related factors—congressional constraints on U.S. ASAT development and an unanticipated degree of restraint on the part of the Soviet Union—

the worst fears of ASAT arms control proponents have not been realized.

It is tempting and not altogether inaccurate to conclude that ASAT arms control advocates offered their ominous projections about an imminent space arms race primarily to jolt the United States into pursuing an ASAT agreement rather than to predict an outcome. But to convict the arms control proponents of "crying wolf" at this point would be premature. The story is not yet over. Although the ASAT competition has not yet escalated dramatically, the possibility that it could do so in the future remains. Trends in technology and military procedure are making further ASAT development a more practical and desirable defense option.[46] The current interest in space-based ballistic missile defense also is inflating the role of ASATs.[47] One former ACDA official who worked on the ASAT negotiations cautions against judging the outcomes prematurely: "In pursuing an ASAT agreement we were not terribly concerned about the ASATs that existed at the time; we were more worried about the types of ASATs that might emerge ten or twenty years down the line—systems that could *really* threaten security."[48] Seen in this light, the outcome of the ASAT talks is still unfolding.

Lulling

The Pentagon believed that, with or without arms control, U.S. satellite survivability needed to be enhanced. The JCS worried that a bilateral antisatellite agreement would give the United States a false sense of security about U.S. satellite safety and would lull Congress into spending less than it should on satellite survivability. This fear contributed to JCS opposition to ASAT arms control.[49] The Carter administration was aware of the Chiefs' concern. As a matter of unstated policy, virtually every administration statement explaining or advocating ASAT arms control stressed that an agreement would in no way diminish the need to upgrade the survivability of U.S. satellites.[50] More to the point, Carter backed his words with cash. A quick examination of satellite survivability funding does not reveal convincing evidence of lulling (see Table 6–1).[51] Inflation-corrected funding for satellite survivability increased at a modest but steady rate throughout Carter's term.

U.S. satellite survivability efforts did not intensify dramatically after the negotiations ended. Had an ASAT agreement been reached,

Table 6-1. Satellite Survivability Funding (*millions of 1972 dollars*).

FY 1978	1979	1980	1981
12.6	14.2	15.1	17.0

Table 6-2. U.S. Space Defense Funding (*millions of 1972 dollars*).

FY 1972	1973	1974	1975	1976	1977	1978	1979	1980	1981
3.1	0.2	0.1	2.2	3.0	9.1	27.7	44.7	45.1	56.4

the price of JCS support quite likely would have included increases in satellite survivability funding to levels higher than those that existed without an agreement. In other words, ASAT arms control, rather than lulling, might well have stimulated the United States to spend more on satellite survivability.

The arms control process unquestionably had a stimulating effect on another component of U.S. space defense: the ASAT system itself. Carter's opposition to antisatellite weapons was well known.[52] According to one aide, the president did not "even want a pea shooter out there [in space]."[53] President Carter surely would have been far less willing to allow U.S. ASAT development had it not been for the negotiations. As Table 6-2 indicates, inflation-corrected funding for U.S. space defense increased dramatically during the period of ASAT negotiations.[54] Although the increases cannot be attributed solely to the existence of the arms control talks, the fact remains that the MV ASAT, which was a bargaining chip in the eyes of the president who permitted its development, accounted for the majority of the increase in spending.

Verification

Verification and compliance concerns were prominent during the ASAT negotiations. ASAT verification issues were complicated by the fact that, compared with other types of arms control, a little cheating on an ASAT ban could go a long way. For example, moderate cheating on a strategic arms accord, though it would have major political implications, would be of relatively minor military significance. The strategic difference between 1,000 Soviet ICBMs and 1,100 Soviet ICBMs, for instance, would be fairly insignificant. Given the small numbers of ASATs and the great reliance of the U.S. military on a limited number of satellites, however, comparable Soviet cheating on an ASAT ban—for example, a few Soviet ASAT weapons instead of none—could be very significant. U.S. analysts also realized that the Soviet Union enjoys a theoretical advantage in the ability to absorb an ASAT attack. Whereas the United States launches relatively few satellites, each of which is comparatively complex and long-lived, the Soviet Union launches greater numbers of cheaper, shorter-lived satellites. Consequently, the chances are good that the Soviet Union would be hurt less by the loss of limited numbers of satellites and/ would be able to replace incapacitated satellites faster and at lower cost. Furthermore, many analysts believe that the United States is more reliant on military satellites than is the Soviet Union.[55] Thus, all other variables being equal—though in actual combat this is rarely the case—the United States would be the net loser in a satellite exchange with the Soviet Union.

For several reasons, opponents of comprehensive ASAT limits were extremely pessimistic about the prospect of verifying compliance with such an agreement. First, even if an agreement could succeed in limiting dedicated antisatellite weapons—weapons designed specifically for use against satellites—no agreement could hope to ban all weapons capable of interfering with satellite functions. Many weapons with other primary uses have residual antisatellite capabilities; ballistic missile defense systems, ballistic missiles themselves, electronic jammers, directed energy weapons, and all vehicles with space-docking potential are capable of inhibiting satellite functions in some way. Unless all of these weapons were banned, arms control opponents argued, U.S. satellite safety would not be assured, and thus an ASAT agreement would be of limited value.

Furthermore, they believed, even compliance with a ban affecting only dedicated antisatellite weapons would be exceedingly difficult to verify. The dedicated Soviet ASAT was launched by the SS-9 missile. Because the ASAT itself was relatively small, dismantlement would be difficult to verify; because the SS-9 served multiple military functions, the United States could not easily determine whether Soviet ASATs were ready to be launched. (The air-launched U.S. ASAT, incidentally, presents similar verification complications.)

Also, directed energy weapons, if ever developed successfully, would pose complex verification problems.

Despite these complications, not all observers at the time agreed that verification was an insurmountable obstacle. Supporters of ASAT arms control believed that certain ASAT agreements could be verified adequately. Limits on ASAT testing would be comparatively easy to verify with confidence; limits on deployment would be more problematic but not necessarily impossible to monitor. Although arms control advocates conceded that no agreement could be verified perfectly, they argued that a sufficient degree of verifiability was attainable. One administration official who favored limitations voiced this opinion:

> The objective is not a completely verifiable ban on anything. The objective is to make the risk of detection an unacceptable risk, and . . . the risk of detection in this instance . . . would be sufficiently high as to make such a ban worth discussing.[56]

Would the Soviet Union have attempted to violate an agreement? Could the United States have detected any such attempt? Nobody knows. The chances that treaty compliance could have been assured would have varied according to the scope of the agreement and the skill with which it was written. U.S. negotiators, operating according to the worst-case assumption that, given the chance, the Soviet Union would cheat, found ASAT verification problems to be particularly intractable. The political and strategic requirements concerning verification and compliance were substantial obstacles to comprehensive ASAT arms control.

Political Support

Even though the ASAT issue itself did not become highly politicized during Carter's presidency, the erosion of the president's political support did affect the negotiations. Had Carter's position been more secure, he could have given more attention and support to ASAT arms control, and the talks quite likely would have continued beyond the inconclusive third round. In a way, thus, the strength of Carter's political opposition preempted the possibility of an ASAT agreement before the issue could even reach the national political agenda in the form of a ratification debate.

Asymmetry

Some people believe that due to the nature of the two societies, the arms control process asymmetrically favors the Soviet Union over the United States. The United States did indeed face some disadvantages in the ASAT talks. Because of the closed nature of Soviet society, and because the Soviet ASAT was operational at the time of the talks, U.S. negotiators had to worry about treaty verifiability much more than their Soviet counterparts did. Furthermore, as the initiator of the talks, the U.S. delegation found itself to be more committed to the idea of ASAT arms control than was the Soviet team. Although the Americans offered most of the proposals, the Soviets were able to sit back and wait until the price was right.

OBSERVATIONS

We have seen that Jimmy Carter initiated the antisatellite negotiations in an attempt to reach an agreement that would reduce the threat facing U.S. satellites and cap a potentially costly and dangerous space arms race before it gained too much momentum. But this attempt failed. Why? No single reason can be considered decisive, but four factors combined to form a major barrier to arms control progress: (1) lack of shared objective, (2) lack of essential equivalency, (3) internal opposition that was tolerated by a passive White House, and (4) verification concerns.

Despite the magnitude of these obstacles, one cannot conclude that an agreement could not possibly have been reached. The talks, after all, did not self-destruct—they were unplugged. Had the negotiations resumed after the third round, as most participants expected, an accord of some sort might well have been reached.

Several observations can be made about the antisatellite negotiations. The first concerns "bargaining chips." A bargaining chip is a weapons system that a country offers to forgo or limit in exchange for commensurate restraint on the part of an adversary. The more valuable that a weapons system is, the more effective it will be at the negotiating table. Herein lies the crux of what might be called the bargaining chip dilemma: if a chip is to entice our competitor to bargain, it must be valuable; but if it is too valuable, or if we have paid too large a price for it, *we* might not be willing to bargain it away. In the ASAT case, this dilemma cut both ways: during the three rounds of talks, the U.S. ASAT program, still in its infancy, was not valuable enough to provoke the desired Soviet concessions. Yet only a few years later, as the MV was approaching the testing stage, the Soviets offered to dismantle their antisatellite system as part of a bilateral ban in order to prevent U.S. deployment. But by that time, the MV had become so valuable that the United States was not willing to give it up. The bargaining chip strategy is truly a difficult one to implement as designed.[57]

Another observation concerns technological "genies": once they are let out of their bottles, even a little bit, arms control is unlikely to be able to tuck them back in all the way. This is especially true of areas such as antisatellite weapons in which verification is uncertain. In such areas, once a weapon is tested, it almost has to be considered deployed. The attempt to use arms control to force the ASAT genie back into its bottle was not successful and in retrospect seems a bit fanciful. No arms control treaty during the nuclear age has succeeded in forcing the complete elimination of a deployed weapons system.[58] Perhaps the talks should have focused more intently on areas in which the genie had not yet begun to emerge. Had this been the case, the negotiations, though more modest, might have been more productive. One possible agreement of this type would be a ban on ASAT testing and activity above a certain altitude: perhaps 3,000 kilometers.[59] Because neither the existing Soviet ASAT nor the prospective U.S. ASAT had a range exceeding that altitude, and neither superpower had immediate plans to develop such a range, an altitude-based ban might well have been acceptable to both sides. Although an agreement such as this one would not have frozen or reversed the ASAT arms race, reduced the threat to low-level satellites, or even decreased the costs of space defense in the short term, it could have served as an upper boundary on the ASAT competition. Above this upper boundary, the security of the benign communications and early warning satellites of high-earth orbit would have been enhanced.

A final observation concerns the amazing capacity of arms control to highlight and transform issues. Before the 1978–79 negotiations, the topic of antisatellite weapons did not inspire much interest or debate. Since the talks, however, every development regarding ASATs has been scrutinized, analyzed, and criticized from all directions. But not only is the issue discussed where once it was all but ignored (a phenomenon that, of course, can be attributed in part to causes other than the negotiations), it is discussed in a certain way: along lines drawn by arms control itself. More often than not, debates about antisatellite matters since the talks ended have really been debates about the very hypotheses under consideration in this study: at issue is the necessity of bargaining strength versus the slippery slope of an uncontrolled arms race; the danger of conciliating with the Soviet Union versus the danger of not doing so; and so on. This is true of the way the topic is approached virtually everywhere on the political spectrum—from left to right and from top to bottom. For better or for worse, the ASAT issue has been swept into the ongoing controversy over arms control itself. This transformation should go down as the most enduring and powerful legacy of Jimmy Carter's ASAT negotiations.

NOTES

1. Donald L. Hafner, "Averting a Brobdingnagion Skeet Shoot: Arms Control Measures for Anti-Satellite Weapons," *International Security* 5 (3) (Winter 1981–82), p. 44. The air force study took place in the mid-1950s, before the 1957 launch of Sputnik.

2. Herbert York, *Race to Oblivion* (New York: Simon and Schuster, 1970), p. 131.

3. Paul B. Stares, *The Militarization of Space: U.S. Policy, 1945–84* (Ithaca, N.Y.: Cornell University Press, 1985), pp. 108–11.

4. In 1964 President Johnson announced that the United States had developed and tested "the ability to intercept and destroy armed satellites circling the earth in space" and affirmed that the systems were "operationally ready" and "on the alert to protect this nation and the free world." Lyndon B. Johnson, Speech on the Steps of the State Capitol, Sacramento, California (Sept. 17, 1964).

5. Stares, *The Militarization of Space*, p. 127.

6. *Ibid.*, p. 135.

7. It is not clear exactly what inspired the Soviets to begin testing again, but some believe that it was a response to the launch of the first Chinese reconnaissance satellite, which occurred in September of 1975. See Marcia Smith, "Satellite and Missile ASAT Systems and Potential Verification Problems Associated with the Existing Soviet Systems," in Bhupendra Jasani, ed., *Space Weapons: the Arms Control Dilemma* (London: Taylor & Francis, 1984), p. 85.

8. For a good account of the uses of U.S. military satellites, see Ashton B. Carter, "Satellites and Antisatellites: The Limits of the Possible," *International Security* 10 (4) (Spring 1986), pp. 46–98.

9. Hafner, "Avoiding a Brobdingnagian Skeet Shoot," pp. 50–51.

10. *The Washington Post*, March 10, 1977, p. 11.

11. U.S. Office of Technology Assessment, *Anti-Satellite Weapons, Countermeasures, and Arms Control*, OTA-ISC-281 (Washington, D.C.: U.S. Government Printing Office, Sept. 1985), pp. 91–94.

12. *The New York Times*, March 31, 1977, p. 11.

13. Stares, *The Militarization of Space*, p. 180.

14. Some administration officials favored ASAT arms control, while others opposed it. Carter's two-track approach, conveniently, was acceptable to both factions. In general, proponents of ASAT arms control were satisfied with the stated commitment to good-faith negotiations, and realized that U.S. ASAT development was a necessary evil—necessary as a bargaining chip for use in bilateral negotiations. On the other hand, those who opposed ASAT arms control, or who were skeptical about its prospects, were satisfied that the United States was developing the capacity to attack Soviet satellites, and realized that arms control negotiations were a necessary evil—necessary to facilitate U.S. ASAT development.

15. For a complete account of the decisionmaking process, see Stares, *The Militarization of Space*, pp. 182–87.

16. "Killer Talks," *Aviation Week and Space Technology* 107 (22) (Nov. 28, 1977), p. 13; *Air Force Magazine* (Jan. 1979), p. 14.

17. There was not a complete consensus within the Defense Department concerning ASAT arms control. Defense Secretary Harold Brown and some other top DOD officials, for example, were open to the prospect of ASAT limitations. But there was a great deal of opposition lower in the ranks. Once stated, DOD opposition was unambiguous. This was due, in part, to a bureaucratic quirk. The air force, having not yet developed a bureaucratic allegiance to ASAT systems, was relatively open to the idea of pursuing ASAT negotiations and possibly even an ASAT ban. The navy, on the other hand, was opposed to any agreement that would prevent the United States from developing the capacity to strike at Soviet sea surveillance satellites. It happened that the OSD representative to the ASAT "backstopping" advisory group was an admiral who, though employed by the Office of the Secretary of Defense, still felt a strong allegiance to the navy, and shared the navy's opposition to ASAT bans. See Herbert F. York, "Negotiating and the U.S. Bureaucracy," in Leon Sloss and M. Scott Davis, eds., *A Game for High Stakes: Lessons Learned in Negotiating with the Soviet Union* (Cambridge, Mass.: Ballinger, 1986).

18. *The New York Times*, Oct. 5, 1977, p. 1.

19. For example, see Henry S. Bradsher, "Do Soviets Have 'Death Ray' Weapon?," *The Washington Star*, March 23, 1977.

20. *Ibid.*

21. Carter's decision was stated in the PRM/NSC Decision Paper of September 23, 1977.

22. National Academy of Sciences, *Nuclear Arms Control: Background and Issues* (Washington, D.C.: National Academy Press, 1985), p. 162; for a more detailed account of the positions of the two sides, see Stares, *The Militarization of Space*, pp. 196–99.

23. Interview with Herbert York, May 8, 1986.

24. Any U.S. optimism about achieving this goal easily must have been dispelled when, according to Malcolm Russell, the Soviet delegation refused to admit that their nation possessed antisatellite weapons. Malcolm Russell, "Soviet Legal Views of Military Space Activities," in William Durch, ed., *National Interests and the Military Use of Space* (Cambridge, Mass.: Ballinger, 1984), p. 208.

25. See, for example, Walter Slocombe, "Approaches to an ASAT Treaty," in Jasani, ed., *Space Weapons*.

26. U.S. Senate Subcommittee on Arms Control, Oceans, International Operations and Environment of the Committee on Foreign Relations, *Hearings on S. Res. 129*, 97th Cong., 2d Sess. (Washington, D.C.: U.S. Government Printing Office, 1982), p. 54.

27. *The Washington Post*, March 20, 1978, p. 18.

28. Sarah B. Sewall, "Carter Administration Two-Track Policy: Antisatellite Arms and Arms Control," Senior honors thesis, 1984, Harvard University, p. 104.

29. *Ibid.*, p. 67.

30. Stares, *The Militarization of Space*, p. 197.

31. Interview with Donald Hafner, former Arms Control and Disarmament Agency official, Chestnut Hill, Mass., Feb. 19, 1986.

32. Stares, *The Militarization of Space*, p. 197.

33. *The New York Times*, July 12, 1979, p. 1; *The New York Times*, June 20, 1979, p. 1.

34. Charles W. Corddry, "SALT Approval Would Expedite Other Arms Accords, Official Says," *The Sun*, May 26, 1979, p. 4.

35. *The New York Times*, March 19, 1978, p. 1; *The New York Times*, Jan. 31, 1978, p. 1; *The New York Times*, April 1, 1978, p. 5.

36. Richard Burt, "U.S. Asks Soviets to Begin Talks on Banning Antisatellite Weapons," *The New York Times*, March 19, 1978, p. 1.

37. In 1979 the U.S. postponed a space shuttle test in an attempt to facilitate "possible moves in Vienna toward a treaty banning use of antisatellite systems." John K. Cooley, "Carter Works to Beef Up US Ability to Monitor

SALT," *Christian Science Monitor*, June 18, 1979, p. 12. The Soviets, for their part, adhered to an ASAT test moratorium throughout the duration of the talks. However, neither of these cases involved a policy area that was truly external to the subject of the negotiations; there is little evidence to suggest that any such areas were affected.

38.   White House Press Release, "Description of a Presidential Directive on National Space Policy." The details of the presidential directive remain classified.

39.   Nicholas Johnson, *The Soviet Year in Space 1983* (Colorado Springs: Teledyne Brown Engineering, 1984), p. 39.

40.   Interview with Donald Hafner, Feb. 19, 1986.

41.   Quoted in James Canan, *War in Space* (New York: Harper & Row, 1982), p. 24.

42.   J.S. Finan, "Arms Control and the Central Strategic Balance: Some Technological Issues," *International Journal* 36 (3) (Summer 1981), p. 455.

43.   Union of Concerned Scientists, *The Fallacy of Star Wars* (New York: Random House, 1984), p. 181.

44.   Ashton B. Carter, "Satellites and Antisatellites: The Limits of the Possible," *International Security* 10 (4) (Spring 1986), p. 89.

45.   U.S. Senate Subcommittee on Research and Development of the Committee on Armed Services, Department of Defense Authorization for Appropriations for Fiscal Year 1980, 92d Cong., 1st Sess. (Washington, D.C.: U.S. Government Printing Office, March 27, 1979), p. 3039.

46.   Aspen Strategy Group, "Anti-Satellite Weapons and U.S. Military Space Policy" (Nov. 13, 1985), p. 1.

47.   For one view of the ASAT-SDI connection, see Union of Concerned Scientists, *The Fallacy of Star Wars*.

48.   Interview with Donald Hafner, Feb. 19, 1986.

49.   Stares, *The Militarization of Space*, p. 199.

50.   Interview with Hafner, Feb. 19, 1986.

51.   The figures, derived from a table in Stares, *The Militarization of Space*, p. 210, have been converted into constant 1972 dollars to correct for inflation.

52.   Kim Willenson, "Arms Race in Space," *Newsweek* (Feb. 13, 1978), p. 53.

53.   Canan, *War in Space*, p. 21.

54.   Stares, *The Militarization of Space*, pp. 204, 209. The figures have been converted into 1972 real dollars.

55.   See, for example, Steven M. Meyer, "Anti-Satellite Weapons and Arms Control: Incentives and Disincentives from the Soviet and American Perspectives," *International Journal* 36 (3) (Summer 1981), pp. 460–84.

56.   U.S. Senate Subcommittee on Science, Technology, and Space of the Committee on Commerce, Science, and Transportation, *Hearings on the*

Future of Space, Science, and Space Applications, 95th Cong., 2d Sess. (Washington, D.C.: U.S. Government Printing Office, Feb. 7, 1978), p. 30.

57. Of course, not all parties involved in the ASAT case considered the MV to be a bargaining chip at all. To the Pentagon, for instance, the U.S. ASAT was not a way to get arms control; it was a way to deter Soviet ASAT attack and to target threatening Soviet satellites.

58. The ABM Treaty did succeed in severely limiting ABMs but still allowed some to be deployed; and even in that case, neither side really wanted to deploy large-scale ABMs.

59. This is suggested by Ashton B. Carter in "Satellites and Antisatellites: The Limits of the Possible," *International Security* 10 (4) (Spring 1986), pp. 96–98.

7 THE SUPERPOWERS AND THE NON-PROLIFERATION TREATY

Joseph S. Nye, Jr.

The Non-Proliferation Treaty originated in a 1958 Irish proposal in the United Nations that was repeated through the early 1960s. It was not until 1968, however, that the two superpowers were able to sign an agreed text. Even then, eight nuclearly significant countries—Argentina, Brazil, China, France, India, Israel, Pakistan, and South Africa—have refused to sign the NPT, usually on grounds that it is discriminatory. Of the eight, only France has indicated it will not undercut the treaty's purposes. Skeptics have dismissed the NPT as a modern equivalent of the infamous Kellogg-Briand antiwar pact because any state can simply quit on three months' notice. Other detractors have argued that the treaty is imperfectly drafted and involves promises that cannot fully be kept. Third World states have complained that the weapons states have not fulfilled their obligations to transfer technology or to curb their own arsenals. Nonetheless, by establishing a normative presumption against proliferation and by creating procedures to verify the peaceful intentions of civilian nuclear programs, the NPT has helped to build confidence and a degree of predictability in states' behavior.[1]

The treaty is relatively simple. Under the first article, weapons states agree not to aid the development of nuclear weapons or explosives. In the second article, the nonweapons states pledge to forgo such development. Under the third article, the nonweapons states agree to put all their peaceful nuclear facilities under international safeguards (that is, inspections). The fourth article promises non-weapons states access to peaceful nuclear technology, and the fifth assures them of access to the potential benefits of peaceful nuclear explosions. In the sixth article, the weapons states pledge good faith efforts to reverse the nuclear arms race.

THE ORIGINS OF THE TREATY

One of the reasons for the slow development of cooperation between the United States and the Soviet Union in nonproliferation was the difference in technological capability and the resultant differences in the perception of how proliferation relates to the overall U.S.-Soviet relationship. After all, the first U.S. nonproliferation plan, the Baruch Plan of 1946, was universal in form but would have prevented the Soviet Union from developing their bomb. Not surprisingly, the Soviets launched a counterproposal in the United Nations and re-jected the Baruch Plan. The Americans were trying to bargain from strength, but they severely underestimated the time that it would take the Soviets to catch up. Stalin was determined to match the U.S. capability and had no interest in plans that would interfere with the development of Soviet capability.

After the failure of the Baruch Plan, the United States followed a policy of restriction and secrecy to prevent the spread of nuclear technology. For example, the Atomic Energy Act of 1946 went as far as to curtail cooperation with the United States' wartime ally, Britain. U.S. policy was changed at the end of 1953. Eisenhower's Atoms for Peace program was to make fissionable materials available under international control and thus check the spread of nuclear weaponry and capitalize on our strong position as a leader in nuclear technology. The Atoms for Peace proposal was meant to advance the United States' interest in its political competition with the Soviet Union.[2] By stressing the peaceful role of the atom, the United States hoped to counter Soviet propaganda aimed at delegitimizing U.S. nuclear weapons. Indeed, a key feature of U.S. policy from 1954 to 1960 was the sharing of nuclear defense capability with NATO allies. Except in the case of Britain (after it had already become a weapons state), this sharing related to the deployment and control of U.S. weapons rather than to the design of independent weapons. Nonetheless, the Eisenhower administration "placed a higher premium on nuclear weapons cooperation with our allies—even at the price of encouraging and stimulating independent atomic weapons programs—than it did on seeking international agreements retarding the spread of nuclear weapons."[3] Until at least 1958 the United States believed that the Atoms for Peace approach to the control of fissionable materials and technological barriers to independent programs would prevent what John Foster Dulles called "promiscuous spread." Thus the United States could design NATO nuclear defenses as it saw fit. In 1953 U.S. nuclear artillery were first deployed in Europe. In 1955 the Atomic Energy Act was loosened to permit NATO allies to have information on the external characteristics of nuclear weapons and training in their use. In 1957 Dulles reassured NATO that "if war comes, they will not be in a position of supplicants, as far as we are concerned, for the use of atomic weapons."[4]

In 1958 the act was loosened again to permit the transfer of fissionable materials and selective sensitive information to allies. After Sputnik, there were fears of a Soviet missile gap advantage, and Eisenhower worried about the pressures on the defense budget. Allied nuclear sharing was seen as an inexpensive way to offset the rising Soviet threat. In Eisenhower's words, it was wasteful for "Allies to command talent and money in solving problems that their friends have already solved—all because of artificial barriers to sharing." Nonetheless, the U.S. Congress was "considerably more conservative and skeptical over extending the areas of atomic cooperation than the White House." Thus Congress restricted the sharing of sensitive information to allies that had already "made substantial progress"—in other words, to Britain. A meeting between John Foster Dulles and General De Gaulle in June 1958 left the French leader with the impression that the United States would not fully share nuclear technology with the French.[5]

At the same time, the United States hoped to restore European confidence by deploying intermediate range ballistic missiles (Thor and Jupiter) in Europe with release authority given to NATO commanders. In addition, changes in the technology of delivery systems created what has been called de facto proliferation in Europe.[6] Long-range NATO aircraft equipped with U.S. nuclear weapons were stationed in European countries under so-called dual control, but in many cases the only barrier to a German pilot's taking off and dropping a U.S. nuclear weapon on the Soviet Union without authorization was a single U.S. sentry who could easily be overcome. As

William Bader describes it, in the 1950s the United States "put flexibility in the use of our nuclear weapons above the first fretful international efforts to erect barriers to the acquisition of nuclear weapons."[7]

Soviet policy in the 1950s went through similar phases but in fore-shortened form. After a period of restriction, the Soviets followed the U.S. lead by sharing nuclear technology with their allies. They went further than the Americans by transferring design information to China, but they learned their lesson and drew back more quickly. In July 1954 the Soviet Union declared that it was willing to share for peaceful purposes both within the Soviet bloc and beyond. But this would be "true sharing," not conditional on military and political restrictions involving inspection.[8] In 1954 a Sino-Soviet science and technology commission was established and in October 1957 a defense agreement was signed that involved the Soviet Union helping China to develop a nuclear weapon.[9] At the same time the Soviet Union suggested devices such as the Rapacki Plan for a nuclear free Central Europe to discourage the proliferation of nuclear weapons to Germany. The Soviet need for Chinese support in the aftermath of events that shook the Soviet system in 1956 may help to explain the contradiction between Soviet proliferation policy in the East and in the West.[10]

At first, the Soviets hoped to control Chinese weapons through military cooperation. They approached China with proposals for bases and joint military command structures. In April 1958 they proposed a joint fleet. They may also have hoped that a test ban would ease their dilemma. But the Soviets met Chinese resistance to all such proposals, and in May the Chinese announced that they intended to acquire their own nuclear weapons. In August the Taiwan Strait Crisis may have stimulated Soviet fears of being drawn into war by reckless Chinese actions. Soviet nuclear cooperation was abrogated in June 1959. Khrushchev later justified his action as a response to a Chinese "smear campaign" and territorial claims. When he finally reneged on his promise to provide a sample bomb to the Chinese, he said that it was all packed up and ready to go.[11]

The end of the nuclear agreement accentuated the Soviet's proliferation dilemma. How could they restore control over the Chinese and also prevent the spread of nuclear weapons to Germany? Cooperation with the United States might help in Europe but might have weakened their efforts to renew control over the Chinese. It might have also required costly political concessions to the West. Faced with this dilemma, Khrushchev adopted a confrontational rather than cooperative strategy for his new nonproliferation policy. Tension with the United States would help solidify the Eastern bloc alliance, and, as he said in his memoirs, Berlin was a "blister" that he could step on to make the Americans feel pain. He could trade stability in the status of Berlin for Western assurances that the Federal Republic of Germany would not get nuclear weapons. This also helps to explain Khrushchev's 1959 proposal of a Far East nonnuclear zone as a means to constrain China, while at the same time the Soviets were very shy about public discussion of proliferation as a universal problem in the United Nations. Despite the failure to alter Chinese policy, Khrushchev pretended that there were no problems between the Soviet Union and China during his 1959 meetings with Eisenhower.[12]

In March 1960, after General Lauris Norstad announced a plan for integrating nuclear forces with the ultimate objective of making NATO a nuclear power in its own right, the Soviet ambassador delivered a protest to Eisenhower threatening similar Soviet behavior. However, the Soviets withdrew their nuclear experts from China in the middle of the year. With the inauguration of President Kennedy in 1961, Khrushchev continued his confrontational policy. He may have hoped that a diplomatic victory over the United States would help him with China and Germany at the same time. When John McCloy visited Moscow in July 1961, Khrushchev continually raised the issue of German nuclear weapons. At the same time the Soviets resisted U.S. multilateral approaches such as the Test Ban Treaty and developing safeguards at the International Atomic Energy Agency (IAEA). In fact they derided the Test Ban as a nonproliferation instrument, arguing that Germany would get weapons by transfer from the United States, not by testing its own.

Khrushchev heightened the tension in 1961 with the Berlin Wall and resumption of particularly large nuclear tests. Nonetheless, for the first time, the United States and the Soviet Union both voted in favor of the Irish U.N. resolution supporting nonproliferation. In July 1962 Soviet representative Zorin told the Eighteen Nation Disarmament Conference of the United Nations (ENDC) that nonproliferation "cannot be discussed in an abstract fashion. It is primarily the question of the spread of nuclear weapons to West Germany."[13] In the East the Soviet Union was trying to create a rapprochement with China by offering trade agreements, jet planes, and subdued rhetoric. In August Khrushchev raised the prospect of a nonproliferation agreement with the Chinese but was rebuffed. At the same time, the first Soviet medium-range ballistic missiles were being sent to Cuba.

Whatever Khrushchev's motives may have been, the Cuban Missile Crisis proved to be a turning point in U.S.-Soviet cooperation on nonproliferation policy. The confrontational approach had failed. China was proceeding toward a nuclear explosion, and the Americans were proceeding with plans to share nuclear capabilities with their NATO allies. Under these circumstances the Soviets turned to détente as a new tactic. In March 1963 the Soviets officially protested the U.S. plans for a multilateral force for NATO (MLF), but to no avail. By June they reversed their policy of opposing U.S. efforts to reach agreement on international safeguards inspections in the IAEA, and in the summer they agreed to the establishment of the Hot Line and quickly negotiated a Limited Test Ban Treaty with the United States.

The Chinese explosion of a nuclear device in 1964 relieved the Soviets of at least part of their dilemma of reconciling their Eastern and Western nonproliferation policy. Henceforth they would try to seek by détente and diplomatic cooperation at least part of what had eluded them in their confrontational nonproliferation policy. From 1964 to 1968 the Soviets sought a nonproliferation treaty as a means of curtailing NATO nuclear cooperation and particularly German access to nuclear capabilities. Much of the diplomacy from 1964 on, when the Eighteen Nation Disarmament Conference began to work on proliferation on a steady rather than an occasional basis, consisted of German efforts to gain some concessions for foreswearing nuclear weapons and Soviet efforts to grant nothing to the Germans and to weaken Germany's political position within NATO.

U.S. policy in the early 1960s is a story of gradual transition in priority from NATO sharing to global nonproliferation. The United States had always been concerned about proliferation, but "during the fifties, the restrictive spirit of the McMahon Act was gradually eroded." Some in the military believed that nuclear weapons "were inevitably the means of modern warfare and that political restriction on their use constituted an inconvenient and even dangerous impediment to military operations."[14] After the French explosion in 1960, there was fear that Germany would be tempted to follow suit. This could be forestalled by giving Germany a sense of greater participation in sharing NATO nuclear planning.

The switch in priority from NATO sharing to a more balanced approach began in the late 1950s when the Joint Committee on Atomic Energy became concerned about the lax control over U.S. weapons in allied countries. Soon thereafter, the Kennedy administration moved to develop and install Permissive Action Links (electronic combination locks) to increase control over such weapons.[15] Also in the late 1950s, some of the State Department officials who developed the idea of a multilateral force (MLF) thought of NATO sharing less as a means of enhancing military capabilities than as a means of reassuring the Germans and thus heading off their incentives for proliferation. This approach became more important after the 1960 election. In May 1961 Kennedy referred to a European seaborne force as a possible nonproliferation measure. After the missile crisis and the meeting with Harold MacMillan at Nassau in late 1962, Kennedy advanced the MLF as a device for solving the European nuclear problem. When he encountered European (particularly French) resistance, he downgraded the priority but did not entirely drop the MLF approach, and many State Department officials continued to give the MLF a top priority. Although Americans saw the MLF as a means of reconciling their nonproliferation and alliance objectives, the Soviets bitterly opposed it.

Kennedy, like Eisenhower before him, also saw the test ban as in part a nonproliferation measure. Harriman was instructed to raise the prospect of Chinese adherence to the test ban during his talks in Moscow. Khrushchev, however, was not willing to discuss China. Kennedy agreed to a quick resolution of the test ban issue despite the absence of time for prolonged consultation with Allies. Johnson continued Kennedy's policy, gradually switching priority from NATO sharing to a nonproliferation treaty. But as late as the U.S. draft treaty of August 1965, the United States was not willing to foreclose for all time the possibility of a European or NATO nuclear force. As Arthur Dean put it in 1966, "Washington has apparently not as yet decided that the time is right for a supreme and unconditional effort to win an antiproliferation agreement."[16]

In 1966 during a political debate, Franz Joseph Strauss asked Robert Kennedy, "NATO or Geneva? What is your priority?"[17] By the end of the year, President Johnson had settled on Geneva, but there was still jockeying over diplomatic details. A section of the U.S.-Soviet joint draft referring to safeguards was left open because of the difficulties of reconciling the EurAtom safeguards arrangements with the new NPT plans. The United States strongly supported West European integration and did not want to undercut the role of EurAtom in inspecting West European facilities. A compromise was reached in the joint draft of early 1968, and the treaty was signed in July.[18] With the signing of the NPT, the Soviets also agreed to the talks on strategic weapons that Johnson had suggested in 1967.

The final diplomatic compromises were facilitated by the increased interest in détente both in the United States and in the Federal Republic of Germany. The entry of the Social Democratic Party into a grand coalition brought to German foreign policy the hope of easing the reunification problem by building bridges and increasing engagement rather than by trying to bargain for reunification as a reward for foreswearing nuclear weapons. In short, détente and the loosening of diplomatic bipolarity eased the U.S. dilemma of balancing alliance interests and pursuing global nonproliferation norms, just as the defection of China from the Soviet alliance had resolved the earlier Soviet dilemma. In that sense the NPT was facilitated by two major trends of the 1960s: the Sino-Soviet split and the development of European détente.[19] These developments allowed the superpowers to redefine their interests by relaxing the constraints imposed on them as alliance leaders. In this sense, détente was an instrument in the continuing larger political competition.

A survey of the efforts at bilateral cooperation also reveals the role of détente. In 1957 Harold Stassen believed that the Soviets might be willing to discuss the nonproliferation issue. He tabled a talking paper at the London Disarmament Conference that suggested that all except three nations be prohibited from manufacturing or using nuclear weapons. This did not address transfer of weapons through NATO. The Soviet rejection was interpreted by Eisenhower as a lack of interest in what he called the "fourth country problem."[20] Also in 1957 the IAEA, which had been proposed in the Atoms for Peace speech, was established within the U.N. system. The Soviets joined but they tended to support Indian and Third World positions, which prevented development of significant agency safeguards capabilities until after the Cuban Missile Crisis. Test ban talks were held in 1958, but they were unsuccessful. In 1958 Ireland first proposed a nonproliferation resolution in the United Nations, but the United States refused to support it because it would have blocked any transfer of nuclear information. Thirty-seven countries supported the resolution, including the Soviet Union; forty-four abstained, including the United States. In 1959 the United States voted in favor of a slightly differently worded Irish resolution, but the Soviet Union (and France) abstained. In 1960 the positions were reversed again, when the Soviets supported another Irish resolution and the United States (and France) abstained. Not until 1961 did both countries vote for the same Irish resolution, but, as we have seen, this did not really signify an underlying change of policy in the cooperative direction. Neither did bilateral talks in 1961 and 1962 lead to significant changes in policy. It was only after the change from confrontation to limited détente in 1963 that the basis was set for cooperation on nonproliferation. Even then the multilateral talks in the ENDC from 1964 to 1966 made little progress until détente eroded the diplomatic constraints that previously inhibited cooperation.

CONTEMPORARY EXPECTATIONS

During the negotiations and the ratification debate in 1967 and 1968, it was generally believed that nonproliferation would benefit U.S. security. The NPT was widely seen as a way to keep most of the world's nuclear weapons genies in their respective national bottles. The means to do so were the creation of a legal presumption against the spread of nuclear weapons and use of IAEA inspections as a means of assuring countries that peaceful nuclear energy facilities were not diverted to military purposes. Both of these features were aimed at reducing uncertainty. Nonweapons states would be less likely to go nuclear if assured that their neighbors and rivals would not, and that there was a means of ascertaining that this was so. In addition, nuclear weapons states would feel less pressured to provide nuclear weapons help to nonweapons states if they felt assured that the other weapons states were not scoring political points by providing such help. The proponents of the NPT expected that the treaty would have a beneficial effect by limiting the spread of nuclear weapons and thus redirecting the arms competition away from potentially dangerous areas. During the Senate hearings on the treaty, one of the dangers frequently cited was that the addition of more countries to the nuclear club would increase the possibility of accidental or catalytic nuclear war by adding complexity to the international situation. Another danger frequently cited was fear that the development of nuclear weapons in one state might lead to preemptive attacks against potential proliferators by their nervous neighbors and adversaries. This, too, could be forestalled by the treaty. A third concern was that further proliferation would complicate superpower efforts at arms control and that the existence of the Non-Proliferation Treaty with its Article 6 requiring superpower efforts to pursue arms control would facilitate such efforts.

Although most of the positions expressed at the time of the ratification hearings were favorable to the treaty, there were also opponents of the NPT. For example, Edward Teller testified that "in this rapid and continuing technological revolution, you won't put any genie back into the bottle. All you can do is to create new genies, and hope that they will be better and more benevolent ones."[21] Teller and other critics were particularly interested in not foreclosing the possibilities of a NATO defense against ballistic missiles. In his words, "I would like to have an arrangement whereby we give to nations that want to defend themselves, . . . nuclear warheads, the design of which need not be known to them."[22] In short, NPT opponents argued that the treaty would redirect the arms competition in counterproductive ways. They feared that if nuclear weapons states could not give benign ABM systems to nonweapons states, those nonweapons states that wanted ABMs would develop their own nuclear warheads and thus get dangerous offensive weapons as they developed defensive systems. Another concern, expressed by Representative Paul Findley, was that European nations should not be left in the cold by the abandonment of the MLF. Others worried that U.S. security guarantees that might have to accompany the NPT might draw the United States into many other countries' disputes.[23]

Proponents argued that the benefits of the NPT were mutual, but opponents, such as Professor Robert Strausz-Hupé, saw the benefits as asymmetrical.[24] He believed that because the Soviet Union distrusted its satellites and did not want them to go nuclear, the United States might benefit if some of its allies got nuclear weapons. Selective proliferation might be in the United States' security interest. Moreoever, the NPT forced the United States to pay a price of NATO goodwill, while the Soviets did not have such a worry about their Warsaw Pact relationships.

As we have seen, concerns regarding effects on alliance relationships severely slowed the negotiation of the treaty during the early

1960s. The U.S. government was internally divided over the issue.[25] The State Department believed that unless European interests were protected, the NPT would lead to potentially large and unacceptable loss in terms of alliance relationships. The Arms Control and Disarmament Agency and the Department of Defense, however, believed that global proliferation would be so dangerous that the NPT was a worthy way to reduce such dangers. Similarly, the Atomic Energy Commission and ACDA advocated strong safeguards by the IAEA, whereas the State Department believed that EurAtom should handle its own inspections. By the time of the ratification hearings, however, these divisions were mostly overcome. The State Department lost the MLF but retained a role for EurAtom in inspections and managed to keep open the option of a nuclear force if a federal Europe were ever created. Thus the alliance interests advocated by the Department of State were clearly protected by the treaty, and Secretary of State Rusk testified to this at the ratification hearings.

In a sense, the NPT and MLF were not necessarily incompatible. Both were designed to limit the spread of nuclear weapons. But from the Soviet perspective, the MLF was not reassuring. The prospects of German fingers near nuclear triggers made the Soviets distinctly uncomfortable, and it was the Soviets who made it clear that the price of the NPT was the abandonment of the MLF. The United States did not see the MLF as a bargaining chip for the NPT, but it had some of that effect. Because the primary Soviet motivation for the NPT at that time was to prevent West Germany from gaining access to nuclear weapons, the MLF increased Soviet incentives to reach an agreement. Without even trying, the United States bargained from strength. This is reflected in the final compromise allowing a federated Europe, if it ever comes into existence, to have nuclear weapons and EurAtom to have an inspection role under the NPT.

Verification was not a major issue at the hearings. Proponents believed that the treaty could be verified effectively. For example, Glenn Seaborg, chairman of the Atomic Energy Commission, testified that "the safeguards adopted for NPT verification will be commensurate with the protection sought under the treaty. The IAEA may need a bit of strengthening, but it is up to it."[26] Some opponents were more skeptical. For example, Congressman Craig Hosmer argued that the NPT had absolutely no safeguards for Articles 1 and 2 (which was correct, for the inspections related only to civil nuclear facilities and not to military facilities). Moreover, he believed that the IAEA was incapable of performing the inspection role called for in relation to civil nuclear facilities under Article 3.[27]

Opponents also expressed concern about the lulling effect of the NPT. For example, Strausz-Hupé argued that the NPT did not provide an effective remedy against nuclear weapons' falling into irresponsible hands, especially in the Communist world. On the contrary, because of the propagandistic claims made on its behalf, the treaty would "lull the free peoples of the world into a false sense of security."[28] In his view, the euphoria of U.S. public opinion masked the true implications of the NPT. In his words, "besides the specifics of the treaty, I am even more concerned with the foreseeable impact on the overall environment of Western security. I am as much concerned about the package in which the treaty is being delivered as with the treaty itself."[29] On the other hand, Deputy Secretary of Defense Paul Nitze denied the specific form of the lulling hypothesis. He testified that "the Department of Defense is under no illusion that we need no longer worry about the proliferation of nuclear weapons. We recognize that the consummation of this treaty will not, of itself, guarantee against any possibility of another nation acquiring nuclear weapons."[30]

In one sense, unilateral restraint was important to the completion of the treaty. After overcoming the temptations and errors of the previous period, neither the United States nor the Soviet Union was about to give nuclear weapons away. Thus the treaty multilateralized a growing unilateral restraint. However, without the treaty, both sides might have remained in the dilemma that they had experienced earlier. Their first preference might be nuclear restraint, but the competition might lead each to give weapons to allies. In a more specific sense, unilateral restraint was not all that difficult to achieve. Because both sides had no intention of giving nuclear weapons away, there was not that much to restrain in seeking to reach an agreement. Nonetheless, the United States did forgo a peaceful nuclear test in the Plowshare Program so as not to complicate the NPT negotiations in 1967, and the United States announced that it would allow the IAEA to inspect its nonmilitary nuclear facilities as a unilateral gesture to ease European worries about the effect of inspections on proprietary commercial information in the nuclear energy industry.

In terms of political support, nonproliferation had always been a popular cause with the U.S. public. In fact, the Congress, reflecting public opinion, had often taken the lead in this area. As we saw earlier, the Joint Committee on Atomic Energy helped to restrain the degree of sharing that the Eisenhower administration wished to undertake with NATO allies in the 1950s. It also helped to promote development of Permissive Action Links. In the autumn of 1965 Senate Majority Leader Mike Mansfield, attempting to break the NPT deadlock, told Soviet leaders during a trip to Moscow that the MLF would never make it through the Congress.[31] Later in the negotiations, Senator Pastore of the Joint Committee on Atomic Energy suggested the critical compromise of combining EurAtom and IAEA safeguards.[32] Although the executive branch had always supported nonproliferation, it did not give it as high a priority as did the Congress. In 1964 Senator Robert Kennedy called proliferation the primary problem facing the United States and the world and urged the signature of a treaty despite the barriers of Vietnam and the MLF dispute. The speech was popular in the Senate, but President Johnson, worried about Kennedy's political appeal, did not move quickly on proliferation for fear of appearing to follow Kennedy's lead. Not until July 1966 did President Johnson decide that he wanted the Non-Proliferation Treaty as a major priority.[33] By the time of the ratification hearings, the Vietnam turmoil had brought Johnson to a low in political popularity, and he hoped that the NPT would bolster his peace image and fortify his political position. The popularity of the treaty did more for the president than the popularity of the president did for the treaty.

There was not much direct linkage between the NPT and other issues, although the absence of progress on the issue in the 1950s and early 1960s was a result of the implicit linkage between nuclear sharing and alliance relationships during a period of confrontation at the height of the Cold War. With the beginnings of détente, that implicit linkage was somewhat relaxed. Of course, the Soviets did link the abandonment of the MLF to their willingness to sign an NPT. There was also an unintended linkage to Vietnam and to Czechoslovakia. The war in Vietnam made progress on U.S.-Soviet arms control more difficult and diverted U.S. executive branch attention away from arms control issues.[34] The Soviet invasion of Czechoslovakia in August 1968 delayed the ratification of the NPT for two years. Thus, unintended linkage resulted in delay rather than derailment of the treaty negotiation and ratification.

IMPLEMENTING THE AGREEMENT

Ironically, one of the first effects of reaching agreement on the non-proliferation treaty was a lower priority given to the issue of nonproliferation in both countries. Insofar as the NPT tied down the West Germans, a major source of Soviet concern about proliferation was relaxed. In the United States, the Nixon administration was critical of the extent to which its predecessor had damaged alliance relationships on "the altar of the NPT." There was a feeling that the United States had been too dogmatic in its approach to nonproliferation. Faced with nonnuclear weapon states' criticism of discrimination, both superpowers wished to avoid damaging their bilateral relations with such countries. For example, they did not cooperate on pressing difficult cases such as India to adhere to the NPT.

On the other hand, cooperation in more technical areas was enhanced by the agreement. The role of the IAEA in safeguards was further strengthened, and the Zangger Committee (named after its Swiss chairman) met from 1971 to 1974 to develop a list of items the export of which would require safeguards. Both the United States and the Soviet Union participated in the Zangger Committee.

Several events in the period 1973–74 dealt shocks to the fledgling NPT regime. The most important was the Indian explosion in 1974 of a nuclear device produced with the use of a Canadian research reactor and heavy water supplied by the United States under the Atoms for Peace program. The Indians proceeded with their explosion despite a unilateral U.S. interpretation that such an act was not permitted under the existing agreement for cooperation between the United States and India. Though the Nixon administration did not respond very strongly to the Indian explosion, the U.S. Congress was quite incensed by what it regarded as a violation of the spirit and perhaps the letter of the agreement for cooperation.

A second event was the energy crisis of 1973–74. The quadrupling of oil prices in the aftermath of the 1973 Middle East War led to exaggerated projections of demand for nuclear energy. Many analysts thought that uranium would be in short supply and that it would be necessary to extract plutonium from spent fuel to run reactors. The projections of widespread reprocessing and commercial trade in plutonium (a weapons useable fuel) caused alarm because of the inadequacy of the current IAEA capabilities for safeguarding such facilities. There was fear that the entire elaborate structure of international safeguards would break down.

The third shock was related to the second. France and Germany both announced plans for significant exports of sensitive nuclear facilities that could be used to produce nuclear weapons materials. France announced the sale of reprocessing plants to South Korea and to Pakistan (which, it was later discovered, did intend to develop nuclear weapons), and Germany announced a massive plan to supply reactors, enrichment plants, and reprocessing facilities to Brazil. This German-Brazilian deal threatened the Argentines, who then advanced their own plans to develop sensitive nuclear facilities.

In this context and in the face of growing congressional and public concern about erosion of the NPT regime, the State Department invited the major nuclear supplier nations to meet in London to discuss the situation. In 1975 seven supplier nations (a group later expanded to fifteen) met to discuss conditions for nuclear exports. They eventually agreed on such measures as safeguards on all transferred materials, restrictions on the export of sensitive facilities such as enrichment and reprocessing plants, a promise not to undercut each others' efforts at sanctions, and promise of consultation in future specific sensitive cases. One of the interesting points about the suppliers' group meetings was that the United States and the Soviet Union often found themselves in closer rapport on policy positions than the United States did with its allies France and Germany. This gave the Soviets a splendid opportunity for provoking difficulties, but in September 1977 when the United States decided to compromise with the French and Germans by not requiring full-scope safeguards in order to get agreement on a set of supplier guidelines that could be forwarded to the IAEA, the Soviet Union resisted the temptation to cause trouble and instead acquiesced in the compromise. The United States held regular bilateral meetings with the Soviet Union (as it did with other member countries) in the context of these supplier group meetings.

The Soviets were not merely responding to U.S. initiatives. On the contrary, it appears that the same three events were forcing them to reevaluate their own policy. Previously the Soviets had "taken care of their own" by requiring the return of spent fuel from the reactors they exported to Eastern Europe. Their initial reaction to the Indian explosion was as mild as that of the Nixon administration. But the prospects of a Pakistani bomb and concern about the German-Brazilian deal seemed to stimulate a more active approach. They cooperated with the United States in preparations for the 1975 NPT Review Conference and resisted temptations to play for Third World popularity. Subsequently, in 1967–77, they insisted on stringent safeguards on a sale of heavy water to India.[35]

Early in 1977 the new Carter administration found itself involved in diplomatic imbroglios with Germany and France as it sought to reverse the Brazilian and Pakistani deals. It also encountered trouble with Japan when its agreement for cooperation required it to give approval for reprocessing in a new plant that the Japanese were building, while at home it had taken steps to halt development of a commercial reprocessing plant in South Carolina. A number of non-nuclear weapon states were also resentful of the restrictions imposed by the nuclear suppliers' guidelines and by the tightened U.S. restrictions being discussed by the Congress for the Nuclear Non-Proliferation Act, which subsequently passed in 1978.

The State Department devised a plan for an international nuclear fuel cycle evaluation (INFCE) to address the various dimensions of how research and commercial nuclear facilities that appeared to be legal under the NPT nonetheless might be involved in the proliferation of nuclear weapons. INFCE was a diplomatic success. Sixty-six countries and organizations came together in Vienna between 1977 and 1979, including consumers and suppliers, both rich and poor, East and West, and most important, a dozen countries that had not signed the NPT. In all, 519 experts from forty-six countries participated in sixty-one meetings of eight working groups producing 20,000 pages of documents. As a diplomatic device, INFCE helped to reestablish a basis for consensus on a more cautious approach to the nuclear fuel cycle. INFCE helped the U.S. government to set the agenda for other governments and helped to defuse the dispute between the United States and its allies.

The Soviet Union could have disrupted the INFCE proceedings and exacerbated the United States' problems with its allies. Fuel cycle issues were not a high priority for them. They supported the development of plutonium for breeder reactors and did not share the United States' concern, in part because they required the return of spent fuel from their Eastern bloc allies. Nonetheless, they were cooperative both in chairing an important working group and in the plenary sessions. Moreover, INFCE provided an opportunity for regular bilateral U.S.-Soviet consultations.

Renewed hostility in the late 1970s and early 1980s caused concern that the nonproliferation regime might be disrupted. In 1978, in reprisal for human rights jailings in the Soviet Union, President Carter halted a science and technology mission to the Soviet Union. This did not, however, interfere with nonproliferation discussions. After the Soviet invasion of Afghanistan in December 1979, however, consultations became more difficult to arrange. Moreover, the incoming Reagan administration had a more suspicious view of the Soviet Union and of the value of the NPT. Presidential candidate Reagan announced that nonproliferation was none of our business, and during the first six months of the Reagan administration, the issue was given low priority. According to National Security Council officials, the Israeli raid on an Iraqi reactor in June 1981 made the proliferation issue more important to the new administration. Now it was a question that could affect other security interests.[36] Nonetheless, there was no rush to reinstitute regular bilateral consultations with the Soviet Union. Some rather technical issues were discussed at IAEA board meetings, but many of the difficult cases were not addressed. Moreover, in 1982 when Arab countries at the IAEA general conference proposed a resolution to expel Israel from the organization, the United States withdrew from the general conference and withheld part of its annual contribution on the grounds that the organization had become too politicized. During this time the Soviet Union supported the Arab position.

In the fall of 1982, however, during the Shultz–Gromyko talks at the United Nations, both countries agreed that their interest in maintaining the nonproliferation regime would be best served by establishing semi-annual bilateral meetings. These have been held about every six months since December 1982. They last several days and cover a wide range of issues. Since then there have been signs of a number of cases of Soviet cooperation or restraint regarding the NPT regime. For example, at the 1982 IAEA general conference, the Soviets moderated their support for the Arab condemnation of Israel's attack on the Iraqi reactor. In 1982 the Soviets followed the U.S. example of making a voluntary offer to put some of their commercial nuclear facilities under IAEA safeguards as a means of proving to nonnuclear weapons states that IAEA safeguards do not impose an unhealthy burden on commercial nuclear activity. At the end of 1983, when the Soviet Union walked out of other arms control talks in protest of NATO's decision to go forward with the deployment of intermediate range nuclear missiles in Europe, they did not interrupt the bilateral talks on nonproliferation.[37]

The 1985 NPT review conference provided another opportunity for the Soviet Union to reap short-run diplomatic gains at the cost of the nonproliferation regime. The Soviet Union had announced its support of a comprehensive test ban, a measure that many of the nonnuclear weapons states regarded as a litmus test for seriousness about compliance with Article 6 (reducing superpower arsenals). The United States announced that it had put CTB negotiations on a back burner and was distinctly uninterested in the more recent Soviet offer. But in an intensive series of diplomatic contacts—both official and unofficial—before the conference, the Soviet Union agreed that it would not be in the interest of the nonproliferation regime for the two superpowers to embarrass each other and thereby provide ammunition to nonnuclear weapons states that might be interested in wrecking the regime.[38]

The rediscovery of cooperation on the NPT by the United States and the Soviet Union in the early 1980s when other areas of security cooperation were disrupted and rhetoric surrounding the overall relationship had become particularly harsh suggests that the institutionalization of a treaty regime with explicit norms and multiple opportunities for contact may help to preserve an area of cooperation when the overall climate has turned sour. The multilateral nature of the treaty probably helps. It provides opportunities for meeting without an explicit bilateral initiative. The universal nature of the norms helps to emphasize more cooperative areas than would come up if only the hard cases were at issue. The multilateral nature of the contact also allows the prospect of intra-issues coalitions developing with the United States and the Soviets on the same side, rather than in strict opposition to each other on all issues. The legal and political obligations that each country has assumed on behalf of the regime seem to have given both sides' more predictability and helped the other to adjust its expectations accordingly. Of course, the very nature of the subject matter—in which the object is to coopt others in a normative framework that limits their sovereign right to the most destructive weapon—creates incentives for the superpowers to maintain the treaty regime. Could cooperation survive or be relearned in the absence of a regime? Possibly. But it certainly would be much more difficult than in a situation in which the structure and expectations of the treaty regime already exist.

It is also worth noting the change in the structure of power within the nuclear issue as an incentive for maintaining the treaty regime. Whereas the United States was the predominant international supplier in the 1960s, by the early 1970s the development of French capability to supply reactors and fuel, a German-British-Dutch consortium to provide fuel, and the prospect of a second tier of subsidiary suppliers in the 1980s made it clear to both superpowers that their leverage within the nuclear supply area was eroding. This diffusion of power made return to unilateral policies less promising than earlier. In short, the incentives to maintain the regime were probably strengthened by the diffusion of power that occurred in the 1970s. All signs, including future evolution of a third tier of nuclear supplier countries, point in the same direction.

Finally, the linkage of the nonproliferation issue to the overall U.S.-Soviet relationship has become progressively looser over time. As we saw with the effort to negotiate the treaty, it was difficult to make progress in the period of tight bipolarity and hostility in the overall U.S.-Soviet security relationship. The need to maintain alliance structures created a tight linkage between the proliferation issue and the overall security relationship. Détente seemed to be a necessary condition for initial progress on nonproliferation. However, by the 1980s détente was no longer a necessary condition for maintenance of the treaty regime.

CONCLUSIONS

Looking at the experience of negotiating and implementing the Non-Proliferation Treaty, what general lessons can be drawn?

Bargaining from Strength

Both sides had a strong interest in negotiating a nonproliferation treaty. Because neither wanted to give away nuclear weapons (at least not after 1959), cooperation via a treaty was a way to avoid a dilemma. It reduced uncertainties about defection and helped to sustain cooperation. Neither side was in an especially stronger position, although the United States may have had a slight edge. Because of its experience with China, the Soviet Union had gone further and learned more quickly the dangers of too much nuclear sharing. At the same time, the United States was trying to resolve its alliance dilemma by creating the MLF. The Soviets concentrated on preventing the spread of nuclear weapons to Germany. They had a strong incentive to get rid of the MLF, which they feared would put a German finger on the nuclear trigger. This may have helped with the final Soviet concessions related to the EurAtom inspections and the possibility of a federated nuclear Europe.

During the implementation of the treaty, neither side seems to have had a stronger position than the other. Both were vulnerable to complaints from Third World countries and client states. Each developed increased concern after the events of the mid-1970s. As a nuclear supplier, the United States was in a weaker position than before, and the Soviets were entering nuclear fuel markets. On the other hand, many of the potential proliferators geographically were closer to the Soviet Union than to the United States. Most remarkable about the period of implementation is that these relative strengths and weaknesses seem to have balanced each other and neither country maximized its short-run advantage at the cost of long-term common interests.

Unilateral Restraint

By the 1960s neither country was interested in giving away or seriously sharing control of nuclear weapons. In that sense, the treaty formalized their unilateral restraint and, for reasons given above, made it possible to implement a cooperative solution. In a narrower sense, there were some instances of unilateral restraint by the United States in regard to a PNE test during the negotiations and in the decision to forgo reprocessing in the later 1970s. The United States' voluntary offer to submit its civil facilities to international inspection was another unilateral measure eventually followed by the Soviet Union in the 1980s. Unilateral restraints may have contributed modestly to the implementation of the treaty but were not major factors in its success.

Linkage

As seen above, the linkage between nuclear weapons and alliance maintenance made progress on negotiating the Non-Proliferation Treaty difficult in the late 1950s and early 1960s, and Soviet linkage of the MLF to the NPT was a critical factor in the mid-1960s. In addition, the unintended linkage of the Vietnam War and the Soviet invasion of Czechoslovakia delayed negotiations and U.S. ratification of the treaty. On the other hand, during the implementation of the treaty, there is surprisingly little linkage. In fact, one of the most striking features of the regime has been the ability to maintain cooperation in nonproliferation when the overall political relationship was marked by renewed hostility and other arms control talks had been halted.

Genies in Bottles

The heart of the argument for the NPT was to keep other nations' genies inside their national bottles. In that sense, the NPT regime differs in that neither the United States nor the Soviet Union wanted others to develop such weapons. Although it is true that there were some in the United States who believed that selective proliferation to our allies would be in our interest, this was a minority view. The Soviet Union, in an earlier period, thought that it was in its interest to help China develop a nuclear weapon. It reversed this position by 1959. Since then both nations have had a common interest in cooperating to keep other genies in other bottles.

Uncertainties

A major purpose of the NPT is to reduce uncertainties, and it seems to have done this. It has created an inertia in favor of one way of approaching the problem of the future by putting the burden of proof on the proponents of nuclear weaponry rather than on those who favor nonproliferation. By creating a presumption against the dissenters, it has reduced the type of uncertainties that could lead to the superpowers or nonweapons states to defect on the agreement and has established a framework in which the rate of proliferation has been considerably slower than was expected in the early 1960s when the treaty negotiations were under way. At that time, President Kennedy estimated that there might be as many as fifteen to twenty-five nuclear nations by the 1970s.

Effect on Arms

Opponents' fears that the Non-Proliferation Treaty would exacerbate the desire of our European allies to develop nuclear weapons and prevent the development of benign ballistic missile defense systems that could be shared with them do not seem to be justified. The treaty does not seem to have redirected arms plans and competition in counterproductive ways. Nor does it seem to have merely codified existing defense plans. Although the Germans and Japanese may not have clear plans to develop nuclear weapons in the 1960s, their adherence to the NPT has helped to solidify antinuclear attitudes in both countries. Discussions of nuclear options are far fewer today than before the NPT. Nor have security guarantees related to the treaty had the feared effect of drawing the United States that much more deeply into other nations' dispute. At the same time the belief of proponents that cooperation in the NPT that stimulates superpower arms control efforts and facilitates further disarmament does not seem to have been a major effect. Although the superpowers have cooperated at NPT review conferences in defending their records against attack for failing to implement Article 6, it is also true that Article 6 of the treaty has not been a major impetus toward significant arms reduction.

Lulling

Lulling has both general and specific connotations. In general, there was fear that the NPT, like any arms control agreement, might lull Americans into not maintaining a strong defense against the Soviet Union. Although it is true that defense expenditures decreased after signing the NPT, that decline was due far more to domestic reactions against the Vietnam War and the desire to change domestic priorities than to the signature of the NPT or other arms control agreements. Moreover, although both sides continued to observe the NPT, defense expenditures went up again in the late 1970s and early 1980s. Thus a general lulling effect is not a sustainable hypothesis. However, in specific terms, there was some lulling effect after the signing of the NPT in that neither the United States nor the Soviet Union paid great attention to followup on the treaty in the early days. For example, neither pressed India very hard for signature and both reacted rather mildly at first after the Indian nuclear explosion in 1974. On the other hand, the shocks of the mid-1970s, including that Indian explosion, lead both sides to take the NPT regime more seriously. Faced with prospects of its loss, both cooperated to shore it up. The addition of the Nuclear Suppliers Group, the INFCE exercise, and the establishing of regular bilateral consultations are cases in point. Thus the specific lulling effect was short-lived and quickly changed as a result of events.

Verification and Compliance

Opponents of the NPT expressed doubts about the capability of the IAEA to verify the agreement. It has turned out that the IAEA inspection system, although far from perfect, seems to be good enough to have deterred countries from using civil nuclear energy programs to advance their military purposes. On the other hand, the inspection system alone may have been insufficient. For example, countries such as Pakistan and South Korea may have intended to use civil reprocessing facilities for eventual military purposes. Effective national intelligence may have forestalled situations that would have burdened the official verification system. Nonetheless, the carefully detailed provisions for IAEA inspections have probably worked quite well in relation to Article 3 of the treaty. At the same time the concerns expressed by some opponents of the NPT that the IAEA was not charged with inspecting military facilities remains true. The treaty is silent on inspections related to a direct, dedicated military path to nuclear weaponry. But this was clear from the start, and again it places emphasis on supplementing verification of international agreements with effective national intelligence means.

Political Support

Nonproliferation has always had widespread public support in the United States. Congress has reflected this concern. In the 1950s it prevented the administration from going as far as it wished in sharing with the allies; in the 1960s, it often prodded the administration to move more quickly on negotiations. During the implementation of the treaty, Congress prodded the administration to more forceful action after the Indian explosion and in the later 1970s insisted on passing tighter legislation than the executive branch desired. In the 1980s Congress took the lead in holding the Reagan administration's feet to the fire in implementing the treaty. The NPT has not depended as heavily on presidential popularity for its negotiation or implementation as many other arms control treaties. Instead, it has rested on its own popular and congressional support.

Asymmetry

It is hard to argue that the NPT has served Soviet or U.S. interests better. Both have strong incentives to prevent the spread of nuclear weapons. Although the Soviets could be the first target of many new proliferators, the United States cannot relax and feel secure. Many of its national interests would be strongly and adversely affected by proliferation. In this sense, the success of the NPT may reflect the strong sense of symmetry that exists. The Non-Proliferation Treaty loosely represents a situation that game theorists call *iterated prisoner's dilemma.* Each has learned that cheating and taking short-run advantage could lead to similar behavior by the other and loss of their common interest in slowing the spread of nuclear weapons. The treaty provides a form of communication that reduces the fears of cheating. It is a good example of what a successful arms control agreement can accomplish.

NOTES

I am grateful to John Wertheimer and William Jarosz for research assistance.

1.   For a discussion, see Joseph S. Nye, Jr., "Maintaining a Non-Proliferation Regime," *International Organization* 35 (Winter 1981), pp. 15–38; and Joseph S. Nye, Jr., "U.S.-Soviet Cooperation in a Non-Proliferation Re-

gime," paper prepared for Stanford University Conference on U.S.-Soviet Efforts at Cooperation in Security. This chapter draws on both papers.

2. Henry Sokolski, "Atoms for Peace: A Non-Proliferation Primer," *Arms Control—The Journal of Arms Control & Disarmament* 1 (2) (September 1980), pp. 99–231.

3. William B. Bader, *The United States and the Spread of Nuclear Weapons* (New York: Pegasus, 1968), p. 26.

4. John Steinbruner, *The Cybernetic Theory of Decision* (Princeton, N.J.: Princeton University Press, 1974), p. 177.

5. Bader, *The United States and the Spread of Nuclear Weapons*, pp. 28–34.

6. George Quester, *Nuclear Diplomacy* (New York: Dunellen, 1970), p. 172.

7. Bader, *The United States and the Spread of Nuclear Weapons*, p. 40.

8. Stephen Sestanovich, "Nuclear Proliferation and Soviet Foreign Policy, 1957–68; The Limits of Soviet-American Cooperation," Ph.D. thesis, Harvard University, 1979, p. 48.

9. John Gittings, *Survey of the Sino-Soviet Dispute* (London: Oxford University Press, 1968), pp. 102–09.

10. Walter Clemmons, *The Arms Race and Sino-Soviet Relations* (Stanford, Calif.: Hoover Institution, 1968), pp. 36ff.

11. Nikita Khrushchev, *Khrushcheve Remembers: The Last Testament*, translated and edited by Strobe Talbott (Boston: Little, Brown, 1974), p. 26.

12. Sestanovich, "Nuclear Proliferation," p. 189.

13. *Ibid.*, p. 221.

14. *Ibid.*, pp. 169, 216.

15. Report of a Conference on Permissive Action Links, Harvard Center for Science and International Affairs, Feb. 1986.

16. Arthur H. Dean, *Test Ban and Disarmament* (New York: Harper & Row, 1966), p. 122.

17. Bader, *The United States and the Spread of Nuclear Weapons*, p. 60.

18. Lawrence Scheinman, "Nuclear Safeguards: The Peaceful Atom and the IAEA," *International Conciliation* 572 (March 1969), pp. 5–64.

19. Sestanovich, "Nuclear Proliferation," p. 181.

20. Dwight D. Eisenhower, *Waging Peace: 1956–1961* (Garden City, N.Y.: Doubleday, 1965), pp. 472–74.

21. U.S. Senate Committee on Foreign Relations, *Hearings*, July 10, 11, 12, and 17, 1968, 90th Cong., 2d Sess. (Washington, D.C.: U.S. Government Printing Office, 1968), p. 182.

22. *Ibid.*, p. 186.

23. *Ibid.*, p. 173.

24. *Ibid.*, p. 129 ff.

25. Harley H. Barnes, Jr., "The Nuclear Non-Proliferation Treaty: Participants, Interests, and Processes in American Foreign Policy Formulation," Ph.D. thesis, Rutgers University, 1976, p. 315.

26. Senate Committee on Foreign Relations, *Hearings*, p. 109.

27. *Ibid.*, p. 164.

28. *Ibid.*, p. 139.

29. *Ibid.*, p. 134.

30. *Ibid.*, p. 56.

31. Barnes, "The Nuclear Non-Proliferation Treaty," p. 315.

32. *Ibid.*, p. 388.

33. *Ibid.*, p. 341.

34. *Ibid.*, p. 247.

35. See Gloria Duffy, "Soviet Nuclear Experts," *International Security* 3 (Summer 1978), pp. 83–111; and W. Scott Spence, "Soviet Strategies for the Non-Proliferation of Nuclear Weapons: 1965–1985," Columbia University seminar paper. Also confirmed in conversations with academicians in Moscow, June 1986. See also William Potter, "Nuclear Proliferation: U.S.-Soviet Cooperation," *Washington Quarterly* (Winter 1985), pp. 141–53.

36. Conversation with NSC official, Autumn 1981.

37. Secretary of State George Shultz, "Preventing the Proliferation of Nuclear Weapons," *Department of State Bulletin* 84 (December 1984), pp. 17–21.

38. Interview, U.S. Arms Control and Disarmament Agency official, Aug. 1985.

8 THE BIOLOGICAL AND TOXIN WEAPONS CONVENTION

Elisa D. Harris

On December 16, 1974, the U.S. Senate unanimously approved the ratification of the 1972 Biological and Toxin Weapons Convention (BWC), banning the development, production, and stockpiling of all biological and toxin weapons. One month later, President Gerald R. Ford signed the instruments of ratification, thus clearing the way for the entry into force, on March 26, 1975, of the first and only disarmament measure of the postwar period. As President Richard M. Nixon pointed out in 1972, when he transmitted the convention to the Senate for its consideration, the BWC was "the first international agreement since World War II to provide for the actual elimination of an entire class of weapons from the arsenals of nations."[1] This characteristic distinguished, and continues to distinguish, the Biological and Toxin Weapons Convention from all other postwar arms control agreements.

A second feature that distinguishes the BWC from other contemporary arms control agreements is that the negotiations that culminated in this treaty were stimulated, in large measure, by an act of unilateral disarmament. On November 25, 1969, President Nixon announced that because of the "massive, unpredictable, and potentially uncontrollable consequences" of biological weapons, including their ability to "produce global epidemics and impair the health of future generations," the United States would destroy its existing

191

stocks of biological weapons, would never use such weapons, and would confine its biological research to defensive measures only. The president also associated the United States with a British draft convention banning the possession and use of biological weapons, which had recently been tabled at the Disarmament Committee in Geneva.[2]

Less than three months later, the president extended his renunciation to include toxin weapons as well. As the White House explained, the president had decided to renounce toxins because their production "in any significant quantity would require facilities similar to those needed for the production of biological agents." Thus, even though "toxins are chemical substances, [and] not living organisms," they would be renounced in order to leave no doubts as to the new U.S. policy concerning biological weapons.[3]

THE ORIGINS OF THE CONVENTION

The Biological and Toxin Weapons Convention of 1972 culminated nearly half a century of efforts to ban biological weapons. In 1925, following the use of chemical weapons in World War I, a protocol was signed in Geneva banning the wartime use of both chemical and biological weapons but not the development, production, possession, or transfer of such weapons. Many of the parties to the Geneva Protocol have reserved the right to retaliate in kind, making the protocol, in effect, a no-first-use agreement.

The United States was instrumental in bringing about the Geneva Protocol. Yet the U.S. Army Chemical Warfare Service's success in mobilizing opposition to the treaty in 1925, and neglect thereafter, prevented the United States from ratifying the agreement for fifty years.[4] This situation changed in 1969 when, in conjunction with his new biological weapons policy, President Nixon promised to return the 1925 Protocol to the Senate for its advice and consent. The president also reaffirmed the U.S. policy not to use lethal chemical weapons first and extended this policy to include incapacitating chemicals as well.[5] On August 19, 1970, Nixon transmitted the Geneva Protocol to the U.S. Senate with a reservation preserving the right to retaliate with chemical weapons against any state that violated the protocol and with an understanding that the protocol did not apply to the wartime use of riot control agents, chemical herbicides, smoke, and napalm.[6]

Chemical and biological warfare (CBW) reemerged as a controversial issue in the mid-1960s because of the use of riot control agents and herbicides by U.S. forces in Vietnam. The domestic debate over U.S. chemical warfare (CW) activities in Vietnam was clearly part of a larger controversy over the legitimacy of the war itself. This debate, which initially focused on the question of whether the harassing and antiplant agents being employed by U.S. forces were prohibited by the Geneva Protocol, eventually stimulated a wider interest in U.S. CBW policy in general and CBW arms control in particular.[7] The Egyptian use of mustard gas, phosgene, and possibly nerve gas between 1963 and 1967 in the civil war in Yemen also contributed to this development,[8] as did reports of U.S. contingency plans for employing biological weapons against Cuba and in other countries.[9]

A number of other incidents further sensitized both the Congress and the general public to CBW issues in the 1960s. A series of earthquakes in Denver, Colorado, were linked to the underground disposal of chemical wastes from the army's Rocky Mountain Arsenal.[10] In March 1968 over 6,000 sheep died in Utah after the accidental release of nerve gas during CW tests at the nearby Dugway Proving Ground.[11] One year later, an army plan to transport tons of obsolete chemical weapons across the country for disposal in the Atlantic Ocean generated further public and congressional concern.[12] Shortly thereafter a nerve gas accident on Okinawa and the subsequent disclosure that U.S. chemical weapons were stored in Japan as well as in the Federal Republic of Germany severely shook U.S. relations with both of the countries involved.[13] Finally, there were reports that the Pentagon had conducted CBW tests in the Pacific without notifying local officials.[14]

These incidents prompted numerous congressional hearings and resolutions on U.S. CBW policy.[15] They also led the Congress, in 1969, to impose a number of serious restrictions on the army's CBW program. The Defense Department was instructed to begin submitting semiannual reports to Congress on its CBW activities. Future CBW open-air testing and transport plans had to be reviewed and approved by the Surgeon General of the Public Health Service. The government was also required to provide foreign countries with advance notice before deploying any additional CBW agents or weapons on foreign soil. Finally, procurement of CBW weapons was banned, and research money for new agents and delivery systems was scaled back.[16]

Media interest in CBW was also on the rise by the late 1960s, as was the interest of the scientific community. Television programs on CBW by CBS and NBC both reflected and contributed to this growing interest,[17] as did a spate of new books on the subject.[18] Members of the scientific community, working with organizations such as the Pugwash Conferences, the American Academy of Arts and Sciences, the National Academy of Sciences, and the Stockholm International Peace Research Institute, helped bring the issue of CBW disarmament to the attention of policymakers. Scientists also wrote most of the major journal articles on CBW in the late 1960s and were frequently called on to testify on the subject before congressional committees. Some scientists, such as Harvard biochemist Matthew Meselson, worked closely with former colleagues who now occupied key positions in the Nixon administration.

Partly in response to the controversy arising from U.S. chemical warfare activities in Vietnam, as well as the other incidents involving chemical weapons, President Nixon, soon after taking office, ordered the National Security Council to undertake a broad review of U.S. chemical and biological warfare policy. This review, which lasted six months and involved every relevant agency of the U.S. government, considered the CBW threat and alternative ways of meeting that threat, the utility of using CBW agents, R&D objectives, U.S. riot control agent and herbicide policy, and the foreign policy implications of U.S. CBW programs. Out of this review emerged the new policy articulated by President Nixon on November 25, 1969.[19]

Although it was widely believed at the time that there was no serious military interest in biological weapons anywhere, including in the United States, the record suggests that at least some in the Pentagon doubted the wisdom of the new BW policy outlined by President Nixon. This was reflected in delays in the implementation of the new policy and, at times, in an outright refusal to undertake the steps necessary for its execution. For example, although the White House had promised that all future defensive research on biological weapons would be unclassified, within months of the president's announcement the army was making plans to transfer hundreds of civilian and military personnel from the biological warfare facility at Fort Detrick to other facilities where they could continue to do biological research on a classified basis.[20]

The United Kingdom played a particularly important role in the negotiations that led to the Biological and Toxin Weapons Convention. A British working paper to the Disarmament Committee in Geneva in 1968 first suggested that biological and chemical weapons be separated in the work of the committee. In 1969 the British followed this initiative with a draft convention on biological weapons.[21] Key provisions of this draft convention, as well as of a draft treaty put forward by the Soviet Union and its allies in March 1971, and of a 1971 working paper from the neutral and nonaligned members of the Disarmament Committee, were eventually incorporated into a draft treaty. The Biological and Toxin Weapons Convention that followed was thus the product of a genuine multilateral negotiating effort within the Geneva Disarmament Committee. Indeed, as then U.N. Ambassador George Bush pointed out, this agreement was "forged with the significant help and through the participation of many countries."[22]

The impetus for the British efforts to ban biological weapons was similar, although not identical, to that in the United States. Presumably part of the explanation for Britain's energetic BW arms control efforts in the late 1960s, while not emphasized at the time, was the realization that the tiny island was completely vulnerable to biological attack. This vulnerability, which was reported publicly for the first time in November 1968, had become apparent during BW tests a decade earlier.[23] Even so, it was not until 1968 that the British government took its first steps to bring about a ban on biological weapons.

As in the United States, public opposition to the British government's CBW policy was very intense by mid-1968. Scientists, Members of Parliament (MPs), students, and the peace movement were all apparently concerned about the secrecy surrounding British CBW research, as well as the relationship between that research and U.S. chemical warfare activities in Vietnam, where the British-developed riot control agent CS was being used. One example of this concern was the May 1968 appeal by twelve leading scientists in Britain, including three Nobel prize winners, for the transfer of the classified British BW research facility at Porton from military to civilian control. In response to this—as well as other protests by Labour Party MPs, students, and various peace groups—the British government announced in June 1968 that it would hold an open house at the biological warfare facility. The government also announced its intention to seek a new international agreement to supplement the Geneva

Protocol.[24] This initiative turned out to be the 1968 British working paper on a biological weapons ban.

Concern about chemical and biological weapons was not, however, restricted to Britain or the United States. In 1968, largely in response to the mounting controversy over U.S. chemical use in Vietnam, as well as the continuing debate about the status of these chemicals under the Geneva Protocol of 1925, the U.N. Secretary General, at the request of the General Assembly, appointed a group of experts to examine the technical characteristics of chemical and biological weapons and the effects of their use. Their report, which was released in July 1969, concluded that "Were these weapons ever to be used on a large scale in war, no one could predict how enduring the effects would be, and how they would affect the structure of society and the environment in which we live." For this reason, both the U.N. group of experts and the Secretary General recommended that all chemical and biological weapons be unconditionally banned.[25] A second, more technical study on the health effects of chemical and biological warfare, undertaken by the World Health Organization in 1969, reached similar conclusions.[26]

THE NEGOTIATIONS

Buttressed by the U.N. experts report and the recommendations of the Secretary General, the Geneva Disarmament Committee began to give serious consideration to CBW arms control in the summer of 1969. From the outset, the deliberations within the committee were hampered by disagreement over a number of issues, including the status of riot control agents and herbicides under the Geneva Protocol and, hence, under future agreements concerning CBW; the desirability of considering a ban on biological weapons separate from one on chemical weapons; and the requirements for adequate verification.

The controversy over the scope of the Geneva Protocol was best illustrated on December 16, 1969, when the General Assembly, by a vote of eighty to three to thirty-six, adopted a resolution declaring the wartime use of any chemical agents "which might be employed because of their direct toxic effects on man, animals, or plants" to be contrary to international law, as embodied in the 1925 agreement.[27] The United States and Australia, which were then employing riot control agents in Vietnam, voted against the resolution, as did Portugal, which was believed to be using similar substances in Angola. Many of the countries that abstained in the vote did so only after considerable pressure from the United States.[28]

The split within the Disarmament Committee on whether to ban chemical and biological weapons separately or simultaneously was clearly reflected in the different draft conventions introduced by Britain and the Soviet Union in 1969. The British draft convention of July 10, 1969, banned the production, possession, transfer, and use of biological weapons, as well as the research, equipment, and delivery systems associated with such weapons.[29] By contrast, the Soviet draft convention of September 19, 1969, banned the development, production, and stockpiling of both chemical and biological weapons.[30]

The West argued that biological weapons should be treated separately from chemical weapons for a number of reasons: the consequences of using biological weapons were so grave, and their military utility so doubtful, that there existed an immediate opportunity to eliminate them;[31] the difficulties of verifying a ban on chemical weapons would delay an agreement covering both types of weapons;[32] biological weapons were more easily banned because they had never been used in modern warfare and had never become established in the arsenals of states;[33] and because the elimination of biological weapons would strengthen the existing restraints on CBW embodied in the Geneva Protocol.[34] Finally, the United States, in particular, could hardly consider a ban on both types of weapons given its ongoing, and highly controversial, riot control agent and herbicide use in Vietnam.

The Soviet Union and its allies, joined by many of the neutral and nonaligned states,[35] argued, on the other hand, that it would be counterproductive to consider a ban on biological weapons separate from one on chemical weapons for the following reasons: both types of weapons had been linked in the past in terms of public perceptions, international law, and military preparations;[36] such an approach could weaken the restraints on CW use embodied in the Geneva Protocol;[37] chemical weapons were already stockpiled by many states and hence posed a serious threat that required immediate action;[38] a ban on biological weapons only could stimulate further efforts to develop chemical weapons;[39] and finally, because partial measures, as evidenced by the Limited Test Ban Treaty, were not always followed by additional arms control agreements.[40]

Verification was clearly at the heart of much of the procedural debate about whether chemical and biological weapons could and should be banned simultaneously. Although a ban on biological weapons could not be properly verified, the West was apparently willing to risk the possibility of noncompliance in order to preclude further developments relating to these weapons. As Fred Mulley, the British representative to the Disarmament Committee, explained,

> we must make a choice—balance the risks of evasion if we go ahead with the formulation of new obligations, against the risks for the world if we do nothing and allow the fears of eventual use of microbiological methods of warfare to continue and intensify. My choice is emphatically to go ahead; we cannot afford to do nothing.[41]

The same was not true of chemical weapons, however. The Western powers believed that chemical weapons were militarily useful in certain circumstances. They were therefore reluctant to eliminate chemical weapons without adequate assurances that other states were doing likewise.[42] The verification procedure embodied in the Soviet draft convention, which essentially left each party to the treaty responsible for its own compliance, was completely inadequate from the Western perspective.

The issue of whether to ban chemical and biological weapons separately or simultaneously stalemated the work of the Disarmament Committee for nearly a year and a half. Then in March 1971 the Soviet Union announced that it was prepared to negotiate a separate agreement on biological weapons and tabled a draft convention to that effect. At the time, the Soviet representative to the Disarmament Committee argued that the Soviet Union had decided to shift its position because Western intransigence on the issue of chemical weapons was blocking progress toward a comprehensive CBW ban. This new position, the Soviet Union hoped, would break the deadlock in Geneva and thereby increase the prospects of at least a modest disarmament success.[43]

There are, of course, other possible explanations for the Soviet decision to accept the more limited ban on biological weapons, explanations that Soviet representatives never mentioned but that are plausible given the time that the decision was made. The Soviet shift came at the same time as General Secretary Leonid Brezhnev's announcement, at the Twenty-fourth Communist Party Congress, of a number of new détente initiatives aimed at both China and the

United States. That both the shift and the Brezhnev proposals occurred at the same time as the first indications of a thaw in U.S.-Chinese relations—as evidenced by Peking's now famous table tennis invitation—probably was not coincidental. A concession on BW, Soviet officials may have reasoned, would be a small price to pay in order to avoid being isolated by a Sino-Western bloc.[44]

Whatever its explanation, the Soviet shift *did* break the deadlock in the negotiations, and within four months the United States and the Soviet Union were submitting identical draft conventions to the Disarmament Committee.[45] A slightly revised joint draft convention—banning the development, production, and stockpiling of all biological agents or toxins "of types and in quantities that have no justification for prophylactic, protective or other peaceful purposes," as well as the delivery systems for such agents—was submitted to the Disarmament Committee in September, 1971.[46] Two months later, in a resolution adopted by a vote of 110 to 0, with France abstaining, the General Assembly recommended that the agreement be opened for signature and ratification at the earliest possible date.[47]

The Biological and Toxin Weapons Convention was signed in Washington, London, and Moscow on April 10, 1972. Four months later, President Nixon submitted the agreement to the Senate for its advice and consent to ratification.[48] Yet it was not until December 16, 1974, that the Senate voted its unanimous approval of the treaty.[49] One reason for the delay was the Senate Foreign Relations Committee's refusal to act on the BWC until the controversy over the status of riot control agents and herbicides under the Geneva Protocol had been resolved.[50] The Watergate affair and subsequent resignation of President Nixon probably also contributed to the delay.

ARGUMENTS

The public record on the Biological and Toxin Weapons Convention is quite limited. The ratification hearing on the convention, for example, was dominated by discussion of the 1925 Geneva Protocol, which was being considered for ratification at the same time. To the extent that the utility and desirability of a ban on biological weapons was debated at all, this debate took place in the period immediately before and after President Nixon's momentous policy announcement of November 1969. In the final analysis, almost no one opposed a prohibition on biological weapons, either during or after the negotiations.

The key military-strategic arguments voiced by both proponents and opponents of a BW ban concerned issues such as deterrence, the military utility of biological weapons, and technological possibilities. The main political-diplomatic considerations involved proliferation, verification and compliance, and the arms control and other potential implications of an agreement prohibiting biological weapons.

Military Arguments

One of the key military arguments for maintaining a biological weapons capability was that of deterrence—the belief that in order to deter the Soviet Union or other potential adversaries from using biological weapons against the United States or its allies it was necessary to possess an ability to retaliate in kind. This was clearly a major tenet of U.S. CBW policy prior to President Nixon's policy announcement in November 1969. As John S. Foster, director of Defense, Research and Engineering, wrote in April of that year, "Unilateral CB disarmament would adversely affect a nation's deterrent capability."[51]

Those who questioned the logic of deterrence with biological weapons did so for a number of reasons. They argued, first, that these weapons were most effective when used against unprotected, and hence unwarned, enemy forces. As Ivan Bennett, a former deputy director of the Office of Science and Technology, explained in 1969, to use biological weapons in retaliation, against an adversary that had initiated the use of such weapons and was thus prepared for an in-kind response, would have considerably less military effect.[52]

Others argued that retaliation with biological weapons was of doubtful military value because of the delay caused by the incubation period for the agents. As the U.S. representative to the Geneva Disarmament Committee, James Leonard, described it: "Few if any, military situations can be imagined in which a state would try to redress a military imbalance by retaliating with weapons whose effects would not show up for days." According to Leonard, for this reason the U.S. government had concluded that retaliation in kind would not be the best military response to a biological attack or, for that matter, even an acceptable or rational response.[53]

Some suggested that nuclear weapons would deter an adversary from using biological weapons, thus making an in-kind response with biological weapons unnecessary. As Howard Furnas, special assistant to the director of ACDA, explained to the House Foreign Affairs Committee in 1969, "in an age of nuclear deterrence, the question" arises as to "whether biological warfare has any military utility and whether, therefore, it makes sense to maintain a capability to retaliate in kind with biological weapons."[54]

Finally, others questioned the deterrence argument on the basis of uncertainty regarding Soviet BW capabilities. Several members of Congress, for example, pointed out that the U.S. intelligence community had no hard evidence that the Soviet Union had developed biological weapons. According to Representative Donald Fraser, intelligence sources had "been unable to identify any facility that would be a counterpart to the facility we have in Arkansas, namely, a production facility of bacteriological agents."[55]

A second consideration in the public debate over whether it was desirable to maintain a biological weapons capability was that of the military utility of such weapons. Before the president's new CBW policy was announced, the Pentagon had argued that biological weapons were militarily useful because they provided the United States with an additional "response option" against attack.[56] Or, to put it somewhat differently, the existence of a biological weapons capability provided the president with the option of using weapons other than nuclear.

Those who questioned the military utility of biological weapons did so on a number of grounds. Probably the most important factor concerned reliability. As Harvard biochemist Matthew Meselson pointed out, the effects of a biological attack would be delayed and unpredictable because of the incubation period for the agents and because of uncertainties regarding the resistance of the target population, as well as the meteorological and atmospheric conditions at the time of attack.[57]

A second and closely related issue was that of controllability, both in terms of intended target and of escalation. Once a biological agent is disseminated over a target, the possibility of infecting friendly forces and populations, indeed of triggering an epidemic, is beyond the control of the attacker. This characteristic of biological weapons was particularly troublesome to the Nixon administration, as well as to many members of Congress.[58] It was also argued that even a limited use of biological weapons carried the risk of escalation to full-scale chemical and biological warfare or even to all-out nuclear war.[59]

Yet another reason for questioning the military utility of biological weapons was the fact that their use could not prevent an adversary from retaliating with nuclear weapons. Although a reduction in collateral damage might be desirable in some circumstances, if weapons of mass destruction were to be employed against a nuclear power, a country would presumably want those weapons to possess a counterforce capability. As Meselson pointed out, "You do not damage Soviet missiles with biological weapons."[60]

A fourth factor that raised doubts about the military utility of biological weapons concerned damage limitation. Maintaining a biological weapons capability, it was argued, was tantamount to a declaration of antipopulation warfare. This perception, whether right or wrong, could severely undermine the possibility of intrawar deterrence, or even of war termination, once hostilities broke out.[61] Han Swyter, a former Pentagon official, pointed out that if the purpose of using biological weapons was, indeed, to inflict massive casualties, then this objective could just as easily (and perhaps more reliably) be achieved through the use of nuclear weapons.[62]

Finally, it was suggested that some military targets could more effectively be dealt with by conventional munitions than by chemical or biological weapons. Ivan Bennett pointed out, for example, that it would be much more useful to destroy a city's factories, railways, docks, storage facilities, and so forth rather than simply poison or infect the population.[63]

A final argument put forward by the Pentagon prior to the president's November announcement was that continued R&D in the field of chemical and biological weapons was necessary in order "to minimize the possibility of technological surprise."[64] However, the administration eventually came to fear that advances in genetics and molecular biology would soon make it possible to develop biological agents of even greater destructive potential than those that already existed. This was a development, from the administration's point of view, which ought to be avoided, rather than encouraged.[65]

Political Arguments

One of the most important political considerations during the debate over U.S. CBW policy in the late 1960s and early 1970s concerned the prospects and implications of the proliferation of these weapons. Chemical and biological agents were viewed as attractive weapons for saboteurs as well as for smaller states that were unable, for financial or technical reasons, to acquire a significant conventional or nuclear capability. As Ivan Bennett pointed out, the use of biological weapons in an act of sabotage—for example, by the release of a small amount of a highly virulent bacteria into the subway system of a major city—could have profound consequences against which there was no effective defense.[66] Han Swyter argued that the spread of biological weapons to smaller states would "tend to change the world's balance of power," reducing the security and power of the United States.[67] A biological weapons disarmament treaty, it was hoped and argued, would discourage such proliferation.[68]

A second political issue that was discussed but received comparatively little attention was that of verification. Jozef Goldblat, of the Stockholm International Peace Research Institute, and Joshua Lederberg, a scientist and consultant for ACDA, argued that by failing to ban research on biological agents and toxins, and by permitting the development, production, and stockpiling of such agents for prophylactic, protective, or other peaceful purposes, the proposed treaty could generate suspicions or lead to actual violations. In the same vein, Goldblat suggested that the absence of explicit standards or criteria for the quantities of agents that were permitted under the convention could also create future problems. He also criticized the treaty because it contained no verification provisions for either the destruction of biological weapons stocks or for the transfer of BW facilities from military to civilian purposes. The ambiguity of the convention's consultation and cooperation provisions, as well as the inherent weakness of a complaints procedure linked to the Security Council, where permanent members could veto any investigation not to their liking, were also pointed out. Finally, Goldblat, Lederberg, and, indeed, the Joint Chiefs of Staff, all criticized the convention for failing to explicitly prohibit the *use* of biological weapons.[69]

Most people agreed that it was impossible to verify a ban on biological weapons adequately. Yet, as Representative Richard McCarthy suggested as early as 1969, policing a ban on biological weapons was irrelevant because it would be contrary to U.S. interests to ever use such weapons, given their uncontrollable effects.[70] Judging from their comments in testimony before the Congress, key figures in the Nixon administration, such as ACDA Director Fred Iklé, apparently held a similar view.[71]

Administration officials also pointed out that because the United States had already unilaterally decided to renounce biological warfare and eliminate its biological weapons stocks, verification considerations had no bearing on the decision to become a party to the convention. Thus, although the administration recognized that the agreement could not be adequately verified, it believed, according to ACDA Director Iklé, that "by failing to ratify [the Convention], we would deny ourselves the benefit of having other countries legally committed not to produce weapons that we have already given up."[72]

In deciding that the benefits of the treaty outweighed its verification limitations, the administration also took into consideration the particularly repugnant nature of biological weapons, as well as concerns about the possible application of new developments in the biological sciences to military ends. ACDA Director Iklé warned in conclusion, however, that "the limited verifiability of this Convention should not be misconstrued as a precedent for other arms limitation agreements where these special conditions would not obtain."[73]

Supporters of the Biological and Toxin Weapons Convention also drew attention to the various arms control implications of the agreement. Although concerned about certain verification aspects of the Convention, Jozef Goldblat noted that it was, undeniably, "the first real disarmament step taken during the whole postwar period."[74] Joshua Lederberg expressed the hope that the treaty would reduce the prospects of a biological weapons race between the United States and the Soviet Union.[75] Finally, nearly everyone hoped that the BWC would enhance the likelihood of additional progress in CBW arms control—more specifically, that it would lead to a similar agreement banning chemical weapons.

On a more general level, proponents of the convention argued that the agreement would help reduce suspicions and tensions between states, and perhaps even contribute to international scientific cooperation in the field of microbiology. In his remarks at the signing ceremony for the treaty, President Nixon expressed the hope that "all of the scientists of the world . . . instead of working to develop biological weapons which one nation might use against another nation, now may devote their entire energy toward working against the enemy of all mankind—disease."[76]

CONCLUSIONS

The Biological and Toxin Weapons Convention of 1972 was the first and only postwar arms control agreement to require the complete elimination of an entire category of weapons from the arsenals of states. Similar efforts with respect to nuclear and conventional weapons in the period immediately after World War II, as well as the more recent nuclear disarmament proposals at the October 1986 Reykjavik summit, received much attention but were never the subject of serious, much less successful, negotiations. It is worth examining, therefore, what the BWC tells us about the prerequisites for, and effects of, arms control and disarmament agreements.

Clearly, one of the primary reasons that states were prepared to eliminate their existing stockpiles of biological weapons or, in the case of nonbiological weapons states, to forgo future developments in this area, was because they doubted whether biological weapons had much deterrent or military value. Moreover, although few countries had made a significant investment in biological weapons, the possibility of proliferation, either as a result of the opportunities created by new technology or because of the ability of biological weapons to provide states with a relatively cheap mass destruction capability, could not be discounted and was in fact greatly feared.

These military and political considerations provided much of the impetus for the new biological weapons policy announced by President Nixon in November 1969. This new policy, in turn, was an important stimulus to the negotiations that culminated in the BWC. As the president described it,

> We are prepared to take any unilateral arms control action that will not compromise our security and will minimize the danger that certain weapons will ever be developed or used by any nation. A good example is the field of chemical and biological weapons. After extensive study, I determined that a new American policy [of unilateral restraint] would strengthen ongoing multilateral efforts to restrict the use of these weapons by international law.[77]

President Nixon's unilateral renunciation of biological weapons and the subsequent achievement of the BWC suggest that unilateral restraint *can* exert a positive influence on the arms control process. Yet the failure to achieve a similar ban on chemical weapons, despite a U.S. moratorium on their production since 1969, likewise suggests that unilateral restraint may be helpful only when the parties to the negotiations have already determined that the weapons concerned do not have much military utility and that their retention may be more harmful to the parties' security interests than might their elimination. Of course, the renunciation of an entire category of weapons is a very different form of unilateral restraint than a moratorium on weapons production. This suggests that different types of unilateral restraint may influence arms control negotiations in different ways.

The Biological and Toxin Weapons Convention also provides insight into the question of the effect of such agreements on weapons programs. As has been shown, the BWC was achieved precisely because many countries, the United States included, had serious doubts about the military value of biological weapons. These doubts were an important consideration in President Nixon's 1969 decision to unilaterally renounce biological and toxin methods of warfare, a decision that preceded the negotiation of the BWC. The BWC would therefore appear to illustrate the hypothesis that arms control agreements simply codify existing defense plans.

During the BWC negotiations, many countries nevertheless feared that a separate ban on biological weapons would redirect the arms competition in counterproductive ways by stimulating further efforts to develop chemical weapons. President Nixon's 1969 decision to impose a moratorium on U.S. production of new chemical weapons was apparently an attempt to meet this concern.[78] Starting in the mid-1970s, however, the Pentagon repeatedly sought congressional approval of a new type of chemical weapon, known as binaries.[79] The Congress finally made funds available for the production of these new chemical weapons in the fall of 1986. According to the Pentagon, the Soviet Union has continued to add to its stockpile of chemical weapons in the years since the negotiation of the BWC.[80] U.S. officials also estimate that at least thirteen other countries now possess chemical weapons and in one case, the Gulf War, their use has been unambiguously confirmed.[81] It seems reasonable to conclude, however, that this expansion of the capabilities and membership of the chemical club probably has had less to do with the achievement of the BWC than with the failure to achieve a similar agreement banning chemical weapons.

The issue of verification received comparatively little attention in the domestic U.S. debate over the Biological and Toxin Weapons

Convention. Although most observers agreed at the time that compliance with the Convention could not be verified, it was also widely believed that such verification was irrelevant because biological weapons had little real military utility. Hence, even if the agreement was not complied with, a violation would have little military significance.

In recent years, U.S. charges of Soviet noncompliance with the BWC have highlighted certain weaknesses in the 1972 Convention.[82] These weaknesses—such as the absence of verification provisions, the toothless compliance provision, and the ambiguous treaty language— have made it exceedingly difficult to determine whether there have been violations of the BWC. The resulting noncompliance controversies have severely undermined confidence in the convention.

The main noncompliance allegation in which the Soviet Union has been implicated involves the use of "yellow rain" in Southeast Asia and Afghanistan. According to the U.S. government, the Soviet Union supplied toxins and other unidentified chemical agents to the Vietnamese for use in Laos and Cambodia, and itself employed the same agents in Afghanistan following its 1979 invasion of that country. These charges are based on the detection of toxins in physical samples from the environment and from victims from the areas concerned; reports from refugees, defectors, and others who have conducted investigations; and other evidence from documentary and intelligence sources.

Vietnam and the Soviet Union have repeatedly rejected the U.S. yellow rain charges. But the most serious challenge to the U.S. accusations has come from other investigations. Neither the British government nor a U.S. army lab has found toxins in any of the yellow rain samples that they have analyzed. Britain, Australia, Thailand, Canada, and a United Nations Expert Group did, however, find *pollen* in environmental samples collected from Southeast Asia. This discovery of pollen led a number of scientists, including Harvard biochemist Matthew Meselson, to conclude that the material known as yellow rain was actually the feces of Southeast Asian honey bees and not a residue from chemical warfare attacks. Meselson and other scientists also speculated that the toxins found in U.S. yellow rain samples were indigenous to the environment and foodstuffs of Southeast Asia but had no evidence to support their theory until May 1986, when the Canadian government acknowledged finding toxins in the blood of several people from Thailand who were not victims of chemical attacks. The Canadian results indicate that the toxins the United States charged the Soviet Union with supplying to the Vietnamese may occur naturally in the environment and food supply of Southeast Asia.

The United States also claims that the Soviet Union has violated the Biological and Toxin Weapons Convention by engaging in a biological warfare research and development program whose purpose is to develop biological weapons. U.S. officials suggest that the anthrax outbreak in the Soviet city of Sverdlovsk in 1979 may have been related to such illegal activities.[83]

From the Reagan administration's perspective, yellow rain, Soviet BW research and development activities, and the Sverdlovsk incident are all tangible proof that, in the words of then Deputy Assistant Secretary of Defense Douglas Feith, "the Soviet Union has not only violated the BWC, but every major prohibition in it."[84] Thus, as far as the Reagan administration is concerned, the experience with the Biological and Toxin Weapons Convention clearly illustrates that the Soviet Union complies with neither the spirit nor the letter of arms control agreements. Despite the Reagan administration's claims, however, the evidence for all three of these noncompliance cases is ambiguous at best.

On the other hand, the administration is correct that the experience with the BWC reveals that ambiguity in agreements does not offer a solution to verification and compliance problems. The failure of the BWC to require procedures for verifying compliance, such as on-site inspection, and to provide for an institutionalized structure for resolving noncompliance concerns, such as the SALT I agreement's Standing Consultative Commission, makes it exceedingly difficult for parties to the agreement to resolve compliance questions satisfactorily. Likewise, the absence of clear guidelines as to the types or quantities of agent that may be retained for "peaceful" purposes makes it nearly impossible to determine whether a country is engaged in activities that violate the convention.

In the final analysis, however, perceptions of the verification and compliance requirements for a treaty reflect both the prevailing view of the military utility of the weapons involved and the political climate between the parties to the agreement. If a weapon is viewed as being of little or no military utility, states may be willing to ban that particular weapon even if the agreement cannot be adequately verified. This was certainly the situation with respect to the BWC. However, if a weapon is believed to be militarily useful, or if perceptions of the military utility of a weapon change, the verification requirements for that weapon will, necessarily, be different. The Reagan administration's recent criticisms of the BWC may in part reflect a new view of the military utility of biological weapons.

Ultimately, however, it is the political climate between the parties to an agreement that is probably most important. As a 1974 House Foreign Affairs Committee report pointed out, when relations between the United States and the Soviet Union are relatively friendly, as during the decade of détente, the requirements for "adequate" verification are perceived differently. During periods of confrontation, however, more demanding levels of verification are expected.[85] The BWC was a product of détente. Much of the current concern about the convention's verification and compliance procedures reflects the tensions in East-West relations that have arisen since the late 1970s. The U.S. charges of Soviet violations of the BWC have both influenced and been influenced by these tensions in East-West relations and have severely undermined support for the convention.

As with verification, the problem of lulling was not a controversial issue during the negotiation or ratification of the BWC. Shortly before President Nixon's November 1969 announcement, the Pentagon pointed out that unilateral CB disarmament would eventually "seriously degrade" the U.S. CB defensive capability.[86] In December 1974, as the Senate Foreign Relations Committee began its consideration of the BWC, the Joint Chiefs of Staff advised Committee Chairman J.W. Fulbright, in a letter of support for the convention, that it was "both prudent and necessary that the United States maintain the effective biological defenses permitted" by the agreement.[87]

An examination of BW research expenditures in the period immediately before and after the United States ratified the BWC suggests that the convention had little independent impact on U.S. biological defense efforts. The first and most dramatic decline in defensive research occurred immediately after President Nixon's 1969 decision to unilaterally renounce biological methods of warfare, when spending fell from $64.6 million in FY 1970 to $15.2 million by FY 1975. In FY 1976, the year after the BWC entered into force, biological defense spending rose to $22 million. Expenditures on biological defense declined again to $18.4 million in the following fiscal year and continued to do so by an average of $1 million per year for the remainder of the decade.[88] These declines were reversed by the

Reagan administration, which nearly doubled biological defense spending between FY 1982 and 1984.[89] The dramatic increase in biological defense spending under the Reagan administration has reflected a combination of concern about possible Soviet violations of the BWC and interest in the potential military implications of new developments in the biological sciences.

The BWC also provides insight into the extent to which public and congressional support for arms control agreements influence the arms control process. As has been shown, CBW reemerged as a controversial issue in the late 1960s as a result of the use of riot control agents and herbicides by U.S. forces in Vietnam and because of a number of other incidents involving chemical weapons. These events, and the concern they aroused both in the United States and abroad, almost guaranteed that any new agreement restricting CBW would be widely supported by both the general public and the Congress. This was certainly the case with the Biological and Toxin Weapons Convention. Although a few observers expressed concern about certain provisions of the treaty, almost no one opposed the agreement itself or the principle on which it was based. This was clear from the unanimous approval that the BWC received from both the Senate Foreign Relations Committee and the full Senate.

Congress was not an active participant in the negotiations on the BWC. But as a result of the efforts of Representative Richard McCarthy and other critics of U.S. CBW policy, as well as the active interest in CBW issues displayed by congressional committees, Congress helped create a climate conducive to the reevaluation of U.S. CBW policy and to the negotiation of further constraints on these weapons. Thus, in the final analysis, political support for the BWC was rooted in public and congressional concern about the direction of U.S. CBW policy.

Finally, the historical record shows that at no time during the negotiation or ratification of the BWC was it ever suggested that this agreement would serve Soviet interests more than those of the United States. President Nixon's unilateral renunciation of biological weapons in 1969 was clearly based on the view that it would be contrary to U.S. interests to ever use such weapons given their unpredictable and uncontrollable effects. Although the United States recognized that the Biological and Toxin Weapons Convention could not be adequately verified, it supported the convention because, as

ACDA Director Iklé suggested, it served U.S. interests to have other countries legally committed to the same renunciation of biological weapons.

In recent years, the Reagan administration has argued that advances in biotechnology now make it possible to develop biological agents that are militarily more useful and to produce and store such agents more easily. According to administration officials, "Because this new technology makes possible a massive and rapid break-out, the treaty constitutes an insignificant impediment at best."[90] Although administration officials promise that the United States will, nevertheless, remain a party to the convention, they emphasize that "the BWC must be recognized as critically deficient and unfixable."[91] The Reagan administration's claims regarding biotechnology, coupled with its charges of Soviet noncompliance with the 1972 Convention, thus implicitly suggest that the Biological and Toxin Weapons Convention now serves Soviet interests more than those of the United States.

No other country has expressed such harsh views of the BWC, although a number of states have raised concerns about the possible implications of biotechnology for the development of BW agents. These concerns were reflected in several working papers at the second review conference for the Convention, held in Geneva in September 1986.[92] Many scientists continue to believe, however, that the stability and reliability problems of traditional biological agents are also likely to plague agents produced using biotechnology.[93] The new technology may make it easier to produce these biological agents, but the problems associated with using such agents for military purposes are, in their opinion, likely to remain. This suggests that from a military point of view, states should not find biological weapons to be any more attractive today than in 1969, when President Nixon unilaterally renounced biological methods of warfare, or in 1975, when the BWC entered into force. Contrary to what the Reagan administration seems to believe, the BWC never was the major impediment to the development of biological weapons. Rather, the convention simply reflected the view that biological weapons had little militarily utility. With a few exceptions, that remains the predominant view today.

NOTES

I would like to thank John Ellis van Courtland Moon and Nicholas A. Sims for their helpful comments on an earlier draft of this chapter, as well as John Wertheimer for research assistance.

1. U.S. Arms Control and Disarmament Agency, *Documents on Disarmament, 1972* (Washington, D.C.: U.S. Government Printing Office, 1974), p. 554 (hereafter cited as *Documents on Disarmament*, with appropriate year).

2. *Public Papers of the Presidents: Richard Nixon, 1969* (Washington, D.C.: U.S. Government Printing Office, 1971), pp. 968–69. In 1969 the membership of the committee was expanded to twenty-six members and the name changed from the Eighteen Nation Disarmament Committee to the Conference of the Committee on Disarmament. To avoid confusion, the term *Disarmament Committee* will be used to identify this multilateral negotiating body.

3. "White House Statement on the President's Decision To Renounce Toxins as a Method of Warfare, February 14, 1970."

4. For a good discussion of the history of this agreement, see George Bunn, "Gas and Germ Warfare: International Legal History and Present Status," *Proceedings of the National Academy of Sciences* 65 (1) (1970), pp. 253–60. See also Joshua Lederberg, "The Control of Chemical and Biological Weapons," *Stanford Journal of International Studies* 7 (Spring 1972), pp. 23–29.

5. *Public Papers of the Presidents: Richard Nixon, 1969*, p. 968.

6. "Message to the Senate Transmitting the Geneva Protocol of 1925 on Chemical and Bacteriological Methods of Warfare, August 19, 1970," *Press Release* (Washington, D.C.: Office of the White House Press Secretary, Aug. 19, 1970). The United States did not ratify the Geneva Protocol until January 22, 1975, because of a dispute between the Nixon administration and the Senate Foreign Relations Committee over the status of riot control agents and herbicides under the Protocol. See, for example, *Congressional Record*, June 8, 1971, pp. S8486–87. The issue was finally resolved in December 1974, when the Ford administration announced a new national policy governing the use of riot control agents and herbicides. U.S. Senate Committee on Foreign Relations, *Hearings on the Prohibition of Chemical and Biological Weapons*, 93d Cong., 2d Sess. (Washington, D.C.: U.S. Government Printing Office, 1974), pp. 11–30. See also U.S. Senate Committee on Foreign Relations, *The Geneva Protocol of 1925*, Executive Report No. 93–95, 93d Cong., 2d Sess. (Washington, D.C.: U.S. Government Printing Office, 1974).

7. Lederberg, "The Control of Chemical and Biological Weapons," pp. 27–28.

8. See, for example, U.S. Senate Committee on Foreign Relations, *Hearings on Chemical and Biological Warfare*, 91st Cong., 1st Sess. (Washington, D.C.: U.S. Government Printing Office, 1969), p. 47. For the text of a report by the International Committee of the Red Cross on the Egyptian use of poison gas in Yemen, see "Text of the Red Cross Report on the Use of Poison Gas in Yemen," *The New York Times*, July 28, 1967, p. 9.

9. See, for example, U.S. House Subcommittee on National Security Policy and Scientific Development of the Committee on Foreign Affairs, *Hearings on Chemical and Biological Warfare: U.S. Policies and International Effects*, 91st Cong., 1st Sess. (Washington, D.C.: U.S. Government Printing Office, 1970), pp. 2, 8, 220.

10. For a detailed discussion of this incident, see Richard D. McCarthy, M.C., *The Ultimate Folly: War by Pestilence, Asphyxiation, and Defoliation* (New York: Knopf, 1970), pp. 99–101.

11. Philip M. Boffey, "Nerve Gas: Dugway Accident Linked to Utah Sheep Kill," *Science* 162 (3861) (Dec. 27, 1968), pp. 1460–64.

12. McCarthy, *The Ultimate Folly*, pp. 102–09. The army plan, which was hotly criticized in congressional hearings, was eventually abandoned. See, for example, U.S. House Subcommittee on International Organizations and Movements of the Committee on Foreign Affairs, *Hearings on International Implications of Dumping Poisonous Gas and Waste into Oceans*, 91st Cong., 1st Sess. (Washington, D.C.: U.S. Government Printing Office, 1969).

13. See Takashi Oka, "Okinawa Report on Gas Provides Windfall for Opposition in Japan," *The New York Times*, July 20, 1969, p. 4; and Ralph Blumenthal, "Bonn Asserts U.S. Has Given No Word on Nerve Gas Stores," *The New York Times*, July 24, 1969, p. 10.

14. Matthew S. Meselson, "Chemical and Biological Weapons," *Scientific American* 222 (5) (May 1970), p. 4.

15. For some of the hearings, see U.S. Senate Committee on Foreign Relations, *Hearings on Chemical and Biological Warfare*; U.S. House Committee on Foreign Affairs, *Hearings on CBW: U.S. Policies and International Effects*; U.S. Senate Committee on Foreign Relations, *Hearings on The Geneva Protocol of 1925*, 92d Cong., 1st Sess. (Washington, D.C.: U.S. Government Printing Office, 1972); and U.S. House Subcommittee on National Security Policy and Scientific Developments of the Committee on Foreign Affairs, *Hearings on U.S. Chemical Warfare Policy*, 93d Cong., 2d Sess. (Washington, D.C.: U.S. Government Printing Office, 1974). For some of the congressional resolutions, see *Congressional Record*, July 23, 1971, pp. S11920–21; *Congressional Record*, Jan. 29, 1973, pp. S1462–65; and U.S. House Committee on Foreign Affairs, *Ratification of the Geneva Protocol of 1925*, Report No. 93–1257, 93d Cong., 2d Sess. (Washington, D.C.: U.S. Government Printing Office, 1974).

16. For a brief discussion of these restrictions, see Bunn, "Gas and Germ War-fare: International Legal History and Present Status," p. 260.

17. Bryce Nelson, "Arms Control: Demand for Decisions . . . CBW," *Science* 162 (3858) (Dec. 6, 1968), p. 1107.

18. See, for example, Seymour M. Hersh, *Chemical and Biological Warfare: America's Hidden Arsenal* (Indianapolis: Bobbs-Merrill, 1968), and Robin Clarke, *The Silent Weapons* (New York: McKay, 1968).

19. See, *Documents on Disarmament, 1969*, pp. 743–44.

20. Samuel Z. Goldhaber, "CBW: Interagency Conflicts Stall Administration Action," *Science* 169 (3944) (July 31, 1970), pp. 454–55. For other reports on delays in the implementation of Nixon's new BW policy, see "Gas and Germ Warfare Renounced but Lingers On," *Nature* 228 (5273) (Nov. 21, 1970), pp. 707–08; and Richard A. Fineberg, "No More Chemical/Biological War?," *The New Republic* 167 (21) (Dec. 2, 1972), pp. 17–19.

21. For the British working paper, see *Documents on Disarmament, 1968*, pp. 569–71. For the draft convention, see *Documents on Disarmament, 1969*, pp. 324–26.

22. "Statement by Ambassador George Bush, United States Representative to the United Nations, in Committee I, on Disarmament, November 11, 1971," *Press Release* (New York: U.S. Mission to the United Nations, Nov. 11, 1971).

23. D. S. Greenberg, "CBW: Britain Holds Open House at Its Biological Weapons Center," *Science* 162 (3855) (Nov. 15, 1968), p. 782.

24. For an interesting discussion of CBW protests in Britain in 1968, see John Walsh, "CBW: British Protests Grow About Porton Center," *Science* 160 (3834) (June 21, 1968), pp. 1318–22.

25. *Chemical and Bacteriological (Biological) Weapons and the Effects of Their Possible Use*, A United Nations Report, No. E.69.124 (New York: Ballantine Books, 1970), pp. xxvi, 156–57. The secretary general also called on the member states of the United Nations to accede to the Geneva Protocol of 1925 and to affirm that the 1925 agreement prohibited the use of riot control agents and herbicides, as well.

26. For a summary of the report "Health Effects of Possible Use of Chemical and Biological Weapons—Report of a WHO Group of Consultants," see U.S. House Committee on Foreign Affairs, *CBW U.S. Policies and International Effects*, pp. 443–50.

27. *Documents on Disarmament, 1969*, pp. 716–17.

28. Matthew Meselson, "Tear Gas in Vietnam and the Return of Poison Gas," *Bulletin of the Atomic Scientists* (March 1971), p. 17.

29. *Documents on Disarmament, 1969*, pp. 324–26. For later British drafts of the convention, see *Documents on Disarmament, 1969*, pp. 431–33, and *Documents on Disarmament, 1970*, pp. 428–31.

30. *Documents on Disarmament, 1969*, pp. 455–57. For a later draft convention, see *Documents on Disarmament, 1970*, pp. 533–37.

31. See, for example, *Documents on Disarmament, 1970*, pp. 101–03.

32. *Ibid.*, pp. 101–06.

33. See, for example, *Documents on Disarmament, 1970*, p. 97.

34. See, for example, *Documents on Disarmament, 1969*, p. 321; and *Documents on Disarmament, 1971*, p. 469.

35. On August 25, 1970, for example, the neutral and nonaligned members of the Disarmament Committee stated in a memorandum that chemical and biological weapons should continue to be dealt with together in the work of the committee. *Documents on Disarmament, 1970*, p. 454.

36. See, for example, *Documents on Disarmament, 1969*, p. 561.

37. See, for example, *Documents on Disarmament, 1970*, p. 75.

38. See, for example, *Documents on Disarmament, 1969*, p. 585.

39. *Ibid.*

40. Stockholm International Peace Research Institute, *The Problem of Chemical and Biological Warfare, Vol. IV, CB Disarmament Negotiations, 1920–1970* (Stockholm: Almqvist and Wiksell, 1971), p. 294.

41. *Documents on Disarmament, 1968*, p. 562.

42. See, for example, *Documents on Disarmament, 1970*, p. 104.

43. *Documents on Disarmament, 1971*, pp. 185–94.

44. Lederberg, "The Control of Chemical and Biological Weapons," p. 31.

45. *Documents on Disarmament, 1971*, pp. 456–60.

46. This revised draft convention reflected the views and recommendations of other members of the Disarmament Committee. *Documents on Disarmament, 1971*, pp. 568–73.

47. *Documents on Disarmament, 1971*, pp. 884–89.

48. *Documents on Disarmament, 1972*, pp. 553–55. See also *ibid.*, pp. 380–86.

49. U.S. Senate Committee on Foreign Relations, *Convention on the Prohibition of Bacteriological and Toxin Weapons*, Executive Report No. 93-36, 93d Cong., 2d Sess. (Washington, D.C.: U.S. Government Printing Office, 1974).

50. U.S. Senate Committee on Foreign Relations, *Prohibition of Chemical and Biological Weapons*, p. 1.

51. U.S. House Committee on Foreign Affairs, *CBW: U.S. Policies and International Effects*, p. 358. Five and a half years later, however, in the context of a discussion of the U.S. decision to unilaterally renounce its biological weapons program, the Joint Chiefs of Staff advised the Senate Foreign Relations Committee that they did not believe that biological warfare was "essential to our deterrent posture." U.S. Senate Committee on Foreign Relations, *Prohibition of Chemical and Biological Weapons*, p. 63.

52. Ivan L. Bennett, Jr., "The Significance of Chemical and Biological Warfare for the People," *Proceedings of the National Academy of Sciences* 65 (1) (1970), p. 275.

53. *Documents on Disarmament, 1970*, pp. 102–03.

54. U.S. House Committee on Foreign Affairs, *CBW: U.S. Policies and International Effects*, p. 184. See also the exchange between Representative Donald Fraser and Representative John Dellenback, and the views of Joshua Lederberg, in the same series of hearings, pp. 23–24 and 88, respectively. See also Bennett, "The Significance of Chemical and Biological Warfare for the People," p. 276.

55. U.S. House Committee on Foreign Affairs, *CBW: U.S. Policies and International Effects*, p. 9. Representative Richard McCarthy made a similar point in the same hearing. See *ibid.*, pp. 38–39. However, in a later hearing, Han Swyter, a former Pentagon official, stated that he believed that the intelligence community did possess information on the Soviet offensive BW program. *Ibid.*, p. 115.

56. See, for example, the written comments of John S. Foster, director of Defense, Research, and Engineering, to Representative Richard McCarthy, in U.S. House Committee on Foreign Affairs, *CBW: U.S. Policies and International Effects*, pp. 353, 358. For one of the few expressions of continued support for biological weapons following President Nixon's 1969 announcement, see the letter to President Nixon from Charles Conrad, speaker of the California Assembly, dated November 27, 1969, reprinted in U.S. House Committee on Foreign Affairs, *CBW: U.S. Policies and International Effects*, pp. 151–54.

57. Matthew S. Meselson, "Behind the Nixon Policy for Chemical and Biological Warfare," *Bulletin of the Atomic Scientists* (January 1970), p. 26.

58. See, for example, *Documents on Disarmament, 1970*, p. 102. The Joint Chiefs of Staff were also apparently concerned about this particular characteristic of biological weapons. U.S. Senate Committee on Foreign Relations, *Prohibition of Chemical and Biological Weapons*, p. 62. For an example of congressional views on this issue, see John Dellenback, Charles A. Mosher, Howard W. Robison, and Fred Schwengel, "CBW and National Security—November 3, 1969," U.S. House Committee on Foreign Affairs, *CBW: U.S. Policies and International Effects*, p. 285.

59. Meselson, "Behind the Nixon Policy for Chemical and Biological Warfare," pp. 28–29. See also Dellenback et al., "CBW and National Security—November 3, 1969," in U.S. House Committee on Foreign Affairs, *CBW: U.S. Policies and International Effects*, p. 286.

60. Meselson, "Behind the Nixon Policy for Chemical and Biological Warfare," p. 26.

61. *Ibid.*, p. 33.

62. See, for example, Han Swyter, "Political Considerations and Analysis of Military Requirements for Chemical and Biological Weapons," *Proceedings of the National Academy of Sciences* 65 (1) (1970), p. 262.

63. Bennett, "The Significance of Chemical and Biological Warfare for the People," p. 274.

64. U.S. House Committee on Foreign Affairs, *CBW: U.S. Policies and International Effects*, p. 353.

65. See, for example, *Documents on Disarmament, 1970*, p. 101. See also *Documents on Disarmament, 1971*, p. 468.

66. Bennett, "The Significance of Chemical and Biological Warfare for the People," pp. 273–74.

67. Swyter, "Political Considerations and Analysis of Military Requirements for Chemical and Biological Weapons," p. 266. This concern was also shared by the Congress. See U.S. House Subcommittee on National Security Policy and Scientific Developments of the Committee on Foreign Affairs, *Chemical-Biological Warfare: U.S. Policies and International Effects*, Report, 91st Cong., 2d Sess. (Washington, D.C.: U.S. Government Printing Office, 1970), p. 7.

68. See, for example, Lederberg, "The Control of Chemical and Biological Weapons," p. 33; Jozef Goldblat, "Biological Disarmament," *Bulletin of the Atomic Scientists* 28 (4) (April 1972), p. 10; and "Outlawing Germ Warfare," *The Washington Post*, Aug. 8, 1971, p. B6.

69. Goldblat, "Biological Disarmament," pp. 6, 8–9; and Lederberg, "The Control of Chemical and Biological Weapons," pp. 32–34; For the Joint Chiefs of Staff's concerns see U.S. Senate Committee on Foreign Relations, *Prohibition of Chemical and Biological Weapons*, pp. 62–63.

70. U.S. House Committee on Foreign Affairs, *CBW: U.S. Policies and International Effects*, p. 38. For a similar view, see the comments of George Bunn, on pp. 74–75.

71. U.S. Senate Committee on Foreign Relations, *Prohibition of Chemical and Biological Weapons*, p. 15. This point was also emphasized by Leon Sloss, deputy director Political-Military Affairs, Department of State, in U.S. House Committee on Foreign Affairs, *U.S. Chemical Warfare Policy*, p. 176.

72. U.S. Senate Committee on Foreign Relations, *Prohibition of Chemical and Biological Weapons*, p. 16. As one of the three depositories, U.S. ratification was essential for the treaty to come into force. See also the comments of Amos Jordan, acting assistant secretary for International Security Affairs, Department of Defense, in U.S. House Committee on Foreign Affairs, *U.S. Chemical Warfare Policy*, p. 168; and of the Joint Chiefs of Staff, in U.S. Senate Committee on Foreign Relations, *Prohibition of Chemical and Biological Weapons*, p. 63.

73. *Ibid.*, pp. 15-16. This warning was also echoed by the Joint Chiefs of Staff, on p. 63.

74. Goldblat, "Biological Disarmament," p. 10. A similar point was made earlier by the U.S. representative to the Geneva Disarmament Committee in reference to the British draft convention. *Documents on Disarmament, 1971*, p. 118.

75. Lederberg, "The Control of Chemical and Biological Weapons," pp. 33-34.

76. "Remarks at the Signing Ceremony of the Biological Weapons Convention, April 10, 1972," *Public Papers of the Presidents: Richard Nixon, 1972* (Washington, D.C.: U.S. Government Printing Office, 1974), p. 525. See also Goldblat, "Biological Disarmament," p. 10.

77. *Public Papers of the Presidents: Richard Nixon, 1970*, p. 185.

78. *Documents on Disarmament, 1970*, p. 106.

79. In the binary chemical weapons, two nonlethal chemicals mix to form lethal nerve agent in the projectile or bomb after it has been fired at a target. The existing U.S. stockpile of chemical weapons contain the lethal nerve agent itself and are known as unitary chemical weapons.

80. See, for example, U.S. Department of Defense, *Continuing Development of Chemical Weapons Capabilities in the USSR* (Washington, D.C.: Department of Defense, October 1983), p. 8; and U.S. Defense Intelligence Agency, Directorate for Scientific and Technical Intelligence, *Soviet Chemical Weapons Threat* (Washington, D.C.: Defense Intelligence Agency, 1985), DST-1620F-051-85, p. 9.

81. Caspar W. Weinberger, *Annual Report to the Congress, Fiscal Year 1986* (Washington, D.C.: U.S. Government Printing Office, 1985), p. 282. For a more detailed discussion of the CW proliferation problem, see Lois Ember, "Worldwide Spread of Chemical Arms Receiving Increased Attention," *Chemical and Engineering News* (April 14, 1986), pp. 8-16.

82. The following discussion on noncompliance is based on a more detailed study of these issues in Elisa D. Harris, "Sverdlovsk and Yellow Rain: Two Cases of Soviet Noncompliance?," *International Security* 11 (4) (Spring 1987), pp. 41-95.

83. See, for example, U.S. Department of Defense, *Soviet Military Power, 1984* (Washington, D.C.: U.S. Government Printing Office, 1984), p. 73; and U.S. Department of Defense, Defense Intelligence Agency, *Soviet Biological Warfare Threat* (Washington, D.C.: U.S. Government Printing Office, 1986).

84. U.S. House Subcommittee on Oversight and Evaluation of the Permanent Select Committee on Intelligence, "Testimony on Biological and Toxin Weapons," Douglas J. Feith, Deputy Assistant Secretary of Defense for Negotiation Policy, Aug. 8, 1986, p. 7.

85. U.S. House Committee on Foreign Affairs, *Ratification of the Geneva Protocol*, pp. 5–6.

86. U.S. House Committee on Foreign Affairs, *CBW: U.S. Policies and International Effects*, p. 358.

87. U.S. Senate Committee on Foreign Relations, *Prohibition of Chemical and Biological Weapons*, p. 63.

88. In constant fiscal year 1979 dollars. The current-year dollar obligations for biological research, development, testing, and evaluation (RDT&E) for fiscal years 1970 to 1973 are from Stockholm International Peace Research Institute, *The Problem of Chemical and Biological Warfare, Vol. II, CB Weapons Today* (Stockholm: Almqvist and Wiksell, 1973), pp. 204–05. The current-year dollar obligations for biological RDT&E for fiscal years 1974 to 1979 may be found in the *Congressional Record* of March 11, 1974, p. S6127; Sept. 12, 1974, p. S31021; March 17, 1975, p. S6910; Sept. 19, 1975, p. S29528; Feb. 11, 1977, p. S4440; March 17, 1978, p. S4025; July 19, 1979, p. S9921; and Aug. 5, 1980, p. S21834. The author was unable to locate budget figures for the final year, fiscal year 1980.

89. For current-year dollar obligations for biological RDT&E for fiscal years 1981 to 1983, see Jonathan Tucker, "Gene Wars," *Foreign Policy* 57 (Winter 1984–85), pp. 68–69.

90. Permanent Select Committee on Intelligence, "Testimony on Biological and Toxin Weapons," p. 10.

91. *Ibid.*, p. 9.

92. See, for example, the following documents from the Second Review Conference of the Parties to the Convention on the Prohibition of the Development, Production and Stockpiling of Bacteriological (Biological) and Toxin Weapons and on their Destruction: "Background Document on New Scientific and Technological Developments Relevant to the Convention on the Prohibition of the Development, Production and Stockpiling of Bacteriological (Biological) and Toxin Weapons and on their Destruction," *BWC/CONF.II/4*, August 18, 1986; "Canadian Paper on General Nature and Magnitude of Biotechnology Activities in Canada and the Extent of Governmental Involvement Therein," *BWC/CONF.II/6*, September 10, 1986; and, "Background Document of New Scientific and Technological Developments Relevant to the Convention on the Prohibition of the Development, Production and Stockpiling of Bacteriological (Biological) and Toxin Weapons and on their Destruction," *BWC/CONF.II/4/Add.1*, August 29, 1986.

93. See, for example, Robert Mikulak, "Possible Improvements in the Biological Weapons Convention." Symposium on Biological Research and Military Policy, AAAS Annual Meeting, May 26, 1984, p. 3.

CROSS-CUTTING
ANALYSES

9 LULLING AND STIMULATING EFFECTS OF ARMS CONTROL

Sean M. Lynn-Jones

The debate over the impact of arms control on U.S. military programs has been dominated by two opposing schools of thought. The first argues that arms control agreements tend to lull the United States into spending less than it should on defense. The second claims that arms control does not reduce military spending but actually stimulates increased and possibly unnecessary military expenditures. This chapter examines these two propositions and the evidence provided by the U.S.-Soviet arms control negotiations considered in this study.

The lulling effect argument holds that arms control in the United States tends to lull the public or Congress into believing that it is no longer necessary to maintain high levels of military preparedness. It suggests that arms control produces a false sense of security that has prevented the United States from responding to the Soviet military build-up. The basic argument has been stated clearly by many defense analysts. William Van Cleave writes: "If there is a strategic arms limitation agreement, there will be a tendency to euphoria in the United States, which might well result in a paralysis of strategic force programs well beyond the actual terms of the agreement."[1] Similarly, Seymour Weiss argues that "an agreement can lull the U.S. into believing that arms control reduces—or even removes—the need for self-help military measures."[2] Few, if any, analysts claim that the Soviet Union is lulled by arms control.

The lulling effect argument is one of the most significant criticisms of U.S.-Soviet arms control for three reasons. First, since the days of the early Cold War it has been one of the most persistently employed arguments against arms control. Former U.S. Ambassador to the Soviet Union Averell Harriman worried in 1946 that the United States would be "lulled to sleep" by apparent Soviet reasonableness.[3] In May 1953 then Secretary of State John Foster Dulles warned that the Soviets might adopt a policy of "making concessions merely in order to lure others into a false sense of security."[4] Further elaborations of the lulling effect argument accompanied the development of theories of arms control in the late 1950s and early 1960s. Robert Bowie, for example, expressed concern that arms control "could create pressures to reduce military spending below the restraints imposed by the agreement."[5] As this chapter will demonstrate, similar arguments have been used against most subsequent U.S.-Soviet arms control agreements.

Second, the argument is significant because it is one of the most general indictments of arms control and, if true, could have profound implications for U.S. policy and negotiating strategy. The lulling effect argument does not rest on specific criticisms of the provisions of a particular arms control agreement. Paul Nitze, for example, claimed that SALT II "will incapacitate our minds and will. And that is more important than the specific provisions of the treaty."[6] The argument suggests that arms control measures inherently have adverse consequences for U.S. security. These costs would have to be weighed against any benefits that might result from an agreement. Even an agreement with provisions that unambiguously conferred a net advantage on the United States might generate a sense of complacency that would lead to reductions in defense spending that would outweigh any benefits obtained through the agreement itself. This prospect could provide a basis for arguing against any attempts to pursue U.S.-Soviet arms control, or it could lead to an insistence on a U.S. negotiating position that ruled out accepting any agreement that would not be so advantageous to the United States that its benefits would offset the impact of any lulling effect. Maintenance of such a negotiating position would probably preclude an agreement in any case, an outcome that might still satisfy those who worried that an agreement might lull Congress and the public. Those who fear a lulling effect might have the United States set such an impossibly

high standard for arms control that no agreement would be negotiable, a result that would guarantee that no lulling would occur. The
lulling effect argument thus provides the basis for an elegant, if somewhat circular, set of arguments against arms control.

Third, the problem of the lulling effect raises fundamental questions about the ability of the U.S. democracy to conduct foreign
policy. As Henry Kissinger has asked, "Can a democracy combine
both resolution and hope, both strength and conciliation?"[7] During
the early Cold War, many thought it was necessary to "scare the
hell" out of the U.S. people to build support for containment of the
Soviet Union.[8] This logic, which assumes that Americans will respond only to extreme threats, lies at the heart of the lulling effect
argument, for it suggests that combining arms control with defense
spending is too subtle for the U.S. public, which allegedly prefers
simplification in foreign policy.

EXPLICATING THE LULLING-EFFECT MODEL

The lulling-effect argument is often developed in the most cursory
manner. It is hard to find a comprehensive statement of the argument because when it appears it is usually intertwined with a number
of other arguments against a particular agreement or against the very
idea of arms control. The argument often remains implicit rather
than explicit. Many discussions of the lulling effect associate it only
with "many conservatives," "critics of the SALT process," or "some
administration circles." Those who adhere to the argument may be
reluctant to state it clearly for political reasons because articulat-
ing the argument might seem like an attack on the entire enterprise
of arms control, which is often thought to be politically popular.[9]

Because complete expositions of the lulling effect are rare, the
following explication draws on various sources to construct a compo-
site model of the process by which arms control is said to produce a
relaxation of defense efforts. There are some variations among different versions of the lulling effect model, but most seem to share the
same three basic stages: (1) arms control takes place; (2) a false sense
of security is thus created; (3) defense efforts are consequently
neglected.

Arms Control Takes Place

Proponents of the lulling effect argument agree that arms control can create complacency about defense in the United States, but they do not always specify what type of arms control actions generate this complacency. Some argue that "the very act of arms negotiations inevitably saps the will of the West."[10] Others identify the lulling effect with the achievement of an agreement.[11] Some defense analysts also apparently distinguish between signature and ratification of an agreement. The belief that ratification—as opposed to mere signature—of SALT II would create an adverse climate for increasing U.S. military strength was evident in the debates over the treaty.[12] This distinction may not be significant if the processes described below generate a false sense of security even in the absence of an agreement. If the U.S. public can be lulled, it may also tend to confuse arms talks with arms control. James Forrestal, the first U.S. secretary of defense, once said, "I am most apprehensive of our people's taking the *discussion* of disarmament for the fact."[13] The difference between the lulling effects of arms control negotiations, signed agreements, and ratified agreements thus may be only a matter of degree. There is, however, a separate argument that holds that the ongoing process of arms control negotiations creates incentives for unilateral U.S. restraint. This process is somewhat different from the basic lulling effect and is therefore treated separately below in connection with this chapter's analysis of the potential lulling effects of SALT II.[14]

Arms Control Creates a False Sense of Security

The false sense of security produced by arms control is the result of the difference between perceptions of the security benefits of arms control and the reality. Proponents of the lulling effect hypothesis suggest that the Congress and public tend to exaggerate the benefits of arms control and thus feel more secure than they should. This exaggeration may be the result of two potentially independent but mutually reinforcing processes.

The Agreement Is "Oversold." If the U.S. president, secretary of state, or other high-ranking administration officials decide to "oversell" an arms control agreement, they may create a sense of complacency about national security.[15] Overselling arms control consists of making claims for an agreement that exceed what can reasonably be expected, thereby inflating public expectations. Even if U.S. leaders recognize this danger, several factors contribute to their tendency to exaggerate their own accomplishments. The need to win support for reelection may encourage such exaggerations. Kenneth Adelman claims that "A glaring deficiency in our system is the unavoidable urge, nay necessity, to exaggerate in order to make an impact."[16] This problem may be accentuated in foreign policy matters because much of the U.S. public is normally uninterested in foreign affairs and will pay attention only to claims of dramatic, major achievements.

The Public "Overbuys" Arms Control.   Even if leaders assiduously avoid exaggerating the benefits of arms control, the U.S. public may still assume that an agreement promises more security than it can offer. In part, this belief is the result of basic attitudes toward international affairs that are prominent in the United States, as well as in other liberal democracies. The U.S. public tends to oppose militarism and power politics and hopes to minimize defense spending.[17] As a result, it may regard arms control "as an escape from the burdens of a national security effort."[18] The tendency to justify arms control agreements on the grounds that they will reduce the need for military spending may contribute to such expectations. This "yearning for peace" produces a "blind and willful optimism" that prevents a realistic appraisal of the impact of arms control agreements.[19] These tendencies may have become more pronounced in the nuclear age, particularly in periods when there is widespread concern about the dangers of a major nuclear war. This argument does not blame leaders for fostering a sense of euphoria but instead holds culpable "a society which extends fame and political rewards to leaders who build bad treaties, rather than urge no treaty at all."[20]

These two factors can operate separately, but the combination of a need to oversell agreements and public willingness to believe optimistic predictions for arms control would seem to make it particularly likely that arms control will foster a false sense of complacency. The Soviet Union, however, is not affected by these factors because its leaders do not have to be sensitive to public opinion or to seek reelection. Even if Soviet leaders were required to be directly responsive to public attitudes, the Soviet population might not share the liberal internationalism prevalent in the West. Thus, it is claimed, the lulling effect inevitably works to the disadvantage of the United States and its allies.

Those who make the lulling effect argument often claim that the Soviets deliberately attempt to use arms control to exploit the above factors so that U.S. defense efforts will be inhibited.[21] These claims may or may not be true, but it should be noted that the lulling effect exists independently of Soviet policy. If the tendency to oversell arms control and to exaggerate its benefits exists in the United States, it will emerge in response to an arms control agreement regardless of Soviet efforts to encourage it.

Complacency Induces Inadequate Defense Efforts

Regardless of how it is induced, the impact of the false sense of security created by arms control should be seen in U.S. public and congressional attitudes to military spending. If the lulling effect argument is correct, arms control will cause the public to oppose adequate levels of defense spending. The same change in attitudes is likely to be seen in Congress, either as a result of constituent pressure or because of the direct effect of inflated claims for arms control. Deluded by a false sense of security and under pressure from constituents who support arms reductions, members of Congress will vote to cut items from the defense budget that they believe are no longer necessary for national security.

Although the magnitude of this shift in public and congressional opinion will depend on various factors, including the extent to which the agreement has been oversold, the result will be a failure to support defense spending that would maximize U.S. military capabilities within any negotiated constraints. Those who adhere to the lulling effect argument do not specify whether this lulling will affect only the categories of weapons limited by the agreement or the entire defense budget. They seem to agree, however, that arms control will lead the public to reduce its support for defense spending to levels lower than it would have supported in the absence of arms control, and they generally claim that these levels are inadequate for U.S. national security. It is important to emphasize that the lulling effect entails reductions below the limits of any negotiated agreement or restraint in areas not limited by an agreement. For many analysts, reducing the financial burden of national security has been one of the canonical objectives of arms control. In theory, an arms control agreement could reduce military spending without adversely affecting national security.[22] Some cuts in spending on military programs might be required to comply with an agreement, but reductions that are a result of the lulling effect exceed those required by an agreement.

ARMS CONTROL AS A STIMULUS TO MILITARY PROGRAMS

Although the lulling effect argument has been prominent among many defense analysts, there are also a number of arguments that contend that arms control has not inhibited U.S. military preparedness but actually has accelerated Pentagon programs. Proponents of this view identify several models of how arms control stimulates military expenditures instead of slowing the arms race.

Intragovernmental Negotiations

One of the most significant processes through which arms control agreements directly stimulate further military expenditures is identified by what might be called the *intragovernmental negotiations model.* This model assumes that congressional support for an arms control agreement is most likely when the Joint Chiefs of Staff give it their support. J. I. Coffey argues that "no President seeking approval of any arms control agreement can afford to go strongly against the recommendation of the Joint Chiefs of Staff and/or the Secretary of Defense."[23]

The need for military support may force an administration to promise to procure new weapons demanded by the military as the price of their favorable testimony on Capitol Hill. The Joint Chiefs may insist on such compensation because they recognize that their backing is essential for Senate consent to ratification and they decide to seize the opportunity to win support for new weapons, or because they fear that the agreement will have a lulling effect and they hope to offset it. In either case, the executive branch may be persuaded to propose higher military spending and to argue that it is necessary to ensure U.S. security in conjunction with the arms control agreement.[24] The negotiation and ratification of an agreement thus stimulates some military spending that probably would not have taken place in the absence of arms control.

Bargaining Chips

A second important explanation of how arms control can serve as an impetus to new weapons involves the use of the bargaining-chip rationale to justify military programs. In the context of continuing arms control negotiations an administration may argue that congressional approval of a weapons system is necessary to make it a bargaining chip to enhance the U.S. negotiating position. This argument may be compelling to representatives and senators, who do not want to be blamed for the failure of negotiations. The bargaining-chip rationale also allows them to claim to be supporting arms control even as they vote for new weapons, thereby enabling them to satisfy several constituencies. The bargaining-chip argument, which would not be available in the absence of arms control negotiations, thus helps to gain funding for weapons that otherwise might have been cut from the budget.[25] In some cases, the weapon justified as a bargaining chip may actually be bargained away during negotiations. More often, however, the weapon may never have been meant as a chip to be traded for Soviet concessions, or it acquires too much momentum and military support to be negotiated away.[26] The cruise missile appears to exemplify the latter category. Although Henry Kissinger initially justified the weapon as a bargaining chip, he later asked, "How was I to know the military would come to love it?"[27]

The Balloon Theory: Rechanneling the Arms Race

A third hypothesis suggests that arms control tends to alter defense programs so that military efforts are accelerated in areas in which there are no constraints. This argument holds that arms control is "little more than squeezing a balloon, causing it to expand elsewhere."[28] Arms control may simply channel military competition into areas that remain unconstrained. Unlike the intragovernmental negotiations and bargaining chip models, however, this theory does not necessarily imply that arms control accelerates defense spending. The redirection of military efforts may have been planned anyway, and the model offers no explanation of why overall expenditures would increase after some programs had been limited by arms control.[29]

THE RELATIONSHIP BETWEEN THE TWO HYPOTHESES

Some analysts argue against the existence of a lulling effect by pointing to the various ways in which arms control agreements can stimulate an acceleration of military programs. Even if true, however, this argument does not necessarily or conclusively refute the lulling-effect hypothesis. The lulling-effect hypothesis and the explanations of how arms control can stimulate military spending seem to contradict one another, but they are not mutually exclusive. It is possible, for example, that arms control negotiations could stimulate funding for weapons justified as bargaining chips while an agreement could lull Congress into reducing the overall defense budget. Determining which effect would be the most important in a given situation may be difficult, much as in economics it is sometimes impossible to say on an a priori basis whether income effects or substitution effects will have the greatest impact. The fact that the two basic hypotheses are not mutually exclusive means that some analysts agree with each simultaneously, apparently believing that they are both part of the case against arms control.[30]

PROBLEMS OF TESTING THE HYPOTHESES

Testing the proposition that arms control has had a lulling or stimulating effect presents several important difficulties. First, if either proposition is stated as suggesting that arms control lulls or stimulates the United States into spending less or more than it *should* on defense, it can be tested only if one knows how much the United States should have spent on defense. Despite the emergence of a fairly broad expert and public consensus on the insufficiency of U.S.

military spending in the 1970s,[31] there is obviously considerable disagreement over the proper level of U.S. military spending during that period and at the present time.[32] Debates over the lulling effect may simply reflect debates over how much the United States should spend or should have spent on defense. One analyst might argue that the United States failed to spend enough in a given year and therefore might have been lulled by arms control, while another might claim that the same level of military spending was excessive and suggest that arms control had stimulated the United States to spend too much.

Second, if either proposition is regarded as suggesting that arms control has led the United States to spend less or more on defense than it would have spent in the absence of arms control, then the proposition is difficult to test because there is no way of knowing for certain how large the defense budget would have been in the absence of an agreement. The argument that a post-arms control change in U.S. defense spending demonstrates that the U.S. public or Congress was lulled or stimulated by an agreement could be answered by the claim that military expenditures would have changed by the same amount without any agreement. It may be difficult or impossible to separate any lulling or stimulating effect from other factors that influence levels of military spending. The determinants of the defense budget are obviously many and varied. They include changing perceptions of U.S. security needs, the relative popularity of the military in the United States, and domestic politics.[33] Any lulling or stimulating effect associated with an arms control agreement is only one of these factors. Even if its existence could be established, its impact may still have been minimal.

Despite these problems, there are several approaches to testing the lulling and stimulating hypotheses that may prove useful. This chapter will look at the following important indicators of the impact of each case of arms control considered by this study.

Overall Military Spending. Total U.S. defense outlays, as shown in Figure 9–1, may provide a very general indication of the effects of an arms control agreement. The lulling effect argument, in its broadest form, would predict a decline or slower growth in military spending in the wake of an arms control agreement, while the stimulating effect argument would predict the opposite. A sudden reversal of an existing trend would suggest that an agreement had an impact, al-

Figure 9-1. U.S. Defense Outlays, FY 1950–86 ($ billions).[a]

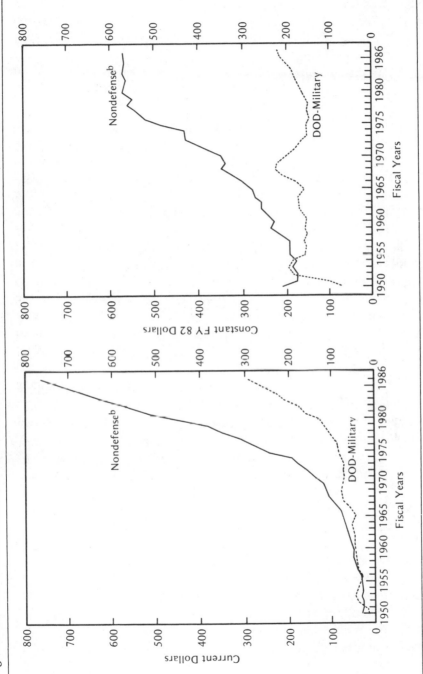

a. Outlays for FY 1982–86 are projected.

b. Includes human resources, education, health, income security, employment, training, veterans benefits, and social services.

Source: Harold Brown, *Department of Defense Annual Report, FY 1982* (Washington, D.C.: U.S. Government Printing Office, 1981), p. 316.

though pressures for changes in military spending may exist autonomously of arms control negotiations and agreements. One must bear in mind that aggregate spending is influenced by many factors other than arms control, and it may not reflect changes in specific programs related to an agreement.

Specific Categories of Military Spending.   Because the most significant cases considered in this study are concerned primarily with strategic arms control, any lulling or stimulating effect is more likely to be seen in this area (Figures 9-2 and 9-3). Increases, decreases, or variations from previous funding trends may offer some evidence for lulling or stimulating effects. This indicator is particularly relevant in assessing whether intragovernmental negotiations or the perceived need for bargaining chips have accelerated some programs. In each case, it is necessary to trace the process by which particular programs are accelerated, delayed, or terminated. As in the area of aggregate spending, many other factors influence decisions on specific strategic programs, but tracing the process can help to identify any relationship between arms control and military programs. In addition, specific changes are more likely to be linked to an agreement if they go against broader trends in aggregate defense spending.

Public Opinion Trends.   Public attitudes toward military spending and defense provide some evidence of whether arms control induces any sense of complacency (see Table 9-1). Although many factors influence public support for defense spending, a shift in attitudes that coincided with an arms control agreement would suggest that the public had become more complacent about U.S. national security.

Congressional and Executive Attitudes.   Congressional and government officials may be influenced by public opinion, or they may draw their own conclusions about the impact of arms control on U.S. security. If they are lulled by an agreement, however, their statements on defense spending or particular weapons systems might include arguments suggesting that arms control has made it possible for the United States to spend less or even to abandon a particular military program. Such statements, combined with reductions in military spending in the aftermath of an arms control agreement, would provide the most convincing evidence for the existence of a

Figure 9-2. Amount of Department of Defense's TOA Allocated to Major Force Programs.

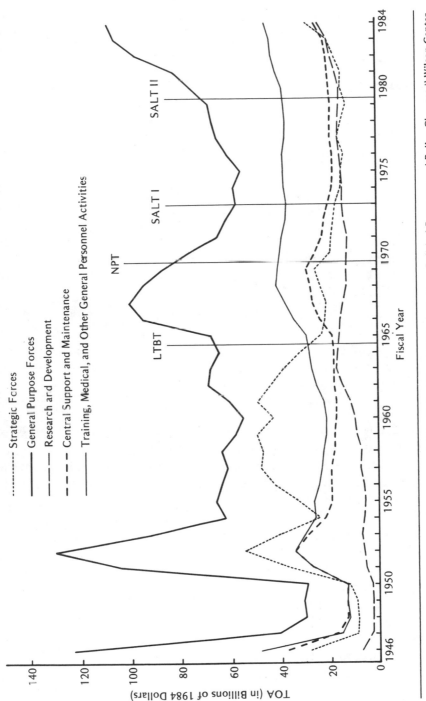

Source: Harold K. Jacobson, "The Determinants of the United States Military Posture: Political Processes and Policy Changes," Wilson Center International Security Studies Program, Working Paper No. 63, Washington, D.C.

Figure 9–3. Strategic Forces Budget Trend.

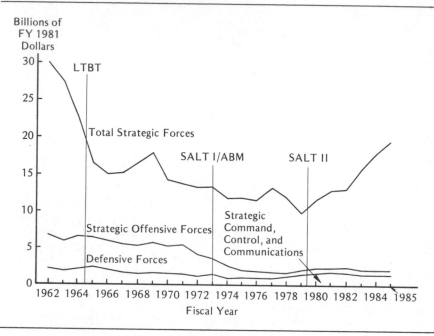

Source: Harold Brown, *Department of Defense Annual Report, Fiscal Year 1981* (Washington, D.C.: U.S. Government Printing Office, 1980), p. 71.

lulling effect, although the problem of defining adequate levels of military spending would continue to complicate the analysis.

Although the indicators employed can offer some evidence on the existence of lulling or stimulating effects of arms control, the problems cited previously make it difficult to offer definitive conclusions. The problem of determining adequate levels of defense spending and assessing what might have happened in the absence of arms control are compounded by the fact that the lulling-effect argument involves a psychological state of complacency or a false sense of security. Even when public statements by representatives, senators, or executive branch officials do not reveal any evidence of complacency or a connection between arms control and decisions on military programs, it may seem impossible to rule out the existence of a mental state of having been lulled. As a result, how one evaluates the evidence depends on where the burden of proof lies. It may be impossible to refute or prove conclusively the lulling or stimulating effect

Table 9-1. Public Attitudes toward Military Spending, 1960–85.

	Percentage Saying That U.S. Military Spending Is:			
Date of Survey	Too Much	About Right	Too Little	No Opinion
March 1960	18	45	21	16
October 1964	4	N/A	N/A	N/A
July 1969	52	31	8	9
November 1969	46	N/A	N/A	N/A
September 1970	49	34	10	7
March 1971	50	31	11	8
August 1972	42	40	9	9
February 1973	42	40	8	10
March 1973	38	45	11	6
September 1973	46	30	13	11
March 1974	31	45	17	7
September 1974	44	32	12	12
December 1974	32	47	13	N/A
March 1975	31	46	17	6
February 1976	36	32	12	12
March 1976	27	42	24	7
March 1977	23	45	24	8
July 1977	23	40	27	10
March 1978	22	43	32	8
November 1978	16	45	32	7
December 1979	22	33	34	12
January 1980	14	14	49	N/A
January 1980	14	23	46	17
March 1980	11	26	56	7
February 1981	15	22	51	12
March 1982	36	36	19	9
March 1982	30	36	29	5
November 1982	41	31	16	12
November 1982	24	52	21	3
January 1983	45	33	14	8
August 1983	42	35	14	9
September 1983	37	36	21	6
January 1985	46	36	11	7
September 1985	50	33	12	5

Sources: Gallup polls cited in Thomas W. Graham, "The Politics of Failure: Strategic Nuclear Arms Control, Public Opinion, and Domestic Politics in the United States, 1945–1985," Ph.D. Dissertation, Massachusetts Institute of Technology, forthcoming, 1987; Tom W. Smith, "The Polls: American Attitudes toward the Soviet Union and Communism," *Public Opinion Quarterly* 47 (2) (Summer 1983), p. 284; *Public Opinion* 2 (2) (March–May 1979), p. 25; and *Public Opinion* 3 (1A) (Feb.–March 1980), p. 22.

argument, and proponents of each may interpret the absence of re-futation as evidence for the continued validity of either proposition.

The overall trends in U.S. defense spending and public opinion shown in Figures 9–1 to 9–3 and Table 9–1 suggest that major changes in the budgets and attitudes do not correlate with arms control agreements. The general pattern does not support the claim that arms control has had either a lulling or a stimulating effect on military programs. Levels of military spending do seem to rise and fall in tandem with public support for the defense budget, but these fluctuations do not seem to be influenced by arms control agreements. Each case must be examined in detail, however, to determine how arms control influenced particular military programs.

THE LIMITED TEST BAN TREATY OF 1963

At the time of its negotiation and ratification, one of the arguments directed against the Limited Test Ban Treaty (LTBT) was the claim that it would induce a sense of complacency and undermine support for U.S. military efforts. Many opponents of the treaty contended that it would lull the U.S. public. This argument was made repeatedly during the Senate hearings on the treaty. Robert McNamara, then secretary of defense, supported the treaty, but he was concerned that it might create a false sense of security. He testified that "the most serious risk of this treaty is the risk of euphoria. We must guard against a condition of mind which allows us to become lax in our defenses."[34] Air Force Chief of Staff Curtis LeMay worried because "we have a tendency to become complacent from time to time."[35]

Defense budgets did decline for fiscal years 1964 and 1965 before increasing rapidly with the Vietnam build-up in FY 1966 (see Figure 9–1). This decline could be due to a sense of complacency after the LTBT went into effect, but a breakdown of the defense budget (Figures 9–2 and 9–3) shows that this decline can be attributed to the rapid decrease in spending on strategic programs that had begun in fiscal year 1962. U.S. strategic programs slowed during this period as many submarines and missiles were completed and deployed. Decisions made in 1962 or earlier were probably responsible for the sharp decline in the strategic forces budget. This decline appears to have been arrested after FY 1965.

The aftermath of the LTBT suggests that the treaty did not exert a lulling effect on U.S. defense programs but instead helped to stimulate increased efforts in the area of underground testing. As Figure 9-4 shows, U.S. underground tests increased after the LTBT was signed. The annual number of underground tests between 1964 and 1970 ranged between twenty-eight and forty. Only in 1958 and 1962 did the United States conduct more tests; in the other years before 1964 the total of U.S. atmospheric and underground tests never exceeded twenty-eight. Moreover, U.S. testing levels consistently exceeded those of the Soviet Union during the first six years in which the treaty was in force. Annual appropriations for Atomic Energy Commission nuclear testing programs rose from $133 million in 1963 to $193 million in 1967.[36] The post–1963 tests, of course, were all conducted underground rather than in the atmosphere, but the increase in this unconstrained area suggests that the treaty had—if anything—a stimulating effect on U.S. defense efforts in the area of nuclear testing.

The intragovernmental negotiations model of how arms control can accelerate military programs seems to fit well with the behavior of the Joint Chiefs of Staff in the LTBT case. On June 14, 1963, JCS Chairman Maxwell Taylor had suggested that the Chiefs might testify against a comprehensive test ban treaty, thereby reminding Kennedy administration officials of the importance of military support for any treaty.[37] After the treaty had been negotiated, the Joint Chiefs called for four safeguards to accompany the end of atmospheric testing. These safeguards included continued underground testing, maintenance of modern nuclear laboratories to attract qualified scientists, the capability to resume atmospheric testing, and an increase in U.S. capabilities to monitor Soviet testing.[38] Testifying before the Senate Foreign Relations Committee, General LeMay argued that the treaty's "disadvantages can only be made acceptable by providing these safeguards."[39] These safeguards were approved by President John Kennedy. In a September 10, 1963, letter to Senate Majority Leader Mike Mansfield and Minority Leader Everett Dirksen, he pledged that "underground testing . . . will be vigorously and diligently carried forward."[40] In his testimony before the Senate Foreign Relations Committee, Chief of Naval Operations David McDonald expressed the hope that "this treaty, together with the safeguards we have laid down, will perhaps stimulate our test programs." Senator Henry Jackson replied, "I would hope that would

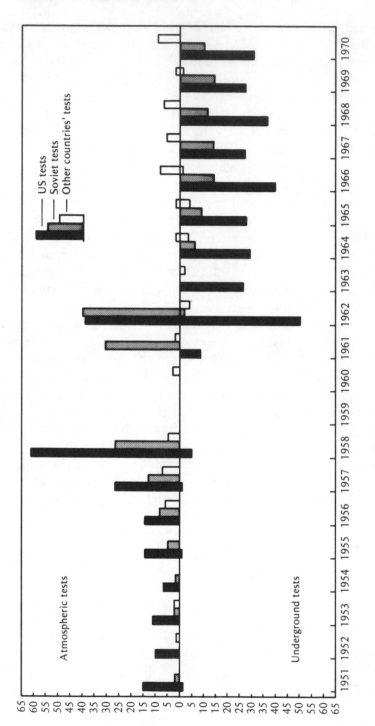

Figure 9-4.   Nuclear Tests Conducted by the United States, the USSR, the United Kingdom, France, and China, 1951–70.

Source: *World Armaments and Disarmament: SIPRI Yearbook 1972* (Stockholm: Almqvist & Wiksell, 1972), p. 408.

be the case, too, Admiral McDonald."[41] Figure 9-4 suggests that such hopes were fulfilled in the years immediately after LTBT ratification. The effect of the LTBT on U.S. nuclear testing also appears to be consistent with the balloon theory of arms control agreements. After tests in the atmosphere were constrained, military efforts were directed to another, unconstrained area. Although it is impossible to know how U.S. testing programs might have evolved in the absence of the LTBT, many defense analysts have noted that the treaty produced an immediate and deliberate acceleration in the rate of U.S. underground tests. Richard Perle, for example, has observed that "Arms control agreements have in the past stimulated development of new technologies to compensate for those limited by agreement. The art of underground nuclear testing, for example, has been rapidly advanced in both the United States and the Soviet Union since the partial nuclear test ban was signed in 1961 [sic]."[42]

The balloon theory itself, however, does not explain why military programs accelerated. A desire to prevent any lulling from taking place and the intragovernmental bargaining process that made Kennedy's approval of the four safeguards a condition for military and congressional support of the LTBT provided the impetus for increased testing efforts. Kennedy worried about a possible lulling effect of the LTBT and took pains to avoid overselling the treaty.[43] The Joint Chiefs also were at least partly motivated by fear of a possible lulling effect from the treaty. Maxwell Taylor testified that

> The most serious reservations of the Joint Chiefs of Staff with regard to the treaty are more directly linked with the fear of a euphoria in the West which will eventually reduce our vigilance and the willingness of our country and our allies to expand continued effort on our collective security.[44]

THE NUCLEAR NON-PROLIFERATION TREATY

The Non-Proliferation Treaty (NPT) differs from the other arms control agreements considered in this study in several respects that have important implications for any possible lulling or stimulating effects. Unlike most of the other agreements considered, it does not seek to remove or reduce threats that the United States and the Soviet Union pose to one another by regulating or limiting the arms of the two countries. Although Article 6 exhorts the superpowers to pursue arms control negotiations, for all practical purposes the treaty imposes no constraints on U.S. and Soviet arsenals. Instead, it attempts to reduce the threat of nuclear proliferation by eliminating the nuclear-weapons capabilities of other countries. In most U.S.-Soviet arms control agreements the two countries cooperate to limit each other's arsenals, but in the case of the NPT they cooperate in an attempt to preclude or at least limit the development of additional nuclear arsenals.

The lulling effect hypothesis suggests that U.S.-Soviet arms control produces U.S. complacency about Soviet challenges to U.S. security. Similar reasoning suggests that if the NPT has had a lulling effect it would consist of excessive complacency about the problem of nuclear proliferation and inadequate U.S. efforts to control the spread of nuclear weapons. This argument was made at the time of the NPT's ratification. In the Senate Foreign Relations Committee hearing on the treaty, Robert Strausz-Hupé claimed that "the present treaty does not provide effective safeguards against the spread of nuclear weapons."[45] Another observer later suggested that the NPT "has doubtless fostered illusions in world opinion as to the security it might provide against future dangers."[46]

Despite the assurances of administration spokesmen at the time of the NPT's ratification that the United States was "under no illusion that we need no longer worry about the proliferation of nuclear weapons,"[47] the treaty does appear to have had some lulling effect. As Joseph Nye points out in his chapter, the United States and the Soviet Union accorded lower priority to the proliferation problem after the treaty entered into effect. Neither superpower attempted to restrain India's nuclear program, nor did they act more firmly after the Indian nuclear explosion of 1974. Secretary of State Kissinger visited New Delhi five months after the nuclear test and pointedly did not criticize India's nuclear program.[48] Such behavior might be evidence of complacency induced by the NPT, but it could also be attributed to concern that excessive efforts to control proliferation had opened fissures between the United States and its European allies. As in other cases of alleged lulling, it is difficult to distinguish between the impact of multiple causes.

Regardless of its causes, this relaxation of efforts to control proliferation appears to have been short-lived. As Nye points out, the Indian nuclear explosion aroused congressional concerns, and the energy crisis led to fears that weapons-grade fissionable materials would become more widely available. These factors contributed to increased U.S. efforts to curb proliferation in the late 1970s.

A second, more general, form of the lulling-effect argument also has been directed against the NPT. If the treaty increases U.S.-Soviet cooperation, it might lull Americans into believing that U.S.-Soviet relations are good enough to enable the United States to reduce military spending. This claim was made in the Senate Foreign Relations Committee hearings. But claims that the NPT could influence more general trends in military spending exaggerate the influence the treaty had on public and congressional attitudes.

Because the negotiation of the NPT was so different from the usual pattern of bilateral U.S.-Soviet arms talks, there is no evidence of any stimulating effects. U.S. and Soviet weapons were not the subject of negotiations, so there was no need for bargaining chips. The U.S. military did not give up any options and thus did not press for compensatory programs in intergovernmental bargaining. Because no U.S. programs were limited, no rechanneling could take place.

THE ACCIDENTS MEASURES AGREEMENT

The Accidents Measures Agreement of 1971 seems to have had little, if any, effect on U.S. military programs. Negotiated in the shadow of the broader SALT talks, it has attracted little attention since. Public information suggests that the agreement has never been invoked, and it is difficult to assess its impact on the risks of nuclear war or on U.S.-Soviet relations. The relative obscurity of the agreement and the fact that it was not submitted to Congress has rendered it exempt from charges that it has had any lulling or stimulating effect on defense programs. Even if the agreement were alleged to have some impact on U.S. military spending, it would be difficult to separate its influence from that of SALT I.

THE BIOLOGICAL AND TOXIN WEAPONS CONVENTION

Like the Accidents Measures Agreement, the 1972 Biological and Toxin Weapons Convention (BWC) has attracted little attention. Generally overshadowed by debates over chemical weapons, it has not provoked substantial debate over whether it has had either a lulling effect or a stimulating effect on U.S. military programs.

Any possible claim that the BWC lulled the United States into spending too little on biological warfare must confront the fact that negotiation of the agreement was preceded by a unilateral U.S. decision to renounce biological weapons in 1969. As Elisa Harris points out in her chapter, this renunciation was based on the judgment that such weapons were of little military utility. Because destruction of existing U.S. stocks of biological weapons and termination of their production took place before the BWC was negotiated, it is impossible to attribute the U.S. decision to any lulling effect of arms control. The real issue at the time was the military utility of biological weapons, not whether arms control had made it possible to disarm unilaterally. It may be possible to argue over the utility of biological weapons, but such debates would reflect differing views of U.S. military requirements, not any potential lulling effects.

The only area in which the BWC might have had a lulling effect is research on defenses against biological weapons. Despite abandoning its offensive biological arsenal in 1969, the United States has continued to conduct research and development on potential vaccines and antidotes to biological agents. In 1986 a Reagan administration official implied that the BWC had led to "neglect [of] BW defense work aimed at developing detection and medical capabilities and protective gear."[49] U.S. spending on defensive BW research and development did decline after the BWC was entered into force in 1975, falling from $22 million in constant 1979 dollars in fiscal 1976 to $16.5 million in fiscal 1979.[50] This pattern, however, had emerged after the unilateral U.S. renunciation of 1969, when funding for BW defense fell from $64.6 million in fiscal 1970 to $15.2 million in fiscal 1975. The earlier decline in research and development expenditures suggests that the ratification of the BWC had little independent impact on U.S. spending trends. If anything, the BWC may have been associated with the slight increase in BW defense funding between FY 1975 and 1976, from $15.2 million to $22.0 million in constant 1979 dollars.[51]

Since 1981 U.S. spending on defensive BW research has increased sharply, from $17 million (in 1984 dollars) in 1981 to $39.1 million in 1984.[52] This increase, which has taken place while the United States has steadfastly proclaimed its adherence to the BWC, suggests that any possible lulling effect associated with the convention can be reversed. The impetus for the increase can probably be traced to concern over possible Soviet violations of the BWC and changing assessments of the utility of biological weapons. In 1980 ACDA Assistant Director Thomas Davies told a congressional committee that "in the case of BW . . . we concluded long before there was a BW convention that it was not a useful weapon, it is counterproductive."[53] By 1982, however, General Niles Fulwyler, director of the nuclear and chemical directorate in the office of the deputy chief of staff for operations and plans, suggested that biological weapons could influence battlefield outcomes. He also suggested that the possible use of DNA to develop new BW agents necessitated increased U.S. research efforts.[54]

There is no evidence to suggest that the BWC has had a stimulating effect on any category of military spending. The U.S. unilateral renunciation of biological weapons precluded any invocation of the bargaining chip argument, and the dubious military utility of such weapons made it unlikely that the U.S. military would seek compensatory increases in other military programs.

THE SALT I INTERIM AGREEMENT AND THE ABM TREATY

SALT I and the Lulling Effect

The SALT I case offers an excellent opportunity to test the claim that arms control has a lulling effect in the United States. There is ample data on public opinion and military spending trends before and after the treaty. Moreover, SALT I is often seen as a classic case of lulling by some defense analysts. Eugene Rostow has offered one of the strongest examples of this argument:

> Lulled by the treaty—as well as by illusions about "overkill," and by the high hopes we had invested in détente—into thinking that the "arms race" was being brought under control, we allowed ourselves to fall behind in most relevant categories of military power: behind in production; behind in research and development; and behind in programming.[55]

During the Senate Foreign Relations Committee hearings on the SALT I agreement, Edward Teller argued, "Now, the treaty has a potential grave danger, that is, if people stand up and say, 'We can reduce our budget; now we can save dollars because we are safe.' Actually we have not been as unsafe ever."[56] Admiral Thomas Moorer, chairman of the Joint Chiefs of Staff in 1972, later argued "that SALT I created a kind of euphoria in the Congress and in the eye of the public, and consequently people more or less kind of sat back in their chairs and the progressive buildup of the Soviets continued while ours went down."[57] Richard Pipes has claimed that "It has been very difficult for U.S. administrations to fund strategic programs even psychologically because SALT I created the impression in this country that we have attained stability and therefore anything we would do would be destabilizing."[58]

Public Attitudes and SALT I. There is little evidence to suggest that SALT I induced a false sense of security among the U.S. public. A June 1972 Harris poll showed that 65 percent of the U.S. public agreed that "the Cold War had not ended."[59] In the years after the SALT I agreements were negotiated, the percentage of the public who worried "a great deal" about the "problem of the Soviet Union" rose from 24 percent in 1972 to 37 percent in 1974 and to 50 percent in 1976. The percentage who said they worried "not very much" declined from 27 to 18 percent during the same period.[60] Measured by attitudes toward the Soviet Union, SALT I was not associated with a euphoric and historic reversal of U.S. views of the Soviet threat. Instead, Americans became more worried about the Soviet Union in the aftermath of SALT I.

Public opinion polls on military spending do not support the claim that the SALT I agreements produced a widespread sense of complacency. Table 9–1 indicates that before and after the SALT agreements the public supported reductions in defense spending. The level of opposition to defense spending peaked in 1968, but the proportions of the U.S. public who believed that U.S. defense spending was "too much," "about right," and "too little" remained remarkably constant between 1969 and 1974. Only in 1976 did a shift toward support for higher defense spending become evident, and in 1977 the percentage favoring increases finally exceeded the percentage calling for further reductions. The overall trend suggests that the SALT I agreements had little impact on the antimilitary spending mood that emerged as the Vietnam War became increasingly unpopular.

SALT I and the Military Budget. As Figures 9-1 and 9-2 show, U.S. defense spending began to decline as the United States withdrew from Vietnam, and it then continued to fall in real terms. This reduction in defense spending was the result of the gradual end of the U.S. involvement in Vietnam and lower budget requests from the executive branch, as shown in Table 9-2, but it also reflects the fact that starting with the fiscal 1969 defense budget, Congress made large reductions in defense budget requests that had already been pruned severely by Secretary of Defense Melvin Laird prior to submission of the budget to Congress. Laird, for example, called the fiscal 1971 proposed spending levels a "rock bottom budget," but it was still cut 3.4 percent in Congress.[61]

These reductions in U.S. military spending could be the result of a lulling effect of the SALT I process, but it seems much more plausible to attribute defense budget cuts to the antidefense climate that emerged in the latter stages of U.S. involvement in Vietnam. It is possible that both factors contributed to calls for reducing defense spending, but congressional cuts in military programs began before the SALT process was underway. Defense spending became more unpopular as the U.S. people increasingly opposed the Vietnam War. Not only did the military requirements of the U.S. presence in Indochina divert funds from modernization programs,[62] but the war created a climate of opposition to military involvements and military spending. A second important factor contributing to the antidefense climate of the early 1970s was the widely held belief that the United States needed to devote a greater share of its resources to domestic

Table 9-2. Congressional Changes in Defense Budget Requests, FY 1969–75.

Fiscal Year	Defense Budget	Nondefense Budget
1969	−6.8%	−10.0%
1970	−7.7	+5.8
1971	−3.4	+2.5
1972	−4.4	+0.1
1973	−7.2	+10.2
1974	−6.3	+2.4
1975	−7.0	+7.4

Source: Lawrence J. Korb, *The Fall and Rise of the Pentagon: American Defense Policies in the 1970s* (Westport, Conn.: Greenwood Press, 1979), pp. 51–52.

problems. The turbulent 1960s revealed flaws in the Great Society and led to calls for a reordering of national priorities.[63] Senators and representatives in the early 1970s called for major reductions in defense spending so that more funds would be available for social programs. During the SALT I hearings, Senator Edward Kennedy argued that "the Defense Department is engaged in a headlong pursuit after additional weapon systems that are irrelevant to our strategic deterrence at this time . . . when our domestic needs are being short changed."[64] The end of U.S. military involvement in Vietnam was expected to yield a "peace dividend" of approximately $20 billion that could be devoted to domestic programs. Defense spending was also held responsible for the inflation and slow economic growth of the late 1960s. A report prepared for a bipartisan group of 105 senators and representatives concluded that "we may isolate the cause for current problems as the failure to cut defense."[65] Reductions in military spending were consistently justified not on the grounds that arms control had eliminated the need for defense expenditures but by the claim that the military budget contributed to inflation, that it was bloated by wasteful expenditures like the C-5A transport plane, and that it was the largest portion of federal discretionary spending that could be reallocated to social programs.

SALT I and the Strategic Forces Budget.   The SALT I agreements appear to have had mixed effects on U.S. spending on strategic forces. Appropriations for strategic forces continued to decline after 1972, although at a much more gradual rate than the general purpose force budget. Between 1971 and 1974 the strategic forces budget declined by 26 percent in real terms. A 1976 Congressional Budget Office study concluded that much of this decline could be attributed to the elimination of the need to continue to fund ABM deployment programs, which were severely constrained by the ABM Treaty.[66] As shown in Figure 9-3, the steep decline in spending on defensive systems was accompanied by a brief but significant increase and then a leveling off of spending on offensive systems.

Although the 1975 congressional decision to deactivate and dismantle the Safeguard ABM site at Grand Forks is sometimes cited as evidence that Congress was lulled by the ABM Treaty and the 1974 Protocol that limited the United States and the Soviet Union to one ABM site each, the rationale offered for this decision does not indicate that Congress was lulled into believing that the ABM site was no longer necessary. Instead, the decision appears to have been based on the argument that the system was of limited effectiveness. The House Appropriations Committee report that recommended eliminating Safeguard funding noted "that the Soviet Union is deploying MIRVed intercontinental ballistic missiles. . . . Because of this, the utility of SAFEGUARD to protect MINUTEMAN will be essentially nullified in the future."[67] The U.S. Army recommended that the site be operated for one year to gain experience with the new system and then be placed on a very low state of readiness, but the General Accounting Office concluded that the experience gained through operating the site would be extremely limited.[68] Senator Edward Kennedy adopted the same argument in proposing a Senate floor amendment that would have deleted Safeguard funding for fiscal 1976. Calling the Grand Forks site an "unnecessary facility" and pointing out that "the Soviet Union is beginning to deploy MIRVs that would render Grand Forks ineffective," he argued that the funding for the ABM site should be "measured against programs of food for the elderly, or lead paint poisoning, or neighborhood youth centers, or community health centers, or educational programs."[69] The Senate did not delete all funding for the Grand Forks site but agreed to deactivate and dismantle the ABM system, retaining only a perimeter acquisition radar system intended to detect attacks from missiles on polar trajectories.[70]

The one area in which there is evidence to suggest that lulling took place, however, is ballistic missile defense research and development. As Table 9-3 shows, Congress made deep cuts in Defense Department proposals for ABM research and development programs in fiscal years 1974-76, the years following the negotiation of the ABM Treaty and subsequent protocol. In approving the fiscal 1975 budget, Congress also directed that the Site Defense Program, which had been directed toward developing a prototype system to defend Minuteman sites, be reoriented to examine systems and component technologies.[71] These cuts were made despite the arguments of Defense Secretaries Elliot Richardson and James Schlesinger that such research was necessary "to prevent technological surprise"[72] and "to provide the Soviet leaders with strong incentives to negotiate additional strategic arms limitation agreements . . . [and] . . . to motivate them to keep the treaties and agreements already made."[73]

This reluctance to fund continued BMD research led to a situation in 1978 in which then Secretary of Defense Harold Brown concluded

Table 9-3. Proposed and Actual BMD Research and Development, 1972–79.[a]

Year	Proposed ($ millions)	Actual	Change
1972	165	156	–9
1973	182	173	–9
1974	270	172	–98
1975	251	212	–39
1976	245	197	–48
1977	225	202.7	–22.3

a. Figures represent combined total of Site Defense/Systems Technology and Advanced Technology Programs for each year.

Source: Department of Defense, *Annual Reports* (Washington, D.C.: U.S. Government Printing Office, 1972–77).

that the "lead enjoyed by the United States in BMD at the time we entered into the ABM Treaty has greatly diminished."[74] In 1984 Assistant Secretary of Defense Richard Perle argued that "We dropped our guard" by not matching the threefold increase in Soviet BMD research after the ABM Treaty.[75] This neglect of BMD research and development appears to reflect a feeling that it would be unwise to devote significant sums to research on systems that could not be deployed in any case.[76] Members of Congress apparently believed that the ABM Treaty and Protocol had eliminated the risks of Soviet steps that might require the United States to deploy rapidly a significant ABM capability, and they therefore limited funding for continued BMD research.[77] This outcome may reflect the fact that the ABM Treaty is unlike the other arms control agreements in that it almost completely bans deployment of a particular weapons system of potential military significance. A complete ban on deployment may generate complacency based on optimism about the durability of an agreement and thus inhibit spending on research and development that might deter the other party from attempting to break out of the accord. Few other agreements fit into this category, with the possible exception of the BWC, which is distinguished by having been preceded by a unilateral U.S. decision to abandon the weapons in question. The apparent lulling effect of the treaty might also be attributed to the difficulty of making judgments about BMD technologies and differing views on U.S. force requirements, not complacency over the benefits of the agreements.

SALT I as a Stimulus to Military Programs

Despite the decline in strategic spending that followed the SALT I agreements, some observers claim that U.S.-Soviet military competition actually accelerated. Laurence Martin argues that "the SALT exercise has done more to accelerate than to restrain strategic arms procurement on both sides."[78] Fred Kaplan contends that "SALT, far from limiting strategic arms, has, in fact, spurred the arms race to a new level of intensity."[79] SALT I did lead to the acceleration of several strategic programs. Shortly after the agreements were presented to Congress, then Secretary of Defense Melvin Laird requested a series of "SALT Related Adjustments to Strategic Programs." These adjustments included a reduction of $711 million in ABM funding for fiscal 1973, but this savings was partially offset by an increase of $168 million due to the addition or acceleration of programs for site defense, SLCMs, bomber rebasing, augmented verification capabilities, improved reentry vehicles, and command, control, and communication improvements.[80] Even before the SALT I agreements had been concluded, the Nixon administration had decided in late 1971 to accelerate the Trident submarine program by requesting additional funds in the FY 1973 budget. The FY 1973 request was for $942 million; only $140 million had been budgeted for Trident in FY 1972. This decision reflected the administration's determination to show that the Moscow summit and the expected SALT agreements would not create the impression that U.S. strength was ebbing.[81]

The administration justified its accelerated military programs by emphasizing that SALT alone could not solve all U.S. security problems. In his June 13, 1972, letter of transmittal of the agreements to Congress, Richard Nixon wrote that "it is now equally essential that we carry forward a sound strategic modernization program to maintain our security."[82] Testifying before the Senate Armed Services Committee, Melvin Laird emphasized that "This is not a time for complacency"[83] and claimed that "The opportunities for peace embodied in the SALT agreements would be nullified and our national security jeopardized unless there is continued strong support for an adequate defense budget."[84] In 1973 then Secretary of Defense Elliot Richardson reminded Congress that "we should have no illusions, however, that the generation of peace is already upon us and that we can now 'beat our swords into plowshares.'"[85]

These arguments in support of strategic military spending suggest that the Nixon administration deliberately attempted to counter any euphoria over SALT I that might have endangered defense programs. As early as August 19, 1970, SALT negotiator Gerard Smith had told Nixon that the "U.S. needs to engage in an educational program both with the Congress and the public to let them realize that a strategic arms limitation agreement is not a panacea to all arms and budget problems." Nixon had agreed that "this last point of Ambassador Smith's was important as we would need to engage in such an educational program at the proper time."[86] During the June 15, 1972, congressional briefing on SALT I, Senator Sam Ervin asked, "Wouldn't ratification of the treaty and the approval of the Limited Arms Agreement make it all the more imperative for us to go forward with the Trident and with the B-1 bomber, and other programs, to keep from being lulled into a dangerous sense of security?" "That," replied Kissinger, "is the position of the Administration."[87]

The SALT-related acceleration in strategic programs is also consistent with the intragovernmental bargaining model of how arms control can stimulate military spending. As they had in the debate over the LTBT, the Joint Chiefs of Staff sought guarantees that congressional approval of the agreements would be accompanied by continued support for military programs. Testifying before the Senate Armed Services Committee, JCS Chairman Thomas Moorer called for three "National Security Assurances in a Strategic Arms Limitation Environment." These assurances included maintenance of capabilities to verify Soviet compliance with agreements, continued strategic modernization programs, and vigorous research and development efforts.[88] Laird repeatedly made it clear to Congress that his support for the SALT I agreements was conditional and depended on congressional approval of the proposed adjustments to the strategic forces budget: "My support of this agreement is of course based upon the implementation of those programs during the next 5 years."[89] Moorer testified on behalf of the Joint Chiefs that "we were in accord provided these actions were taken."[90]

The SALT I negotiations also provided a context in which the Nixon administration was able to win support for weapons systems by justifying them as bargaining chips. This argument was made to Congress both before and after the agreements were concluded in 1972. Prior to the treaty, ABM funding was frequently justified as necessary to strengthen the hand of the U.S. SALT negotiators. In

1970, when the Senate appeared ready to delete all funds from the Safeguard ABM program, Gerard Smith was persuaded to send a telegram to senators affirming the importance of the ABM system in the SALT negotiations. Kissinger suggests that this telegram "saved the day for 'Safeguard.'"[91] In 1972 Senator Symington said, "I never thought the ABM was worth the staggering price. We would have knocked it out last year, in my opinion, except that the argument developed that it was a bargaining chip for SALT."[92]

The ABM was the only bargaining chip that was actually cashed in during the SALT I process. Other military programs were justified as necessary for the success of the negotiations, but none was actually bargained away. Secretary of State William Rogers called for a "sound strategic modernization program to maintain our security and to insure that more permanent comprehensive arms limitation agreements can be reached,"[93] but he did not suggest that specific weapons could be traded for reciprocal Soviet concessions. It is important to distinguish between weapons meant as explicit bargaining chips and those intended to provide more general bargaining leverage. The Trident submarine program, for example, was sometimes linked to the need to continue strategic modernization to enhance the chances of a favorable outcome in the upcoming SALT II negotiations, but Laird told the Senate Armed Services Committee that "I have never referred to the [Trident] submarine construction program as a bargaining chip."[94] Even if Trident, the B-1 bomber, and other systems were not explicitly described as bargaining chips, the linkage between them and the SALT negotiations may have contributed to the (grudging) congressional support for strategic force modernization in the early and mid-1970s.

THE SALT II PROCESS

The SALT II Treaty is unique among U.S.-Soviet arms control agreements for two reasons. First, until November 1986 it occupied an ambiguous status as an unratified agreement that the United States decided not to "undercut."[95] Second, the treaty was negotiated over a seven-year period by three administrations. Few observers expected in 1972 that negotiation of a SALT II Treaty would take this long; most apparently believed that the five-year SALT I interim agreement would provide ample time for the negotiation of an accord with a longer duration. SALT I negotiator Gerard Smith testified that "People shorthandedly say this is a five-year agreement. I hope it won't be. It may be a one-year agreement; it may be a two-year agreement, depending on when we succeed in the follow-on negotiations."[96] During the lengthy negotiation of SALT II, the Vietnam War ended, there was conflict in the Middle East, the Soviet Union became more active in the Third World, and the superpower détente of the early 1970s gradually eroded. These events influenced the SALT II negotiations and also affected U.S. strategic force modernization programs. Given the complex context of the negotiations, it is difficult to assess the impact of SALT on U.S. military programs in the 1970s. The political changes that occurred during the SALT II negotiations may have caused the arms control process to produce different effects at different times. In addition, analysis of this period is complicated by the intermingling of the consequences of the negotiation of the SALT I agreements and the process of negotiating SALT II.

SALT II and the Lulling Effect

Those who argue that the United States was lulled by the SALT II process often attribute U.S. unilateral restraint to the desire to enhance the prospects for U.S.-Soviet arms control. Richard Perle claims that "in the nine years since SALT got underway, there have been repeated efforts, by individuals in and out of the U.S. government, to halt or delay the procurement of weapons systems in the United States in the belief that the prospects for U.S.-Soviet arms control would be thereby brightened."[97] Richard Burt argues that "The importance attached to gaining agreement at SALT has naturally led some decision-makers to question the development and deployment of weapons that might complicate the process of negotiation and the methods for monitoring compliance."[98] Unilateral restraint is not synonymous with lulling. The former could, at least in theory, be a useful means of facilitating a U.S.-Soviet agreement, but it could be evidence of complacency if it is based on excessive optimism about the benefits or likelihood of reaching an anticipated agreement. The argument that the SALT II process exerted a lulling effect can be made without any reference to how unilateral restraint results from the desire to reach an agreement. William Van Cleave, for example, contends that "on-going SALT negotiations have a dampening effect on American options and programs far beyond the direct limitations themselves."[99] Because it is often difficult to distinguish between these arguments—the two sometimes appear to be made simultaneously—the following analysis will examine important decisions of the Carter administration to determine how the SALT II process influenced military programs without attempting to draw a sharp line between unilateral restraint and the lulling effect. It is important to point out, however, that both arguments link U.S. decisions on military programs to the SALT II process. Other defense analysts, however, criticize the Carter administration for its purportedly inadequate defense efforts without attributing this restraint to any possible lulling effect of the arms control process.[100]

To assess the competing arguments on the adequacy of the Carter administration's defense program is beyond the scope of this chapter. Critics of the Carter policy cite the growth in Soviet strategic forces and the slow pace of U.S. modernization programs as evidence of "inexcusable restraint."[101] Carter's defenders, on the other hand, point out that there was a real increase in defense spending during the Carter years and that this pattern would have continued during a second Carter administration.[102] To determine whether the lulling effect was responsible for possible excessive U.S. unilateral restraint in the 1970s, it is necessary to examine the factors that caused delays and cuts in various military programs. If weapons systems were delayed or cancelled on the grounds that they were not effective, such decisions do not provide evidence that lulling took place.

The B-1 bomber is often cited as an example of a weapon cut by the Carter administration in hopes that such restraint would enhance the prospects for an arms control agreement. President Carter and Secretary of Defense Harold Brown, however, justified the discontinuation of the B-1 program on the grounds that improvements in Soviet air defenses would make it difficult for the B-1 to serve as a penetrating bomber. They argued that cruise missiles carried by B-52 bombers or other aircraft would provide a more effective means of modernizing the air-breathing leg of the U.S. strategic triad. In his FY 1979 *Annual Report*, Brown argued that "the B-52/cruise missile combination is the better choice on the grounds of expected cost and effectiveness."[103] When asked if he thought the cancellation of the B-1 would signal to the Soviets that the United States was eager for progress toward a SALT II agreement, Carter replied, "I can't deny that's a potential factor. But that has not been a reason for my decision. I think if I had looked upon the B-1 as simply a bargaining chip for the Soviets, then my decision would have been to go ahead with the weapon."[104] Even some critics of Carter's defense policies recognized that the B-1 was cancelled "independently of SALT" although they may have felt the bomber should have been used as a bargaining chip.[105] (Ironically, the cruise missile—the weapon that Carter felt had made the B-1 unnecessary—initially had been justified as a bargaining chip.)

Although Carter argued that he was cancelling the B-1 because the cruise missile would provide a more effective deterrent, he was criticized for delaying the cruise missile program in order to avoid complicating the arms control negotiations. Advocates of the cruise missile program feared that SALT II would eventually restrict cruise missiles, an area in which the United States appeared to have a clear technological lead over the Soviet Union. The cruise missile did raise a number of verification problems, and advocates of arms control expressed concern that unlimited deployments of unverifiable, dual-capable cruise missiles would undermine the entire process of nuclear arms control. The Office of Management and Budget did recommend slowing the cruise missile program pending the outcome of the SALT II negotiations, arguing that the United States should "Defer 1979 procurement of both the anti-ship and land-attack sea-launched cruise missile in view of uncertainty as to how SALT protocol provisions affecting these systems will be reflected in future agreements."[106] Nevertheless, the Carter administration continued to plan the deployment of ALCMs, GLCMs, and SLCMs, and negotiated a protocol to the SALT II Treaty that would have expired before planned deployments began. The OMB recommendation probably reflected the budgetary concerns of that agency more than any widespread belief that SALT II would make any cruise missile programs unnecessary.

The MX missile also was delayed repeatedly during the SALT II negotiations. Critics of the Carter administration argue that these delays were the result of excessive hopes for an arms control agreement or too much concern over making MX deployments compatible with the eventual SALT II verification provisions. Analysis of the history of the MX, however, suggests that the fundamental problem was the difficulty of finding a basing mode that would be survivable and also politically acceptable in the United States. Numerous alternatives were rejected on the grounds that they would not solve the problem of ICBM vulnerability or that their costs exceeded the benefits of increased ICBM survivability.[107] The Reagan administration faced the same difficulties and has similarly delayed MX deployment, first reversing the Carter decision to deploy the missiles on mobile platforms that would shuttle between shelters and then debating many other basing modes before deciding to place the MX missile in Minuteman silos.

The Carter administration also has been criticized for delaying the Trident submarine program during the late 1970s. Harold Brown noted in his FY 1980 *Annual Report* that the rate of Trident construction was being slowed from three ships every two years to one per year.[108] This change, however, reflected "cost escalation caused by extremely high inflation in the shipbuilding industry"[109] and many management and labor problems at the Electric Boat Division of General Dynamics. In July 1977 General Dynamics had claimed that the first Trident submarine would be six months late, and the navy had concluded shortly thereafter that the delay would be at least twelve months.[110]

The 1977 decision to close the Minuteman III production line could also be cited as an example of SALT-induced unilateral restraint. In justifying the decision, however, Harold Brown pointed out that the United States already had more than enough spare missiles and that upgrading additional Minuteman II missiles made little sense if those missiles already were becoming vulnerable to Soviet ICBMs.[111]

The overall pattern of the Carter administration's strategic procurement decisions indicates that the desire to progress toward an arms control agreement and any sense of complacency induced by the process of negotiations were not important factors in the cancellation or postponement of strategic modernization programs. With the exception of the restoration of the B-1 bomber and the president's Strategic Defense Initiative, most of the Reagan administration's strategic programs represent accelerated continuations of plans that were made by the Carter administration.[112] Carter may have underestimated the Soviet threat and pursued an inadequate defense policy, but many of his decisions appear to have been made on the basis of personal conviction or criteria unrelated to arms control.

There is little evidence to suggest that the lulling effect was an important deleterious influence on U.S. defense planning in the late 1970s.

Potential Lulling Effects of the SALT II Treaty.   As the debate over SALT II ratification began, opponents of the treaty raised the possibility that it would have a lulling effect that would slow strategic modernization. This view was prominent in the Senate Foreign Relations Committee hearings on the SALT II Treaty. JCS Chairman David Jones echoed Maxwell Taylor's 1963 testimony on the LTBT, stating that "The most serious concern of the Joint Chiefs of Staff in this regard is the risk that SALT II could be allowed to become a tranquilizer to the American people."[113] Paul Nitze argued that "To accept the case that is being made for the Vienna terms, with all its fallacies and implausibility, can only incapacitate our minds and wills for doing the things necessary to redress the strategic balance."[114] Nitze later contended "that we have been living somewhat under the illusion that the SALT agreement somehow or other would fix this problem of the strategic nuclear threat."[115] Senator S. I. Hayakawa wondered "if there is not a danger that the ratification of SALT II will lull the United States into a false sense of security which will cause the United States not to take the required actions to maintain its relative defense position."[116] Admiral Moorer predicted "that we are going to see the same thing that happened in SALT I; namely the fact that you have the words 'arms limitation' in the SALT creates a euphoria in the country."[117]

Because the SALT II Treaty was never ratified, it is impossible to say whether formal ratification would have led to lulling. The negotiating and signing of the treaty, however, do not appear to have induced a sense of complacency about U.S. security. As Table 9-1 above indicates, polls during this period showed a sharp increase in support for higher military spending. The proportion of the U.S. public supporting increased defense expenditures rose from 12 percent in 1976 to 34 percent in December 1979 and 49 percent in January 1980. During the same period the number of Americans who felt that the United States was spending "too much" on defense fell from 36 percent to 14 percent, the lowest level since 1964. The conclusion of the SALT II negotiations may have been unrelated to these trends, which were obviously influenced by broader political developments, but it does not appear to have altered them significantly. Indeed, polls conducted before the signing of SALT II suggest that the public saw no contradiction between strategic arms control and increased defense spending. In February 1979, in an NBC/Associated Press poll, 26 percent of those surveyed supported Carter's increases in the defense budget, 13 percent wanted even higher increases, and only 16 percent favored reducing defense spending. The same NBC/AP poll revealed that 81 percent of the public favored "a new agreement between the United States and Russia which would limit nuclear weapons." This percentage was the highest recorded between January 1978 and October 1980. The second highest was 74 percent in January 1978. Harris polls conducted in January, April, and October 1979 showed that the number of Americans believing that "it is vital for the two countries to reach an agreement to limit nuclear arms" remained constant at approximately 86 percent. The public did not, however, expect that such an agreement would enable the United States to reduce military spending. In November 1978, when asked "Do you think a treaty with the Soviet Union limiting weapons will or will not enable the United States to spend less money for defense?" 45 percent said that it would not and 39 percent said that it would enable the United States to cut defense spending.[118]

SALT II as a Stimulus to Military Programs

Far from lulling the U.S. public, the debate over SALT II seems to have actually fostered awareness of U.S. defense deficiencies. The Senate ratification debate helped to forge a consensus on the need for increased military spending. Arthur Metcalf, chairman of the U.S. Strategic Studies Institute and a critic of SALT II, recognized what he called the "paradox of SALT": Instead of lulling the U.S. public, the treaty debate was calling attention to U.S. defense needs.[119] In its report on the SALT II Treaty, the Senate Foreign Relations Committee concluded that "the SALT debate in the Senate has increased the awareness of the Congress that certain steps must be taken to modernize and strengthen our strategic, theater and conventional forces."[120] Committee Chairman Senator Frank Church said, "I have never attended lengthy or extensive hearings on this committee having to do with a so-called arms control agreement that involved such a vigorous presentation for a much larger American arms budget."[121] Senator George McGovern wondered "whether SALT II is really a formula for arms limitation or arms escalation."[122]

As in previous cases of arms control, the conclusion of the SALT II treaty provided an opportunity for those who worried about the possibility of a lulling effect to win approval for military programs that would offset any potential reductions in military spending. In the case of SALT II, however, the already strong support for increased military spending probably reduced the likelihood that any lulling would take place. With or without SALT, the defense budget would have increased in fiscal years 1980 and 1981. Fears that SALT would create a false sense of security may have only added to the prevailing mood that the United States needed to increase military spending and undertake major modernization programs. In testimony before the Senate Foreign Relations Committee, JCS Chairman David Jones claimed that Congress and the executive branch "for 15 years, have been underfunding our defense requirements."[123] Harold Brown emphasized that SALT "will have to be accompanied by substantial U.S. defense programs and specifically by expanded ones in the strategic field."[124] Figures 9-1 and 9-3 show that a second Carter administration would have continued the rapid increase in military spending, and particularly spending on strategic systems, that began during the final stages of the SALT II negotiations. The Reagan administration, of course, has exceeded Carter's planned spending levels.

The reaction to SALT by the military and congressional proponents of increased defense spending appears to fit into the intra-governmental bargaining model. The Joint Chiefs of Staff gave their endorsement to the agreement, but only after Carter had made clear his commitment to the MX missile and broad increases in military spending. Indeed, Carter's decision to make the MX as large as possible under the terms of the treaty reflected a desire to satisfy senators who might otherwise oppose SALT.[125] Many members of Congress saw the SALT ratification debate as an opportunity to press for guarantees of further increases in the Pentagon budget. Although the fate of the SALT treaty in the Senate remained in doubt in late 1979, it was obvious to most observers that the price of Senate consent would be an increase in the defense budget.

ANTISATELLITE NEGOTIATIONS

The 1978-79 antisatellite (ASAT) negotiations, like the SALT II process, failed to produce a ratified treaty. Unlike SALT II, however, they did not even lead to a signed U.S.-Soviet accord. The talks simply ended in 1979, leaving various observers and participants with widely differing perspectives on what might have been achieved. Any discernible lulling or stimulating effects would have to be attributed solely to the negotiations.

Possible Lulling Effects of the ASAT Talks

In the absence of unclassified information on either the internal ASAT decisions of the U.S. government or the U.S.-Soviet negotiations, it is difficult to assess the overall effects of the negotiations on U.S. ASAT programs. There is little evidence to suggest that the negotiations lulled the United States into reducing spending for space defense and satellite survivability. In current dollars, U.S. space defense funding rose from $12.8 million in fiscal year 1977 to $110.4 million in FY 1981. The increase in constant 1972 dollars was from $9.1 million to $56.4 million. Despite the fears of the Joint Chiefs of Staff that the very existence of ASAT negotiations would lull Congress into underfunding measures to protect U.S. satellites from attack, between fiscal years 1978 and 1981 nominal spending on satellite survivability rose from $19 million to $33.3 million—from $12.6 million to $17.0 million in constant 1972 dollars.[126]

If there is any evidence to suggest that the United States was lulled into spending less than it should on space defense, it appears in fiscal years 1973-76, when funding declined from $3.1 million to $0.1 million, before returning to $3.0 million. This change could be attributed to the overall climate of détente, the 1971-76 suspension of Soviet ASAT tests, and U.S. hopes that the SALT I provisions affirming the importance of national technical means of verification would prevent the Soviet Union from interfering with U.S. satellites.[127] The decline in U.S. space defense spending does not, however, appear to be connected with ASAT negotiations for the simple reason that there were none during this period. Although U.S. SALT negotiator

Raymond Garthoff has argued that an ASAT agreement might have been possible in 1972, he points out that "Neither side proposed a ban or even raised the matter."[128] Only when negotiations began during the Carter administration did space defense funding increase as ASAT development was accelerated.

Possible Stimulating Effects of the ASAT Talks

It is impossible to know how much the United States would have spent on satellite survivability and space defense if U.S.-Soviet ASAT negotiations had not taken place. President Carter, however, was reluctant to deploy ASAT systems, and the possibility of negotiating a ban on such weapons provided the impetus for his support of ASAT development to enhance the U.S. negotiating position.[129] ASAT and satellite survivability funding increases also may have been intended to assuage fears of the Joint Chiefs that the negotiations or a possible agreement would not lull the United States. As in the case of the LTBT, SALT I, and SALT II, concern over a potential lulling effect appears to have generated a compensatory increase in U.S. spending.

Judgments of the net impact of the ASAT negotiations on U.S. ASAT programs are probably influenced by the observer's position on the need for U.S. ASAT weapons. Those who believe that a vigorous ASAT program is essential for U.S. national security are likely to contend that ASAT negotiations impeded the development of vital weapons systems. On the other hand, critics of ASAT weapons are more likely to argue that the ASAT negotiations stimulated the development of ASAT systems for use as bargaining chips. Although no agreement was achieved, the case of the ASAT negotiations exemplifies the difficulty in making judgments about the impact of arms control on military programs.

CONCLUSIONS

Arms Control and the Lulling Effect

The experience of the United States with U.S.-Soviet efforts to reach agreements examined in this study casts doubt on the more extreme forms of the lulling effect argument. Military spending did not decline precipitously after U.S.-Soviet arms control agreements were negotiated, and public opinion polls do not show that agreements or negotiations increased opposition to defense outlays. The possibility that some lulling took place cannot entirely be excluded, however, particularly in the case of BMD research and development. Much of the available evidence is subject to conflicting interpretations, and it is difficult to assess what military spending levels would have been in the absence of arms control. In general, the difficulty of finding clear evidence that arms control has actually had a lulling effect on U.S. military programs should give pause to those who claim that arms control agreements have been responsible for inadequate U.S. levels of military spending.

Advocates of the lulling effect hypothesis appear to exaggerate its significance in influencing military spending. The public record of debate on arms control reveals very few statements that claim arms control has increased U.S. security to such a point that unconstrained military programs can be slowed down or eliminated. Instead, U.S. attitudes toward military spending have been shaped by many other factors. After the SALT I and ABM agreements, for example, the public and Congress continued to oppose increased military spending, but these attitudes represented a continuation of previous opposition to defense programs. This opposition had its roots in public reaction against the Vietnam War, increasing concern about U.S. domestic problems, reduced respect for the military, and skepticism about executive branch calls for increased Pentagon budgets. Even if these factors had not existed, Americans historically have been reluctant to maintain wartime levels of military expenditures during peacetime. Calls for reductions in defense spending may have followed the Vietnam War even if it had been popular, much as they followed World War I and World War II.

In the case of SALT II, on the other hand, most observers agree that military spending would have increased even if ratification of the agreement had been approved by the Senate. Public support for higher military spending was increasing during the SALT II negotiations and may have continued to rise. The debate over SALT II may have even contributed to this trend by calling attention to perceived U.S. defense deficiencies.

The existence of other factors that influence U.S. attitudes toward military spending suggests that the lulling effect argument should be regarded skeptically. Given its potentially limited or nonexistent impact on prevailing support or opposition for defense programs, it would be a mistake to argue against future arms control agreements on the grounds that they will inevitably lull the United States into reducing military expenditures.

One apparent reason for the absence of evidence of lulling is that concern over a possible false sense of security has led to efforts to control and to compensate for any lulling effect. The LTBT, SALT I, and SALT II were all accompanied by accelerated military programs. In each case the president, leading administration officials, and military leaders attempted to prevent the emergence of any false sense of security by emphasizing the limits of the agreement and the need for continued military efforts. Indeed, it may be that the prominence of the lulling effect argument has prompted such a compensatory response that arms control agreements have accelerated U.S. military spending. Leaders can educate the public and Congress about the necessity of integrating arms control into defense policy and not placing sole reliance on arms control agreements.

Alleged lulling during arms negotiations is often attributed to the belief that unilateral restraint by the United States can contribute to the negotiation of U.S.-Soviet arms control agreements. If it is recognized that unilateral restraint may not always induce the Soviet Union to reciprocate, it is less likely that the United States will delay or cancel military programs in hopes of furthering arms control. The real issue here is not lulling but determining when restraint can enhance the prospects for an agreement and when it will encourage Soviet intransigence. This issue is a difficult one, but no more difficult than many other problems of U.S.-Soviet negotiations or diplomacy in general.

The Stimulating Effect of Arms Control

Although the usual caveats about our inability to determine what would have happened in the absence of arms control apply, arms control agreements do appear to have served as an impetus for some military programs. In some cases, such as the LTBT, SALT I, and SALT II, increased spending has been part of a deliberate attempt to counter any possible lulling effect. Intragovernmental bargaining and the invocation of the bargaining chip justification also have contributed to support for military programs that might otherwise have gone unfunded. U.S. ASAT and ABM programs probably would not have been supported as much as they were if they had not been the subject of arms control negotiations. This type of increase in spending may offset any reductions due to the lulling effect, but the two processes may occur simultaneously. The evidence of a relationship between arms control and accelerated military programs seems to be stronger than that of the lulling effect, but the acceleration is generally confined to specific programs related to the negotiations or agreement. Moreover, determining whether accelerated programs are necessary or not remains a difficult matter of judgment.

Arms control negotiations and agreements may have contributed to inadequate or excessive defense spending, but they seem to have reinforced existing trends in most cases. The evidence for the stimulating effects of arms control seems to be slightly stronger, but defense spending would probably have been increased in the late 1970s, for example, even in the absence of the SALT debate. The irony of the debate over the impact of arms control on military spending is much like what Colin Gray has called the *arms control paradox*—the fact "that arms control agreements of an unambiguously substantial character tend to be negotiable only between states whose mutual relations are sufficiently good that arms control is irrelevant."[130] In a similar fashion, arms control agreements tend to be followed by reductions or increases in military spending only when there were already pressures to reduce or increase the defense budget. Observers who blame arms control for inhibiting or accelerating defense spending probably exaggerate the impact of the arms control process and arms control in general.

NOTES

1. William R. Van Cleave, "Implications of Success or Failure of SALT," in William R. Kintner and Robert Pfaltzgraff, eds., *SALT: Implications for Arms Control in the 1970s* (Pittsburgh: University of Pittsburgh Press, 1973), p. 327.

2. Seymour Weiss, "The Case against Arms Control," *Commentary* (Nov. 1984), p. 21.

3. Quoted in Walter Isaacson and Evan Thomas, *The Wise Men: Six Friends and the World They Made* (New York: Simon and Schuster, 1986), p. 378.

4. Quoted in John Lewis Gaddis, *Strategies of Containment* (New York: Oxford University Press, 1982), p. 141.

5. Robert R. Bowie, "Arms Control and United States Foreign Policy," in Louis Henkin, ed., *Arms Control: Issues for the Public* (Englewood Cliffs, N.J.: Prentice-Hall, 1960), p. 72.

6. U.S. Senate Committee on Foreign Relations, *Hearings on The SALT II Treaty*, 96th Cong., 1st Sess., Part 1 (Washington, D.C.: U.S. Government Printing Office, 1979), p. 511.

7. Henry A. Kissinger, *White House Years* (Boston: Little, Brown, 1979), p. 1246.

8. See Isaacson and Thomas, *The Wise Men*, p. 395; Gaddis, *Strategies of Containment*, pp. 107–08; and Ernest R. May, "The Cold War," in Joseph S. Nye, Jr., ed., *The Making of America's Soviet Policy* (New Haven: Yale University Press, 1984), pp. 226–27.

9. See John F. Lehman and Seymour Weiss, *Beyond the SALT II Failure* (New York: Praeger, 1981), p. 99.

10. Kenneth L. Adelman, "Arms Control with and without Agreements," *Foreign Affairs* 63 (2) (Winter 1984–85), p. 250.

11. See, for example, Bowie, "Arms Control and United States Foreign Policy," in Henkin, ed., *Arms Control*, pp. 71–72; William R. Kintner and Robert L. Pfaltzgraff, Jr., "The Strategic Arms Limitation Agreements of 1972: Implications for International Security," in Kintner and Pfaltzgraff, eds., *SALT*, p. 393; and Weiss, "The Case against Arms Control," p. 21.

12. See below, p. 258.

13. Walter Millis, ed., *The Forrestal Diaries* (New York: Viking, 1951), pp. 290–91, quoted in May, "The Cold War," in Nye, ed., *The Making of America's Soviet Policy*, p. 227.

14. See below, pp. 254–258. In addition, some argue that U.S.–Soviet détente, not arms control in particular, produced a lulling effect. See, for example, Norman Podhoretz, "The Future Danger," *Commentary* (April 1981), p. 39; and Lawrence J. Korb, *The Fall and Rise of the Pentagon: American Defense Policies in the 1970s* (Westport, Conn.: Greenwood Press, 1979), pp. 140, 150. A large majority of the U.S. people evidently agrees with this proposition. A 1984 poll found that 67 percent of those surveyed agreed with the statement, "The Soviets used détente as an opportunity to build up their armed forces while lulling us into a false sense of security." See Public Agenda Foundation, *Voter Options on Nuclear Arms Policy: A Briefing Book for the 1984 Elections* (New York: Public Agenda Foundation, 1984), p. 31. The effects of détente and SALT are linked, as SALT formed the centerpiece of the Nixon-Kissinger strategy for improving U.S.-Soviet relations. This chapter will focus on the impact of arms control, however, as many versions of the lulling effect argument specifically blame arms control for adverse trends in U.S. defense spending.

15. See, for example, Graham T. Allison, Albert Carnesale, and Joseph S. Nye, Jr., *Hawks, Doves, and Owls: An Agenda for Avoiding Nuclear War* (New York: Norton, 1985), p. 244. Overselling arms control may also lead to disenchantment when the agreement fails to satisfy inflated expectations.

16. Adelman, "Arms Control with and without Agreements," p. 243. See also Kissinger, *White House Years*, p. 1255.

17. See George F. Kennan, *American Diplomacy, 1900-1950* (Chicago: University of Chicago Press, 1951), for a classic statement of this view.

18. Barry M. Blechman, "Do Negotiated Arms Limitations Have a Future?," *Foreign Affairs* 59 (1) (Fall 1980), pp. 113-14; and Ithiel de Sola Pool, "Public Opinion and the Control of Armaments," in Donald G. Brennan, ed., *Arms Control, Disarmament, and National Security* (New York: George Braziller, 1961), pp. 340-41.

19. Eugene V. Rostow, "The Case against SALT II," *Commentary* (Feb. 1979), p. 23.

20. Frank Barnet, preface to Paul H. Nitze, James E. Dougherty, and Francis X. Kane, *The Fateful Ends and Shades of SALT* (New York: Crane Russak, 1979), pp. viii-ix.

21. See, for example, Rostow, "The Case against SALT II," p. 31.

22. For a discussion of this issue, see Roger Zane George, "The Economics of Arms Control," *International Security* 3 (3) (Winter 1978-79), pp. 94-125.

23. J.I. Coffey, "American Interests in the Limitation of Strategic Armaments," in Kintner and Pfaltzgraff, eds., *SALT*, p. 70. See also Joseph Kruzel, "From Rush-Bagot to START: The Lessons of Arms Control," *Orbis* 30 (1) (Spring 1986), pp. 204-05. It is possible, of course, that Congress will seek increased military spending as the price of its support for arms control even if the Joint Chiefs of Staff do not make it a condition of their support.

24. See George Rathjens, Abram Chayes, and J.P. Ruina, *Nuclear Arms Control Agreements: Process and Impact* (Washington, D.C.: Carnegie Endowment for International Peace, 1974); Colin Gray, *The Soviet-American Arms Race* (Lexington, Mass.: Heath, 1976; reprinted by Saxon House, Farnborough, Great Britain), p. 184; Bruce Russett, *The Prisoners of Insecurity* (San Francisco: Freeman, 1983), p. 178; W.K.H. Panofsky, *Arms Control and SALT II* (Seattle: University of Washington Press, 1979), p. 17; and Weiss, "The Case against Arms Control," p. 20.

25. See Gray, *The Soviet-American Arms Race*, p. 184; and Rathjens, Chayes, and Ruina, *Nuclear Arms Control Agreements*, p. 21.

26. See Robert J. Bresler and Robert C. Gray, "The Bargaining Chip and SALT," *Political Science Quarterly* 92 (1) (Spring 1977), pp. 65-88.

27. *The New York Times*, Feb. 17, 1976, p. 8.

28. Graham T. Allison and Frederic A. Morris, "Armaments and Arms Control: Exploring the Determinants of Military Weapons," *Daedalus* 104 (3) (Summer 1975), p. 101. See also George, "The Economics of Arms Control," p. 123; and Kruzel, "From Rush-Bagot to START," pp. 207–08.

29. Roger Zane George, for example, attributes the acceleration in military programs to a vaguely defined "technological imperative," but such imperatives need not be connected to arms control. See his "Economics of Arms Control," p. 123.

30. See Weiss, "The Case against Arms Control," pp. 20–21.

31. In 1984 a poll showed that 62 percent of the U.S. public agreed that "The buildup of our military defenses is long overdue." See Public Agenda Foundation, *Voter Options on Nuclear Arms Policy*, p. 34.

32. These divergent perspectives are illustrated by Colin S. Gray and Jeffrey G. Barlow, "Inexcusable Restraint: The Decline of American Military Power in the 1970s"; Robert Komer, "What Decade of Neglect?"; and Melvin R. Laird, "A Strong Start in a Difficult Decade: Defense Policy in the Nixon-Ford Years"; all in *International Security* 10 (2) (Fall 1985), pp. 5–83.

33. See Korb, *The Fall and Rise of the Pentagon*, pp. 5–17. Even some observers sympathetic to the lulling effect argument admit that it "is difficult to document and, to be sure, much of the evidence is subject to conflicting interpretations." See Steven L. Rearden, *The Evolution of American Strategic Doctrine: Paul H. Nitze and the Soviet Challenge* (Boulder, Colo.: Westview, 1984), p. 69.

34. U.S. Senate Committee on Foreign Relations, *Hearings on the Nuclear Test Ban Treaty*, 88th Cong., 1st Sess. (Washington, D.C.: U.S. Government Printing Office, 1963), p. 109.

35. *Ibid.*, p. 403.

36. Ronald J. Terchek, *The Making of the Test Ban Treaty* (The Hague: Martinus Nijhoff, 1970), p. 198.

37. Glenn T. Seaborg, *Kennedy, Khrushchev, and the Test Ban* (Berkeley: University of California Press, 1981), p. 221.

38. *Nuclear Test Ban Treaty*, pp. 274–75.

39. *Ibid.*, p. 348.

40. Seaborg, *Kennedy, Khrushchev, and the Test Ban*, p. 279.

41. *Nuclear Test Ban Treaty*, p. 367.

42. Richard Perle, "Superpower Postures in SALT: The Language of Arms Control," in Morton A. Kaplan, ed., *SALT: Problems and Prospects* (Morristown, N.J.: General Learning Press, 1973), pp. 129–30.

43. See Kennedy's address of July 26, 1983, and his message transmitting the LTBT to the Senate, in U.S. Arms Control and Disarmament Agency, *Documents on Disarmament* (Washington, D.C.: U.S. Government Printing Office, 1964), pp. 250–57; 299–302.

44. *Nuclear Test Ban Treaty*, pp. 275–76.

45. U.S. Senate Committee on Foreign Relations, *Hearings on the Nonproliferation Treaty*, 90th Cong., 2d Sess. (Washington, D.C.: U.S. Government Printing Office, 1968), p. 129.

46. Elliot R. Goodman, *The Fate of the Atlantic Community* (New York: Praeger, 1975), p. 386.

47. Paul Nitze, in *Nonproliferation Treaty*, p. 56.

48. Joseph J. Kruzel, "The Preconditions and Consequences of Arms Control Agreements," Ph.D. dissertation, Harvard University, 1975, pp. 296–97.

49. Douglas J. Feith, Deputy Assistant Secretary of Defense for Negotiations Policy, "Testimony on Biological and Toxin Weapons before the Subcommittee on Oversight and Evaluation of the House Permanent Select Committee on Intelligence, August 8, 1986," mimeo, p. 11.

50. See U.S. Department of Defense, *Annual Reports on Chemical Warfare and Biological Research Programs* for fiscal years 1976-1979, in *Congressional Record—Senate*, February 11, 1977, p. 4440; *Congressional Record—Senate*, March 7, 1978, p. 4025; *Congressional Record—Senate*, July 19, 1979, p. 59921; and *Congressional Record—Senate*, August 5, 1980, p. 21384.

51. For data on 1970-72 spending, see Stockholm International Peace Research Institute, *The Problem of Chemical and Biological Warfare*, Vol. II, *CB Weapons Today* (Stockholm: Almqvist and Wiksell, 1973), p. 205. For 1973–1975 spending, see U.S. Department of Defense, *Semiannual Reports on Chemical Warfare and Biological Research Programs* for periods January 1–June 30, 1973, July 1–December 31, 1973, January 1–June 30, 1974, July 1–December 31, 1974, and January 1–June 30, 1975, in *Congressional Record—Senate*, November 2, 1973, p. 35745; *Congressional Record—Senate*, March 11, 1974, p. 6127; *Congressional Record—Senate*, September 12, 1974, p. 31021; *Congressional Record—Senate*, March 17, 1975, p. 6910; and *Congressional Record—Senate*, September 19, 1975, p. 29528.

52. Erhard Geissler, "A New Generation of Biological Weapons," in Erhard Geissler, ed., *Biological and Toxin Weapons Today* (Oxford: Oxford University Press, 1986), p. 25; and Jonathan B. Tucker, "Gene Wars," *Foreign Policy* 57 (Winter 1984–85), p. 69.

53. U.S. House Subcommittees on International Security and Scientific Affairs and on Asian and Pacific Affairs of the Committee on Foreign Affairs, *Hearings on the Strategic Implications of Chemical and Biological Warware*, 96th Cong., 2d Sess. (Washington, D.C.: U.S. Government Printing Office, 1980), p. 37.

54. U.S. House Committee on Armed Services, *Hearings on Military Posture and H.R. 5968 [H.R. 6030], Department of Defense Authorization for Appropriations for Fiscal Year 1983*, 97th Cong., 2d Sess. (Washington, D.C.: U.S. Government Printing Office, 1982), pp. 828–29; 848. See also

Feith, "Testimony on Biological and Toxin Weapons," p. 7; and Tucker, "Gene Wars," pp. 58–79.

55. Rostow, "The Case against SALT II," p. 25. See also Lehman and Weiss, *Beyond the SALT II Failure*, p. 8.

56. U.S. Senate Committee on Foreign Relations, *Hearings on the Strategic Arms Limitation Agreements*, 92d Cong., 2d Sess. (Washington, D.C.: U.S. Government Printing Office, 1972), p. 221.

57. *The SALT II Treaty*, Part 4, pp. 45–46.

58. *The SALT II Treaty*, Part 3, p. 57.

59. Louis Harris, "82% Approve Summit Trip," *The Washington Post*, June 27, 1972, p. A3.

60. Gallup-Potomac Associates poll, cited in Tom W. Smith, "The Polls: American Attitudes toward the Soviet Union and Communism," *Public Opinion Quarterly* 47 (2) (Summer 1983), p. 280.

61. Melvin R. Laird, Secretary of Defense, *Fiscal Year 1971 Defense Program and Budget* (Washington, D.C.: U.S. Government Printing Office, 1970), p. 1.

62. See Lawrence J. Korb and Linda P. Brady, "Rearming America: The Reagan Administration Defense Program," *International Security* 9 (3) (Winter 1984–85), p. 8; and Korb, *The Fall and Rise of the Pentagon*, p. 34.

63. See Korb, *The Fall and Rise of the Pentagon*, pp. 15–17; 69–70; and Coffey, "American Interests in the Limitation of Strategic Armaments," p. 66.

64. *Strategic Arms Limitation Agreements*, p. 246.

65. See Kissinger, *White House Years*, pp. 199–200; and Members of Congress for Peace through Law, *Economics of Defense: A Bipartisan Review of Military Spending* (New York: Praeger, 1971), p. 13.

66. U.S. Congressional Budget Office, *SALT and the U.S. Strategic Forces Budget*, Background Paper No. 8 (Washington, D.C.: U.S. Government Printing Office, 1976), pp. ix, x, 22.

67. U.S. House Committee on Appropriations, *Department of Defense Appropriations Bill, 1976*, Report No. 94–517, 94th Cong., 1st Sess. (Washington, D.C.: U.S. Government Printing Office, 1975), p. 270.

68. *Ibid.*, p. 271.

69. *Congressional Record*, Nov. 11–18, 1975, pp. 36755–56.

70. "$90.7-Billion Defense Bill Sent to Conference," *Congressional Quarterly Weekly Report*, Nov. 22, 1975, p. 2555.

71. James R. Schlesinger, *Annual Defense Department Report, FY 1976 and FT 197T* (Washington, D.C.: U.S. Government Printing Office, 1975), p. II–46.

72. Elliot L. Richardson, *Annual Defense Department Report, FY 1974* (Washington, D.C.: U.S. Government Printing Office, 1973), p. 64.

73. James R. Schlesinger, *Annual Defense Department Report, FY 1975* (Washington, D.C.: U.S. Government Printing Office, 1974), p. 71.

74. Harold Brown, *Department of Defense Annual Report, FY 1979* (Washington, D.C.: U.S. Government Printing Office, 1978), p. 124.

75. U.S. Senate Committee on Armed Services, *Hearings on Soviet Treaty Violations*, 98th Cong., 2d Sess. (Washington, D.C.: U.S. Government Printing Office, 1984), p. 22.

76. See Van Cleave, "Implications of Success or Failure of SALT," p. 327; and Weiss, "The Case against Arms Control," p. 21.

77. See R.L. Maust, G.W. Goodman, Jr., and C.E. McLain, "History of Strategic Defense," Final Report SPC 742, prepared by System Planning Corporation for the Defense Science Board (Sept. 1981), pp. 16, 17–19.

78. Quoted in Stephen Ambrose, *Rise to Globalism*, 3d ed. (Harmondsworth, Great Britain: Penguin, 1983), pp. 316–17.

79. Fred M. Kaplan, "SALT: The End of Arms Control," *The Progressive* (Jan. 1978), p. 22.

80. U.S. Senate Committee on Armed Services, *Hearings on the Military Implications of the Treaty on the Limitation of Strategic Offensive Arms*, 92d Cong., 2d Sess. (Washington, D.C.: U.S. Government Printing Office, 1972), p. 17.

81. See John Steinbruner and Barry Carter, "Organizational and Political Dimensions of the Strategic Posture: The Problems of Reform," *Daedalus* 104 (3) (Summer 1975), p. 140; Kissinger, *White House Years*, p. 1129; and Melvin R. Laird, *National Security Strategy of Realistic Deterrence: Annual Defense Department Report, FY 1973* (Washington, D.C.: U.S. Government Printing Office, 1972), pp. 68–69.

82. *Military Implications*, p. v.

83. *Ibid.*, p. 5.

84. *Ibid.*, p. 140.

85. Richardson, *Annual Defense Department Report, FY 1974*, p. 2.

86. Quoted in Elmo R. Zumwalt, Jr., *On Watch* (New York: Quadrangle, 1976), p. 391.

87. *Strategic Arms Limitation Agreements*, p. 409.

88. *Military Implications*, p. 146.

89. *Ibid.*, p. 60.

90. *Ibid.*, p. 62.

91. Kissinger, *White House Years*, p. 551.

92. *Strategic Arms Limitation Agreements*, p. 16.

93. *Ibid.*, p. 13.

94. *Military Implications*, p. 156.

95. See Leo Sartori, "Will SALT II Survive?," *International Security* 10 (3) (Winter 1985–86), pp. 147–74.

96. Quoted in Roger P. Labrie, ed., *SALT Hand Book: Key Documents and Issues 1972–1979* (Washington, D.C.: American Enterprise Institute, 1979), p. 75.

97. Richard Perle, "Echoes of the 1930s," *Strategic Review* 7 (1) (Winter 1979), p. 13.

98. Richard Burt, "Arms Control and Strategic Forces: The Risks of Asking SALT to Do Too Much," *Washington Review of Strategic and International Studies* 1 (1) (Jan. 1978), p. 31.

99. William R. Van Cleave, "U.S. Strategic Forces in the 1980s," in Gordon Humphrey, *et al.*, *SALT II and American Security* (Cambridge, Mass.: Institute for Foreign Policy Analysis, 1980), p. 20. As evidence, Van Cleave cites Secretary of Defense Donald Rumsfeld's 1978 *Annual Report*, which states, "Force planning under current policy is constrained by those limitations *anticipated* in light of the Vladivostok accords." This statement, however, does not necessarily suggest that the United States was lulled. Van Cleave apparently objects to the fact that the United States decided not to violate an agreement signed by Presidents Ford and Brezhnev.

100. See, for example, Gray and Barlow, "Inexcusable Restraint."

101. See *ibid.*,; and David Sullivan, *The Bitter Fruit of SALT* (Houston: Texas Policy Institute, 1982).

102. See, for example, Komer, "What Decade of Neglect?"

103. Brown, *Department of Defense Annual Report, FY 1979*, p. 115.

104. See Carter and Brown statements in Labrie, ed., *SALT Hand Book*, pp. 468–73.

105. Paul H. Nitze, "The Merits and Demerits of a SALT II Agreement," in Nitze, Dougherty, and Kane, *The Fateful Ends and Shades of SALT*, p. 45.

106. "The Now and Forever Protocol," *The Wall Street Journal*, Jan. 17, 1979, p. 22.

107. See Albert Carnesale and Charles L. Glaser, "ICBM Vulnerability: The Cures Are Worse Than the Disease," *International Security* 7 (1) (Summer 1982), pp. 70–85.

108. Harold Brown, *Department of Defense Annual Report, Fiscal Year 1980* (Washington, D.C.: U.S. Government Printing Office, 1979), p. 121. Secretary of Defense James Schlesinger also twice reduced the rate of Trident procurement. See Congressional Budget Office, *SALT and the U.S. Strategic Forces Budget*, p. 24.

109. Brown, *Department of Defense Annual Report, FY 1980*, p. 121.

110. Brown, *Department of Defense Annual Report, FY 1979*, p. 113; see also D. Douglas Dalgleish and Larry Schweikart, *Trident* (Carbondale and Edwardsville: Southern Illinois University Press, 1984).

111. Brown, *Department of Defense Annual Report, FY 1979*, p. 108.

112. See Komer, "What Decade of Neglect?"

113. *The SALT II Treaty*, Part 1, p. 373.

114. *Ibid.*, p. 438.

115. *Ibid.*, p. 497.

116. *Ibid.*, p. 154.

117. *The SALT II Treaty*, Part 2, p. 177.

118. Smith, "The Polls: American Attitudes toward the Soviet Union and Communism," pp. 287–88; NBC News, "Poll Results," No. 39 (Feb. 6, 1979), pp. 8, 10; and *Public Opinion* 2 (2) (March–May 1979), p. 27.

119. A.G.B. Metcalf, "The SALT II Paradox," *Strategic Review* 7 (4) (Fall 1979), pp. 9–12.

120. U.S. Senate Committee on Foreign Relations, *Report on The SALT II Treaty*, 96th Cong., 1st Sess. (Washington, D.C.: U.S. Government Printing Office, 1979), p. 160.

121. *The SALT II Treaty*, Part 3, p. 57.

122. *The SALT II Treaty*, Part 1, p. 132.

123. *Ibid.*, p. 429.

124. *Ibid.*, p. 110.

125. See John Edwards, *Super Weapon: The Making of MX* (New York: Norton, 1982), pp. 202–03.

126. See Paul B. Stares, *The Militarization of Space: U.S. Policy, 1945–84* (Ithaca, N.Y.: Cornell University Press, 1985), pp. 204, 209–10.

127. *Ibid.*, pp. 162–66.

128. Raymond L. Garthoff, *Détente and Confrontation: American-Soviet Relations from Nixon to Reagan* (Washington, D.C.: Brookings Institution, 1985), pp. 189–90.

129. See Stares, *The Militarization of Space*, pp. 181, 192–93.

130. Colin S. Gray, "The Purpose and Value of Arms Control Negotiations," in U.S. Senate Committee on Foreign Relations, *Perceptions: Relations between the United States and the Soviet Union* (Washington, D.C.: U.S. Government Printing Office, 1978), p. 365. This argument may or may not be correct, but assessing it is beyond the scope of this chapter.

10 LINKAGE

Kiron K. Skinner

The tie between arms control and the larger U.S.-Soviet relationship is complex. This tie can be understood in a broad sense—that is, whether arms control negotiations and agreements tend to promote more moderate Soviet (or from Moscow's perspective, U.S.) behavior in other realms such as regional diplomacy and human rights, in which case the overall relationship would clearly improve. It can similarly be asked whether improvements in these other spheres of U.S.-Soviet relations lubricate the arms control process. In both cases, one can also ask about adverse connections: whether difficulties in arms control spill over and exacerbate tensions elsewhere in the superpower relationship and whether differences over the pursuit of regional objectives or Soviet treatment of its citizens creates problems for arms control efforts.

The tie between arms control and the larger U.S.-Soviet relationship can also be understood more directly. The question arises as to whether arms control negotiations can be used to further interests in other realms of the relationship; similarly, there is the possibility of using these other interests and interactions to further arms control ends. These and other notions are often characterized as *linkage*. This essay will examine the various forms of linkage and assess what impact linkage has had on both arms control and U.S.-Soviet relations.

ESTABLISHING A LINKAGE FRAMEWORK

A useful framework for assessing the role and impact of linkage differentiates among three basic forms of connections between arms control and other arenas of superpower relations. Linkage can be understood as a strategy to influence the behavior of the other party. As such, linkage can take two forms. Arms control progress can be made contingent on political concessions from the target country in some other area of rivalry. Arms control is used as a lever in this linkage strategy. An example of this type of linkage is as follows: "If you want progress in arms control, then you must curb your aggressive behavior in country X or reform your behavior domestically." Alternatively, other incentives can be offered in exchange for concessions in arms control. Extending economic benefits in return for compromises at the negotiating table would constitute an example of this approach. In this approach, progress in arms control is the object of the exercise.

What characterizes linkage as a bargaining strategy—that is, the use of arms control as lever or object—is the purposeful employment of linkage as a policy by one party attempting to manipulate the behavior of the other party to its own advantage. The second basic type of linkage is fundamentally different. It can best be described as unintended. Sometimes it is simply described as a fact of political life. Unintended linkage occurs when developments within the overall U.S.-Soviet relationship but outside the realm of arms control affect the ability of governments to pursue the arms control policies of their choice. The opposite pattern is possible too: one can imagine arms control developments having a positive or negative impact on the larger relationship.

A third form of linkage, termed here *delinkage*, is related to both forms already defined. Like linkage as a bargaining strategy, delinkage is purposeful and intended. Its purpose, however, is not to exploit arms control for other policy ends or vice versa but rather to isolate particular arms control enterprises from other aspects of the U.S.-Soviet relationship. The principal objective is to insulate arms control from the often disruptive impact of geopolitical competition. In short, delinkage is a policy that would forgo any possible benefits of using linkage as a strategy to avoid the possible costs of unintended linkage. An additional rationale for a delinkage policy is to inhibit the other party's potential use of a linkage strategy.

Much of what follows is devoted to assessing the impact of each of the three linkage variants.[1] Particular attention is devoted to linkage as a strategy (as opposed to unintended linkage and delinkage) not because it constitutes the most significant form of linkage but because it is the form of linkage most often referred to and debated. In addition, this chapter both examines the prerequisites for implementing strategies of linkage and delinkage and assesses the relationship between arms control and other aspects of U.S.-Soviet competition.

LINKAGE AS A STRATEGY: ARMS CONTROL AS LEVER

The promise of progress in arms control—that is, arms control as lever—in exchange for seemingly unrelated political concessions from the target country has frequently, although rarely successfully, been used by U.S. and Soviet leaders in the course of arms control negotiations. President Richard Nixon and his national security advisor Henry Kissinger initially adopted this strategy. Aware that the Soviet Union wanted to begin strategic arms negotiations and that the United States needed to end the Vietnam War, Nixon and Kissinger devised a secret mission early in the new administration to link progress on SALT I to Soviet cooperation in Vietnam. According to Kissinger, "Vance would be sent to Moscow to begin SALT discussions and on the same trip meet secretly with a senior North Vietnamese representative. Vance would be empowered to make rapid progress in *both* areas, while seeking to keep them in tandem."[2] It took the Soviets several months to respond. When they did, they claimed that they could not get the North Vietnamese to participate. Thus, the mission never took place. Although Kissinger claims that the administration "never made a comprehensive proposal to the Soviets on Vietnam," it did seek to use the promise of arms control as leverage for Soviet aid in resolving the Vietnam War.[3] The attempted use of SALT I as a lever for Soviet cooperation in Vietnam underscores the difficulty of meeting the requirements for using linkage as a bargaining strategy. It is probably the case that the Soviets did not have as much influence on the North Vietnamese as Nixon and Kissinger believed. Moreover, Soviet leaders understood that the United States sought strategic arms talks for their inherent value and could not long insist that they be put off because of Vietnam. History shows all too clearly that the Vietnam War continued—and that the SALT process went ahead—despite U.S. pressure for Soviet assistance to end the war in Vietnam.

The attempt to exploit Soviet interest in arms control as leverage for changes in Soviet external behavior was not limited to Vietnam. The 1970 Cienfuegos incident is another example. In August and September 1970 U.S. U-2 reconnaissance planes spotted what was believed to be the construction of a naval facility at Cienfuegos Bay, Cuba, along with a submarine tender and two barges. On learning of these activities, Kissinger met with Soviet Ambassador Anatoly Dobrynin and told him that the United States viewed the Soviet "construction at Cienfuegos unmistakably [as] a submarine base. . . . We would not shrink from other measures including public steps if forced into it."[4] Kissinger noted that such Soviet behavior was in violation of the 1962 Kennedy-Khrushchev understandings prohibiting Soviet creation of an offensive base in Cuba. In response to the adverse implications for détente suggested by Kissinger, Dobrynin reportedly turned ashen; more important, within a matter of weeks, he assured the White House that the Soviet Union was not building a base at Cienfuegos.[5] Although caution must always be taken in interpreting Soviet behavior, it is highly plausible that U.S. linkage did affect Soviet calculations in this episode.

The Nixon administration also linked SALT and détente to Soviet external behavior in an attempt to limit the 1971 India-Pakistan War. During what was supposed to be a meeting to discuss U.S. grain sales to the Soviet Union, Nixon told Soviet Minister of Agriculture Vladimir Matskevich that "If India moved forces against West Pakistan, the United States would not stand by" and that "all progress in U.S.-Soviet relations was being threatened by the war on the subcontinent."[6] In part owing to Soviet aid, the Indians won the war. Although Bangladesh was born in the process, Indian war aims turned out to be limited. Quite possibly, Soviet influence was one factor in New Delhi's decision not to continue the war against what remained of Pakistan; it remains unclear, however, whether U.S. pressures had any effect on Soviet behavior.

The Soviets also sought to use arms control for extrinsic purposes. During the Harriman-Khrushchev summit on the Limited Test Ban

Treaty (LTBT), for example, the USSR sought to unsuccessfully link the Test Ban Treaty with a NATO-Warsaw Pact nonaggression pact.[7] There may also have been Soviet attempts to use arms control as a means of influencing U.S. policy in Vietnam, although it is difficult to determine how serious the Soviets were about this tie. Moscow might have been reluctant to begin strategic arms limitation talks in the mid-1960s because of the Vietnam War (although wanting to continue their own military build-up is a more likely explanation), but once the SALT talks began in earnest, Soviet linkage of arms control and Vietnam subsided.[8] What is clear is that any linkage on their part failed to affect U.S. strategy in Indochina.

During SALT I both the Soviet Union and the United States sought to link arms control with the Berlin talks. Kissinger writes that when he "linked Berlin to SALT, the Soviets linked Berlin to a summit."[9] A U.S. exercise in object linkage turned out to be a Soviet attempt at using arms control as leverage. Another possible Soviet linkage during the SALT I negotiations involved the May 20, 1971, SALT compromise that included such Soviet concessions as the decision not to include U.S. forward-based aircraft in any freeze. It has been suggested that this diplomatic move was directly related to the Soviet interest in increased grain sales. According to Seymour Hersh, "Nixon had accomplished his backchannel SALT breakthrough only after assuring Moscow that he would end the grain embargo and once again sell American wheat to the Soviet Union."[10] Despite Hersh's confidence, however, and as is often the case, there is no way of knowing that U.S. arms control diplomacy was in fact influenced by a Soviet desire for expanded U.S. exports.

The Soviet linkage of grain and SALT may be true, but it may also be the case that Nixon and Kissinger promised the much needed grain sales to the Soviet Union to induce Moscow to make SALT I compromises. For instance, in June 1971 Nixon rescinded the 1963 order that 50 percent of U.S. grain sold to the Soviet Union had to be loaded in U.S. ships.[11] Although appearing to accept the argument that grain and SALT were linked, Raymond Garthoff writes, "Neither the official documents that have been released nor the memoirs of either Nixon or Kissinger disclose that the agreement on SALT reached in early May and publicly announced on May 20, 1971, had been privately linked to an American agreement on major grain sales to the Soviet Union and on the provision of credits for those sales."[12]

Linkage is difficult to identify. If the linkage between grain and SALT actually took place, it is an example of successful linkage for both Washington and Moscow because it led to something both countries wanted: progress in arms control and expanded trade in grain. The question is whether the Soviets were able to affect U.S. political behavior as Nixon increased grain sales to the country or whether the United States succeeded in using grain to bring about Soviet compromise in arms control. Again, it is difficult if not impossible to distinguish between the simultaneous exercise of leverage and object linkage.

In the examples of arms control as a lever cited above, the linking party made rather specific demands of the target country. The linkage strategy of arms control as lever is not always used in this way. In some instances the linker has more general objectives. Handicapped by the lack of U.S. domestic support for extensive military involvement in the Third World and by the Jackson-Vanik Amendment to the 1974 Trade Reform Act that took away the option of using the economic carrot of increased trade with the Soviet Union, Presidents Gerald Ford and Jimmy Carter had to readjust the strategy of arms control as lever to fit domestic political constraints. This readjustment primarily meant casting linkage proposals in very general terms—and arguing, for instance, that arms control progress could be hurt by Soviet political behavior but then not requiring of the Soviet Union that it take some specific action as was done in the Cienfuegos crisis. This approach to linkage comes close to an attempt to stimulate linkage as a deterrent within the USSR.

The U.S. reaction to Soviet involvement in the 1975 Angolan civil war illustrates the difficulties in attempting to use arms control as a lever for general purposes. In October 1975, "long after both superpowers were deeply involved militarily," the United States began to raise the Angolan problem with Moscow.[13] The administration turned to linkage following its unsuccessful attempt to convince Congress to provide aid to two of the political factions involved in the struggle. Kissinger warned the Soviets that their involvement in Angola could have severe consequences: "we have made clear that a confrontation of actions like those in Angola must threaten the entire web of Soviet-U.S. relations. In this sense, both [SALT] negotiations and the overall relationship are in long-term jeopardy unless restraint is exercised."[14] Kissinger's goal in making this statement, which came too late in the conflict to be effective, might well have been to serve notice to the Soviets that U.S.-Soviet relations could not withstand any more Angolas than to exact some type of political concession from them. This is especially plausible when considering the fact that shortly after the Angolan dispute Kissinger traveled to Moscow in an attempt to salvage SALT II.

One of the most significant problems of using linkage as a way to send warnings or messages to the target country is that it often lacks credibility. Many leaders use linkage in this way when they do not have the domestic resources to make specific demands of the other party. The U.S. linkage of Angola and SALT II supports this reasoning. By 1975 support for détente in the United States was eroding; the Soviets may have harbored doubts as to Ford's political strength and his ability to build a domestic consensus favoring renewed détente; the United States possessed too few economic "carrots and sticks" to manipulate in an attempt to shape Soviet behavior; and the Soviet Union was already too deeply invested in conflict to change course. As Dimitri Simes has written of the Soviet Union's perception of its stakes in Angola: "by 1975, while still remaining optimistic about the long-term prospects of the U.S.-Soviet relationship, the Politburo in all likelihood felt neither so enthusiastic about the advantages of cooperation nor so concerned about the dangers of confrontation that it was willing to forego intervention in Angola."[15] In light of these realities, the Soviet Union most likely did not feel compelled to respond to U.S. linkage proposals.

The Soviet conception of détente also affected how Moscow responded to U.S. linkage diplomacy. The Soviets embraced a different, more narrow notion of détente. General Secretary Leonid Brezhnev made this plain in his address to the Twenty-fifth Party Congress: "Détente does not in the slightest abolish and cannot abolish or alter the laws of the class struggle. Some bourgeois leaders affect surprise over the solidarity of Soviet communists, of the Soviet people, with the struggle of other people for freedom and progress. This is either outright naiveté or more likely a deliberate befuddling of minds."[16]

Despite the Carter administration's stated policy of eschewing linkages between arms control and other aspects of U.S. relations, several attempts were made at using arms control as leverage on Soviet political behavior. In response to Soviet support of the Ethiopian army as it fought against Somalia in the Ogaden War, National Security Advisor Zbigniew Brzezinski told the press (on March 1, 1978) that Soviet activities in the Ogaden "would inevitably complicate SALT."[17] The next day President Carter attempted to clarify Brzezinski's statement by explaining that SALT II and the Ogaden were "linked because of actions by the Soviets. We don't initiate the linkage."[18] Months later, in a "Meet the Press" interview, Brzezinski argued that Soviet behavior in the Third World was not "compatible with what was once called the code of détente."[19]

The Carter administration's African linkages were largely ineffective. The Soviets did not withdraw support for the Ethiopians; to the contrary, Soviet involvement in the Ogaden dispute on behalf of Ethiopia increased over time. There was no compelling incentive for the Soviet Union not to court Ethiopia. It was never clear that the United States was prepared to link the Ogaden to SALT II. Carter wavered in support of Brzezinski's linkage statement. Secretary of State Cyrus Vance opposed it; in his memoir Vance noted, "I favored making it clear to the USSR that its behavior was undermining our ability to follow a balanced policy . . . but carrying the linkage idea far beyond that had serious drawbacks."[20] And although the administration cancelled the Indian Ocean talks after only four rounds of Soviet activities in the Horn, the Carter administration remained interested in signing the SALT II treaty.[21]

Bureaucratic divisions were not the only factors weakening the potential influence of a linkage strategy. In December 1977 Representatives Bonker and Tsongas published a report based on their visit to the Horn of Africa. One recommendation was that "the United States should not provide direct or indirect military assistance to Somalia."[22] The report appeared to reflect widespread congressional sentiment toward U.S. involvement in the Ogaden conflict;[23] once again legislative opposition to any direct response to Soviet adventurism left the United States with little more than rhetoric to fall back on. Also, by 1978 the administration had few other instruments to turn to in hopes of affecting Soviet calculations. As Marshall Shulman (Vance's Soviet advisor) noted at the time, "Economic relations are not a feasible instrument because we don't have the trade agreement in force and we aren't able to put, say, limits on credits because those simply aren't granted."[24]

It may also be the case that in several instances the Soviet Union sought to use arms control as leverage to discourage U.S.-China rapprochement. Although the United States "played the China card" at least in part to heighten Soviet commitment to arms control and détente, the Soviets may have played their own version of the China card, seeking to use progress in SALT I negotiations to deter U.S.-Chinese rapprochement.[25]

Moscow appeared again to use arms control as a lever during SALT II—much as the United States attempted vis-à-vis Angola and the Ogaden—in relation to the China/Vietnam conflict in 1979. Two weeks before Chinese troops entered into Vietnam in mid-February 1979, Chinese Deputy Premier Deng Xiaoping was on an official visit to the United States and proclaimed that the Chinese might fight Vietnam, a Soviet ally. The USSR quickly spoke of linking SALT II to U.S. support of the Chinese. In February 1979 Soviet Foreign Minister Andrei Gromyko said, "The Central Committee of the Communist Party of the Soviet government have drawn attention more than once to the fact that such actions by the United States as playing 'the China card,' which has become so dear to those in Washington who think little of the future, in no way met the purposes of the [SALT] agreement or the goals of peace in general."[26] Strobe Talbott maintains that political linkage had an adverse affect on U.S.-Soviet relations: "There was nothing ambiguous about the effect of China's behavior on Soviet-American relations and on SALT. It was unquestionably and unmitigatedly damaging. . . . In back-channel conversation both in Washington and Moscow, there were dark hints that the Soviet leadership might be undertaking a fundamental reassessment of its policy toward the U.S., including a reassessment of the desirability of concluding a SALT agreement at all."[27] Although Soviet discussions on linking arms control to U.S. external political behavior did not result in the country's pulling out of the arms talks, the linkage by both countries dampened support for what remained of U.S.-Soviet détente.

ARMS CONTROL AS THE OBJECT OF LINKAGE

Object linkage is another bargaining strategy that was used by the United States and the Soviet Union during SALT I. The Nixon administration turned to nonmilitary inducements such as trade, credits, and U.S. political behavior to obtain arms control concessions from the Soviet Union. Kissinger recounts that "We sat on a scheme for an American firm to sell gear cutting machinery for a Soviet civilian truck plant on the Kama River for two years in the face of massive pressures from our economic agencies and the Congress . . . after the Soviets agreed to the May 20 compromise on SALT, the plant was quickly approved."[28]

In addition to economic levers, Nixon and Kissinger believed that U.S. rapprochement with China would make the Soviet Union more amenable to establishing détente with the United States and concluding the SALT talks. They saw an opportunity for linkage in the deterioration of Sino-Soviet relations, especially after the border clashes during the spring and summer of 1969. Garthoff contends that "Nixon and Kissinger did not want to press ahead in developing relations with the Soviet Union without parallel movement with China and leverage gained through linkage of those developments."[29]

The Carter administration also used linkage to strengthen the U.S. bargaining posture vis-à-vis Moscow by exploiting U.S. relations with the People's Republic of China. Indeed, one of the important foreign policy accomplishments of the Carter period was to normalize relations with China. Carter speaks directly of linking the normalization of relations with the People's Republic of China to SALT II in a diary entry before the May 1978 Brzezinski trip to China: "I had a meeting with Brzezinski, Brown, Vance, Mondale, and Jordan to discuss Zbig's trip to China, and decided that we would move to normalization this year if the Chinese were forthcoming. Our preference is to take final action after the November election. We all agreed that a better relationship with the PRC would help us with SALT."[30] Ironically, this U.S. exercise in object linkage led the Soviets to put forward linkage of their own as they postponed the SALT II summit for six months. The incentives were low for the Soviet Union to act otherwise: the prospects for SALT II ratification in the United States looked increasingly grim with each passing month, and there were no economic ties in force to induce the Soviet Union to alter its behavior.

It appears that the Soviets also attempted object linkage. Jewish emigration was a major concern for many Americans. During the negotiation process of SALT I, Soviet emigration policy was not a major public issue, but there were private discussions between U.S. and Soviet leaders on Jewish emigration. It is possible that Soviet leaders used the promise of a steady increase in Jewish emigration (which did occur from 1969 to 1972) if arms control progress took place. Indeed, one political analyst maintains that during SALT II object linkage was a Soviet bargaining strategy: "the large increase in out-migration in 1979 clearly had much to do with Soviet hopes for successful ratification of SALT II. Thus, it remains a possible bargaining chip for Soviet negotiators."[31] An alternative perspective would view the increase in emigration from the USSR in the early 1970s as a successful example of U.S. practice of arms control as leverage on some unrelated dimension of Soviet behavior.

UNINTENDED LINKAGE

Unintended linkage, or linkage as a fact of life, could well be the most important form of the phenomenon under study in this chapter. Although for the most part such linkage has proved to be an obstacle to the arms control process, in at least one instance it was an impetus. The Cuban Missile Crisis had a sobering effect on all who lived through it; it clearly increased the determination of the Kennedy administration to seek an improvement in relations with the Soviet Union and in particular to press ahead for some form of limits on nuclear testing.

The more prevalent pattern, however, has been that of events beyond the realm of arms control creating difficulties for the political management of the arms control process. The Johnson administration's attempt to start what ultimately became the SALT process was aborted by the August 1968 Soviet invasion of Czechoslovakia. Progress on the Non-Prolferation Treaty was similarly affected for a time. And much more seriously, the Carter administration's efforts to gain public and Senate support for the SALT II Treaty was undermined by a series of events, including the 1979 "discovery" of the Soviet brigade in Cuba, the fall of the Shah of Iran and the subsequent hostage taking, and the later 1979 Soviet invasion of Afghanistan. In both instances, the U.S. administration pulled back from arms control reluctantly; what was being done reflected bowing to domestic political realities rather than any attempt to use arms control as a lever to affect Soviet policy.

DELINKAGE

In the wake of the 1962 Cuban missile crisis, President Kennedy became especially committed to delinking the Limited Test Ban

Treaty from Soviet external behavior. In a memo to Kennedy, one policymaker suggested that the United States should "not accept a Summit meeting to sign the . . . test ban treaty unless: the Soviet troops are out of Cuba; and Moscow either honors its commitment to the Geneva Accord of 1962 or stands back while we enforce it on North Vietnam."[32] Kennedy disagreed, believing that the Limited Test Ban Treaty was too important to be held hostage to the resolution of conflicts in other areas. The administration also succeeded in helping to defeat a Senate attempt to postpone ratification of the treaty until all Soviet troops were removed from Cuba.

To be sure, the Soviets were carrying out policies, such as in Laos, which were opposed by the U.S. administration of the time. Yet Kennedy was successful in his delinkage strategy. This was due largely to the widespread desire to stabilize core U.S.-Soviet competition in the wake of the missile crisis and to the existence of widespread sympathy for a partial test ban. But it was also due to Kennedy's strength as a president.

Kennedy's successor, Lyndon Johnson, shared his desire to negotiate arms control with the Soviet Union. In the spring of 1967 tension between Syria and Israel mounted and the North Vietnamese sent a greater number of forces into the south. Nevertheless, Johnson was determined to begin strategic arms limitation talks. In a May 19, 1967, letter to Prime Minister Kosygin, he wrote, "Beyond these points of danger and conflict, there are two areas of opportunity where I deeply believe it is our common interest and common duty to humanity to achieve constructive result: the achievement of understandings which would limit our respective deployments of ABMs and ICBMs and the negotiation of a non-proliferation treaty."[33]

Although there was some domestic opposition to beginning arms control talks with the Soviet Union because of its geopolitical activities, Johnson still hosted Kosygin at Glassboro with the hope of setting up strategic arms talks. At the Glassboro meeting, Johnson's eagerness to begin arms control negotiations was obvious, with his reportedly saying to Kosygin, "Give us a date—next week, next month. We will be there. Secretary [of Defense] McNamara is ready now."[34] And although Johnson cancelled his summit meeting with Kosygin in Leningrad in response to the Soviet invasion of Czechoslovakia in 1968—there were limits to his ability to resist unintended linkage—two months later he proposed to president-elect Nixon that the two of them go to Moscow for an arms control summit. (Nixon did not agree to this plan.) In a last-ditch effort, Johnson authorized Ambassador Llewellyn E. Thompson in Moscow to begin SALT talks with the Soviets in Geneva. The now lame-duck administration received a cool response. The Soviets decided to wait for the incoming administration.

Despite the strong association of the Nixon-Kissinger years with the practice of linkage as a strategy, the reality is more complex. Even if one does not endorse fully the following assessment of John Newhouse—"Nixon had started by talking about an era of negotiation, but also, to Moscow's annoyance, by linking SALT to progress on other matters, especially the Middle East and Vietnam. By autumn [1969] the linkage notion, if not entirely discarded, was declining in fashion. In May 1972, the Moscow summit agreements would bury it once and for all."[35]—the administration did at times move in the direction of implementing a delinkage strategy when it suited its purposes. Most notably, the SALT talks were largely unhampered by superpower regional competition and despite the fact that Soviet military assistance to allies in both the Middle East and Southeast Asia continued unabated.

There were as well other examples of delinkage in practice. Although both Ford and Kissinger spoke of linkage near the end of the Angolan Civil War, they also advocated delinkage. In early 1976 Kissinger argued that "As for strategic arms limitation talks, we have never considered these to be a favor which we grant to the Soviet Union to be turned on and off according to the ebb and flow of our relations. The fact is that limiting the growth of nuclear arsenals is an overriding global problem that must be dealt with urgently for our own sake and for the sake of world peace."[36] Similarly, as regarded manipulating economic relations for political purposes, Kissinger noted that "economic measures take too much time to affect a fast moving situation like Angola."[37] The fact that 1976 was an election year further diminished the enthusiasm of the Ford administration for linkage, as President Ford himself argued that linking grain sales to the Angolan conflict would not serve "any useful purpose whatsoever."[38]

Jimmy Carter initially sought to delink SALT II from other issues. His delinkage strategy was unsuccessful for a number of reasons. Support for delinkage was uneven within the administration, with Secretary of State Vance and Marshall Shulman showing more interest in it than National Security Advisor Brzezinski. Carter was widely perceived as weak on dealing with the Soviet Union, and thus many domestic political actors in the United States interpreted his delinkage strategy as evidence of the administration's inability to cope with the Soviet challenge. As the Soviet Union became more assertive in Third World conflicts from 1976 to 1980, Carter's attempt to carry out a delinkage strategy became increasingly difficult to sustain. He abandoned it altogether after the Soviet Union invaded Afghanistan. In response to this event he asked the United States Senate to stop SALT II ratification proceedings, imposed an embargo on U.S. grain sales to the Soviet Union, and cancelled U.S. participation in the Moscow Olympics. Carter's response did not constitute an embrace of linkage as a strategy as much as simple acknowledgment of political realities. Once again, unintended linkage had overwhelmed a strategy of delinkage.

Until the Soviet invasion of Afghanistan, Congress and the executive did not link negotiations on antisatellite weapons (ASAT) to Soviet external behavior. To the contrary, ASAT talks were highly insulated from other issues. So too years before was the negotiation of the Biological Weapons Convention (BWC) and the Accident Measures Agreement (AMA). The lack of linkage in these cases is due in large part to the unique nature of these undertakings. Most of the attention was focused on the larger arms control negotiations, SALT I and SALT II. The AMA, the BWC, ASAT—all were seen as relatively modest or technical negotiations carrying little political symbolism of the sort associated with the principal inventory agreements. Neither Congress nor the executive sought to use these negotiations as bargaining chips to extract unrelated political concessions from the USSR. Similarly, the United States (and the Soviet Union as well) insulated their efforts to prevent the proliferation of nuclear weapons from the vicissitudes of their overall relationship. At stake here were arrangements not only technical but also mutually perceived to be in the common interest.

The USSR also may have embraced delinkage at times. The most illustrative case of Soviet attempts to insulate arms control from other issues came during SALT I negotiations from 1969 to 1972. Two U.S. actions in the Third World could have resulted in the Soviet Union slowing or even abandoning the SALT talks but did not. In the spring of 1970 U.S. forces moved into Cambodia to destroy Communist sanctuaries. Although the U.S. action constituted a significant escalation of the conflict, no serious reprisal against SALT was taken by the Soviet Union. Although from a U.S. perspective this looks like Soviet delinkage, it is possible that the Soviets never considered seriously the notion of linking Cambodia and SALT.

A second U.S. action that the Soviet Union did not link to SALT was the U.S. mining of Haiphong harbor in May 1972, just two weeks before President Nixon was scheduled to meet with Soviet General Secretary Brezhnev in Moscow. Here both the timing and the magnitude of U.S. activities make it certain that Soviet behavior was in fact conscious delinkage. The Soviets publicly assailed U.S. actions, but they did not interrupt the conclusion of the SALT talks. Similarly, the Soviets did not use the 1972 U.S. breakthrough with the People's Republic of China as grounds for halting the SALT process; indeed, Soviet delinkage can be viewed in this case as the result of successful U.S. use of object linkage.

Soviet willingness to practice delinkage may have had its limits, however. Moscow's reaction to the passage of the Jackson-Vanik amendment to the Trade Reform Act comes to mind; so too does President Carter's human rights policy. Carter apparently believed that his human rights policy toward the Soviet Union would not affect SALT II prospects. After the unfavorable outcome of the trials of Soviet dissidents Anatoly Shcharansky and Aleksandr Ginzburg, Carter cancelled the sale of a Sperry Univac computer to TASS, the Soviet news agency. According to one source, "the link between the Shcharansky trial outcome and the sale appeared to be explicit."[39] The administration also tightened controls on the sale of oil-drilling equipment to the Soviet Union.[40] The Soviets resisted separating U.S. attempts to change their internal political structure from the rest of the relationship. On February 26, 1977, Pravda refuted Secretary Vance's earlier statement that U.S. support for dissidents would not hurt superpower relations. On June 7 TASS severely attacked what is termed President Carter's interference in Soviet internal politics and cautioned that relations could be harmed. When Vance visited Moscow to present the SALT II proposal, Brezhnev objected to continued U.S. emphasis on Soviet human rights policy.[41] Soviet statements and actions may simply have constituted an attempt at leverage, to use U.S. interest in arms control to persuade the Carter administration to back off its human rights policy; alternatively, Carter's human rights policy may actually have had a negative impact on SALT prospects given Soviet unwillingness to delink the two issues.

PRECONDITIONS FOR SUCCESSFUL USE OF LINKAGE AND DELINKAGE

There are several requirements for putting forward credible linkage and delinkage proposals. The first relates to the stakes for both parties.[42] Neither the United States nor the Soviet Union is willing to give up what it considers vital interests no matter how attractive the inducement or how distasteful the punishment from the linking country. The United States, for example, has demonstrated its unwillingness to curtail its activities in a major regional dispute, such as in Vietnam in 1972, because of superpower summitry. There must be a credible correlation between what is at stake and what is threatened or promised. As Helmut Sonnenfeldt has said, "Nobody in his right mind would say get out of Poland for Eximbank loans."[43]

When there exists an asymmetry of stakes favoring the would-be linker, however, the opportunity for linkage is brighter. It is generally argued that the Soviet "investment" in Cienfuegos was more of a concern to the United States than the Soviet Union. The Soviet Union may well have been testing the United States on the issue of acceptable Soviet submarine activities in Cuba. This said, calculating the stakes of the target country is not always an easy task. It was, for example, difficult to identify U.S. stakes in a conflict despite the relative openness of the U.S. political process. During the early phases of the 1975 Angolan Civil War, Kissinger apparently believed that it was a low-level conflict that would not lead to a significant degree of superpower competition. When the war intensified and the Cubans became heavily involved, Kissinger decided that the United States had more significant stakes in the outcome of the war. By that time, it was too late. Congress barred military aid to political factions in Angola by passing the Clark Amendment, while the Soviet Union was unwilling to forgo an opportunity to gain an African ally.[44]

How linkage is attempted can also be critical. Sometimes the target country may not have high stakes in a conflict, but if the linkage proposal is made in such a way that the target country will appear to be succumbing to another superpower, it may create stakes for itself so as not to lose face by backing down. The Jackson-Vanik and Stevenson Amendments to 1974 trade legislation are examples of overestimating the price that the Soviets were willing to pay for the political and economic benefits of détente with the United States. The passage of both the Jackson-Vanik Amendment, which made U.S. granting of most-favored-nation status to the Soviet Union contingent on increases in Jewish emigration levels, and the Stevenson Amendment, which restricted Export-Import Bank loans to the Soviet Union to $300 million—far below Soviet expectations—led the Soviet Union to repudiate the October 18, 1972, bilateral trade agreement. Soon thereafter, they decreased emigration levels. The linkage appeared to work, however, when the amendments were being debated, for emigration levels reached their historic peak.

Successful linkage can also require the ability to make "side payments" to the target country. The would-be linker often needs more than one bargaining chip. The uncertain promise of arms control is not always enough to make the target country make specified concessions. But if the linker can wield a range of levers—arms control, trade, technology transfer—the target country may be more inclined to strike a deal. Also, if one lever proves ineffective in a particular situation, the linker has other levers to serve as inducements.

Beginning with the Kennedy administration, bolstering East-West trade was seen as a way to improve bilateral relations. On the day the Senate approved the Test Ban Treaty, high-level officials in the Kennedy administration began meetings to discuss U.S. wheat sales to the Soviet Union. As a result of those deliberations Kennedy approved both a major grain sale to the Soviet Union and Ex-Im bank loans to finance the purchase in October 1963. Foremost among Kennedy's foreign policy goals was to "demonstrate to the Soviet leaders that the improved climate of agreement could serve the interests of both nations."[45]

President Johnson also attempted to use trade as a way to improve political relations with the Soviet Union and to begin arms control negotiations. Johnson's Special Committee on United States Trade Relations with Eastern Europe and the Soviet Union reported in April 1965 that "trade is a tactical tool to be used with other policy instruments for pursuing our national objectives."[46] These recommendations reaffirmed Johnson's support of the East-West Trade Relations Act introduced in May 1966 and Reciprocal Trade Act of 1968. Both of these bills fell victim to congressional linkage. In 1966 consideration of the East-West Trade bill was delayed because of the Vietnam War and congressional elections. Again in 1967 Republican leaders opposed the bill because of Soviet support for the North Vietnamese and for the Arabs in the Six-Day War. The Reciprocal Trade Act of 1968 met a similar fate. Thus, Johnson was unsuccessful in attempts to improve economic relations with the Soviet Union, something that might have facilitated progress in arms control and other areas where he sought agreement.

Manipulating the availability of economic instruments to foster Soviet flexibility on political matters was to be a cornerstone of the Nixon-Kissinger strategy of shaping Soviet behavior. Yet various executive departments and the constituencies they serve posed problems for the president's linkage policy. The Departments of Agriculture and Commerce often opposed Nixon's strategy of linking trade to Soviet political behavior. Commerce pushed to increase exports to the Soviet Union despite the state of political relations.[47] Also during the Nixon years, the Department of Agriculture violated the president's linkage strategy. Ignoring Nixon's plans, the Department of Agriculture approved the selling of large amounts of wheat to the Russians. This action, according to John Lewis Gaddis, had the effect of "undercutting any possibility of linking such sales to political concessions. 'Linkage' thus required tighter coordination within the bureaucracy than even the highly centralized Nixon administration was able to achieve."[48] Department of Agriculture and Department of Commerce cooperation with executive linkage strategies may largely depend on the financial fortunes of their constituencies. There is a domestic political cost to using economic relations as leverage on the Soviet Union; only the president can determine whether the price is worth paying.

Effective implementation of a linkage strategy also requires intergovernmental discipline. Differences within an administration can diminish the effectiveness of a president's linkage strategy. This was the case during the early months of the Nixon administration. Two months after Nixon's first press conference as president where he advocated linking SALT to the resolution of regional disputes, Gerard Smith, the chief SALT negotiator, told a Soviet negotiator, Alexei Roshchin, that SALT "need not be tied, in some sort of package formula, to the settlement of specific international problems."[49] Secretary of State William Rogers made similar comments. However, Nixon and Kissinger planned to hold out on SALT as long as possible so that it could be used as leverage on other issues. As Kissinger writes, "The cumulative impact of all the bureaucratic indiscipline, with media and Congressional pressures added, was that we had to abandon our attempt to use the opening of SALT talks as a lever for other negotiations."[50] For instance, without presidential approval, Gerard Smith told the chief Soviet negotiator Vladimir Semenov, that "the South Asia situation [referring to the India-Pakistan war] could have negative implications for Soviet-American relations and SALT." President Nixon, despite his own similar warnings, was "alarmed" that Smith made such a linkage and told him not to continue such discussions.[51] Similarly, the Carter administration was not well served by the differences over linkage between Secretary Vance and National Security Advisor Brzezinski. Although Brzezinski argued that SALT II was "lost in the sands of the Ogaden," Vance suggested that the Ogaden conflict did not have to be linked to SALT II but that Brzezinski created the linkage.

As this discussion shows, the U.S. Congress has also had an important if uneven impact on U.S. ability to carry out a linkage policy. Soviet international activity was not a major issue during Senate ratification hearings on the Limited Test Ban Treaty. Some senators such as Strom Thurmond questioned the treaty on the grounds that it was incompatible with Soviet behavior in countries like Laos. These views, however, did not attract a majority of the Senate. SALT I also did not meet with sustained congressional pressures for linkage. President Johnson wrote that from 1966 to 1968 some members of Congress opposed his attempts to negotiate with the Soviet Union on strategic arms limitations talks and trade because of Soviet external policies.[52] Yet congressional opposition to strategic arms limitation talks was not as great as to prevent the Glassboro meeting between Johnson and Kosygin from taking place during the same month as the Arab-Israeli Six-Day War in June 1967. When SALT I negotiations got seriously underway during the Nixon years, most of the linkages emanated from the White House. Cienfuegos and the India-Pakistan conflict were linked to arms control and détente by Nixon and Kissinger and not by the Congress. Also, most of the dialogue during Senate committee hearings on SALT I focused on substantive aspects of those agreements. There was very little consideration of the relationship between SALT I and superpower competition in the Third World.[53]

Senator Jackson's human rights campaign is an example of congressional linkage that constrained executive options. Early in his administration, Nixon had rejected the idea of human rights linkage.

In 1970 he said, "I cannot in good conscience recommend as a principle of American foreign policy that our entire foreign policy should be made dependent on [a] particular aspect of the domestic structure of the Soviet Union."[54] In a April 1973 congressional report, representatives supporting the Jackson-Vanik amendment put forth their ideas on how linkage should be used: "We are convinced that improved relations with the Soviet Union—and specifically improved trade ties—are useful to both countries and to the cause of world peace. But both the President and the Soviets must understand that normal relations between our countries cannot proceed while Jews and others in the Soviet Union are harassed and prevented, by whatever means, from exercising the right of emigration."[55] In the end, the Jackson-Vanik Amendment was passed by Congress in December 1974, and the administration was denied a possible instrument to affect Soviet behavior.[56]

The Ford administration was unsuccessful as well in delinking human rights from trade relations. Kissinger argues that in addition to the inability to delink human rights from other issues, Congress undercut executive use of linkage as a strategy: "Our policy toward the Soviets was based on a balance between the carrot and stick. But we had failed to produce MFN [Most Favored Nation] status; we seemed to be unable to organize the financial mechanisms for even such trade as there was—and all this despite Soviet concessions on Jewish emigration that would have been considered inconceivable a few years earlier. By the summer of 1974, the carrot had for all practical purposes ceased to exist."[57]

SALT II marked an even more important period of congressional involvement. In 1979, after learning of the "discovery" of 2,600 Soviet troops in Cuba, Chairman of the Senate Foreign Relations Committee Frank Church directly spoke of linkage: "I see no likelihood that the Senate would ratify the SALT II treaty as long as Soviet combat troops remain stationed in Cuba."[58] This only reinforced congressional opposition to SALT II that was mounting before the Cuban brigade discovery. Soviet military support of political factions in Angola, Ethiopia, and South Yemen made many senators skeptical about ratifying the SALT II Treaty. The minority report of the Senate Foreign Relations Committee (filed by Senators Howard Baker, Richard Lugar, S. I. Hayakawa, and Jesse Helms) opposed the treaty partly on linkage grounds: "We disagree with the Administration's contention that SALT and our consideration of this treaty should not be linked to the overall geopolitical relationship between the Soviet Union and the United States."[59] The Committee on the Present Danger argued that U.S. relations with the Soviet Union should consider "the world balance of forces" because the Soviet Union takes "advantage of every opportunity to expand its political and military influence throughout the world."[60] It was not only the Soviet military build-up, they argued, that threatened U.S. security but also the Soviet Union's demonstrated commitment to aggression in the Third World.

Behind these words were strong views on the Soviet Union and on what strategy the United States should follow in regard to its principal antagonist. Some advocates of linking arms control to Soviet international activities contend that until the Soviet Union changes its political behavior, the United States should not conclude an arms control agreement with that country. Richard Pipes argued that SALT II "must be placed against the background of relentless Soviet anti-American hate propaganda inside the Soviet Union and the Third World, Soviet armed interventions in Afghanistan, Ethiopia, Vietnam and, more recently, the Caribbean, and against Soviet support of terrorism all over the globe. . . . Linkage means that until and unless the Soviet Union radically modifies its thinking and external policies, we cannot count on SALT enhancing our security and diminishing the probability of war."[61]

According to another perspective on linkage, arms control may lead to a lessening of Soviet expansionist drive. This view is supported by groups such as the American Committee on East-West Accord. The American Committee maintains that progress on arms control and trade will push the Soviet Union in the direction of policy change. Robert Schmidt (a member of the American Committee) thus argued that "The Soviets are great imitators of the United States. You see them imitate the United States in a military environment. You see them imitate the United States in our industrialization process, and if we were to ratify SALT II and stabilize our trade with them, I think you would see a greater emphasis on their part to imitate the United States in our mutually beneficial trade relationships."[62] Donald S. Zagoria advocated a similar view when he argued that by engaging in both SALT and trade with the Soviets, they would have a stake "in improving relations with us, that at some point the leaders will have to sit around with each other and say, well comrades, we have a choice that we have to make. Who is more important? What is more important, our relationship with the Americans, technology, trade, developing Siberia, and so on or Angola and South Yemen?"[63]

The assumption underlying these perspectives is that arms control can be used as leverage to change unrelated Soviet policies. Both perspectives suggest that by concluding an arms control treaty with the Soviet Union, the leadership in that country would begin to rethink its foreign policy. This assumption appears flawed for the most part. For the Soviet Union is no more willing to abandon its historical and political goals for arms control negotiations such as SALT than is the United States. One analyst has cautioned against viewing arms control as a way to change Soviet behavior: "Arms control cannot change the Soviet view of history. It cannot make Moscow accept what it considers threatening change in its sphere of influence or forgo significant opportunities to support what it seems as historical progress in the Third World."[64] Indeed, over the last two decades, the Soviets have increased their Third World commitments in new and significant ways despite U.S. use of linkage. Neither arms control nor attempts at linkage has made the Soviet Union (nor for that matter the United States) abandon its external political ambitions. Linkage as a strategy has not only proven difficult to orchestrate owing to the nature of the United States but uncertain in its impact owing to the nature of the USSR.

CONCLUSIONS

Linkage as a strategy—whether as a lever to affect Soviet behavior in third areas or as an effort to effect Soviet compromise in the realm of arms control—has had but a modest impact. In part this is because linkage in this form is so difficult to identify and demonstrate; in part because it is so difficult to implement. But even the examples of alleged or possible linkage described in this study indicate that it is easy to exaggerate the historical impact of linkage strategies. Few developments within arms control or without can be traced to its successful use.

Several related conclusions can be drawn from the historical record. There is little evidence to suggest that arms control accomplishments contribute to a broader improvement in relations. The 1972 agreements, for example, were followed by such events as the

October 1973 Middle East conflict and Soviet support for Egypt and Syria that went beyond the bounds of what the United States considered to be "acceptable" behavior; continuing support for North Vietnam and new involvement in Angola; and heightened repression at home. Parallel to the negotiation of SALT II and the multitude of lesser forums initiated by the Carter administration were such Soviet activities as destabilization of Africa's Horn, promotion of a coup in South Yemen, and an invasion of Afghanistan. Soviet support of "forces of national liberation" on behalf of the "class struggle" around the world does not appear to have been constrained by either the process or products of arms control.

Linkage as a strategy is problematic for other reasons as well. U.S. ability to use arms control as a lever to moderate Soviet behavior at home or around the world is weakened by the U.S. stake in arms control. It is not simply that arms control can bestow certain benefits on the United States but also that certain political constituencies in the public, in the Congress, and among the allies limit the ability of any administration to forgo arms control progress in an attempt to affect some other aspect of Soviet behavior. Knowing this, the Soviets are less likely to be affected by U.S. attempts at leverage.

Similarly, the United States is not in a position to offer up arms control concessions to bring about Soviet restraint in other areas. Any arms control accord must be able to withstand on its merits the scrutiny of informed constituencies; thus the only leverage derives from Soviet interest in achieving arms control agreements. The same point can be made about object linkage; no U.S. administration could garner public support for a policy that compromised valued regional interests for arms control. Thus, any administration seeking to practice a linkage strategy cannot escape the fact that each of its own initiatives will be judged on its own merits.

Perhaps the greatest impediment to the conduct of an effective linkage strategy by the United States is its own composition; quite simply, the United States is not well structured for linkage. To be successful, linkage requires not only a clear, common sense of priorities but also the ability to apply (or credibly threaten to apply) the various incentives and penalties (or carrots and sticks) needed to attempt to shape Soviet behavior. Divisions within administrations; differences between executive and Congress; farmers, businesspeople, and labor each going their own way; the allies pursuing their own separate economic and political interests with the Soviet Union; an active press and the difficulty of carrying out private diplomacy often necessary for linkage to be effective—all detract from the capacity of the United States to conduct a strategy of linkage. The Carter administration, for example, lacked internal consensus on the desirability of linkage, enjoyed little confidence in the Congress, possessed few economic inducements to hold out to the Soviets, and could not threaten military intervention in much of the world; in such circumstances it is not surprising that linkage as a strategy could not succeed. Nor given the overall impression of weakness is it surprising that this administration was especially vulnerable to the emergence of unintended linkage.

The most potent form of linkage is ironically enough the one form not intentionally used by policymakers. Unintended linkage, as seen both in the delay of SALT I and the defeat of SALT II, possesses the capacity to obstruct and ultimately undermine the arms control process. Not all administrations are equally vulnerable to its force, however; perceptions of strength and trends in the overall political and military balance affect the potential for unintended linkage, especially because Congress remains the principal vehicle through which such linkage acts in the U.S. political system.

Because of this tendency, delinkage—which can often be nothing more than the management or avoidance of unintended linkage—is difficult to sustain. The record suggests that delinkage is politically realizable when the president and his administration are strong or when the agreement in question is viewed as relatively minor or technical. Confidence-building arrangements designed to reduce the risk of war through accident or miscalculation are examples of the kind of past less vulnerable to unintended linkage.

It is difficult to exaggerate the importance of delinkage. Given the inevitability of U.S.-Soviet competition around the world and the propensity of the Soviet Union to rely on the threat or use of force to maintain order at home, in Eastern Europe, and around the world, the ability of a U.S. administration to delink arms control from the adverse domestic reactions to such Soviet behavior would appear to be a prerequisite for achieving arms control. The Soviet Union has demonstrated its willingness and capacity to "look the other way" when it served its political and military interests to do so; such willingness and capacity on the part of the United States is likely to be a price of arms control.

NOTES

This chapter is based on research and interviews conducted by Kiron Skinner and was written by Ms. Skinner and Richard Haass.

1. There could well be another form of linkage, one related to both the strategic and the unintended varieties in the sense that a country, fearing strong reactions, might forgo certain activities or behavior so as not to antagonize the other. Thus, the Soviet Union, having witnessed the U.S. propensity for unintended linkage, might decide against some action likely to anger the United States. Such possibilities can be signaled so as to encourage restraint and in fact were by the Nixon administration. This phenomenon could be described as linkage as a deterrent. The problem for analysts is that it cannot be discerned. It is the proverbial dog in the night failing to bark.

2. Henry Kissinger, *White House Years* (Boston: Little, Brown, 1979), p. 266.

3. *Ibid.*, p. 266.

4. *Ibid.*, p. 647.

5. Marvin Kalb and Bernard Kalb, *Kissinger* (Boston: Little, Brown, 1974), p. 211.

6. Kissinger, *White House Years*, p. 904.

7. Walter C. Clemens, Jr., *The Superpowers and Arms Control* (Lexington, Mass.: Lexington Books, 1973), p. 66.

8. Harry Gelman makes a similar point in *The Brezhnev Politburo and the Decline of Détente* (Ithaca, N.Y.: Cornell University Press, 1984), p. 106: "it is important to recall that during the Vietnam War the Soviet leaders evaded several overtures from the Johnson administration seeking to improve the atmosphere of bilateral relations. This Soviet stance was allegedly a consequence of Moscow's moral abhorrence of U.S. behavior—an abhorrence that mysteriously became less important when the balance of perceived profit and loss changed several years later."

9. Kissinger, *White House Years*, p. 833.

10. Seymour Hersh, *The Price of Power: Kissinger in the Nixon White House* (New York: Summit Books, 1983), p. 343.

11. Garthoff, *Détente and Confrontation: American-Soviet Relations from Nixon to Reagan* (Washington, D.C.: Brookings Institution, 1985), p. 92.

12. *Ibid.*, p. 92.

13. See Bruce D. Porter, *The USSR in Third World Conflicts: Soviet Arms and Diplomacy in Local Wars, 1945-1980* (Cambridge, Cambridge University Press, 1984), p. 173.

14. Quoted in Garthoff, *Détente and Confrontation*, p. 524.

15. Dimitri Simes, "Soviet Policy towards the United States," in Joseph S. Nye, Jr., ed., *The Making of America's Soviet Policy* (New Haven: Yale University Press, 1984), p. 310.

16. The text of Brezhnev's speech is in *Pravda* of February 25, 1976, and reprinted in English in *Current Digest of the Soviet Press* 28 (March 24, 1976), pp. 3–32. For an excellent analysis of Soviet thinking at this juncture about expanding the reach of their influence, see David Holloway, *The Soviet Union and the Arms Race* (New Haven: Yale University Press, 1984), esp. pp. 90–95.

17. Quoted in Garthoff, *Détente and Confrontation*, p. 592.

18. Quoted in *The New York Times*, March 3, 1978, p. 3.

19. Text of interview can be found in *Department of State Bulletin* 78 (2016) (July 1978), p. 27.

20. Cyrus Vance, *Hard Choices: Critical Years in America's Foreign Policy* (New York: Simon and Schuster, 1983), p. 85. For Brzezinski's alternative approach, see his memoirs, *Power and Principle: Memoirs of the National Security Advisor, 1977–1981* (New York: Farrar, Straus and Giroux, 1983), esp. pp. 178–90.

21. See Jimmy Carter, *Keeping Faith: Memoirs of a President* (New York: Bantam Books, 1982).

22. See *War in the Horn of Africa: A Firsthand Report on the Challenges for United States Policy*, Report of a fact-finding mission to Egypt, Sudan, Ethiopia, Somalia, and Kenya, Dec. 12–22, 1977, to the House Committee on Foreign Affairs, 95th Cong., 1st Sess. (Washington, D.C.: U.S. Government Printing Office, 1978), p. 49.

23. See Larry Napper, "The Ogaden War: Some Implications for Crisis Prevention," in Alexander L. George, ed., *Managing U.S.-Soviet Rivalry: Problems of Crisis Prevention* (Boulder, Colo.: Westview Press, 1983), p. 233.

24. Quoted in *The New York Times*, April 16, 1978, sec. 4, p. 4.

25. Michael Nacht makes a similar point in *The Age of Vulnerability: Threats to Nuclear Stalemate* (Washington, D.C.: Brookings Institution, 1985), pp. 126–27: "By sustaining the SALT process and other elements of détente, the Soviets no doubt hoped to generate the complications in American decisionmaking that Nixon and Kissinger had tried to introduce into Soviet policy formulation. The Soviets might have reasoned that the Americans would hesitate to move too close to China if such a move would jeopardize strategic arms control with the Soviet Union."

26. Quoted in Strobe Talbott, *Endgame: The Inside Story of SALT II* (New York: Harper & Row, 1980), p. 251.

27. *Ibid.*, p. 251.

28. Kissinger, *White House Years*, p. 840.

29. Garthoff, *Détente and Confrontation*, p. 73.

30. Carter, *Keeping Faith*, p. 194.

31. James R. Millar, "The Impact of Trade and Trade Denial on the U.S. Economy," in Bruce Parrott, ed., *Trade, Technology and Soviet-American Relations* (Washington, D.C.: Georgetown University Center for Strategic and International Studies, 1985), pp. 340–41.

32. Memorandum of Walt Rostow, July 5, 1963, Kennedy Papers, NSC Files, Box 265, "ACDA—Disarmament Harriman Trip III."

33. Lyndon Baines Johnson, *The Vantage Point: Perspectives on the Presidency 1963-1969* (New York: Holt, Rinehart, and Winston, 1971), p. 480.

34. *Ibid.*, p. 484.

35. John Newhouse, *Cold Dawn: The Story of SALT* (New York: Holt, Rinehart, and Winston, 1973), p. 169.

36. *Department of State Bulletin* 74 (Feb. 19, 1976), p. 180.

37. *Ibid.*, p. 180.

38. *Department of State Bulletin* 74 (Jan. 26, 1976), p. 98.

39. John Hardt, "United States-Soviet Trade Policy," in Joint Economic Committee, *Issues in East-West Commercial Relations* (Washington, D.C.: U.S. Government Printing Office, 1979), p. 281.

40. Joan Edelman Spero, *The Politics of International Economic Relations* (New York: St. Martin's Press, 1981), p. 319.

41. Garthoff, *Détente and Confrontation*, pp. 572-73.

42. For important theoretical discussions on issue linkage, see Robert D. Tollison and Thomas D. Willett, "An Economic Theory of Mutually Advantageous Issue Linkages in International Relations," in *International Organization* 33 (4) (Autumn 1979), pp. 425-49, and James K. Sebenius, "Negotiating Arithmetic: Adding and Subtracting Issues and Parties,'" in *International Organization* 37 (2) (Spring 1983), pp. 281-316.

43. Interview, May 30, 1986, Washington, D.C.

44. Alexander George writes specifically of the difficulty policymakers experience in determining the United States' stakes in the Angolan War. "Often it is only when a situation has deteriorated or is on the verge of serious deterioration—for example, as a result of the unexpected Soviet-assisted Cuban intervention in Angola—that the broader ramifications for American interests or for the domestic political standing of the administration become evident in Washington, forcing consideration of a strong response." See Alexander George, "Political Crises," in Nye, ed., *The Making of America's Soviet Policy*, p. 151.

45. Theodore C. Sorenson, *Kennedy* (New York: Harper & Row, 1965), p. 741.

46. *Department of State Bulletin* 54 (1405) (May 30, 1966), p. 846.

47. John Lewis Gaddis, *Strategies of Containment: A Critical Appraisal of Postwar American National Security Policy* (New York: Oxford University Press, 1982), p. 314.

48. *Ibid.*, p. 314.

49. Henry Kissinger, *White House Years*, p. 137.

50. *Ibid.*, p. 138.

51. Gerard Smith, *Doubletalk: The Story of the First Strategic Arms Limitation Talks* (Garden City, N.Y.: Doubleday, 1980), pp. 341-42.

52. Johnson, *Vantage Point*, pp. 470-81.

53. Senate Committee on Foreign Relations, *Hearings on the Strategic Arms Limitation Agreements*, 92d Cong., 2d Sess. (Washington, D.C.: U.S. Government Printing Office, 1972), p. 137. One instance when the connection between arms control and U.S.-Soviet relations was mentioned was during the testimony of Robert C. Tucker: "So long as the United States and Soviet Russia continue to view the Third World as an arena of political competition for influence, their attempts to cooperate in arms control, trade, science and technology, will be in perpetual jeopardy. The whole structure of Soviet-American cooperation will remain fragile."

54. Quoted by Strobe Talbott, "Social Issues" in Nye, ed., *The Making of America's Soviet Policy*, p. 199.

55. Quoted in Henry Kissinger, *Years of Upheaval* (Boston: Little, Brown, 1982), p. 252.

56. The best treatment of this issue is to be found in Paula Stern, *Water's Edge: Domestic Politics and the Making of American Foreign Policy* (Westport, Conn.: Greenwood Press, 1979).

57. Kissinger, *Years of Upheaval*, pp. 997–98.

58. Quoted in Talbott, *Endgame*, p. 285.

59. *The SALT II Treaty*, Report of the Senate Committee on Foreign Relations, together with Supplemental and Minority Views, 96th Cong., 1st Sess. (Washington, D.C.: U.S. Government Printing Office, 1979), p. 491.

60. See Charles Tyroler II, ed., *Alerting America: The Papers of the Committee on the Present Danger* (Washington, D.C.: Pergamon-Brassey's, 1984), p. 3.

61. Senate Committee on Armed Services, *Hearings on the Military Implications of the Treaty on the Limitation of Strategic Offensive Arms and Protocol Thereto (SALT II Treaty)*, Part 3, 96th Cong., 1st Sess. (Washington, D.C.: U.S. Government Printing Office, 1979), p. 1308.

62. *The SALT II Treaty*, part 4, p. 183.

63. *Ibid.*, part 3, p. 111.

64. Joseph S. Nye, Jr., "Restarting Arms Control," in *Foreign Policy* 47 (Summer 1982), p. 113.

11 VERIFICATION AND COMPLIANCE

Richard N. Haass

An axiom guiding the U.S. approach to arms control is that agreements with the Soviet Union cannot be entered into and adhered to by the United States on the basis of trust; rather, the United States must possess the means to observe and judge relevant Soviet military activities. In recent years the concern over whether the Soviet Union is complying with the spirit (that is, the object and purpose) as well as the letter of the pacts that it has signed has become a dominant one in the United States. The political and potential military stakes are considerable; to cite a U.S. Arms Control and Disarmament Agency report, "Soviet violations of arms control agreements could create new security risks. Such violations deprive us of the security benefits of arms control directly because of the military consequences of known violations, and indirectly by inducing suspicion about the existence of undetected violations that might have additional military consequences."[1] Beyond such military and political effects of real or suspected noncompliance, there is the related matter of whether and if so how the United States ought to respond to specific Soviet actions that may be in violation of arms control undertakings. As a result, not only arms control but the entire fabric of U.S.-Soviet relations are tied up with the compliance issue.[2]

Before proceeding it is necessary to define some commonly used (and abused) terms. *Monitoring* refers to collecting and processing information about Soviet activities. *Verification*, while literally

303

meaning the process of establishing the truth or accuracy of something, in the arms control context refers to the matching of information collected through monitoring against the provisions of an agreement in order to determine the degree of *compliance*.[3] Thus, whereas monitoring is solely a technical endeavor, verification is both technical and political in nature. At the same time, it is important to note that the verification process does not itself explicitly determine the standard of compliance sought. Nor does it determine the approach to enforcement—that is, how to respond in the event that the process yields the conclusion that possible or certain illegal behavior has been observed. These are political judgments to be reached outside the more limited verification context.

The relationship between arms control and compliance is complex. No agreement requires a party to demonstrate compliance; rather, what is "required" is the ability to refute a charge of noncompliance to the satisfaction of the side making the charge. In so doing it is important to distinguish between *violations* and *circumvention*. The former normally refers to actions taken contrary to specific provisions of an agreement—that is, violations of the letter of a pact. The latter, often used interchangeably with the phrase "violation of the spirit" (or "violation of the object and purpose"), refers most often to exploitation of imprecise treaty language, loopholes, omissions, or ambiguities. Although only violations have legal standing, both violations and circumventions possess political and possibly military significance.[4]

Compliance has long been a part of the U.S. debate regarding the negotiation of arms control arrangements with the USSR. Concern over possible Soviet cheating or noncompliance has always existed; more than anything else, this concern led to emphasis on verification capacity and procedures. Verification issues figured in the post–World War II consideration of the Baruch Plan, the 1950s discussion of Eisenhower's Open Skies proposal, the early 1960s debate over the Limited Test Ban, and then again a decade later when the United States considered the strategic arms limitation agreements.

Concerns over verification were sufficiently strong to have precluded any comprehensive test ban pact in the absence of a sufficient number of on-site inspections. The significance of Soviet refusal to accept a demanding level of intrusive verification dwindled when the test ban became partial. The emergence of highly capable national technical means of verification (NTM) gave the United States the confidence that it could detect all militarily significant cheating of a partial test ban; the Kennedy administration's argument was not that the Soviets would fail to look for advantage or that the United States could be certain to detect every instance of Soviet noncompliance but simply that the United States possessed more than enough overall military strength and more than enough reconnaissance capacity so that any act of Soviet cheating that could go unnoticed would be sufficiently small as not to threaten U.S. security.[5] This line of argument, coupled with the limited nature of the treaty undertaking, carried the day over those who opposed the treaty based on predictions of Soviet cheating.

Related arguments carried the day during consideration of U.S. policy towards the proposed ban on biological and toxin weapons. The Nixon administration signed the 1972 Convention despite the almost total absence of measures to enhance verification and the presence of provisions that allowed signatories to produce biological agents and toxins for "prophylactic, protective or other peaceful purposes." The administration did so only because the nature of biological agents and toxins made them poor candidates for military use; even so, officials emphasized that U.S. willingness to adhere to this multilateral arrangement in no way constituted a precedent or readiness to enter into other undertakings with similar potential for undetected noncompliance.[6]

In the public debates over SALT I and the ABM Treaty, concerns over verification and compliance with few exceptions played a less central role than did unhappiness with the unequal quantitative ceilings enshrined in the agreements themselves.[7] Several factors account for this relative lack of anxiety. Nixon administration officials did not inherit a large arms control record with controversial compliance claims. Moreover, these arms control agreements constituted a new venture in the early, promising days of détente. Perhaps most important, the Interim Agreement and the ABM Treaty were ventures undertaken by a president with a widespread reputation for being both tough with the Soviets and supportive of U.S. military strength. The public perspective on compliance thus tended to blend confidence in U.S. verification capabilities with a belief that the Soviets were unlikely to violate the new undertakings.[8] Henry Kissinger's briefing of Congress captured this dual optimism:

> we advocate these agreements not on the basis of trust, but on the basis of the enlightened self-interests of both sides. This self-interest is reinforced by the carefully drafted verification provisions in the agreement. Beyond the

legal obligations, both sides have a stake in all of the agreements that have been signed, and a large stake in the broad process of improvement in relations that has begun. The Soviet leaders are serious men, and we are confident that they will not lightly abandon the course that has led to the summit meeting and to these initial agreements.[9]

The public debate aside, verification concerns received considerable attention in both U.S. preparations for the negotiations and the negotiations themselves. SALT I established a number of important precedents affecting verification and compliance: Article XII of the ABM Treaty (along with Article V of the Interim Agreement) not only explicitly endorsed the central role of national technical means of verification to assure compliance but precluded both parties from either interfering with the national technical means of the other or deliberately concealing measures that would impede verification. The ABM Treaty also established the Standing Consultative Commission (SCC) to among other things "consider questions concerning compliance with the obligations assumed and with related situations which may be considered ambiguous."[10] Within the U.S. government, the Nixon administration created a number of bodies to oversee compliance issues—including a special intelligence committee charged with producing quarterly reports on Soviet compliance with SALT I and the Verification Panel, an administrationwide collection of key senior officials to consider verification matters and arms control issues more generally both during and after the negotiations.[11] Perhaps more important, the U.S. position in the negotiations themselves—for example, the selection of launchers as the principal unit of account for ballistic missiles—reflected a commitment to limiting what could be readily verified.

By the time of SALT II, concern over U.S. verification capacity had increased to the point of dominating the initial public debate. In part this development reflected the deteriorating state of U.S.-Soviet relations; in part it was a result of more than a decade of arms control experience. The SALT II Treaty text itself—its length, the proportion of language devoted to verification-related functions, the attempt to include data characterizing current inventories so that meaningful modernization limits could be established, counting rules intended to ease verification of MIRV ceilings and subceilings—all testify to heightened awareness of the salience of verification and compliance concerns.[12] In addition, senior Carter administration officials spoke publicly of their confidence that the treaty as negotiated could be adequately verified.[13]

Yet the loss of valuable monitoring posts in Iran, the controversial record of Soviet compliance with SALT I, and the existence of allegedly insufficiently narrow or specific language in the proposed treaty combined to leave unsatisfied a large and possibly decisive body of senators. Citing provisions relating to the Soviet Backfire bomber, cruise missile ranges, warhead numbers on heavy ICBMs, possible conversions of medium-range into long-range missiles, deployment of mobile ICBMs, telemetry encryption and the testing of "new types" of ICBMs, a majority on the Senate Armed Services Committee concluded

> The treaty . . . cannot be said to be "verifiable" or even "adequately verifiable." However confident we might be that the Soviets would not cheat or that the consequences of their cheating would be minimal or that they could cheat to a degree that would alter the strategic balance, the fact remains that there are a number of provisions of the treaty, the compliance with which we cannot even expect adequately to monitor, much less verify.[14]

For reasons of verification SALT II was in deep trouble in the Senate long before Soviet behavior in Cuba or Afghanistan eliminated any chance of passage.

Today, some years later, not simply verification but compliance has become the subject of a major debate. Why has this come to be? There are a number of possible explanations: Soviet compliance behavior has deteriorated; U.S. ability to monitor accords has improved, and we are catching the Soviets in more violations; U.S. ability to verify compliance has declined (given the emergence of new technologies and practices such as MIRVing and mobility), and we are therefore less likely to detect noncompliance; our verification standards have gone up; past agreements were rife with ambiguities and interpretations not commonly held; the United States is more critical than before owing to domestic political factors or more general disillusionment with U.S.-Soviet relations. But whatever the reason or reasons, the fact is that compliance has emerged as an issue to an extent not foreseen by the negotiating history or the political debates of the initial postwar decades.

The bulk of the contemporary compliance debate concerns three agreements: the two SALT pacts and the ABM Treaty. The debate does, however, gather momentum from alleged Soviet circumventions and violations of such agreements as the 1925 Geneva Protocol relating to chemical and toxic weapons, the 1972 Biological Weapons Convention, the 1974 Threshold Test Ban Treaty, and the 1975 Helsinki Final Act provisions dealing with prior notification of large-scale exercises. Only one aspect of the Limited Test Ban Treaty has garnered attention in this context—namely, the provision that prohibits any venting (the release of radioactive debris) beyond the borders of the testing state. Soviet venting beyond the borders of the USSR has repeatedly taken place; the United States has protested such behavior, particularly in those instances when the amount of debris indicated a blatant disregard for the treaty's venting provisions.

At the same time, the United States has reacted with some restraint. This relative restraint is worth noting. It may as much as anything reflect the fact that the United States for a time vented relatively small quantities of radioactive matter across its borders. But perhaps more important, the U.S. reaction is significant because it underscores the dual nature of compliance. A violation of a provision, even if it provides insight into how conscientiously a party fulfills its legal obligations, may not be seen as significant if it does not violate the principal intent of the agreement—in this case to ban all nuclear tests except those below ground—and, perhaps most important, if the activity is of no military consequence.

It is difficult to speak of noncompliance with regard to the Accidents Measures Agreement. The first of its three principal articles—that each party maintain and improve its command and control capacities to reduce the chance of accidental or unauthorized use of nuclear weapons—allows the signatories total discretion as to what if any steps are to be taken. Similarly, the articles requiring notification of the other in the event of accidental or unauthorized launches or detection of unidentifiable objects by warning systems also provide for a huge amount of discretion in that notification is required only if the country doing the launching (or in the latter case monitoring) believes that there is a risk of nuclear war breaking out. Lastly, the only nondiscretionary provision—Article 4's requirement that the other party be notified in advance of planned missile launches with a trajectory both beyond the launching country's borders and in the direction of the other—has never come into play as both sides have eschewed such launches.

The history (or rather lack of one) of the Accidents Measures Agreement points out the difficulty in holding any party accountable to an arrangement that allows that much discretion and unilateral interpretation. In this instance, the triggering mechanism or circumstances governing when either party is meant to contact the other are so imprecise (with the exception of Article 4) that no charge of noncompliance has been levied despite the fact the agreement has never been implemented during false alarms or crises. Compliance concerns are easiest to advance when there is precise language available by which to judge behavior.

The United States has charged the Soviet Union with several violations of the 1925 Geneva Protocol and the 1972 Biological and Toxin Weapons Convention. The Soviets have been charged with violating both pacts by using toxins and other chemical warfare agents in Afghanistan and with transferring and supervising their use by Vietnamese and Laotian forces in both Cambodia and Laos. The United States has also stated that the Soviets maintain a biological weapons and production program that can be characterized only as offensive and thereby in violation of the 1972 convention. The Soviets have denied all accusations; in the absence of a dedicated mechanism for dealing with alleged noncompliance, no provision for on-site inspection, and allowance for peaceful production of otherwise proscribed agents, no means exist to settle this dispute.

THE SALT I INTERIM AGREEMENT

One of the first compliance issues arising under the new agreement came in 1973, when U.S. intelligence revealed that the Soviets appeared to be constructing additional ICBM launch silos—the so-called III-X silos—in apparent contravention of SALT I's ban on new ICBM launchers. The Soviets responded to U.S. inquiries by claiming that these silos were for command and control functions and hence permissible, a claim later supported by information (provided by the Soviets and confirmed by U.S. NTM) that demonstrated certain unique design features of these silos. Another issue arose in 1976, when the Soviets faced the necessity of dismantling a number of SS-7 and SS-8 silos if their planned deployment of new ballistic missile submarines was not to put them over permitted ballistic missile launcher totals. In this instance the Soviets actually took the initiative in raising the issue with the United States in the SCC and agreed to the U.S. position that it hold off sea trials of their new SSBN until the required dismantling had been carried out.

The principal Soviet compliance-related concern with SALT I involved U.S. conversion of Minuteman II to Minuteman III launchers. This work required the temporary covering of selected silos; the Soviets charged that this activity interfered with their NTM. The United States claimed that its activity was not illegal because the SALT I agreement (Article V, paragraph 3) precluded only "deliberate concealment measures" and explicitly exempted "current construction, assembly, conversion or overhaul practices." The issue was not resolved until SALT II, when in the Third Common Understanding to Article XV the two sides agreed that no shelters impeding verification were to be used over ICBM silo launchers.[15]

Far more controversial was (and remains) the Soviet decision to modernize its ICBM force by replacing the SS-11 missile with the SS-19. The background to this controversy is tangled but crucial to any appreciation of the contemporary compliance debate. In the course of the SALT I negotiation the U.S. delegation sought to persuade the Soviet side to agree on a definition of heavy missile. The United States wanted to limit the size of any successor to the light SS-11 so that the threat to land-based U.S. missiles would not be increased significantly by a new generation of large, MIRVed Soviet missiles; the Soviets wanted to protect their planned modernization and in particular their soon-to-appear SS-19 ICBM. Thus, although the Soviets would agree that no light missile could be replaced with a heavy missile and that the SS-9 was a heavy missile and the SS-11 was not, they would not sign on to the more restrictive U.S. notion of what constituted a heavy missile. Unable to get the Soviets to agree, the United States issued a unilateral interpretation of what it believed to be intended by the treaty.[16]

Whatever else the Soviet behavior might have been—sharp or even deceptive negotiating, exploitation of imprecise treaty language, circumvention of the light-to-heavy conversion prohibition—the fact is that in this instance the U.S. government did not accuse the Soviets of violating the Interim Agreement. The Soviets could not legally replace the SS-11 with the heavy SS-18 (which was a follow-on to the heavy SS-9), and they did not; they could legally introduce the SS-19, and they did. Their behavior was inconsistent with the unilateral U.S. interpretation, but this U.S. statement was not legally binding on the Soviet Union. There was a political price to be paid nonetheless. The SS-19 accelerated the emergence of the perceived vulnerability of U.S. land-based missiles and the parallel disillusionment with an arms control process that seemed unable to do anything about it.

THE ANTI-BALLISTIC MISSILE TREATY

The most severe test of compliance issues has concerned the 1972 Anti-Ballistic Missile (ABM) Treaty. This is not surprising. Undetected violations of the 1972 Treaty could have an impact on the strategic balance more significant than violations of any of the agreements limiting offensive arms. Violations of the latter might increase Soviet capabilities by a few percentage points, not enough by itself to alter significantly the strategic balance; violations of the ABM accord could provide a defensive capability and thereby weaken the condition of mutual vulnerability on which stability in the nuclear age has thus far been premised.

Article VI(a) of the ABM Treaty prohibits the testing of air-defense radars in "an ABM mode." In the early years of the treaty, the Soviets followed a practice of turning on their SA-5 radars located near or at ballistic missile test ranges at times of ballistic missile tests. Such "concurrent operations" could help provide the SA-5 radar (an air defense radar) with ballistic missile tracking capabilities. The United States challenged the Soviets on their behavior, only to be told that the SA-5s were being used for air safety purposes. Subsequent discussions in the SCC to delimit concurrent use of air defense radars at missile test ranges narrowed but did not close the loophole.[17] Unless a system is banned altogether (or banned from operating at certain locations or in specified circumstances), a loophole is created by which a system with more than one potential purpose can be deployed legally even if one possible use is prohibited. The entire matter is further complicated by the fact that certain existing Soviet surface-to-air missile (SAM) systems, above all the SA-12, possess some antiballistic missile capability. As long as there are dual-purpose systems, and as long as parties are permitted discretion in their use, the potential exists for treaty provisions to be violated in a manner in which other parties to the agreement are left with little or no means by which to press a claim of noncompliance.

A second ABM radar-related compliance issue also emerged in the mid-1980s. The treaty limited ABM testing to those ranges that existed at the time that the treaty was signed; testing could occur at new or additional ranges only by subsequent mutual agreement. In 1975 the United States observed that the Soviets were constructing an ABM radar on the Kamchatka Peninsula ballistic missile test range. When the United States challenged the USSR, the Soviets claimed that the facility had in fact existed at the time that the treaty was signed and therefore did not constitute a new facility requiring U.S. approval. During the negotiations, however, the United States asked the Soviets to confirm that the radar facility at Shary Shagan was their single range, only to be told by the Soviets that national technical means of verification were sufficient to assess the situation. The Soviets never contradicted U.S. statements that the Soviets had only one test range at the time of the treaty's signing. The Soviet Union was guilty either of attempting to mislead the U.S. side or of misrepresenting years later what had in fact existed at the time. In 1975 there was no way to prove what was the case, there being no annex to the treaty that listed those facilities existing when the treaty was signed. Here as in other instances a lack of specificity precluded the establishment of an effective compliance regime.

A third ABM radar-related compliance issue stems from Article V of the treaty and its prohibition of mobile radars—that is, those not being of a "permanent fixed type." The specific Soviet systems at issue are the Flat Twin and Pawn Shop radars. Although the radars in question may not be truly mobile—the intent of the treaty provision was to prevent the accumulation of radars that could be fielded quickly and thereby provide either side with the potential to break out rapidly of the treaty limits—they are capable of being transported without too much difficulty and require little site preparation before becoming operational. They are as a result relatively movable. The components do not violate the treaty per se but brush up close against the treaty's letter strictly defined; by so doing, the radars point up the difficulty in proscribing systems with specified characteristics when actual systems possess traits that do not necessarily conform to the categories established by negotiated agreements.[18]

The most well-known compliance issue affecting not only the 1972 Treaty but indeed all arms control concerns the Soviet radar in Krasnoyarsk, Siberia. What is at issue again is a familiar dilemma for arms controllers: how to permit a system in one set of circumstances while prohibiting it in another. As the mere existence of the debate suggests, it is a dilemma that continues to confound.

Limitations on large, phased-array radars (LPARs) constitute a key element of the restrictive regime created by the ABM Treaty. Such radars were and remain an essential component of an antiballistic missile system; because they take years to construct and are easily visible to satellites, limitations on them are both necessary and relatively easy to monitor. The problem stems from the desire of both parties to have such radars for other purposes—principally for early warning, space-tracking, and intelligence gathering.

In addition to limiting each party's ABM radars (initially to two sites at least 1,300 kilometers apart, later to only one site each), the treaty permits the construction of additional LPARs for early-warning purposes as long as they are located on the periphery of the country's territory and oriented outward. Moreover, the ABM Treaty does not prohibit the construction of LPARs anywhere in the country as long as they are for other purposes such as space-tracking or intelligence collection.

In the case of the Krasnoyarsk radar, the United States has charged that both the siting and the orientation of the radar make it a poor candidate for space-related functions and that as a result it violates the treaty's provisions governing early-warning radars. The Soviet Union has countered in part by claiming that the new radar is not subject to the constraints on early-warning radars because its purpose is to track objects in space; the Soviets have also countered by charging the United States with violating the 1972 Treaty. The Soviets charge that not only the thrust but many of the specifics of the U.S. Strategic Defense Initiative are inconsistent with the 1972 Treaty. The Soviets have also stated that the United States is illegally developing mobile ABM radars, testing ICBMs to give them an ABM capability, developing ABMs with multiple warheads, and laying the groundwork for a territorial ABM network.[19] The Soviets also claim that U.S. upgrading of ballistic missile early warning radars at Thule, Greenland, and Fylingdales, United Kingdom, contravene the 1972 Treaty. The United States has denied the claim, arguing that these two early warning radars, already in existence in 1972, were exempt from the treaty's provisions.[20] This again highlights the value of agreed data bases accompanying any pact.

The Krasnoyarsk case points out once more the danger of negotiating arms control agreements that allow the construction of systems possessing more than one application when one or more of the applications is restricted. The problem is compounded when the treaty allows the deploying party to declare what the purpose of the system is; not surprisingly, the Soviets declare the purpose of the system to be one falling outside the treaty's purview. (By such reasoning the Soviets could justify the deployment of an unlimited number of LPARS anywhere in the USSR as long as they could demonstrate some space or intelligence-related function. Yet it was precisely the deployment of a large number of LPARs with their potential to provide the basis of a nationwide, territorial ABM system that the treaty was designed to prevent.) The alternatives in such situations are several: to ban any system with certain potential applications either entirely or in specified circumstances; to permit deployments only as mutually agreed, thereby giving all parties a veto; to require the addition of truly functionally related observable differences (FROD) characteristics that would limit a system's potential to be used for unwanted purposes while not allowing it to be easily modified, or to share intelligence data demonstrating the illegal application of a system once it is operational.[21] Because the last of these approaches raises major problems for intelligence agencies and may in any case not be conclusive, the answer appears to lie in one or more of the other approaches. Asking the SCC to decide such issues, as was apparently the case here, is to expect too much of this forum.

SALT II

There are three principal U.S. compliance issues concerning the SALT II pact.[22] The first is that of encryption, or the process by which a country testing a system conceals through the use of codes the test data being transmitted by the system during the test. If such data are essential to the country doing the testing so that it can discover whether the system meets operational requirements, the data are also essential to others so that they can determine whether the characteristics of the new system are compatible with the stipulations of existing agreements. (There are even more basic military reasons for learning about the characteristics of an adversary's new weapons, and more often than not such requirements are more demanding than those for verification.) Needless to say, no party is anxious to make available to the other such information, yet arms control agreements require access to a good deal of information that can be gleaned only from telemetry.

Under SALT II the United States and the Soviet Union attempted to square this circle by allowing encryption except when it impeded verification of compliance with the provisions of the treaty.[23] Yet the permitted level of encryption was to be determined largely by the country doing the encrypting; as such it was an approach based more on consent than obligation. Although the potential to work out mutually acceptable levels of encryption exists because both sides presumably know what telemetry is required to verify treaty provisions, in reality the Soviets have encrypted to an extent that has reduced the ability of the United States to verify compliance with the treaty.[24] This effect notwithstanding, the alternatives of a total ban or more specific guidelines are not without drawbacks: the former would obligate the United States to provide data that would be militarily useful to the Soviets though not required to verify U.S. compliance with the agreement, and the latter would require a degree of specificity about intelligence techniques and needs that the intelligence community would likely balk at.[25] Yet if political discussion—that is, emphasizing to the Soviet Union that domestic U.S. support for arms control pacts will wither in the absence of sufficient Soviet restraint on encryption—cannot persuade the Soviets to reduce their encryption, and if the United States continues to depend on telemetry for verification purposes, some specifying of guidelines could well be necessary. The intelligence risk of doing so must be offset against the loss of information and the undermining of arms control if most or all telemetry is denied.

A second SALT II-related compliance problem stems from the agreement of the two parties to limit the modernization of their respective ICBM inventories. What emerged after years of arduous negotiation was an agreement to limit each side to one "new type" of ICBM. Not surprisingly, the compliance issue focuses on just when a "new" ICBM is also a "new type" of ICBM.

Treaty language defines a new type as any missile that would change an existing missile's fuel type, number of stages, *or*, by 5 percent or more, its length, largest diameter, launch-weight, or throw-weight. An increase or decrease in throw-weight by 5 percent or adding an additional stage would cross over the "new type" threshold; improving missile accuracy by any factor would not. An additional provision of the agreement precluded either party from deploying new single-warhead ICBMs if the warhead weight was less than half of the overall throw-weight. The intention in this latter instance was to prevent the sudden emergence of MIRVed missiles through the rapid addition of warheads to what had been single-warhead missiles; the overall intention was thus to limit qualitative improvement but to confine the limits to those characteristics that could be verified.

The Soviets declared the SS-X-24 (a new MIRVed ICBM that can be deployed on a mobile launcher) as their one permitted new type; the controversy surrounds the single warhead SS-25. The Soviets claim this missile to be a variant of the older SS-13, with new characteristics falling within the permitted SALT II guidelines. The United States has charged that the SS-25 constitutes a second (and hence illegal) new type because its throw-weight, even after taking into account U.S. uncertainties as to the data base, differs from that of the SS-13 by more than 5 percent. The United States has also charged the missile would not be permitted because its warhead-to-throw-weight ratio falls below the necessary 50 percent threshold. The Soviets claim that U.S. throw-weight estimates are off and that the SS-25 payload meets the 50 percent rule if one excludes (as the Soviets argue should be the case) on-board telemetry equipment. With no agreed data base, there is no apparent way to settle this issue to mutual satisfaction; as James Schear has noted, "If the SS-25 turns out to be illegal under the terms of SALT II, the Soviets may well have misjudged what they could do under SALT. Conversely, if it is legal under the terms of the agreement, the SS-25 will have disappointed—as did the SS-19 with SALT I—expectations in the U.S. regarding what an arms control agreement was supposed to prevent. Either way, someone loses."[26] What this points up is the need to include in arms control agreements a more complete data base (as well as data that can be independently verified) so that alterations to existing inventories, if they are to be effectively constrained, can be checked against a common standard.

The remaining SALT II-related compliance issue concerns the SS-16. The treaty is clear here: the SALT II agreement bans the production, testing, and deployment of the SS-16 (a three-stage mobile ICBM whose first two stages are identical to the two-stage SS-20 mobile IRBM) as well as the production of its unique components. (The intention was to prevent the emergence of mobile ICBMs through a break-out of SS-16s by the marrying up of the SS-16's third stage to the SS-20.) What is at issue are two matters: whether existing SS-16 boosters—boosters left over from the testing program carried out in the mid-1970s—at the Plesetsk missile-test facility constitute a circumvention of the treaty's ban on producing the SS-16 (no one is charging the Soviet Union with producing new SS-16s or with testing them) and, more important, whether those SS-16s that were stockpiled at Plesetsk were operational and thereby in violation of the treaty's deployment ban. The treaty itself is silent on the matter of dismantling existing SS-16 components, while the Soviets deny the latter deployment charge. The January 1984 and February 1985 compliance reports found the activities at Plesetsk to be a probable violation of SALT II; the December 1985 report to the Congress indicated the issue may have been resolved.[27] Quite possibly, the entire matter could have been avoided with a more detailed dismantling provision or possibly by an exchange of data regarding existing components; in the absence of such provisions, only NTM and in principle consultations are left to manage compliance-related disputes.

LESSONS OF THE PAST/LESSONS FOR THE FUTURE

The purpose of this chapter is not to add yet another voice to the large chorus debating whether and if so how significantly the Soviets are guilty of not complying with existing arms control arrangements.[28] Rather, the objective is to discern the sources of past and present compliance-related disputes and to determine what if any lessons can be derived from experience in order to reduce the scope of such compliance problems in the future.

The controversy surrounding compliance suggests avoiding substantial reliance on the use of ambiguity as a solution to negotiating impasses. This advice is easier said than heeded, however. The Soviets tend to resist U.S. attempts to reduce ambiguity, while in some circumstances the United States is loathe to specify certain activities for fear of compromising sensitive intelligence sources and methods. Specificity also brings with it another problem: much as is the case with a tax code that seeks to detail conditions under which tax must be paid only to create avenues for avoidance, so too can detailed agreements create opportunities to "design around" precise provisions.[29] Perhaps most important, the process of negotiation often requires a degree of ambiguity if agreement is to be reached between the two parties—the same ambiguity that can plague the implementation of agreements. This is a dilemma for which there is no easy resolution.

Yet compliance has emerged as a major issue not simply because of Soviet actions or textual ambiguities but also because of a change in elite attitudes in the United States. In the early years of the arms control process—that is, in the 1960s and 1970s or from the Kennedy through the Carter administrations—the U.S. government adhered to a posture of adequate verification. Adequate verification had as its premise the notion that absolute verification was impossible but that some uncertainty (and as a result some undetected noncompliance) could be tolerated as long as U.S. verification capacity was able to detect significant violations of agreements in sufficient time to allow the United States to mount the necessary response.[30] Implicit in this approach to arms control was the primacy of security over political concerns, that what mattered most was not the principle of noncompliance but the actual effect, and that some actions inconsistent with treaty provisions (or suspected to be) would matter much more than others.

More recently the official U.S. position has evolved toward one in which the fact of noncompliance—that is, the political act itself—is as important as the military impact. "A treaty may be said to be verifiable if behavior inconsistent with the treaty can be detected by the other party," wrote Richard Perle in 1980.[31] Five years later, President Reagan stated to Congress that "In order for arms control to have meaning and credibly contribute to national security and to global or regional security, it is essential that all parties to agreements fully comply with them. Strict compliance with all provisions of arms control agreements is fundamental, and this Administration will not accept anything less. To do so would undermine the arms control process and damage the chances for establishing a more constructive U.S.-Soviet relationship."[32] Tolerance for any sign of noncompliance is thus extremely low; the requirements for verification consequently extremely high. Adequate verification has been largely superseded by a desire for high confidence that the Soviet Union is abiding by all provisions of agreements regardless of the degree of military significance.

What follows from these three developments—a Soviet pattern of circumvention and apparent violation, the disutility of ambiguity when it comes to assessing compliance, and the heightened requirements for verification and compliance in the United States—are several important conclusions for future arms control negotiations and agreements:

The United States should eschew unilateral statements whose thrust is to affect Soviet behavior beyond terms stated in the treaty. Such expressions, even if unanswered, have no legally binding effect and no impact on Soviet behavior, but they do have an undesirable impact on U.S. perceptions and politics. As the SS-19 heavy-missile controversy makes readily apparent, such statements raise expectations that will inevitably be dashed, thereby diminishing support for agreements and what they do accomplish. Better to fail to reach agreement and either break off negotiations or explain the limits of what has been agreed than to issue proclamations that only confuse the issue of just what the Soviets can be expected to do.

Future agreements should build on the precedent of SALT II but make greater use of agreed data bases. The lack of such commonly accepted information has given rise to major compliance disputes in those areas where modernization or new deployments are constrained; both the disputes over new types of ICBMs and ABM radars and radar ranges might have been averted if accords had included a more complete set of agreed information on the size and characteristics of inventories at the time the treaties were signed. It should be recognized, however, that negotiating such agreed data bases is likely to become a difficult and prolonged exercise; indeed, the MBFR negotiations offer a dramatic example of how data disputes can all but preclude progress on arms control.

If agreements seek to restrain systems in certain circumstances but not in others—that is, if the restraints affect activity or purpose and not inventory or deployment—imprecise drafting or the allowance for exceptions is a recipe for compliance problems down the road. The several disputes over ABM-related radars point this up. So too do U.S. objections to alleged Soviet production of biological and toxin agents on grounds the Soviet program goes beyond the "types and quantities" permitted by the 1972 convention. If certain exceptions are unavoidable, the criteria for compliance ought to be capability (or some other attribute that can be verified by NTM), not the intention as stated by the side deploying the system in question. Wherever possible, functionally related observable differences (FRODs) ought to be insisted on. Other so-called cooperative measures—whether a reliance on third-party arbitration or intrusive (on-site) inspection—hold less promise; neither party would accept a decisive role for outsiders who would in any case lack an independent means of verifying behavior, while the Soviets have largely resisted the notion of on-site inspection. Even if the Soviets were to modify their thinking about inspections, it is far from certain that such access (presumably to be carefully circumscribed) would actually decrease the scope for behavior inconsistent with treaty undertakings.

Similarly, the degree of desired restraint ought to be specified in as much detail as possible and not to be left to the discretion of the parties themselves. Disagreement over what levels of development, testing, and deployment are permitted under the 1972 ABM Treaty are an inevitable result of not having definitions of such key terms as *system* and *components*. Similarly, the approach to encryption that leaves obligations open to varied interpretations is a poor precedent. The United States might have to be prepared to discuss intelligence sources and methods in greater detail than it would prefer if obligations are to be specified; the potential compromise of intelligence methods or targets needs to be weighed against the loss of intelligence through increased encryption.

It is unrealistic to expect too much of the Standing Consultative Commission (SCC). Even if one does not go as far as a recent Department of Defense indictment of the SCC—"Far from resolving disputes over compliance, the SCC has become a diplomatic carpet under which Soviet violations have been continuously swept, an Orwellian memory hole into which our concerns have been dumped like yesterday's trash"[33]—it is folly to look to the SCC to resolve differences that years of arduous negotiations could not. The SCC can contribute mostly on those occasions when treaty language is clear and some activity is questionable; dismantling provisions come to mind. It is less able to contribute when the parties disagree as to the facts regarding activities and capabilities or when the text itself is at issue.

In the end, there will be no doing away with compliance issues. Existing agreements provide more than ample scope for behavior that raises a full range of compliance issues. Future agreements, regardless of how precisely drafted, will inevitably produce new compliance concerns given verification uncertainties, evolving technologies (from increased missile mobility to greater miniaturization and potential for concealment) that are likely to exacerbate verification challenges, and differing interpretations (often patently self-serving) of obligations. Moreover, no treaty can be expected to provide a definition of what constitutes "adequate" verification; much less will any agreement dictate whether the United States ought to pursue compliance concerns privately or publicly, within the SCC or without. Nor will any future treaty settle the matter of whether the United States ought to respond to unresolved compliance concerns by taking identical or proportionate steps, withdrawing from or abrogating the pact, doing nothing at all, or retaliating in some other sphere of U.S.-Soviet relations.

Arms control without compliance controversies is unattainable. Indeed, the more that arms control produces new agreements, the more it will be threatened by its own success; contending with contested compliance of existing agreements and negotiating verification provisions of new ones could well come to dominate the arms control agenda for the foreseeable future. In addition, agreements establishing lower ceilings for forces will tend to increase the salience of compliance concerns as ostensibly modest violations could assume greater military significance. Yet informal or tacit arrangements are no panacea, for if they avoid some of the compliance-related problems inherently associated with formal agreements, they also fail to yield many of the political and military benefits that only formal agreements can confer. The only thing that is certain is that surmounting the twin challenges of negotiating mutually acceptable verification provisions for future agreements and meeting mutually acceptable standards of compliance regarding existing agreements will require a sustained commitment by the political leadership of both the United States and the Soviet Union.

NOTES

1. U.S. Arms Control and Disarmament Agency, *Arms Control: U.S. Objectives, Negotiating Efforts, Problems of Soviet Noncompliance* (Washington, D.C.: U.S. Government Printing Office, 1984), p. 10.
2. This chapter makes use of a large number of sources central to an appreciation of the current compliance debate. The key documents include President Reagan's January 23, 1984, February 1, 1985, and December 23, 1985, reports to the Congress, the report by the General Advisory Committee on Arms Control and Disarmament, *A Quarter Century of Soviet Compliance Practices under Arms Control Commitments: 1958-1983*, published in October 1984, and U.S. Arms Control and Disarmament Agency, *Soviet Noncompliance* (Feb. 1, 1986). The best overview articles I have read on the debate are James A. Schear, "Arms Control Treaty Compliance," *International Security* 10 (2) (Fall 1985), pp. 141–82 and Jeanette Voas, "The Arms-Control Compliance Debate," *Survival* (Jan.–Feb. 1986), pp. 8–31. Other pieces drawn on here include David Sullivan, "The Legacy of SALT II: Soviet Deception and U.S. Retreat," *Strategic Review* (Winter 1979); Walter Slocombe, "A Salt Debate: Hard but Fair Bargaining," *Strategic Review* (Fall 1979); Carnegie Panel on U.S. Security and the Future of Arms Control, *Challenges for National Security* (Washington, D.C.: Carnegie Endowment, 1983); Richard Perle, "What Is Adequate Verification?," in Gordon J. Humphrey, et al., *SALT II and American Security* (Cambridge, Mass.: Institute for Foreign Policy Analysis, 1980); Federation of American Scientists, "Changes of Treaty Violations: Much Less Than Meets the Eye," *Public Interest Report* 37 (3) (March 1984), pp. 1–20 and Michael Krepon, "Decontrolling the Arms Race: The U.S. and the Soviets Fumble the Compliance Issues," *Arms Control Today* 14 (3) (March–April 1984), pp. 1–3, 12. This essay also makes heavy use of the various case studies in this volume.
3. For useful discussions of verification, see William F. Rowell, *Arms Control Verification: A Guide to Policy Issues for the 1980s* (Cambridge, Mass.: Ballinger, 1986), and Mark M. Lowenthal, *SALT Verification* (Washington, D.C.: Congressional Research Service, Library of Congress, July 10, 1978).
4. Henry Kissinger articulated a somewhat different version of what constitutes a violation. He suggested as many as six types: (1) deliberate violations aimed at increasing strategic capacity in ways the agreement in question was intended to preclude; (2) actions inconsistent with the spirit of the agreement that tend to undermine its viability even though not expressly prohibited; (3) unintended violations occurring through negligence; (4) actions not banned but that complicate verification; (5) ambigu-

ous activities resulting from differing interpretations of provisions; and (6) activities assessed as ambiguous due to inadequate information or misinterpretation of information that suggests a violation where in fact none exists. See Kissinger's news conference of Dec. 9, 1975, reprinted in *Department of State Bulletin* (Jan. 5, 1976), pp. 1–12.

5. This was precisely the argument used by President Kennedy with the Senate. See, for example, U.S. Arms Control and Disarmament Agency, *Documents on Disarmament, 1963* (Washington, D.C.: U.S. Government Printing Office, 1964), p. 301.

6. See Senate Committee on Foreign Relations, *Hearings on the Prohibition of Chemical and Biological Weapons*, 93d Cong., 2d Sess. (Washington, D.C.: U.S. Government Printing Office, 1974), pp. 15–16, 63.

7. The principal protagonist raising verification-related matters was Senator Henry Jackson. Jackson was worried that the Soviets would exploit the Interim Agreement's ambiguity and lack of agreed data to introduce additional offensive systems. He also raised the possibility that in the absence of considerable on-site inspection the Soviets could violate the ABM Treaty's ban on the development of certain types of ABM systems. See Senate Committee on Armed Services, *Hearings on Military Implications of the Treaty on the Limitations of Anti-Ballistic Missile Systems and the Interim Agreement on Limitation of Strategic Offensive Arms*, 92d Cong., 2d Sess. (Washington, D.C.: U.S. Government Printing Office, 1972), pp. 205–08, 439–42 (hereafter cited as *Military Implications*). For a useful compendium covering verification and the principal modern arms control pacts see William C. Potter, ed., *Verification and SALT: The Challenge of Strategic Deception* (Boulder, Colo.: Westview Press, 1980).

8   See, for example, the statements of Secretary of State Rogers and Secretary of Defense Laird about the adequacy of U.S. NTM in Senate Committee on Foreign Relations, *Hearings on the Strategic Arms Limitation Agreements*, 92d Cong., 2d Sess. (Washington, D.C.: U.S. Government Printing Office, 1972), pp. 37, 64. Chief Negotiator Gerard Smith echoed this confidence, going as far as to state that he preferred dependence on NTM to on-site inspection. See *Military Implications*, p. 100.

9. The text of the briefing is reprinted in Senate Committee on Foreign Relations, p. 401. Here as elsewhere Kissinger made it clear that poor Soviet compliance would affect the entire range of U.S.-Soviet relations. In another briefing Kissinger stated "any country which contemplates a rupture of the agreement or a circumvention of its letter and spirit must now face the fact that it will be placing in jeopardy not only a limited arms control agreement, but a broad political relationship" (reprinted in *Military Implications*), pp. 117–18.

10. All excerpts of treaties and other agreements taken from U.S. Arms Control and Disarmament Agency, *Arms Control and Disarmament Agree-*

ments: Texts and Histories of Negotiations (Washington, D.C.: U.S. Government Printing Office, 1982).

11.   President Nixon established the Verification Panel in the spring of 1969, designating Henry Kissinger as chairman and the under secretary of state, the deputy secretary of defense, the chairman of the Joint Chiefs of Staff, and the directors of the Central Intelligence Agency and the Arms Control and Disarmament Agency as members. Kissinger's description of the panel's function is worth repeating: "The Verification Panel analyzed each of the weapons systems which could conceivably be involved in an agreement. It compared the effect of different limitations on our program and on the Soviet programs, and weighed the resulting balance. It analyzed the possibilities of verification, and the precise risk of evasion, seeking to determine at what point evasion could be detected and what measures would be available for a response." See Senate Committee on Foreign Relations, p. 396.

12.   The Senate Select Committee on Intelligence, for example, concluded that "in most cases, monitoring requirements were given high priority during Treaty negotiations, and that monitoring necessities were reflected in the Treaty provision. . . . overall . . . the SALT II Treaty enhances the ability of the United States to monitor those components of Soviet strategic forces which are subject to the limitations of the Treaty." See Senate Select Committee on Intelligence, *Report on Principal Findings on the Capabilities of the United States to Monitor the SALT II Treaty* (Washington, D.C.: U.S. Government Printing Office, Oct. 1979), pp. 1, 5.

13.   Testimony of Defense Secretary Harold Brown and Under Secretary William Perry in Senate Committee, *Hearings on The SALT II Treaty*, Part 2, 96th Cong., 1st Sess. (Washington, D.C.: U.S. Government Printing Office, July 1979), pp. 231–87.

14.   See Senate Committee on Armed Services, *Hearings on the Military Implications of the Proposed SALT II Treaty Relating to the National Defense* (Washington, D.C.: U.S. Government Printing Office, 1980), pp. 13, 17.

15.   See "The U.S. Violates Its International Commitments," *Pravda*, Jan. 30, 1984 (reprinted in *The Current Digest of the Soviet Press* 36 (4) (Feb. 22, 1984), p. 4).

16.   For background into the U.S. attempt to get the Soviets to accept the U.S. approach to the heavy missile issue, see Gerard Smith, *Doubletalk: The Story of the First Strategic Arms Limitation Talks* (New York: Doubleday, 1980), esp. pp. 389–91 and 413–17. The U.S. delegation proposed to President Nixon that he authorize a unilateral statement only when it became clear the Soviets would not accept language that would seriously constrain SS-11 modernization. U.S. delegation head Gerard Smith made the proposal knowing that the statement itself—"The United

States would consider any ICBM having a volume significantly greater than that of the largest light ICBM now operational on either side to be a heavy ICBM. The U.S. proceeds on the premise that the Soviet side will give due account to this consideration"—would likely have little effect; indeed, he told Washington at the time that "A unilateral statement by us may have some slight deterrent effect on any such new Soviet program, but I wouldn't put a very high estimate on the value of such deterrence" (see above, p. 400).

17. A June 1985 "Common Understanding" reached in the SCC established a mechanism under which either party could challenge the other on alleged illegal concurrent testing of air defense radars in an ABM mode. The understanding does not prohibit the existence of air defense radars at ABM ranges or even their operation during missile tests as long as the radar is being used for purposes of range air safety—that is, to prevent aircraft in the vicinity from straying into danger amid tests of ABMs. Thus, at least in principle, banned ABM-related concurrent testing could occur under the cover of permitted air defense activities. For a more generous interpretation of this understanding, see R. Jeffrey Smith, "Arms Agreement Breathes New Life into SCC," *Science* (Aug. 9, 1985).

18. Definitional questions also are at the core of another relatively minor ABM Treaty–related compliance issue. Article V prohibits those systems allowing rapid reload of ABM launchers. The Soviets have reportedly fired two SH-08 interceptor missiles from a single launcher within two hours. At issue is whether this rate crosses the "rapid" threshold. See Voas, "The Arms-Control Compliance Debate," p. 25.

19. See, for example, "The U.S. Violates Its International Commitments," *Pravda*, Jan. 30, 1984. (The full text of this official memorandum is reprinted in *The Current Digest of the Soviet Press* 36 (4) (Feb. 22, 1984), p. 4.) See also "Don't Sabotage Commitments, Observe Them," *Pravda*, Feb. 9, 1985 (reprinted in *The Current Digest of the Soviet Press* 37 (6) (March 6, 1985), p. 7).

20. The United States is said to have rejected one Soviet proposal to resolve the Krasnoyarsk issue when in late 1985 the Soviets reportedly offered to halt construction of the controversial radar in exchange for the United States' halting its upgrading of the two early warning radars. See Leslie H. Gelb, "Moscow Proposes to End a Dispute on Siberia Radar," *The New York Times*, Oct. 29, 1985, p. 1.

21. Concerns such as these could well have precluded any agreement banning all antisatellite systems. In addition to dedicated antisatellite weapons, a large number of systems including ballistic missiles, antiballistic missiles, and surface-to-air missiles have or could have "residual" or potential antisatellite capabilities. As a result, any agreement in this realm would have

had no choice but to focus on dedicated systems or testing of any system in an antisatellite mode or both. Obviously, the challenges to verification would have been considerable and the potential for noncompliance great.

22. I do not include here several compliance issues, such as the Soviet refusal to reduce to lower strategic nuclear delivery vehicle (SNDV) limits (from 2,504 to 2,400 to 2,250) or the U.S. charge that Soviet SNDV totals are above the level of 2,504 existing when SALT II was signed, which are peculiar to the uncertain status of the SALT II pact. It should also be noted that there are a number of Soviet compliance-related charges against the United States. U.S. deployment of long-range cruise missiles is seen by the Soviets as inconsistent with the intent of the protocol, while the deployment in Europe of a new generation of intermediate range nuclear forces (INF) is seen as inconsistent with the clause prohibiting circumvention of the treaty by transferring relevant systems to third parties. The United States has also been accused of intending "to create" a second "new type" of ICBM. (For the Soviet charges see "The U.S. Violates Its International Commitments," *Pravda* and *Izvestia*, Jan. 30, 1984, reprinted in *The Current Digest of the Soviet Press* 36 (4) (Feb. 22, 1984), p. 4.) The first two of these Soviet charges are groundless: the protocol and its constraints on long-range cruise missiles were due to expire at the end of 1981, while the deployment of new INF missiles by the United States in Europe does not involve the transfer of control of these systems to any third party. As for the third charge, the Soviet Union is correct that the United States is developing a second "new type" of ICBM (the Midgetman), but the United States argues that it is relieved of the agreement's restrictions in this area (the SALT II Treaty prohibits both the flight-testing and deployment of more than one "new type" of ICBM) because of alleged Soviet flight-testing of a second "new type."

23. This approach to encryption was consistent with the SALT I provision that prohibited concealment measures impeding verification by the NTM of either party. The United States had occasion to challenge the Soviets on their behavior in this realm. In 1974 the United States noticed an increase in concealment activity by the Soviets that while not impeding U.S. ability to verify compliance might have if continued and expanded. The United States raised this concern with the Soviets in 1975, after which the United States noted an end to the expansion of concealment activities. See Senate Committee on Foreign Relations, *Hearings on Briefings on SALT Negotiations*, 95th Cong., 1st Sess. (Washington, D.C.: U.S. Government Printing Office, 1978), p. 68.

24. The president's December 23, 1985, compliance report states that Soviet encryption "impedes our ability to verify the Soviet Union's compliance with its political commitments" (p. 4), while a second official document alleges that continued Soviet violation of the encryption provision "is certain to diminish still further our ability to monitor Soviet activities and

to verify their compliance with Treaty obligations." See "Responding to Soviet Violations Policy (RSVP) Study," Memorandum for the President from Secretary of Defense Caspar Weinberger (Dec. 1985), p. 8.

25. A total ban on encryption would also raise the issue of constraining or even banning "encapsulation," a means by which test-related data can be obtained through the release of capsules containing information from the system in question, thereby reducing the need for telemetry.

26. See Schear, "Arms Control Treaty Compliance," p. 167.

27. The President's "Unclassified Report on Soviet Noncompliance with Arms Control Agreements" (Dec. 23, 1985) notes "Soviet activity in the past year at Plesetsk seems to indicate the probable removal of SS-16 equipment and introduction of equipment associated with a different ICBM" (p. 10).

28. For their part, the Soviets claim full compliance with agreements they have signed. See the "Response by the Soviet Government" from the Soviet Embassy in Washington to Congressmen Aspin, Solarz, et al. of April 23, 1985. Also see Marshal S.L. Sokolov, "Preserve What Has Been Achieved in Strategic Arms Limitation," *Pravda*, Nov. 6, 1985 (excerpts reprinted in *The Current Digest of the Soviet Press* 37 (45) (Dec. 4, 1985), pp. 24–25. For some insight into possible motivations behind Soviet compliance behavior, see *Explaining Soviet Compliance Behavior* (Digest of a One-Day Conference, Project on Compliance and the Future of Arms Control, Center for International Security and Arms Control, Stanford University, Feb. 14, 1986.)

29. Another analogy that comes to mind here is the debate over the "correct" interpretation of the U.S. Constitution. Advocates of "states rights" would reserve to the states all powers not explicitly attributed to the federal government. The record of Soviet arms control behavior suggests their adhering to a view that at a minimum permits them to go ahead with any activity not specifically prohibited. Indeed, it is this trait that lies at the heart of U.S. charges of Soviet circumvention.

30. Defense Secretary Harold Brown, testifying on behalf of the SALT II Treaty, presented the case for "adequate verification":

> Our impressive monitoring capability does not mean that we can be certain of detecting every conceivable treaty violation—or every conceivable change in Soviet strategic forces—as soon as it occurs. That is an impossible and unnecessary standard to meet, either for verification or for intelligence generally. No arms limitation agreement can ever be absolutely verifiable. The relevant test is not an abstract ideal, but the practical standard of whether we can determine compliance adequately to safeguard our security—that is, whether we can identify attempted evasion if it occurs on a large enough scale to pose a significant risk, and whether we can do so in time to mount a sufficient response. Meeting this test is what I mean by the term "adequate verification."

The remarks are excerpted from Senate Committee on Foreign Relations, *Hearings on the SALT II Treaty*, p. 241.

31.   Richard N. Perle "What Is Adequate Verification?," in Gordon J. Humphrey, et al., *SALT II and American Security*, p. 53.

32.   See President Reagan's February 1, 1985, report on Soviet compliance to the Congress. The December 23, 1985, report from President Reagan to the Congress further developed the administration's thinking about verification:

> In a fundamental sense, all deliberate violations are equally important. As violations of legal obligations or political commitments, they cause grave concern regarding Soviet commitment to arms control, and they darken the atmosphere in which current negotiations are being conducted in Geneva and elsewhere. In another sense, Soviet violations are not of equal importance. While some individual violations are of little apparent military significance in their own right, such violations can acquire importance if, left unaddressed, they are permitted to become precedents for future, more threatening violations. Moreover, some issues that individually have little military significance could conceivably become significant when taken in their aggregate.

(memo from The White House Office of the Press Secretary, p. 3). The logic is akin to the accountant analogy, in that one does not want to employ an accountant (no matter how much money he may save for the client overall) who is somewhat dishonest because it creates a strong sense of anxiety.

33.   See "Responding to Soviet Violations Policy (RSVP)," memorandum from Secretary of Defense Weinberger to the President (Dec. 1985), p. 9. For a rebuttal, see Gloria Duffy, "Administration Redefines Soviet 'Violations,'" *Bulletin of Atomic Scientists* (Feb. 1986). Also see the article by Sidney Graybeal and Michael Krepon, "Making Better Use of the SCC," *International Security* 10 (2) (Fall 1985).

12 CONCLUSIONS
Weighing the Evidence

Albert Carnesale and Richard N. Haass

The public debate about arms control discloses more about the debate participants than about arms control. Individuals and organizations tend to bring to the debate strongly held beliefs about the pros and cons of arms control processes and agreements. The purpose of this study has been to identify and elucidate the principal beliefs, which we call hypotheses, that have shaped the debate and to examine their validity in the context of the important U.S.-Soviet arms control negotiations and agreements—namely, the Limited Test Ban Treaty (LTBT), the Accidents Measures Agreement, the SALT I Anti-Ballistic Missile (ABM) Treaty and Interim Agreement on Offensive Arms, the SALT II Treaty, the 1977–79 negotiations on anti-satellite (ASAT) weapons, the Nuclear Non-Proliferation Treaty (NPT), and the Biological Weapons Convention (BWC).

In this final chapter, we seek under each of the ten hypotheses to gather the important case-specific findings and to draw some general lessons from the arms control experience. Five of the hypotheses deal primarily with the prerequisits for and processes of arms control, and five with its effects. Each hypothesis is considered in turn below.

The emphasis here is on gathering and analyzing evidence relevant to the hypotheses in order to discern any lessons that might be learned from the arms control experience. It is not our objective simply to prove or disprove each hypothesis. Indeed, because each hypothesis represents a belief held by an important participant or constituency in the arms control process and disbelieved (or at least doubted) by another, it is hardly surprising that the historical evidence of their validity is mixed. Such hypotheses rarely can be unambiguously demonstrated to be either true or false: some evidence can almost always be found to support either contention. But often the weight of evidence tips the balance strongly one way or the other, at least in the eyes of those willing to view the scale objectively.

HYPOTHESIS 1. BARGAINING FROM STRENGTH

Progress in arms control takes place only when

1. The United States has the advantage.
2. Neither side has an advantage.
3. The Soviet Union has the advantage.

Arms control agreements have been concluded only when neither side had an appreciable advantage—that is, only when there already existed rough parity in the relevant forces of the two sides. Although the United States has demonstrated greater flexibility than the Soviet Union on this matter, neither side has been willing to enter into an agreement in which it would suffer enduring inferiority by any meaningful measure. This assertion is supported by all of the cases considered in this study.

In the instance of the Limited Test Ban Treaty, the absence of restraints on underground tests enabled both sides to enter into the agreement without any significant sacrifice in the benefits of nuclear testing. As for the Accidents Measures Agreement, which imposed no constraints on forces, there is little meaning to the notion of relative advantage.

It is instructive to observe that no serious negotiations on strategic nuclear forces—offensive and defensive—even began until the end of the 1960s, by which time the Soviet Union had achieved rough parity (or essential equivalence) with the United States. When the 1972 ABM Treaty was concluded, neither side had a capacity (or even a potential capacity) for ballistic missile defense in which it could be confident. The Soviet Union had an advantage in deployed capability in its Galosh system at Moscow, but that system could be overwhelmed easily by a small fraction of the then deployed U.S. offensive force. Although the United States had not yet deployed its Safeguard ABM system, the technologies characteristic of that system were clearly superior to those employed by the Soviets. This U.S. technological advantage may well have been offset by opposition in the Congress and the engaged public to U.S. ABM deployment. On balance, however, the absence of any clear, militarily significant inequality in either actual or near-term potential capability for defense against ballistic missiles appears as much as anything to have made agreement on the ABM Treaty possible.

Although the treaty permitted each side to maintain active ABM deployments at two (later reduced to one) sites, for the past decade only the Soviet Union has exercised that option. Yet this asymmetry in practice has not undermined support for the treaty among arms control advocates and publics in the United States and elsewhere. Nor has the absence of evidence suggesting Soviet embrace of a condition of mutual assured destruction eroded Western public support for the ABM Treaty, which many consider to be the cardinal accomplishment of arms control.

The early 1970s brought essential equivalence of U.S. and Soviet offensive nuclear capabilities, although there were important differences in the structures of the forces. The United States enjoyed substantial advantages in the size of its long-range bomber force, in the numbers of warheads on its ICBMs and SLBMs (made possible by multiple independently targetable reentry vehicles (MIRVs), which the United States was deploying but the Soviets had not yet even tested), and in its forward-based systems within range of the Soviet homeland. The Soviet Union, on the other hand, had more ICBM launchers, more ballistic missile submarines and SLBM launchers, and far more missile throw-weight (which provided substantial potential for deployment of future Soviet MIRVs). The SALT I Interim Agreement placed no constraints on bombers, numbers of warheads, forward-based systems, throw-weight, or MIRVs. Only long-range missile launchers were subject to limitations, and these limits were intended to apply for a period of only five years. Areas of important asymmetry were omitted from the Interim Agreement. By the mid-1970s the Soviets had tested and were deploying their own MIRVs, making it possible to reach agreement on a SALT II Treaty that constrained numbers of warheads in addition to limiting numbers of strategic launchers.

Failure of the ASAT negotiations lends further credence to the proposition that arms control agreements are reached only when neither side has an advantage. Segments of the Carter administration opposed an ASAT pact that would leave the USSR with a demonstrated capacity to intercept and destroy some low-orbit U.S. satellites while preventing the United States from obtaining comparable capability. At the same time, the Soviet Union rejected the notion that it should dismantle its deployed ASAT system as a price for achieving a formal accord precluding any U.S. ASAT. The Soviets' interest in progress toward agreement appears to have increased markedly when the United States moved closer to testing an ASAT system substantially more effective than their own. It is only a slight oversimplification to say that the United States was uninterested in an ASAT agreement that would preserve its disadvantage, and the Soviet Union was uninterested in an ASAT agreement that would eliminate its advantage. Even if the two sides might have perceived as roughly equivalent the extant Soviet ASAT and the potential U.S. ASAT, it is doubtful that a meaningful agreement could have been reached. Other problems intrinsic to the negotiation (notably verification) and extrinsic (especially the general deterioration of U.S.-Soviet relations) effectively terminated the diplomatic effort.

Although progress in arms control generally takes place only when neither side has an advantage, this does not imply that success comes only when the forces subject to negotiation are identical. Overall parity does not require precise equality in every relevant measure of military strength. Although there are numerous instances in which a given Soviet system has a direct analogue in the U.S. inventory, overall parity is also the "result" of numerous inequalities that balance out. Such inequalities are the inevitable result of the asymmetrical force structures of the two countries, asymmetries that in turn are largely the result of unilateral force decisions of the two governments. The process of negotiation thus tends to become a series of tradeoffs, in which the advantages of one party in one or more particular categories of weaponry are in some sense compensated for by the advantages of the other party in other categories, despite the inherent incommensurability of the asymmetries. Yet it is an irony of arms control that the offsetting asymmetries that make negotiation possible also make any U.S. administration vulnerable to charges that it agreed to an unsatisfactory arrangement in which the USSR emerged with one or more advantages.

There exist clear limits to the potential for tradeoffs, however. Overall parity is not enough; some elements of the strategic balance are perceived to be so central that disadvantages cannot be legitimized. Where no acceptable tradeoff exists, the inferiority cannot be formalized by agreement and can be rectified only by unilateral effort.

HYPOTHESIS 2. GENIES IN BOTTLES

Meaningful constraints on any particular category of weapons can be achieved only if neither side

1. Really wants the weapon.
2. Has tested the weapon.
3. Has invested heavily in the weapon.

This examination of U.S.-Soviet arms control history confirms that militarily significant constraints on any particular category of weapons eludes negotiations if either side strongly prefers unfettered freedom of action with regard to the weapon in question. Put simply, each side has a veto on such constraints. If either party has tested the weapon or invested heavily in it, the difficulties confronting arms control are compounded. In and of itself, however, technological change is not an insurmountable obstacle to the achievement of meaningful limitations.

That the Limited Test Ban Treaty is limited rather than comprehensive is related in large part to the mutual desire of the U.S. and Soviet governments not to forgo all nuclear testing. Verification considerations also were a factor in precluding a comprehensive ban, but their relative importance in determining the limited outcome often is overstated. Both sides wished to continue testing, whether to modernize offensive weapons or to develop defensive ones. Indeed, it may be that the partial test ban was attainable only because policymakers believed that prospects were bleak for a ballistic missile defense system that itself employed nuclear explosives. Had this not been the case, resistance to the limited ban (prohibiting the atmospheric nuclear bursts essential to full testing of an ABM system) would have been far greater than it was.

The ability of the United States and the Soviet Union to conclude an ABM Treaty that all but eliminated ballistic missile defenses testifies to the importance of technological promise as a factor in arms control. Despite the desire of both sides to attain a capability to destroy incoming ballistic missiles, extensive testing of ABM proto-types, and considerable investment by the Soviets in a limited de-ployment around Moscow, the ABM Treaty was achieved when both sides concluded that competition in this area would prove costly, possibly destabilizing, and in the near term technologically futile. It is worth noting that the ABM Treaty, for all its comprehensiveness, did not prohibit testing of the fixed land-based ABM systems then judged most promising, nor did it require the Soviets to abandon the Moscow ABM deployment in which they had invested so heavily.

The MIRV experience is relevant to the genies-in-bottles hypothe-sis. During the SALT I negotiations, the United States enjoyed a con-siderable lead in MIRV technology and was actively testing, produc-ing, and deploying MIRV systems. The Soviets were still in the devel-opment stage and had not yet flight-tested MIRVs. Neither side offered a serious proposal for constraining MIRVs. This can be ex-plained in part by the Soviet desire to narrow or close the MIRV gap and the U.S. desire to maintain or widen it. An equally important obstacle to meaningful MIRV constraints was posed by the military attractiveness of MIRV technology. MIRVs are "technically sweet": they offer a cost-effective means for increasing target coverage and for overwhelming traditional kinds of ABM systems.

SALT II offers a mixed record of efforts to constrain emerging weapons and technologies. Both sides agreed, for example, not to produce submarine-based or land-mobile launchers for heavy ballistic missiles—systems neither side had indicated any desire to acquire. More interesting was the Soviet willingness to forgo the SS-16 mo-bile ICBM, indicating that the Soviets were not impressed with the potential of their own system or were willing to sacrifice it to in-crease the likelihood of obtaining a long-term ban on deployment of mobile ICBMs. The most important emerging technology of the SALT II era—medium-range and long-range cruise missiles—was "lim-ited" by the protocol, a separate part of the treaty designed to run through the end of 1981. (The treaty was slated to remain in force until the end of 1985.) At least in principle the protocol was de-signed to buy time for arms control negotiators to devise a means for constraining key new technologies such as cruise or land-mobile mis-siles; yet there is no reason to believe that the two parties would have been able to reach agreement on a ban on all but short-range cruise missiles beyond the end of 1981. These systems may simply have been too attractive to the United States and its allies to be given up.

ASAT is another genie whose bottle has not been capped by arms control. Several factors account for the failure of the ASAT negotiations to achieve agreement: the fact that the Soviets alone had demonstrated and deployed an actual ASAT interceptor missile, verification difficulties, the deterioration of U.S.-Soviet relations, and the promise of technological advance toward an effective U.S. ASAT system. Yet the possibility for some constraints on these devices (such as a ban on testing high-altitude ASATs) remains, suggesting that if technology emerges sufficiently gradually and at comparable rates on both sides, arms control can have considerable opportunity to curb it.

The Biological Weapons Convention was achieved at a time when all three conditions of this hypothesis were satisfied. Neither the United States nor the Soviet Union was deeply committed to biological or toxin weapons; neither had invested heavily in their development; and given the inherent uncontrollability of the agents in question, testing on a large scale was all but impossible. It is instructive to note here the contrast with chemical weapons. Although the United States and the Soviet Union are parties to the 1925 Geneva Protocol banning the use of chemical and biological agents, both have insisted on maintaining the right to develop, test, produce, and stockpile various forms of chemical agents and associated delivery systems, many of which are perceived to have substantial military utility. Moreover, the United States made clear that its adherence to the Geneva Protocol would not restrict its use of certain categories of chemicals, specifically herbicides, riot-control agents, and napalm—all of which were in use at the time of U.S. ratification (1975).

Much of this history suggests that the superpowers were able and willing to forgo development and deployment of certain technologies or activities when the costs of these activities appeared high and payoffs uncertain. That "preclusive" regimes were agreed to for outer space, Antarctica, the seabed, and environmental modification supports this thesis. So too does the fact that a regime could not be reached for controlling the highly promising MIRV technology. Interestingly, agreement was reached to limit severely antiballistic missile technology at a time when prospects for successful defense appeared poor; today, with the prospects appearing to some to be brighter than they were, the regime is coming under sustained pressure. The conclusion to be drawn is that arms control has far more difficulty in coping with weapons programs that are underway and show promise, despite the tendency for each side to fear that the other side will make greater progress and therefore will eventually gain some advantage.

HYPOTHESIS 3. UNILATERAL RESTRAINT

Unilateral restraint by the United States

1. Induces reciprocal restraint by the Soviet Union.
2. Induces counterproductive action by the Soviet Union.
3. Increases the likelihood of achieving bilateral arms control agreement.
4. Decreases the likelihood of achieving bilateral arms control agreement.

There are those who believe that a promising mechanism for contributing to arms control progress—whether by means of a tacit regime of mutual denial or a formal agreement—is the exercise of unilateral constraint by the United States. The historical record offers little basis on which to test this hypothesis, for there are few (if any) instances of one side's abstaining from an activity of significant military utility over a period of time sufficiently long to induce an observable and unambiguous response by the other side. The little evidence that can be gleaned, however, gives little encouragement to those who would argue that "arms control by example" or unilateral denial by the United States is likely to induce similar behavior by the Soviet Union or pave the way to a successful accord. An apparent exception is the decision by President Nixon in 1969 to forgo unilaterally all biological and toxin weapons, which was followed soon thereafter by achievement of the Biological Weapons Convention. However, this episode probably reflects less the value of unilateral restraint than it does the fact that arms control prospects are brightest when neither party sees military utility in a particular weapons system, activity, or environment.

The Soviets' formulation of their security plans and programs obviously takes into account more than just corresponding U.S. plans and programs. Their decision to resume nuclear testing in 1961 took place despite the absence of any evidence indicating that the United States was preparing to resume testing. There is no evidence that the slow pace of U.S. ABM development in the 1960s had an appreciable effect on the pace of Soviet efforts. The subsequent U.S. decision to forgo any active ABM deployment despite the ABM Treaty's allowance for doing so was in no way reciprocated by Moscow; to the contrary, the Soviet Union not only maintained but upgraded the Galosh ABM system around Moscow.

Similarly, there is no reason to believe that the Soviets respond positively to claims of U.S. unilateral restraint in the area of offensive weaponry. Unilateral U.S. decisions to cap the number of land-based and submarine-based ballistic missile launchers in what became the U.S. totals for SALT I did not prompt the Soviets to curtail their own efforts once numerical equality was realized. The Soviets introduced the SS-20 IRBM in the absence of any actual or planned deployment of a new generation of comparable U.S. missiles in either Europe or Asia. And neither the Carter administration's decision not to proceed with the B-1 bomber (for which the stated rationale was cost-effectiveness rather than restraint) nor U.S. forbearance in the development of antisatellite systems in the 1960s and 1970s appear to have affected the pace of Soviet efforts in these areas.

In many of the areas cited above, however, arms control agreements have been achieved. It may well be that while unilateral restraint by the United States does not noticeably affect Soviet actions or lead directly to bilateral accords, it does in some instances create opportunities for the Soviet Union to gain relative to the United States, which in turn may create a condition of parity and thereby increase the Soviet (and, indeed, the U.S.) appetite for formal agreements.

HYPOTHESIS 4. LINKAGE

The arms control process influences and is influenced by

1. Soviet behavior in other policy areas.
2. U.S. behavior in other policy areas.

To the extent that the arms control process influences and is influenced by Soviet or U.S. behavior in other policy areas, linkage can be employed as an active form of diplomacy—introduced by one party to affect the behavior of the other, either by manipulating arms control to modify behavior elsewhere or to manipulate behavior elsewhere to shape arms control positions. Linkage can also be unintended, when events extrinsic to arms control have an unplanned impact on one side's ability to manage a negotiation or its aftermath. Related to this last notion is yet another linkage variant—a conscious policy to insulate, or delink, arms control negotiations from developments in other realms of the relationship.

Examples of linkage diplomacy, with arms control as either the lever or the object of policy modification and manipulation, are difficult to identify. Moreover, even when participants claim the successful use of linkage, it is not certain that the policy of the other party was in fact determined by the alleged link. It is difficult to see evidence of the Soviets' restraining their client India in its 1971 conflict with Pakistan for the sake of in-progress U.S.-Soviet arms control negotiations, unless one credits to Soviet urgings the absence of an Indian dismemberment of West Pakistan. There is also the possibility that the Soviets sacrificed their desire to use the Cuban facility at Cienfuegos to service their submarines (an activity that from the U.S. perspective would have been inconsistent with the post-Cuban Missile Crisis Soviet undertaking not to station offensive nuclear systems in Cuba) so as not to jeopardize the prospects for the then under way SALT I and ABM negotiations.

What is clear is that both President Nixon and his National Security Advisor Henry Kissinger sought to improve U.S.-Soviet relations across a broad front, hoping in particular that the Soviets would moderate their global ambitions and to a lesser extent their repression at home so that arms control progress could be realized. Yet for the most part the Soviets resisted compromising their regional objectives for the sake of arms control. Both before and after the signing of the 1972 agreements, aid flowed in large quantities to North Vietnam, Cuba, the Arab confrontation states, and other Soviet friends and allies while the Soviet navy was actively promoting Soviet interests around the globe. The Soviets were free to pursue their regional aims and their arms control objectives independently and simultaneously; the United States not only had an interest in promoting arms control progress in its own right, but owing to the West's fundamental pluralism and divided political authority, the Nixon administration lacked the means to impose linkage on the Soviets. Indeed, the most successful example of linkage—tying Soviet emigration policy to the threat of legislation denying the Soviets Most Favored Nation (MFN) trade status—appeared to work because the Congress could act on its own; even then, this linkage worked as desired only as long as it remained a threat. Once the legislation was adopted, the flow of Jewish emigrants from the USSR decreased substantially.

Far more extensive are examples of what has been termed in this study *unintended linkage* or linkage between arms control and other developments in the relationship that were unplanned and usually unanticipated. The Limited Test Ban came about in part because the Cuban Missile Crisis created a constituency favoring that more be done to pull the two nuclear powers back from the brink of direct confrontation. Yet events far removed from the test ban also had the effect of delaying negotiations; talks could well have gotten under way sooner had it not been for other events, notably the downing of the U.S. U-2 reconnaissance aircraft and the resulting cancellation of the scheduled four-power summit.

This last example of outside events creating an environment unfriendly to arms control is by far the more common pattern. External events—in this case the August 1968 Soviet invasion of Czechoslovakia—also delayed the start of strategic arms limitation talks until a new U.S. administration had come into office. The 1968 decision to postpone the start of the negotiations was not inevitable, however; rather, it was a conscious political choice by the U.S. side that it would be inappropriate to meet with the Soviets at such a juncture. It is noteworthy that the Nixon administration did not allow the SALT I/ABM negotiations (or for that matter the Accidents Measures Agreement) to be affected by Soviet support for North Vietnam or its late 1971 support for India in its war against U.S. friend Pakistan. Similarly, such connections between regional behavior and arms control were not drawn at the time by the Soviets. Indeed, what is perhaps most interesting about the Soviet approach to these negotiations was the Soviet willingness not to invoke linkage when the United States acted with such determination against an important Soviet ally. The May 1972 U.S.-Soviet summit went ahead despite the large-scale U.S. bombing of North Vietnam's Haiphong Harbor. That the Soviets did not cancel the summit appears not only to have reflected a stake in arms control but their genuine interest in reaping the perceived political benefits of the scheduled meeting, one of which may have been to demonstrate to the world (and above all to the People's Republic of China) that only the Soviets enjoyed a relationship with the United States founded on a basis of equality.

The history of SALT II (and in a less important way the history of other arms control efforts then underway, including the antisatellite weapons talks) above all attests to the power of inadvertent linkage. The Carter administration attempted to conduct a policy of delinkage in which arms control would constitute a separate and insulated track of the relationship, to be pursued on its own merits, unaffected by other aspects of U.S.-Soviet competition or disagreement. Yet the U.S. disillusionment with détente, which had been gaining currency beginning with the October 1973 Middle East conflict and gathered momentum during the Ford and Carter administrations, created an atmosphere in which virtually any undertaking with the Soviets, including arms control, was suspect. The Angolan conflict, the Ogaden war, the "discovery" of the Soviet brigade in Cuba, the Soviet invasion and resulting occupation of Afghanistan—these and other developments proved too much for Nixon's successors to manage. Gaining domestic support for arms control, whether the process of negotiations or the resulting accord, became all but impossible.

Overall, the last few decades indicate that active linkage diplomacy is often beyond the capacity of the United States to choreograph. The United States simply lacks the requisite degree of political consensus and institutional centralization to manipulate rewards and penalties to affect Soviet arms control and regional behavior. Moreover, the notion of trading off objectives in arms control and regional affairs is flawed: the United States cannot afford to reward the Soviets in the arms control arena for their restraint in some regional competition. Nor does the United States possess the leverage to penalize the Soviets in the arms control arena in the absence of restraint; walking away from negotiations or agreements, as the United States did in the late 1970s, penalizes the United States as well if arms control is in the U.S. interest.

As history demonstrates, conducting a policy of delinkage (or avoiding unintended linkage) is a difficult task for any U.S. president. Some would argue that such a policy would be unwise, that arms control cannot be divorced from the larger political relationship; others would simply say that such linkage is unavoidable given the power of the media, public opinion, and the Congress. Yet as noted earlier there are examples of a U.S. president—Richard Nixon, for one—who successfully resisted (or managed) unintended linkage. And every president since Lyndon Johnson has successfully insulated the Non-Proliferation Treaty from the vicissitudes of U.S.-Soviet relations. U.S. leaders, like their Soviet counterparts, have obviously believed that the spread of nuclear weapons would be contrary to their country's interests. The prospects for delinkage in this case, however, were enhanced markedly by the existence of a consensus on this point across the U.S. domestic political spectrum. The fact that there are more examples of unsuccessful management, coupled with the power of precedent, indicates just how vulnerable arms control has been and is likely to remain to problems in U.S.-Soviet relations. To borrow from nautical imagery, arms control appears to have the worst of all worlds: while it must rest on its own bottom, it is clear too that a falling tide lowers all boats.

This last discussion introduces a related but somewhat distinct question: whether the arms control process influences or is influenced by U.S.-Soviet relations more broadly. There is evidence that this was at times the hope of various U.S. administrations. Kennedy hoped that the successful completion of the test-ban negotiations would lead to an improvement in the relationship across the board; Nixon and Kissinger embraced a similar approach to the relationship between the SALT process and détente in that the two were seen as mutually reinforcing.

It is difficult to demonstrate that gains in arms control led to such an improvement in relations. U.S.-Soviet rivalry continued unabated in the wake of the agreements covered by this study; indeed, the moment of greatest arms control accomplishment—the early 1970s— quickly gave way to an era of worsened overall relations as détente soured. Just as significantly, the Soviets showed little restraint in the wake of SALT II's signing even though evidence was widespread that the agreement would have difficulty weathering any further deterioration in bilateral relations. Afghanistan comes to mind above all in this regard.

The case seems somewhat stronger that arms control has been influenced to a degree by the state of the U.S.-Soviet relationship. At a minimum, successful negotiations require in-depth, sustained, and often confidential negotiations—all to some extent characteristic of good working relations. Moreover, as has been noted, events beyond the immediate realm of arms control can make negotiations impossible, a fact that suggests that the absence of a crisis in the relationship is a prerequisite for arms control progress. One should not make too much of this, however, because the Limited Test Ban can be said to have followed an improvement in relations only if one compares the level of U.S.-Soviet relations in 1963 to what they were in October 1962. Similarly, SALT II was negotiated and signed amid a secular decline in the state of the relationship. Overall, the tie between arms control and the larger relationship appears weak in both directions: arms control does not tend to lead to improved ties overall, nor does it necessarily require them, although it benefits from them. On balance, other factors appear to account much more in determining arms control prospects.

HYPOTHESIS 5. EFFECT ON ARMS

The arms control process and arms control agreements

1. Redirect the arms competition in productive ways.
2. Codify existing defense plans.
3. Redirect the arms competition in counterproductive ways.

The alleged effects of arms control—both the process of negotiations and any agreements that might result—continued to be highly controversial. Some believe that it redirects the arms competition in important ways, although there is disagreement among them on whether the redirection is favorable, and others believe that arms control has virtually no effect on the competition but tends rather to codify the existing defense plans of the two sides. (The role of arms control in reducing uncertainties in estimates of each other's defense plans is the subject of Hypothesis 6.)

Neither the Limited Test Ban Treaty nor the Accidents Measures Agreement had any discernible effect on the arms competition. Conclusion of the LTBT and the resulting cessation of atmospheric tests may have accelerated the trend toward underground testing, but that transition already was well underway.

The SALT I Interim Agreement often is cited as a pact that merely codified the existing inventories and plans of the two signatories. The facts tend to support this view. The Interim Agreement required no changes in either U.S. force structures or modernization plans. In particular, it did nothing to affect the emergence of the new MIRV technology. Regarding the Soviets, the Interim Agreement codified not only existing strategic forces but also those under construction.

(This allowance strongly influenced the permitted numbers of Soviet launchers for ICBMs and SLBMs and numbers of ballistic missile submarines.) With no limit on MIRVs, the accord did not prevent the marriage of multiple-warhead technology with heavy Soviet intercontinental ballistic missiles. On the other hand, even though the Interim Agreement required no reductions on the inventories extant at its entry into force, there is no doubt that in the ensuing years each party could have built forces far beyond the Interim Agreement's ceilings had it so chosen. Moreover, the pressure to have done so would likely have been considerably greater in the absence of an arms control pact.

Much the same can be said about SALT II; it appeared essentially to codify existing forces and plans to modernize them. No limits were placed on the modernization of submarine or bomber forces, while each side was limited to one new type of ICBM. Intermediate-range and long-range cruise missiles were constrained only in the protocol, due to expire two years after the agreement was signed and four years before the SALT II Treaty was slated to run out. The sub-ceilings on MIRVed systems were sufficiently high that each side could (and did) build up to them; there were no direct limits on overall warhead numbers, only an agreement that specified systems could not be tested with more than a designated number of warheads.

There were some exceptions to this tendency to codify rather than limit. U.S. planning for basing the MX ICBM was complicated by treaty constraints on land-based missile mobility. The Soviets agreed not to deploy the three-stage mobile SS-16 ICBM. Moreover, over time, the SALT II pact even though never ratified did force the two parties to retire systems—in some cases before their useful active life had expired—that might otherwise have remained operational. And as was the case with the SALT I Interim Agreement, it is likely that in the absence of the treaty each side may have been tempted to upgrade or increase even more the size of its inventories. In short, if SALT II at its inception did little more than to codify existing and planned programs, over time it did compel the two signatories to choose between systems, a choice that allowed modernization while requiring retirement.

The 1972 Anti-Ballistic Missile Treaty is commonly cited as the best example of an arms control pact that directed competition in productive ways (or at least closed off competition in a counterproductive direction). The general perception is that the treaty maintained confidence in mutual vulnerability and assured retaliation and thereby strengthened deterrence. But it is far from certain that in the absence of the treaty the United States would have fielded a large-scale ballistic missile defense. It is quite possible that technological uncertainty and concerns about stability would have convinced a majority in the Senate to oppose funding; indeed, it can even be argued that it was the negotiations that led a reluctant Senate to continue funding for ABM development. Were there no treaty, Soviet efforts might have increased the pressure on the United States to follow suit. In this connection, it is noteworthy that Soviet civil defense and air defense efforts have not been seriously emulated by the United States, although they have stimulated active measures to counter them. The treaty also permits research (often hard to distinguish from development) to continue; it may have codified the existing situation, but it did not establish permanent obstacles to reaching a new situation. Lastly, there are those who argue that the ABM Treaty may not have had a uniformly productive or stabilizing impact. By closing off the deployment of virtually all ABM systems, including those that might have been deployed to protect land-based missiles increasingly vulnerable to the ever more accurate missiles of the other superpower, the treaty blocked one possible path (using large numbers of ground-based local or point defenses) to stem the growing problem of ICBM vulnerability. That the ABM Treaty had an impact on the arms competition is widely agreed; but just how much of one, and whether it was desirable, is less so.

In sum, all of the arms control agreements examined in this study were consistent with existing military force structures—that is, none required substantial changes in the nature or size of those forces. Moreover, with the possible (and, in any event, debatable) exception of the ABM Treaty, these accords also have been consistent with known aspects of the modernization programs of the two sides.

HYPOTHESIS 6. UNCERTAINTIES

The arms control process and arms control agreements reduce uncertainties in estimates and projections of each other's forces.

The historical record tends to support the contention that arms control negotiations and outcomes serve to reduce uncertainties in the estimates and projections that each participant makes about the other's forces. It is somewhat surprising that this aspect receives little attention in public debates about specific negotiations and accords. Indeed, reduction of uncertainty and enhancement of predictability may well be the principal contribution of the arms control experience. This benefit is especially valuable to the United States because, in the absence of arms control agreements, U.S. knowledge of Soviet defense plans is and would be far less complete than Soviet knowledge of U.S. defense plans.

Of the cases examined in this study, only the Limited Test Ban Treaty provides contrary evidence. Underground nuclear tests are inherently more difficult to monitor than atmospheric ones. Thus, by driving all tests underground, the LTBT may have decreased the information available to each side about the other side's detonations. This is only marginally attributable to the LTBT, however, because the transition to underground testing had started well before the agreement was reached. Moreover, the effect was mitigated over time by improvements in monitoring of underground explosions.

The Non-Proliferation Treaty, by strengthening international norms against proliferation and by establishing mechanisms for deterring diversion of nuclear materials and technologies from civilian to military uses, probably has slowed the spread of nuclear weapons. In this way, it has helped delay the emergence of a world with many nuclear weapons states—a world that would be inherently more dangerous and less predictable than the current one.

The Accidents Measures Agreement may have contributed modestly to improving current estimates and projections. More valuable than the central provision calling for prior notification of any ballistic missile flight test outside one's own territory and in the direction of the other—which has never been implemented—is the possibility that the negotiation itself led to a mutual recognition of the desirability of avoiding such a potentially provocative and destabilizing action. Arms control negotiations themselves can provide for increased understanding and transparency as to motives, intentions, and concerns. They can also create a venue for reassurance. Achievement of the Accidents Measures Agreement was, in itself, a confidence-building measure.

The Biological Weapons Convention introduced a degree of predictability into a unique area of weaponry. Indeed, despite the inherent uncontrollability that has made biological agents and toxins untttractive for weapons use, it is quite possible that in the absence of a formal agreement one or both of the superpowers would have proceeded with a serious weaponization effort, either because of organizational pressures or faulty assessments of the capabilities and plans of the other.

The ABM Treaty provided a good deal of predictability about the overall strategic environment. Offense would clearly dominate defense, populations would remain vulnerable, and missiles that could survive a first strike would get through to critical targets. (Prior to the signing of the ABM Treaty, the United States estimated that by 1980 the Soviets might deploy as many as 10,000 ABM interceptor missiles. The treaty (as modified by a 1974 protocol) limited each side to only 100 such interceptors.) The treaty's constraints on large phased-array radars (LPARs, a critical component of any ABM system and one whose construction is both time consuming and easy to monitor) also enhanced confidence against the ability of either side to break out rapidly of its treaty commitments and thereby threaten to upset the strategic order.

Both SALT agreements on offensive weapons also contributed to predictability. The United States was considerably more certain of what Soviet capabilities would be in 1977 with the Interim Agreement than it would have been otherwise. The same can be said for predictions of where the USSR would be today in the absence of SALT II. Projections of opposing forces would have included a large margin of error—a margin far larger than anything caused by compliance-related controversies—without these pacts in place. In addition, the establishment of verification rules—most notably the principle of noninterference in each party's national technical means of verification and to a lesser but not insignificant extent the creation of the Standing Consultative Commission (SCC)—provided both principles and procedures for increasing the transparency (and reducing the natural state of uncertainty) of one another's forces. A world without negotiations, agreements, and rules to promote verification would be one of far greater uncertainty and far more prone to unrestrained and potentially destabilizing arms competition.

HYPOTHESIS 7. VERIFICATION AND COMPLIANCE

1. The Soviets do not comply with the spirit or the letter of agreements.

2. The political requirements for verification and compliance are more demanding than the security requirements.
3. Ambiguity does not offer a solution to verification and compliance problems.

Concerns about the United States' ability to verify arms control accords, coupled with doubts over Soviet willingness to abide by the same, have been a feature of the arms control debate since its inception. Such concerns figures prominently in the preliminaries to the test ban negotiations and explain in part why the agreement was partial rather than comprehensive. Verification concerns played a modest part in the SALT I and ABM Treaty debates but dominated the debate over SALT II. In all cases verification considerations affected the substance of the U.S. approach to the negotiations. They similarly figured prominently in the development of the U.S. approach to the antisatellite talks. Today, verification concerns are if anything greater than ever, in large part because of the increasingly controversial debate over Soviet compliance with agreements entered into thus far. Concerns over compliance have contributed to a souring of the U.S.-Soviet relationship and have become an obstacle in and of themselves to future arms control undertakings.

The bulk of the compliance debate centers on the two SALT agreements limiting offensive arms and the 1972 ABM Treaty. (Noncompliance charges have been leveled against the Soviets for a number of arms control agreements not examined here, such as the 1975 Helsinki Final Act (CSCE). In addition, the United States has charged the Soviet Union with violating the Biological Weapons Convention's prohibitions against both development and use. Similarly, Soviet venting or release of radioactive debris beyond its borders has constituted a politically but not militarily significant violation of the Limited Test Ban.) The purpose of this study has not been to assess whether and to what extent the Soviets are circumventing or actually violating arms control undertakings—such determinations are inevitably subjective and in many instances require access to highly classified data—but to discern the sources of compliance-related concerns and to determine what if anything can be done about them.

What is clear is that ambiguity does not offer a solution to verification and compliance problems. Ambiguity creates opportunity for circumventions (or violations of the spirit or intent) of pacts if not outright violations of explicit provisions. Such ambiguity cannot be compensated for by unilateral statements that are not legally binding; nor can the Standing Consultative Committee or other such bodies be relied on to solve in the implementation phase of an accord what years of negotiating could not. The possible solutions are several: increased use of agreed data bases, the avoidance of discretion on such activities as the encryption of telemetry, the eschewal of limits on systems in some situations but not others. But even these "solutions" have their drawbacks: data disputes can block progress indefinitely in negotiations; intelligence concerns can limit what the United States might choose to discuss about encryption; and some weapons systems will inevitably retain the capacity to perform more than one kind of mission. Moreover, ambiguity often is seen as the only means available to bridge negotiating differences. Paradoxically, excessive detail and specificity also can create opportunities for circumvention because provisions drawn too narrowly often can be "designed around" by those inclined to do so.

The entire verification and compliance problem has become difficult for another reason as well: the political requirements for verification and compliance are increasingly more demanding than are the security requirements. This was not always the case; at the time of the Limited Test Ban, the Kennedy administration did not predict absolute Soviet compliance or even total confidence in U.S. ability to detect any violation. Rather, Kennedy promised only that the United States possessed the capability to detect any militarily significant Soviet violation early enough so that the United States would be in a position to take any necessary corrective action on its own to preclude any meaningful change in the military balance. This relativist approach to verification and compliance was applied to the SALT I Interim Agreement and the ABM Treaty but began to give way to more demanding requirements for verification during the SALT II debate. Since then, in part because of compliance problems and the deterioration in U.S.-Soviet relations, the requirements for verification confidence have continued to rise, while the tolerance for noncompliance has been strained.

The act of noncompliance, regardless of its military significance, has taken on major political implications. Noncompliance has eroded confidence in and support for the arms control process. It may well be that compliance issues, if not resolved, will prove to be a major (perhaps insurmountable) barrier to significant progress in arms control.

HYPOTHESIS 8. LULLING

The arms control process and arms control agreements

1. Lull the United States into spending less than it should on defense.
2. Stimulate the United States to spend more than it should on defense.

There are those whose primary concern about arms control relates to its indirect effect on U.S. vigilance. Did the negotiations and agreements—that is, both the promise and the product of arms control efforts—lull the U.S. public and government into a false sense of security? Or did arms control have the opposite effect—that is, to stimulate the United States into taking unnecessary steps it would otherwise have forgone?

The more common critique is that the arms control process—whether through exaggerated expectations of what it might accomplish or in fact has accomplished—would somehow lead the United States to be less robust on defense than it should. Measuring this alleged loss of robustness—whether through levels of defense expenditure, public opinion data indicating popular support for defense, or some other index—is inherently imprecise. Moreover, the level from which the loss is to be measured is unknown and unknowable: there are wide ranges of views on what the United States should or would have spent on defense in the absence of arms control, and on what would have been the trends in public opinion. History does not reveal its alternatives. Nevertheless, the lulling critique is a powerful one in the sense that it is often cited and appears to have considerable influence.

Indeed, the critique (or prediction) has been a part of the entire arms control experience covered by this study. Opponents of the Limited Test Ban Treaty feared that the euphoria that was expected to greet the pact in the United States would lead to a dangerous loss of U.S. will. As a result, the Kennedy administration went to great rhetorical lengths to demonstrate it would not. The pace of U.S. testing actually increased in the wake of the treaty. Indeed, if there was any lulling associated with the test ban, it was not with the treaty but rather with the four-power moratorium that preceded the treaty by several years. When the Soviet Union unexpectedly resumed atmospheric testing soon after the French explosion, the United States found itself ill prepared to initiate a new series of tests.

There is little evidence to suggest that either of the agreements limiting strategic offensive arms produced a direct lulling effect in the United States. Neither the SALT I negotiation nor its outcome lulled the United States into forgoing MIRV, the development of the new B-1 bomber, the Trident submarine, or cruise missiles. If anything, the debate surrounding the Interim Agreement—a debate both dominated and symbolized by the Jackson Amendment and its call for equal ceilings in future pacts—all but ensured that there would be no lulling on account of the agreement. If there was any signal emanating from the Nixon administration that the world had become a less dangerous place, it was less because of SALT I per se than because of the alleged overall improvement in U.S.-Soviet relations, symbolized above all by the overly ambitious May 1972 Basic Principles intended to regulate their competition for influence around the world. Moreover, to the extent that U.S. defense efforts were inadequate in the 1970s, it is far more plausible to associate this with the drain of the Vietnam conflict and the heightened hostility of Congress and a majority of the U.S. people to high levels of defense spending.

It is if anything more difficult to make a case that the SALT II agreement promoted a sense of undeserved complacency. The very controversy of the Senate's review of the treaty and the larger public debate all but transformed consideration of the treaty into a referendum on U.S. strategic modernization. The United States proceeded with the Trident C-4 missile deployment, the upgrade of the warheads on the Minuteman III missile, the development of the MX and Trident D-5 missiles, and three long-range cruise missile programs and carried out research and development of an advanced (Stealth) technology long-range bomber. The decision to cancel the B-1 bomber appears to have been motivated more by narrow calculations of defense spending and force planning (President Carter opted for going ahead with a cruise missile option over the B-1) than any belief of what arms control might bring in the way of increased security. Long-range cruise missile development continued despite the protocol ban on deployment, while the delay in MX deployment resulted not from any conscious exercise in self-restraint but from technical and parochial political problems associated with finding a viable basing mode.

Lulling seems likewise not to have been at work amid the ASAT negotiations. The Joint Chiefs of Staff were reported to have feared that the talks would lead to a reduction in the ongoing U.S. effort to reduce the vulnerability of U.S. satellites to possible hostile action. Money continued to be authorized for this purpose at modest levels; more important, funding grew considerably during the negotiations for the development of the U.S. antisatellite system.

Where lulling may have happened was in the aftermath of the 1972 ABM Treaty, where the United States (unlike the Soviet Union) reduced its expenditures on permitted ABM research. (This is distinct from the decision to dismantle the one permitted ABM site at Grand Forks, North Dakota—a decision made by Congress on the basis of cost effectiveness.) Similarly, in the wake of the Non-Proliferation Treaty there may have been some decline in efforts to slow the spread of nuclear weapons. If this was indeed the case, it was short lived because any complacency would have been shattered in 1974 by India's "peaceful" nuclear explosion.

A different facet of the ABM record indicates that arms control can produce the opposite of lulling. The negotiations, rather than lulling U.S. ABM-related efforts, stimulated them, as the Nixon administration marshalled support for programs on the basis that failure to support development would undermine the U.S. negotiating position and diminish any Soviet incentive to reach agreement. This is the classic bargaining chip phenomenon, where systems are promoted less for their contribution to force planning than for their contribution to a credible negotiating position. Related to this phenomenon are those systems that are funded in order to gain political support within the executive branch (notably to gain the approval of the Joint Chiefs of Staff) or to convince members of the Congress that a particular arms control pact will not diminish U.S. security. Indeed, this latter tendency to demonstrate continued willingness to support weapons programs effectively preempts the lulling effect; concern that arms control might in fact lead to less vigilance ensures that a political price for arms control is a commitment to undiminished or increased spending on relevant defense programs.

HYPOTHESIS 9. POLITICAL SUPPORT

1. Political support for an arms control agreement depends less on the provisions of the agreement than on other factors.

2. Congressional support for an arms control agreement depends on the extent of congressional participation in the arms control process.
3. The public will support any negotiated arms control agreement.

Arms control is a political endeavor; its success requires broad support from participants and constituencies. The cases examined in this study indicate that, by and large, (1) political support for an arms control agreement depends on many factors, some of which are given greater weight than the specific provisions of the accord; (2) congressional support has not depended on the extent of congressional involvement in the arms control process; and (3) the public and the allies have been positively disposed toward every negotiated agreement.

The key factor determining the degree of support for arms control is the president himself, and yet his power is by no means total. Indeed, support from the Department of Defense, and above all the uniformed military, is a prerequisite to gaining the needed larger support outside the executive branch. Here the key actors are the Congress, the public and media, and the allies.

The process of accumulating political support for a negotiating approach and for a treaty or some other form of international agreement is fundamentally different for actors within the government than it is for those outside. Within the government, and in particular with regard to the key constituency of the military, what matters to a great extent are the provisions of the agreement, especially those constraining U.S. forces and actions. Thus, the Joint Chiefs of Staff (JCS) were opposed to a comprehensive test ban and were wary of the Carter administration's interest in bargaining away the U.S. antisatellite program. What might matter to the military even more, however, are the force modernization programs that would complement arms control. Indeed, history suggests that the Joint Chiefs tend to be well disposed toward arms control because of its contribution to bounding the threat and introducing an element of predictability, which in turn assists U.S. force planning. At the same time, they are wary of constraints on emerging U.S. programs and often bargain their support for arms control for a White House commitment to force modernization.

Public support tends to be even more well disposed in principle toward arms control. In contrast to their importance to the views of elites, specific provisions and the technical details appear to count for little in the formation of public opinion. The public welcomed the Limited Test Ban Treaty both as a breakthrough in U.S.-Soviet relations and as a means to lessen the health risk associated with atmospheric testing. Public support for the SALT I Interim Agreement and ABM Treaty was considerable; support for SALT II was somewhat more lukewarm, in part because arms control did not appear to reduce tensions in the U.S.-Soviet relationship or the level of arms. Moreover, the general disposition of the public to support the SALT II Treaty was offset by the activities of well-informed and motivated elite groups opposed to the treaty as negotiated.

Congress has grown more critical of arms control over time. Interestingly, the degree of congressional participation in the negotiating process in no way assuages congressional fears; to the contrary, there seems to be some correlation between higher involvement in and increased opposition to arms control. Senator Henry Jackson was more involved in the SALT I and ABM negotiations than any of his colleagues, yet he emerged as the most knowledgeable and persistent critic of the accords once they were before the Senate. Similarly, congressional participation in delegations—introduced by the Carter administration—had no discernible effect on congressional opposition to SALT II. By way of contrast, the almost total absence of congressional knowledge of the Accidents Measures Agreement in no way diminished support for the agreement once concluded.

The reasons for this critical congressional attitude are several. In part it is simply another manifestation of the post-Vietnam, post-Watergate emergence of the legislative branch as a more active and often more critical participant in the national security policy process. Congress is more aware than the general public of the details of proposed arms control agreements because of its access to information and highly motivated elites. Above all, though, Congress is likely to be influenced in its behavior by its perception of the president's ability to bargain effectively with the Soviets and to gather support from the public for whatever emerges from the negotiation at issue. Thus, Kennedy in the aftermath of the 1962 Cuban Missile Crisis possessed considerable freedom of action, as did Nixon at the time of SALT I and the ABM Treaty. But a Nixon weakened by Watergate and Presidents Ford and Carter had trouble in gaining congressional support for their arms control initiatives. Doubts about their negotiating ability, disillusionment with détente, disappointment with arms control accomplishments, concern over verification and alleged Soviet noncompliance—all decreased the support for arms control while making it more vulnerable to vagaries in the U.S.-Soviet relationship and to what has been termed here *unintended linkage.* Yet it is difficult if not impossible to attribute this decline in support for arms control solely to the state of U.S.-Soviet relations or the content of the proposed accords. To the contrary, a case can be made that Soviet global behavior was deteriorating in the early and mid-1970s or that SALT II offered no worse and probably a better agreement to the United States than did SALT I. Even with the Congress, perceptions of presidential strength can be more important than external developments or specific provisions of the proposed pact.

Allied attitudes have tended to be supportive of arms control. This must be qualified by two points: the allies demonstrated certain discomfort over appearances of superpower condominium in which deals might be struck not only over the heads of the allies but at their expense, and a particular concern over the fate of systems directly relevant to the European (or, in the case of Japan, Asian) theater. The allies thus supported the SALT process but were wary that U.S. forward-based systems might be counted against U.S. force totals. These concerns proved manageable through a combination of consultations and U.S. resistance to provisions viewed as being aimed at European security interests. For the most part, U.S. allies have thus proved to support the arms control process, more often decrying its lack of accomplishment than its potential to harm their more narrow interests.

HYPOTHESIS 10. ASYMMETRY

The arms control process and arms control agreements serve Soviet interests more than U.S. interests.

This last hypothesis concerns the overall effect of arms control— namely, whether on balance the arms control process and the agreements it has produced have served Soviet interests more than those of the United States or vice versa. The evidence is inadequate to make a case either way. Both sides have benefitted from the reduced uncertainty and enhanced predictability the process has engendered.

Neither has been forced to compromise important interests or capabilities. Without arms control, both U.S. and Soviet force totals probably would be higher than they are now.

The arguments suggesting that the United States is worse off tend to be more theoretical than real. The United States, as a democracy possibly more prone or vulnerable to a lulling effect, appears to have avoided this danger through conscious effort and perhaps even more because of the domestic politics of the arms control process. Specific strategic modernization programs are promoted as a means of reassuring and gaining the support of key constituencies in and out of government. The openness of U.S. society, in contrast to that of the Soviet Union, raises special barriers to U.S. noncompliance; yet even if Soviet cheating is as serious as has been alleged, the military consequences would thus far be minimal. Lastly, it is pointed out that the arms control age has witnessed a shift in the strategic balance toward the Soviet Union. This may indeed be a correct assessment, but to point out that arms control reflects this change is not to hold it responsible.

What is most striking about the arms control experience surveyed here is what it did not do. Those who hoped arms control would bring about major reductions in existing or planned inventories or slow the introduction of new and more capable technologies have little grounds for satisfaction. Nor do those who looked to arms control as a means for constraining the emergence of a large, modern Soviet arsenal capable of destroying a significant proportion of U.S. strategic retaliatory forces. Even the contributions of the ABM Treaty, arms control's chief accomplishment, are of uncertain durability. The treaty may merely have codified the postponement of a race in defensive systems until advancing technologies made effective defenses possible.

What emerges above all is the modesty of what arms control has wrought. Expectations, for better or worse, for the most part have not been realized. The stridency of the debate, however, provides little clue to this modest reality; proponents and critics, liberals and conservatives, hawks and doves—all seem to exaggerate the potential and actual impact of arms control. If the history reveals anything, it is that arms control has proved neither as promising as some had hoped nor as dangerous as others had feared.

AFTERWORD
The INF Treaty

Albert Carnesale and Richard N. Haass

On December 8, 1987—fewer than three months after the initial publication of this book—Ronald Reagan and Mikhail Gorbachev met in Washington, D.C., to sign the Treaty Between the United States of America and the Union of Soviet Socialist Republics on the Elimination of Their Intermediate-Range and Shorter-Range Missiles. This agreement (usually referred to as the Intermediate Nuclear Forces Treaty, or INF Treaty for short) raises a host of questions for our study. How does the INF Treaty comport with the historical record of arms control negotiations and accords examined in this book? Is this Treaty just another U.S.-Soviet arms control agreement, or does it differ significantly in scope and purpose? Which of our previously derived conclusions are reinforced by the INF experience? Which must be modified, and how?

THE HISTORY OF THE NEGOTIATIONS

It is inherently arbitrary to choose a starting date for the history of the INF accord. One could go back to the early years of the Atlantic Alliance, for in significant ways the INF experience is but the most recent chapter in the ongoing story of U.S. and West European efforts to cope with the realities of extended deterrence. In a sense, the INF Treaty resulted from Western deployment of U.S. nuclear

357

systems designed to counterbalance Soviet military improvements in order to enhance the credibility of the U.S. pledge to extend its nuclear umbrella to cover its West European allies.

For our purposes, however, it is more useful to begin in early 1977, with the initial Soviet deployment of the SS-20 missile, a mobile ballistic missile carrying three nuclear warheads. The SS-20's 5,000-kilometer range is sufficient to hold all Europe at risk but falls below the 5,500-kilometer strategic threshold established in the strategic arms limitation talks (SALT). West European leaders, particularly Helmut Schmidt (then the chancellor of the Federal Republic of Germany), were understandably apprehensive, especially as the new Soviet deployments came against a backdrop of more general concern about the military strength of the United States and its commitment to Europe.

Several years of intense NATO consultations ensued, culminating in the December 1979 decision that the United States would deploy a new generation of intermediate range nuclear missiles in Western Europe while simultaneously pursuing negotiations with the Soviets aimed at creating a balance at the lowest possible level. NATO thus embarked upon the so-called two-track policy: a deployment track that beginning in December 1983 would introduce 464 ground-launched cruise missiles (to be distributed among five European countries) and 108 Pershing II ballistic missiles (in West Germany), and a negotiating track beginning as soon as possible that would limit these deployments or even render them altogether unnecessary.

The Soviets sought to head off NATO deployments even before the two-track decision was formally adopted. In October 1979, General Secretary Leonid Brezhnev proposed a freeze on Soviet SS-20 deployments (then totaling some 130 missiles with 390 warheads) if NATO forswore its counterdeployments on the basis that a balance already existed. This gambit failed. Nearly a year later, in July 1980, the Soviets agreed in principle to participate in formal INF negotiations, but owing to an inability to agree on the specific focus, as well as the change in U.S. administrations, no formal talks began.

The real anticedent to the INF negotiation begins with President Ronald Reagan's November 1981 "zero option" proposal to cancel the planned U.S. INF deployments in exchange for Soviet elimination of all their SS-4, SS-5, and SS-20 INF missiles. The position was put forward only after fierce debate in Washington. Advocates viewed the zero option as the best means to capture the public relations high ground in Europe, an essential move if allied governments were to fend off the powerful peace movements. The option was also seen as a major disarmament step that distinguished the Reagan administration from its predecessors. Opponents within the executive branch argued that the proposed deal was too unequal to be credible—that few in Western Europe would take seriously the U.S. offer not to deploy missiles in exchange for Soviet destruction of missiles already deployed—and that support for deployments would evaporate in the face of certain Soviet rejection. In addition, there was concern that the zero option might not be in the interest of the West, as it would weaken the nuclear link that coupled the United States to Western Europe—a connection that lies at the heart of the Atlantic Alliance.

Within weeks, formal negotiations between the United States and the Soviet Union opened in Geneva. The U.S. side tabled the zero option; the Soviets responded with a proposal for equal ceilings of 300 "medium-range" missiles and nuclear-capable aircraft, with the additional factor that British and French nuclear forces would be included in the U.S. count. (Given Soviet estimates of British and French systems, this left no room for new U.S. deployments.) Months later, the Soviets sought to increase the attractiveness of their offer by announcing a moratorium on new SS-20 deployments. This bid for support accomplished little once it became clear that a good deal of work on SS-20 sites was continuing despite the moratorium.

With the two sides far from agreement in the formal negotiations, the principal negotiators at the Geneva talks, Paul Nitze for the United States and Yuli Kvitsinky for the USSR, developed an alternative package (the so-called "walk in the woods" formula) key elements of which would establish equal levels of INF missile launchers in Europe, preclude U.S. deployment of the Pershing II, and freeze Soviet SS-20 deployments in Asia. (The net result would have allowed the Soviet Union to deploy in Europe seventy-five SS-20s with a total of 225 warheads, the United States seventy-five GLCM "launchers" with a total of 300 missiles.) Neither government was satisfied with the approach: the Soviets were unwilling to accept the legitimacy of any Western INF deployments, and the Americans believed a cruise missile-only deployment for the West would give the USSR an advantage since it would still be permitted to deploy ballistic missiles.

The formal negotiating channel remained deadlocked. The Soviet Union opposed any U.S. deployment of new missiles and sought inclusion of British and French systems. The Soviets appeared to be less interested in negotiations per se than in using them to raise public opposition in Western Europe (and especially West Germany) to the U.S. deployments. The United States, which wanted equality of rights between the two superpowers, exclusion of third parties, and global limits, also sought to use the negotiations to win over the European publics and governments. Thus, to demonstrate it was not inflexibly tied to a zero-option–only position, the United States introduced another option in March 1983. This proposed "interim agreement" in effect would have established equal global levels of U.S. and Soviet warheads on INF launchers at any level.

The initial interim proposal met with Soviet rejection, as did a second one put forward in September of 1983. The negotiations themselves came to a sudden end in November 1983, when the Soviet delegation walked out in the wake of the arrival in Europe of the first GLCM components. The Soviet strategy to prevent Western deployments had failed; with the negotiating track ending in stalemate, the United States began to implement INF deployments.

Negotiations did not resume until early 1985, when the two sides agreed to establish a new comprehensive arms control framework that would discuss not only INF but also strategic offensive forces along with defense and space issues. The first sign of real progress came that October, when Mikhail Gorbachev, the new Soviet general secretary, waived the Soviet insistence that all Western INF deployments be cancelled. Instead, he called for a freeze in both Soviet and U.S. INF deployments, to be followed by the "deepest possible" reductions. Gorbachev also stated that the Soviets were phasing out their older SS-4s. Because a freeze would have codified Soviet superiority, this proposal was unacceptable to the United States. President Reagan did, however, note its positive elements and outlined a modification of the U.S. position, suggesting that both sides might want to consider an interim agreement with equal ceilings of 140 launchers and 420 warheads, which would allow a Western mix heavily weighted toward GLCMs and would approach meeting the Soviet concern over the Pershing II.

INF was a prominent topic at the November 1985 summit in Geneva, after which Gorbachev wrote to Reagan suggesting that all long-range INF (LRINF) be eliminated from Europe within five to eight years as part of a goal to rid the world of nuclear weapons over a fifteen-year period. (By now the negotiations began to focus increasingly on shorter range INF, or SRINF, systems with a range between 500 and 1,000 kilometers.) Less than a year later, at the October 1986 Reykjavik summit, the two leaders agreed in principle to deploy no LRINF warheads in Europe and to establish equal global ceilings of 100 LRINF warheads apiece, the Soviet share to be in Asia and the U.S. share in the United States. As they had done since early 1985, however, the Soviets linked progress on INF to resolution of U.S.-Soviet differences on what sort of testing would be allowed under the 1972 ABM Treaty.

Several months later, though, after the Reagan administration continued to refuse tying the INF to strategic defense, the Soviets dropped this linkage, thereby clearing the way to what became the final phase of negotiations. In June the United States formally proposed that all SRINF be eliminated as part of any INF Treaty. This "double zero" option, which effectively eliminated all INF missiles with ranges between 500 and 5,500 kilometers, was accepted by the USSR in July 1987.

Two issues remained. The first was the status of the seventy-two U.S. Pershing IA nuclear warheads located in the Federal Republic of Germany. Although these weapons fell within the SRINF range and included U.S. warheads, they were unique in that the missiles belonged to West Germany. The United States refused to compromise on its long-held position that third-party systems fell outside the scope of the negotiations; the Soviets refused to budge on their demand that the Pershing IA systems be included. The issue was finally resolved in August 1987 when German Chancellor Helmut Kohl announced his government's decision to dismantle its Pershing IAs and not to replace them with more modern missiles.

The second outstanding issue, verification, was hardly a new one. Eliminating the systems (rather than limiting them to some level other than zero) eased verification challenges since it is generally easier to verify the absence of a system than to verify that the number of deployed weapons does not exceed a specified limit (especially if the weapons are mobile). Nonetheless, the verification problems were significant coming as they did against a backdrop of past compliance disputes and the ongoing START negotiations, for which the INF Treaty would establish precedents. In the end, a regime emerged calling for highly detailed data exchange and a considerable degree of intrusive on-site inspection.

THE TREATY

The essence of the Treaty is relatively simple. It covers all U.S. and Soviet land-based missiles with ranges from 500 to 5,500 kilometers. Upon entry into force, the Treaty bans immediately all production and flight testing of existing INF missiles or "new types." It also requires the elimination of all U.S. and Soviet INF ballistic and ground-launched cruise missile systems and related facilities within three years.

The Treaty also includes a number of provisions intended to facilitate verification. All SRINF systems must be moved to elimination facilities within ninety days after the Treaty goes into effect. Deployment and movement of INF systems prior to their elimination require prior notification. An associated Memorandum of Understanding includes substantial data on the location, number, and technical specifications of all INF systems and support structures; there is also a requirement for updating these data. Procedures are given for eliminating missiles, launchers, and related equipment and facilities. Finally, there is an intrusive set of on-site inspections of key sites and facilities—arrangements intended to last for thirteen years, or ten years after the last INF missiles are to be eliminated—and the creation of a Special Verification Commission to address questions and challenges.

Given the content of the INF Treaty and its evolution, what then can be concluded about its likely consequences for arms control or for U.S.–Soviet relations more broadly? The best way to answer this question is to measure the INF agreement against our ten hypotheses.

Bargaining from Strength

Simple bean-counting would indicate that the Treaty is inconsistent with our earlier finding that arms control agreements have been concluded only when there was rough parity in the relevant forces of the two sides. Indeed, when the agreement was signed, the Soviets had a two-to-one advantage in deployed INF missiles (i.e., 857 to 429) and a four-to-one advantage in warhead-carrying capacity (i.e., 1667 to 429). Despite this substantial numerical asymmetry favoring the Soviets, the two sides have agreed to eliminate these military forces.

Why might the Soviets have chosen to forgo this advantage? Two plausible reasons are apparent. First, there is a substantial geographic asymmetry: *none* of the 1667 warheads on Soviet deployed INF missiles were within range of U.S. territory, whereas *all* of the 429 warheads on U.S. INF missiles could reach the Soviet homeland. It should not be surprising to learn that Soviet leaders were willing to give up four Soviet warheads threatening Western Europe for each American warhead threatening Mother Russia. Moreover, the Pershing II warheads could reach Soviet targets in as few as ten to fifteen minutes. Thus, taking into account not only the numbers of deployed weapons affected by the INF Treaty but also the asymmetries in geography and the quality of the forces, it appears that the Treaty is more like than unlike past arms control agreements; that is, neither side entered or emerged from the negotiations with an appreciable advantage.

Genies in Bottles

U.S.-Soviet nuclear arms control agreements prior to the INF Treaty generally had not imposed meaningful constraints on categories of weapons in which one or both sides had made a substantial investment or that offered promise of military utility. The INF accord represents a departure from this trend. The vast majority of the weapons to be destroyed under the Treaty, particularly the Soviet SS-20 and SS-23 missiles and the U.S. Pershing II and ground-launched cruise missiles, are modern missile systems in the prime of their operational lives, and they probably would have remained deployed for some time to come. Both sides seemed to perceive these weapons as militarily significant: the Soviets expressed vigorous and often grave concerns about the high accuracy of both U.S. systems and the short flight time of the Pershing IIs, and correspondingly the West groaned about the mobility and accuracy of the MIRVed SS-20 and the short flight time of the SS-23.

The political and economic investments in these weapons also were substantial. Deployment of the Soviet missiles antagonized Western Europe governments and publics just as the Soviets were beginning to woo them. U.S. deployments had similarly shaken America's relations with the same Western European governments and publics. As for the economic costs, the United States spent approximately

$8 billion developing, producing, and deploying its INF systems, and probably will spend additional billions to destroy them and to verify Soviet compliance with the Treaty. The INF missiles may be the first of the nuclear genies to be put back into their bottles.

Why are both parties willing to bear these considerable costs? The United States and its NATO allies have little choice; any problems caused by the INF Treaty pale in comparison to the crisis that would ensue in the Atlantic Alliance were the United States to back off the zero option at this late date. NATO sees itself as hoist on the petard of its own proposal.

Soviet calculations are more complex. The Soviets apparently decided that it was worth giving up their INF missiles in exchange for the United States eliminating missiles that could reach the USSR with great accuracy and in the case of the Pershing II great speed. The fact that other Soviet missiles not affected by the Treaty could still threaten Western European targets diluted the military significance of destroying the SS-20. And the Soviets may also have reasoned that the accord serves their larger objective of reducing the role of nuclear weapons in Europe, thereby placing a premium on conventional forces (a domain of Soviet advantage) and complicating U.S.-West European relations.

Unilateral Restraints

The history of nuclear arms control provides little evidence of militarily meaningful unilateral restraint and virtually none to support the notion that such action induces reciprocal restraint. The INF accord adds to the body of evidence of unreciprocated restraint.

In 1977 the Soviet Union began to deploy the SS-20. NATO's response was the 1979 dual-track decision, calling for deployment in Europe of U.S. INF missiles and a simultaneous attempt to negotiate limits on U.S. and Soviet INF missiles at the lowest possible level. In 1981, with no U.S. missiles yet deployed, the United States stated its preference for the "zero outcome," a global ban on all U.S. and Soviet INF missiles. Enjoying their initial unilateral advantage, the Soviets insisted that NATO must renounce its planned deployments as a precondition for negotiations. Soon thereafter the Soviets proposed a moratorium under which they could retain (and even expand) their INF missile monopoly. In November 1983, one month before the first U.S. INF missiles were deployed in Europe, the Soviets walked out of the negotiations, only to return two years later when the U.S. deployments were well under way. For so long as the West was restrained unilaterally from deploying INF missiles, the Soviets showed no interest in an INF agreement. Only when it became clear that the planned NATO INF deployment of 572 missiles would indeed be made did the Soviet Union consent to the zero outcome. The U.S. deployment accomplished the Western arms control objective that unilateral restraint had been unable to achieve.

Linkage

The INF record, like that of earlier U.S.-Soviet arms control negotiations, offers no evidence of the successful use of linkage as a deliberate strategy. The Soviet attempt to hold the INF agreement hostage to U.S. concessions on strategic defense can be seen as a failed attempt at linkage. As with previous accords, the INF agreement seems less to have improved U.S.-Soviet relations than to have been a product of such improvements.

Effects on Arms

Whereas previous nuclear arms control agreements were consistent with then-existing forces and (with the possible exception of the ABM Treaty) modernization plans, the INF Treaty clearly is not. Under the INF accord, both the United States and the Soviet Union are to destroy substantial numbers of modern missiles. Moreover, the U.S. deployment of 429 missiles had not yet reached the planned level of 572 (464 GLCMs and 108 Pershing IIs). In this sense, the INF Treaty, unlike previous accords, appears not simply to have codified existing defense plans but to have brought to fruition the broader plan of NATO expressed in the 1979 dual-track decision—namely, to limit U.S. and Soviet INF missiles to the lowest possible level. Zero *is* the lowest possible level.

It is difficult to predict whether the INF accord will redirect the arms competition and, if so, whether in productive or counterproductive ways. Will new, longer range weapons be produced to cover the old INF targets? Will additional air- or sea-launched cruise missiles be assigned to the task? Will the INF accord push us onto the "slippery slope" leading to denuclearization of Europe, or will it contribute to further modernization of the arsenals of short-range nuclear forces? Will the agreement facilitate mutual reductions in conventional forces in Europe, or will it stimulate increases in those forces? These questions remain to be answered.

Uncertainties

The INF Treaty, like its arms control predecessors, has several mechanisms to reduce uncertainties in estimates and projections of the other side's forces. First, the INF Memorandum of Understanding incorporates the data exchanged by the United States and the Soviet Union on the locations, numbers, and characteristics of their INF missiles, associated launchers, support structures, and equipment. Second, the Treaty prohibits production and flight-testing of INF ballistic and cruise missiles. Third, it institutes restrictions on the deployment and movement of INF missiles during the three-year period allocated for their elimination, and it calls for regular updating of the data in the Memorandum of Understanding. Fourth, the Treaty provides a complex regime, including several kinds of on-site inspection, to assist in the verification of compliance. All of these measures serve to increase each side's confidence in its knowledge of the other side's INF missile forces, both during the three-year transition to the zero level and thereafter.

Verification and Compliance

Concern about the Soviet predisposition to cheat on arms control accords and the U.S. ability to detect such violations remains a crucial issue. Recognition of this reality was undoubtedly the major factor underlying Soviet (and American) willingness to incorporate a verification regime of unprecedented proportion and complexity into the INF Treaty. And, as with previous agreements, much of the U.S. debate over ratification focused on verification issues.

Surprisingly, the alleged Soviet violations of the ABM Treaty and the (unratified) SALT II agreement presented no substantial political barriers to ratification of the INF Treaty. In his formal statement before the Senate Foreign Relations Committee on January 25, 1988, Secretary of State George Shultz described the Soviet violations as "selective and specific" rather than "wholesale," and made clear the Reagan administration's view that they should not impede ratification of "the INF Treaty [that] is in the security interests of the United States." Our concern that compliance issues would be a major, perhaps insurmountable, barrier to significant progress in arms control appears not to have applied to the INF case.

Despite the two sides' rejection of ambiguity as a useful negotiating approach, however, the potential exists for significant differences in interpretation and compliance. In particular, and as the Senate debate suggested, future disagreements over data, developments at non-designated facilities, exploitation of exotic technologies, or production or transfer of missiles or missile components just above or below the Treaty's thresholds can be expected to incur charges of circumvention or even violation of the accord.

Lulling

Despite claims to the contrary from conservatives and liberals alike, the arms control process and arms control agreements have had no observable effect on U.S. defense expenditures. The INF Treaty is unlikely to cause a departure from this pattern. Any savings that might accrue from eliminating INF missiles are likely to be redirected to compensating forces, both nuclear (other than INF missiles) and conventional. In any event, these relatively small perturbations in spending will almost certainly pale in comparison with the effects on the defense budget of the state of U.S.-Soviet relations and the health of the domestic economies of the United States and its allies.

Political Support

As with previous arms control accords, political support for the INF Treaty stems more from the power of the president and from the inherent appeal of arms control to the public and the allies than from the specific terms of the Treaty or from the extent to which Congress was involved in negotiating it.

Only the staunchest of ideological conservatives fear that a U.S.–Soviet arms control agreement acceptable to Ronald Reagan, whose anticommunist credentials are impeccable, could plausibly favor the Russians. And despite the almost complete absence of congressional participation in the negotiating process, congressional approval was overwhelming, with the Senate voting 93–5 on May 27, 1988 in favor of ratification. Indeed, the most controversial issue that arose—the Senate's adding a "condition" to the Treaty stating that any reinterpretation of the Treaty at variance with the text, the resolution of ratification, or "authoritative representations" by the executive branch would require Senate approval—had less to do with INF than it did with the ongoing debate over the correct interpretation of the 1972 ABM Treaty.

The allies, too, support the INF Treaty, although with mixed feelings. The governments of NATO nations where the U.S. missiles were to be located—Belgium, the Federal Republic of Germany, Italy, the Netherlands, and the United Kingdom—had already paid high political prices to gain domestic acceptance of the deployments. There is considerable concern too that the accord might dilute the credibility of the U.S. pledge to Western Europe. On the other hand, these governments took part in NATO's unanimous 1979 decision to pursue the dual-track strategy, which includes seeking the zero outcome. The allies, like the United States, see no realistic alternative to accepting the Soviets' positive response to our own proposal.

Asymmetry

Those who believe that the arms control process and arms control agreements serve Soviet interests more than U.S. interests, or vice versa, are unlikely to change their views on the basis of the INF record. As with previous agreements, the effects of the INF Treaty are modest. Observers most strongly in favor of the Treaty hope that it establishes important precedents in its requirements for actual reductions and in its demanding verification provisions, and will pave the way to a comprehensive and significant arms control regime; those most strongly opposed fear that the path thus paved will lead in the wrong direction. There is also danger that the Treaty might weaken the tie between the United States and Western Europe; for those who see removal of INF missiles as a step (however small) toward a denuclearized Europe, the Treaty raises doubts about deterrence and coupling alike. That said, it is easy to exaggerate any potentially adverse impact of the Treaty, and just as easy to find ways of offsetting it, whether through new military deployments or arms control initiatives or both. To the extent that the future of arms control can be expected to rhyme with its past, neither the highest hopes nor the worst fears are likely to be realized.

INDEX

ABOUT THE EDITORS

Albert Carnesale is a professor of public policy and the academic dean at Harvard University's John F. Kennedy School of Government. His teaching and research interests are in international security and U.S.-Soviet relations, with emphasis on policies and issues associated with nuclear weapons. He consults for several agencies of the U.S. government, served on the U.S. delegation to the Strategic Arms Limitation Talks (1970–72), and is a co-author of *Hawks, Doves, and Owls: An Agenda for Avoiding Nuclear War, Living with Nuclear Weapons*, and *Fateful Visions: Avoiding Nuclear Catastrophe*.

Richard N. Haass is a lecturer in public policy at Harvard University's John F. Kennedy School of Government and a senior research associate at Harvard University's Center for Science and International Affairs. Previously, he was an official in the Departments of State and Defense, a research associate at the International Institute for Strategic Studies, and a legislative assistant in the U.S. Senate. He is the author of *Congressional Power: Implications for American Security Policy* and *Beyond the INF Treaty: Arms, Arms Control, and the Atlantic Alliance*.

ABOUT THE CONTRIBUTORS

Andrew Bennett is a doctoral student in public policy at Harvard University's John F. Kennedy School of Government and a predoctoral fellow at the School's Center for Science and International Affairs.

Ivo H. Daalder, a Dutch national, is a Harvard MacArthur Fellow at the Center for Science and International Affairs in Harvard University's John F. Kennedy School of Government and a doctoral candidate in political science at the Massachusetts Institute of Technology. He is the author of *The SDI Challenge to Europe*.

Stephen J. Flanagan is the executive director of the Center for Science and International Affairs and an adjunct lecturer in public policy in the Kennedy School of Government at Harvard University. He has been a fellow of the Council on Foreign Relations, a research associate of the International Institute for Strategic Studies (IISS), and a professional staff member of the U.S. Senate Select Committee on Intelligence. He is the author of *NATO's Conventional Defense Options* and a co-editor of *Securing Europe's Future* (With Fen Osler Hampson).

Fen Osler Hampson is a research associate at the Canadian Institute for International Peace and Security and an assistant professor at The Norman Paterson School of International Affairs, Carleton University, in Ottawa, Canada. He is author of *Forming Economic Policy: The Case of Energy in Canada and Mexico* and co-editor of *Securing Europe's Future* (with Stephen J. Flanagan).

Elisa D. Harris is a doctoral candidate in International Relations at the University of Oxford and a predoctoral research fellow in the Center for Science and International Affairs, John F. Kennedy School of Government. She was formerly on the professional staff of the Committee on Foreign Relations in the U.S. House of Representatives.

Sean M. Lynn-Jones is a doctoral candidate in Harvard University's Department of Government and a Harvard MacArthur Fellow in International Security at the Center for Science and International Affairs. Starting in September 1987 he will be managing editor of *International Security.*

Joseph S. Nye, Jr., is a professor of government and the director of the Center for Science and International Affairs at Harvard University. He is a senior fellow of the Aspen Institute and director of the Aspen Strategy Group and a member of the Trilateral Commission. He served as deputy to the under secretary of state of security assistance, science and technology, and also chaired the National Security Council Group on Non-Proliferation of Nuclear Weapons. His most recent book is *Nuclear Ethics.*

Kiron K. Skinner is a Ph.D. candidate in Harvard University's Department of Government and a predoctoral fellow at the Center for Science and International Affairs at Harvard's John F. Kennedy School of Government.

John Wertheimer is pursuing a Ph.D. in history at Princeton University. He spent the academic year 1985–86 as a research assistant at the Center for Science and International Affairs at Harvard University's John F. Kennedy School of Government.